# REGIONAL WAGE VARIATIONS
# IN BRITAIN, 1850–1914

# REGIONAL WAGE VARIATIONS IN BRITAIN

## 1850-1914

E. H. Hunt

CLARENDON PRESS
OXFORD
1973

*Oxford University Press, Ely House, London W.1*

GLASGOW  NEW YORK  TORONTO  MELBOURNE  WELLINGTON
CAPE TOWN  IBADAN  NAIROBI  DAR ES SALAAM  LUSAKA  ADDIS ABABA
DELHI  BOMBAY  CALCUTTA  MADRAS  KARACHI  LAHORE  DACCA
KUALA LUMPUR  SINGAPORE  HONG KONG  TOKYO

PRINTED IN NORTHERN IRELAND AT THE UNIVERSITIES PRESS, BELFAST

# ACKNOWLEDGEMENTS

THIS book is a revised version of a doctoral dissertation submitted to the University of London. Its preparation has benefited from the assistance of several people whose contribution it is a pleasure to acknowledge. My greatest debt is to Professor D. C. Coleman who supervised the early stages of research and gave unstintingly of advice and encouragement long after his formal obligations had ended. I have profited enormously from discussion with other colleagues and ex-colleagues at the London School of Economics and the Queen's University of Belfast and in this respect I should like to thank especially Mr D. E. Baines, Dr L. A. Clarkson, Dr C. J. Erickson, and Professor F. J. Fisher, each of whom read and criticized an earlier version of this work; for any errors and other shortcomings that remain I am entirely responsible. I am grateful also to Professor W. Ashworth, Professor E. H. Phelps Brown, Dr M. Knott, and Mr O. M. Westall who provided advice on specific problems; to Mrs E. Wilson and her colleagues of the drawing office at L.S.E. for help with the preparation of maps and scatter diagrams; to Mrs G. A. McClare and Mrs J. M. Maxwell who typed the manuscript; to my wife who assisted in numerous ways; and to students of labour history at L.S.E. for their constant stimulus. Parts of Chapter Five and Chapter Six were published earlier in a different form and thanks are due to the editors of the *Economic History Review* and to the Exeter University Press for permission to incorporate this material.

E. H. H.

*L.S.E.*
*March, 1973*

# CONTENTS

# LIST OF TABLES

## LIST OF MAPS AND ·FIGURES

# ABBREVIATIONS

| | |
|---|---|
| *Ec.H.R.* | *Economic History Review* |
| *J.E.H.* | *Journal of Economic History* |
| *J.R.Ag.S.* | *Journal of the Royal Agricultural Society* |
| *J.R.S.S.* | *Journal of the Royal Statistical Society* |
| *M.C.* | *Morning Chronicle*, Survey of Labour and the Poor, 1849–51 |
| *Pop.Stud.* | *Population Studies* |
| *P.P.* | *Parliamentary Papers* |
| *V.C.H.* | *Victoria County History* |
| *Yks.Bull.* | *Yorkshire Bulletin of Economic and Social Research* |

*Note*  All references cited were published in London unless otherwise stated.

# INTRODUCTION

## I

THE AIM of this book is to provide an outline of the nature and causes of regional variations in the wages of adult males in Britain between the middle of the nineteenth century and the First World War. James Caird, in his mid-century tour of rural England, found farm labourers earning 12s. to 15s. in south Lancashire but only half as much on Salisbury Plain: in Wiltshire, he noted, 'great pinching must be endured.'[1] Half a century later differences in earnings of farm labourers, ranging from 14s. 6d. in Oxfordshire to 22s. 6d. in Durham, were still 'astonishingly great'.[2] Variations of similar magnitude existed in most occupations; fitters' rates in central London were double those in parts of Cornwall and the Webbs noted that members of the Amalgamated Society of Carpenters were paid 20 different rates varying between 5d. and 10d. per hour.[3] These figures show that wage differentials between regions at any one time were as great as the over-all improvement in wages between 1850 and 1914, and the increase then was probably more rapid, and more sustained, than at any time since the seventy or eighty years after the Black Death.[4]

1. J. Caird, *English Agriculture in 1850–51* (1852), pp. 84, 284.
2. J. H. Clapham, *An Economic History of Modern Britain* (Cambridge, 1950–2 edn.), iii. 97–9.
3. E. H. Phelps Brown, *The Economics of Labor* (New Haven, Conn., and London, 1962), p. 176; S. and B. Webb, *Industrial Democracy* (1920), p. 321.
4. E. H. Phelps Brown and S. V. Hopkins, 'Seven Centuries of the Prices of Consumables, compared with Builders' Wage-Rates', *Economica*, N.S. xxiii (1956), 302–6. There are various estimates of the increase in the standard of living between 1850 and 1900, most fall between 50 and 100 per cent.

Moreover, inter-regional differentials in Britain in the nineteenth century were also almost certainly greater than the differential between average British and average United States real wages at that time.[1] Historians of wages in Britain have always devoted the greater part of their effort to measuring changes in wages over time, but large variations in payment for similar work in different areas also merit attention and have received very little.[2]

The extent and persistence of wage variations in this period, when railways and improvements in education were reducing barriers to mobility and when trade unions, with their egalitarian tendencies, became a power in the land, raise wider questions about the nature and efficacy of these and other influences on the level of wages. How mobile was labour in Britain at this time and what was the influence of railways upon mobility? What became of trade union egalitarianism when it entered the market-place? What were the consequences of Irish and alien immigration upon regional wage variation, and does their influence in this respect add anything to existing interpretations of their contribution to the British economy? Investigation of these questions should help to answer others which have recently been asked more than once: how appropriate are historical generalizations which assume a near-monolithic economy and to what extent are significant regional trends obscured by national aggregates? If farm labourers in Lancashire in 1850 could earn up to twice as much as those in Wiltshire whereas farm labourers' wages in the two counties were almost the same in 1921, then is not a great deal obscured

1. D. R. Adams, 'Some Evidence on English and American Wage Rates, 1790–1830', *J.E.H.*, xxx (1970), 511; H. J. Habakkuk, *American and British Technology in the Nineteenth Century* (Cambridge, 1967), pp. 11–14; E. H. Phelps Brown and M. H. Browne, *A Century of Pay* (1968), pp. 159, 165.
2. The same cannot be said of the United States. Although wide differentials might be considered less remarkable in a country the size of the United States they have received considerable attention. For a recent survey and reference to some of the better-known works see R. Perlman, *Labor Theory* (New York, 1969), Ch. VI. In Britain regional wage variations in the eighteenth century have been more studied than those in the nineteenth century, see E. W. Gilboy, *Wages in Eighteenth Century England* (Cambridge, Mass., 1934).

INTRODUCTION 3

by averages purporting to show increases in wages throughout
Britain as a whole?[1] Similarly, if in the first half of the century
unskilled labourers were paid markedly different rates according
to where they worked, no more than a small proportion could
have received the subsistence income formulated by the 'iron
law of wages'; and the enormous intellectual investment devoted to tracing chronological changes in the standard of
living after 1815 is both unlikely to find a single satisfactory
answer and likely to produce unsatisfactory answers every time
wages from different areas are combined in a single index. In
addition to whatever light the investigation of regional wage
differences might cast upon these various aspects of British
economic history, the analysis and conclusions have some
relevance to the debate among regional economists concerning
regional inequalities, the magnitude of inequality at various
stages of economic development, and whether or not, in the
absence of government intervention, there is a natural tendency
for these inequalities to diminish.[2]

II

The investigation that follows falls into three broad parts:
the first three chapters examine the pattern of wages and consider whether it was much affected by compensating differentials in prices or family earnings; Chapters Four and Five
examine demand for labour and the way demand for labour
was influenced by variations in productivity; the remaining
chapters deal with various aspects of labour supply.

1. Caird, op. cit., pp. 84, 284; A. L. Bowley, *Prices and Wages in the United
Kingdom, 1914–1920* (Oxford, 1921), pp. 171–2.
2. Those economists who challenge neo-classical general equilibrium theory
emphasize the possible cumulative advantages of initially favoured loca-
tions, or 'growth-poles', and the vicious circle of impedimenta or 'backwash'
effects which may perpetuate the disadvantages of less fortunate regions.
The 'convergence school', by contrast, emphasizes the potency of 'spread'
or 'trickling down' effects. For an introduction to the debate see, H. W.
Richardson, *Regional Economics: Location Theory, Urban Structure and
Regional Change* (1969), Ch. 13.

Wage levels in each part of Britain between 1850 and 1914 are examined in Chapter One. The pattern is described at some length because, while there are several accounts which show wages in one part of the country, the pattern as a whole has never been examined in detail[1]—readers more interested in the causes of spatial differentials than the details of the pattern itself might prefer to omit all but the concluding section of Chapter One. The pattern described is characterized by a very gradual reduction in spatial differentials throughout the period and a remarkable constancy in the relative position of different areas. In broad terms there were two high-wage areas in 1850: the London area; and the counties of the north of England together with parts of the Midlands as far south as Birmingham. In 1914 the position was similar except that these two areas had been joined by South Wales and much of southern and central Scotland.

The investigation is based upon the level of wages in four occupational groups. Considerable use is made of agricultural wages because farm labourers' earnings are probably the most useful single guide to wage levels in different parts of Britain. At the beginning of the period more than one man in four worked in agriculture and in the following half-century it was an important reservoir of labour for the rest of the economy. Farm wages were a reference point by which others fixed their position,[2] a significant consideration at a time when customary differentials between occupations enjoyed a greater sanctity than they do today, and when some autonomous influence affected the urban labour market migration from rural areas and farm wages were affected also. There is the further advantage that agriculture, unlike many other occupations, afforded employment in all parts of Britain and its nature changed little

1. Variations in wages over very short distances, from one farm or village to the next, will not be considered separately. Many of these variations owed their survival to the force of custom.
2. E. J. Hobsbawm in A. Briggs and J. Saville (eds.), *Essays in Labour History* (1960), p. 115. On the same point see A. L. Bowley: 'There is no doubt that agricultural wages are in close sympathy with wages that can be obtained for unskilled labour in the same neighborhood . . .' 'Rural Population in England and Wales', *J.R.S.S.*, lxxvii (1914), 617.

and gradually. Moreover, farm wages were more often and more competently investigated than earnings in any other occupation. Skilled and unskilled building wages, which are also used extensively in Chapter One, share many of the advantages of agricultural wages and building labourers' rates are a good guide to the relative level of all unskilled wages in any particular district.[1] Coalmining and police wages are less suitable guides to the level of wages in different parts of the country but are used because in these occupations evidence of regional rates is fairly readily available. The sources and reliability of wage evidence for these four occupational groups are shown in the appendix to Chapter One. In addition the survey of spatial differentials draws upon less systematic investigation of wages in a number of other occupations including printing, tailoring, dockwork, the shipbuilding and engineering trades, boot and shoe manufacture, box making, retailing, domestic service, and the manufacture of cotton, silk, lace, and woollen goods.

For purposes of presentation and analysis wage rates are discussed in the context of the thirteen regions shown in Map 1. The regions are not rigorously defined and they are certainly not areas in which all men in any particular occupation received an identical wage. They reflect a compromise between areas with similar wage characteristics, those usually considered as distinguishable economic regions, and the necessity to avoid a plethora of very small regions. Further compromise is imposed by the necessity that regional boundaries coincide with county boundaries because most of the statistics used in Chapters Four, Six, and Seven, and many of those used in Chapter One, are available only in county units. For these reasons the regions are less rigorously defined than those which might be constructed to investigate mid-twentieth-century regional problems;[2] there are substantial wage variations within the regional

1. On the representativeness of building wages see A. L. Bowley, *Wages in the United Kingdom in the Nineteenth Century* (Cambridge, 1900), pp. 58–9.
2. In fact, the difficulties of working with other than political boundaries are such that most studies of twentieth-century problems are subject to similar constraints. On the definition of regions see, H. W. Richardson, op. cit., pp. 223–31.

boundaries and the indices of regional wages shown in the appendix to Chapter One should be used in conjunction with the notes in the same appendix and the detailed analysis of spatial variations in Chapter One. It is, of course, possible that variations in men's wages were compensated by variations in the earnings of their wives and children, or that money wages simply reflected local prices. These possibilities are examined in Chapters Two and Three. Chapter Four attempts an assessment of demand for labour in different regions and the way this affected wage rates; Chapter Five examines the relationship between productivity and wages; Chapters Six and Seven deal with two important influences on the supply side of the market, population growth and migration; and Chapters Eight and Nine with the influence of particular groups of workers, Irish and alien immigrants and trade unionists.

# 1

## WAGES

### I

REGION ONE (London and Home Counties—see Map 1)

LONDON and the Home Counties illustrate some of the problems raised in the Introduction, in particular the fact that the administrative areas for which statistics are available were not homogeneous economic regions. For whereas wages in parts of Essex, Kent, and Surrey were sufficiently affected by London's influence to be considered within the metropolitan economy, wages in other parts were no more affected than those in counties at a much greater distance.[1] In the region as a whole wages were a little above the national average,[2] but the most remarkable aspect of wages in the region was their diversity. This small area contained some of the best- and worst-paid labour in Britain.

In the eighteenth century London wages were almost certainly the highest in Britain,[3] Adam Smith and Arthur Young both noted that wage rates fell the further one moved from the capital.[4] This advantage was probably retained in the first half of the nineteenth century and there can be little doubt that London was the highest-wage centre after 1850. In 1886 London carpenters received 9d. per hour; in Manchester

1. Another possible arrangement, viz. considering London and its neighbouring counties as two separate regions, was rejected because of the complications which arise from changes in London's boundary.
2. Tables 1–4, 1–6, 1–8. The appendix to this chapter shows town, county, and regional wages in several occupations together with notes on the nature and reliability of the wage statistics. All references to the national average refer to Britain.
3. Gilboy, op. cit., Parts 1 and 4 passim.
4. Ibid., p. 39; A. Smith, The Wealth of Nations, ed. E. Cannan (1950 edn.), i. 76–7.

MAP 1. BRITAIN: WAGE REGIONS

## KEY TO MAP 1

### REGIONS

Region  1 London and Home Counties
Region  2 Southwest
Region  3 Rural Southeast
Region  4 South Wales
Region  5 Rural Wales and Herefordshire
Region  6 Midlands
Region  7 Lincs., Rutland, E. and N. Ridings
Region  8 Lancs., Cheshire, and the W. Riding
Region  9 Cumberland and Westmorland
Region 10 Northumberland and Durham
Region 11 South Scotland
Region 12 Central Scotland
Region 13 Northern Scotland

### COUNTIES

| | | | | | |
|---|---|---|---|---|---|
| Aberdeenshire | Ab | Essex | Es | Orkney | Or |
| Angus | Angu | Fifeshire | Fife | Oxfordshire | Ox |
| Anglesey | Angl | Flintshire | Fl | Peebles | Pee |
| Argyll | Ar | Glamorgan | Gla | Pembroke | Pemb |
| Ayr | Ay | Gloucestershire | Glo | Perthshire | Per |
| Banff | Ba | Haddingtonshire | Had | Radnorshire | Rad |
| Bedfordshire | Bed | Hampshire | Ha | Renfrew | Re |
| Berkshire | Berk | Hereford | Hf | Ross and | |
| Berwick | Berw | Hertfordshire | He | Cromarty | RC |
| Brecknockshire | Bre | Huntingdonshire | Hunt | Roxburgh | Ro |
| Buckinghamshire | Buc | Invernesshire | Inv | Rutland | Ru |
| Bute | But | Kent | Ke | Selkirk | Se |
| Caithness | Cai | Kincardine | Kinc | Shetland | Sh |
| Cambridgeshire | Cam | Kinross | Kinr | Shropshire | Shr |
| Cardiganshire | Card | Kirkcudbright | Kir | Somerset | S'set |
| Carmarthenshire | Carm | Lancashire | Lanc | Staffordshire | Sta |
| Carnarvonshire | Carn | Lanarkshire | Lana | Stirling | Sti |
| Cheshire | Che | Leicestershire | Le | Suffolk | Suf |
| Clackmannan | Cl | Lincolnshire | Linc | Surrey | Sur |
| Cornwall | Corn | Linlithgow | Linl | Sussex | Sx |
| Cumberland | Cu | London | L | Sutherland | Suth |
| Denbighshire | Den | Merionethshire | Mer | Warwickshire | Wa |
| Derbyshire | De | Middlesex | Midd | Westmorland | We |
| Devonshire | Dev | Monmouthshire | Mo | Wigtown | Wig |
| Dorset | Do | Montgomeryshire | Mont | Wiltshire | Wil |
| Dumfries | Dum | Nairn | Na | Worcestershire | Wor |
| Dunbartonshire | Dun | Norfolk | Norf | Yorkshire E.R. | ER |
| Durham | Dur | Northamptonshire | N'hant | Yorkshire N.R. | NR |
| Edinburgh | Ed | Northumberland | Nort | Yorkshire W.R. | WR |
| Elgin | El | Nottinghamshire | Nott | | |

the rate was 8*d*. and in a great many provincial centres rates of
pay were less than two-thirds of the London wage.[1] Taunton
carpenters were paid 5*d*., which was a penny less than the wage
received by London labourers.[2] Twenty years later the relative
positions were much the same, although in percentage terms
London's advantage had narrowed.[3] The building trade was
typical of many others. The *Tenth Abstract of Labour Statistics*,
for example, shows wage rates for over thirty occupations in a
number of different centres; London occupied first or second
position in every case but one, and in most cases London wages
were above those in any provincial centre.[4]

From London towards the rural parts of the Home Counties
wages fell steeply; 25 miles from Westminster there were wages
well below the national average, fifty miles away were some of
the lowest-wage districts in Britain. 'Approach London from
the south or west', wrote one of the provincial correspondents
of the *Morning Chronicle*'s survey of 'Labour and the Poor' in
1850, '. . . and you find the scale of wages gradually rising from
the moment that you enter within the circle of its influence.'[5]
The same could be said of other approaches to the capital and
it was probably to the north that wage contours were closest
together. In Kent and Surrey at this time farm labourers were
considerably better paid and nourished than those in counties
further west.[6] In north Essex, however, the *Morning Chronicle*
investigator found labourers strangers to butchers' meat and
wages 'extremely low'.[7] Fifty years later the relationship

1. Table 1–5.
2. Ibid.
3. Ibid. Wages had risen but London carpenters were still paid only a penny
   more than the Manchester rate and the advantage over Taunton had been
   reduced from 4*d*. to 3½*d*.
4. P.P. 1905, LXXVI, pp. 40–51. The general position can be verified by
   reference to any of the more detailed wage sources—several are given below,
   pp. 61, 66. On shipyard wages in London and provincial centres see S.
   Pollard, 'The Decline of Shipbuilding on the Thames', *Ec.H.R.*, 2nd Ser.,
   iii (1950–1), 80.
5. *M.C.* 13 Feb. 1850.
6. Ibid. 13 Feb., 6, 30 Mar. 1850.
7. They were paid 6*s*. to 7*s*.; nearer to London the rate was 10*s*. The survey
   gave few useful details of labourers' wages in Kent and Surrey although they
   were said to be about 2*s*. 6*d*. a day in the hop districts. In west Sussex
   and east Hampshire, which were compared unfavourably with Kent
   and Surrey, wages were 7*s*. to 8*s*., rather more than rates in the north of
   Essex. Ibid. 26, 29 Dec. 1849; 26, 30 Jan. 1850.

between wages in London and the Home Counties was much
the same. Labourers at Romford in 1903 earned between 16*s*.
and 18*s*. a week, more if they worked on a market garden. At
Stansted, hardly 25 miles further from London, the rate was
between 11*s*. and 12*s*.; it was much the same at Steeple Bumstead and between 12*s*. and 13*s*. in the vicinity of Halstead.[1]
Several rural districts elsewhere in England had rates as low as
this but none were lower.[2] Similarly in the building trades;
Halstead bricklayers received 6*d*. per hour in 1906, about 60
per cent of the London rate and as little as bricklayers almost
anywhere else in Britain. Of the large number of towns shown
in Table 1–5 only St. Austell in Cornwall had a lower rate;
only one other, Dorchester (Dorset), had the same rate and
bricklayers in towns as far removed from the economic mainstream as Carnarvon (Carnarvonshire) and Peterhead
(Aberdeenshire) received rather more.

A further aspect of wages in Region One should be noted:
although by the standards of the time most London workers
were well paid, there were considerable numbers whose pay
compared less favourably with provincial rates and who form
a significant qualification to the description of London as a
high-wage centre. This group has been carefully investigated,
most notably by Mayhew, Booth, and in several official
inquiries.[3] London's distress, compared with that of other
areas, and especially when compared with conditions in the
rural south, was less than the amount of attention it has
attracted since the 1880s might suggest. No large town was
free of distress; the problem was probably more pressing in
London than in most, but, as today, nowhere was better placed

1. *Second Report by A. Wilson Fox on the Wages, Earnings and Condition of
   Agricultural Labourers*, P.P. 1905, XCVII, Appendix III, p. 156. (Subsequently referred to as *Second Report on Wages . . . Agricultural Labourers*.)
   The figures are for cash wages only but it is unlikely that the general
   impression would be much affected by the inclusion of payments in kind.
2. Ibid., pp. 151–9.
3. H. Mayhew, *London Labour and the London Poor* (1861–2); C. Booth,
   *Life and Labour of the People in London* (1902–3 edn.); among the official
   inquiries see, in particular, *S.C. on the Sweating System*, P.P. 1888, XX,
   XXI; 1889, XIII, XIV; 1890, XVII and the *Report to the Board of Trade
   on the Sweating System at the East End of London*, P.P. 1887, LXXXIX.
   On the size of the 'residuum' see G. Stedman Jones, *Outcast London*
   (Oxford, 1971), Ch. 3.

to catch the eye of politicians, the press, and sociologists. Moreover, to the extent that poverty in London was a consequence of poor wages[1] the major problem was women's wages and our main concern is with men;[2] and of the badly paid males a considerable proportion were Jewish immigrants, a rather special group.[3]

Part of the trouble in London was competition from provincial factories; another part, as Mayhew never ceased to remind his readers, was the competition of cheap foreign labour; the boot and shoe makers and the Spitalfields silk weavers suffered both.[4] Another cause of low earnings was short-time working, particularly in the clothing, footwear, and other trades where demand was subject to fashion. How much distress was a consequence of fluctuating demand for labour, how much of general over-supply, cannot be determined. Demand was unsteady, but at the same time London was a great attraction for the unemployed, the unemployable, the footloose, the idle, and the petty criminal.[5] A few skilled workers were affected by these conditions but for the most part low earnings were confined to the unskilled.[6] Some of these were

1. The outcry over the sweating system was concerned as much with working conditions as with wages and sweating was in part an attempt to offset the competitive disadvantages of London's high wages. The wages and working conditions of London's 'distressed' workers are discussed in greater detail in Ch. 3 (below, pp. 109–11) and Ch. 8 (below, pp. 312–18).
2. Women's wages, however, often influenced men's. Family earnings are considered in Ch. 3.
3. P. G. Hall described London's pool of unskilled labour as consisting of two main elements; 'First is the army of female labour . . . The second element is the immigrants', *The Industries of London since 1861* (1962), p. 118. Immigration and its influence on the London labour market are considered in Ch. 8.
4. For some notes on the wages and conditions of silk weavers and boot and shoe makers see Mayhew in the *Morning Chronicle*, 23, 26 Oct. 1849; 4, 7, 18 Feb. 1850; D. F. Schloss, Ch. 4 in Booth, *Life and Labour*, 1st Ser., iv.
5. The size, wealth, and vitality of the capital were themselves an attraction; so were the availability of casual work and London's numerous and liberal charities. Many of those women who made up the greater part of the 'depressed' sector were the wives and daughters of the casual labourers of the East End. For more details on the nature of this class and on London charities see Booth, *Life and Labour*, 1st Ser., iii, Chs. II and III; 1st Ser., iv, Chs. III and IX; Mayhew in the *Morning Chronicle* for 21 Dec. 1849; 11, 25 Jan. 1850, and below, pp.109–11, 148 n. 1, 313–4.
6. *M.C.* 21 Dec. 1849; Hall, op. cit., pp. 59–60.

employed in the service trades of the West End, hanging upon the skirts of wealth and ministering to luxury,[1] but the great centre of low earnings and short-time work was the East End, particularly in the tailoring trade and in and about the London docks.

The largest single group among London's less-well-paid male workers was probably the casual dockers: and while it is extraordinarily difficult to make useful generalizations about wages in London's 'depressed' sectors, beyond the fact that they compared less well with provincial wages in the same occupations than most London wages,[2] dockers' earnings illustrate the position of one important group.[3] By the autumn of 1889, after the strike of that year, their pay was 6d. per hour. Few, if any, builders' labourers outside London received as much as the 'dockers' tanner' and even the best-paid farm labourers fell considerably short of this amount.[4] Nevertheless, the dockers were not better paid, and were probably worse paid, than those on the Mersey, Clyde, Tyne, and Humber.[5] But dockers, the sweated workers in the clothing trades, and others like them were not typical of London labour.[6] Booth himself,

1. Booth, *Life and Labour*, 1st Ser., i. 228.
2. The changing membership of the sector, the influence of short-time, and opportunities for 'dovetailing' two or more seasonal occupations create great difficulties; there is a wealth of detailed information in Mayhew and Booth.
3. Casual dockwork was a 'residual' employment: 'a man who is coming down in the world filters through all the grades of labour, till he arrives at the bottom of all as a dock casual', Booth, *Life and Labour*, 1st Ser., iii. 88–9. On the character of casual dockers see also P. de Rousiers, *The Labour Question in Britain* (1896), pp. 346–51.
4. See Tables 1–4, 1–5; and building labourers' wages in G. H. Wood, unpublished wage collection, Library of the Royal Statistical Society. There were usually more casual dockers than the port required and in respect of annual earnings the building and farm labourers' pay probably compared less unfavourably with London dock rates than hourly earnings might suggest.
5. *R.C.* on *Labour, Secretary's Report*, P.P. 1894, XXXV, pp. 144-S, para. 168–9; see also de Rousiers, op. cit., p. 349.
6. It is worth noting also that by no means all workers in London's 'depressed' trades were badly paid. Male rates in the ready-made-clothing trade in 1906 were the highest in the country. *Report of the War Cabinet Committee on Women in Industry*, P.P. 1919, XXXI, p. 50.

although preoccupied with the poor, never lost sight of the
generally favourable circumstances of most labour in the
capital: 'Turning to the general question of wages and hours of
work', he said, 'we find that compared with any standard in
England, or still more on the Continent, London rates of wages
are high.' [1] This was the most remarkable feature of London
wages, i.e. they were higher than most elsewhere. London's
high wage level was also one of the two outstanding characteristics of wages in the region as a whole; the other was the
sharp decline in rates between London and the rural parts of
the Home Counties.


II


REGION TWO (South-west—see Map 1)

The south-west, unlike Region One, had no major wage
variations within its boundaries; the whole of Region Two was
characterized by low wages throughout the period. Farm
labourers in parts of Devon and Wiltshire were paid 6s. to 7s. in
1849–50, the same 'extremely low' wage of the north Essex
labourers.[2] The more usual wage in the region at this time was
between 7s. and 8s. with up to 9s. 6d. (including payments in
kind) near the tin and copper mines, around the Dorset clay
mines, and in the vicinity of the Somerset and Forest of Dean
coalfields.[3] The regional average, including cider and other
payments in kind, was probably about 8s. 3d. or slightly more
than half the rate in Northumberland and Durham.[4] Poor
wages resulted in poor diets. The *Morning Chronicle* investigator
found labourers in Dorset living on 'bread, cabbage and turnips'
with butchers' meat 'out of the question'.[5] Those in Devon

1. Booth, *Life and Labour*, 1st Ser., iv. 336.
2. See above, p. 10.
3. *M.C.* 10, 14, 28 Nov. 1849, 26 Jan. 1850; T. D. Acland, 'On the Farming of
   Somersetshire', *J.R.Ag.S.*, xi (1850), 750; R. Molland in *V.C.H. Wiltshire*
   iv (1959), 81.
4. *M.C.* 16 Jan. 1850.
5. *M.C.* 28 Nov. 1849; 26 Jan. 1850.

and Wiltshire were scarcely better off and the same investigator
compared their diet unfavourably with workhouse diets and
the diets of slaves in Virginia.[1]

Tables 1–3 and 1–4 suggest that the gap between farm
earnings in the south-west and in counties like Northumberland
and Durham narrowed between 1850 and 1870. Even so, in
1870 earnings were the lowest in Britain; they were 13 per cent
less than the national average and about two-thirds of the rates
in Lancashire, Cumberland, Northumberland, and Durham: it
was at this time that Canon Girdlestone was busy dispatching
Devon rustics to the high-wage north.[2] During the next 30
years wages in the south-west continued to improve relative to
wages elsewhere in Britain. In 1898 farm earnings in the region
were 9 per cent below the national average.[3] In 1907 they were
8 per cent below average and the south-west was no longer the
worst-paid region; county rates for agricultural labourers were
then three-quarters or more of those in the north, although
there were still districts in the north where men received twice
as much as was paid for similar work in parts of the West
Country.[4]

No other group in the south-west was as badly paid as farm
labourers, but pay in other occupations compared no more
favourably with pay for similar work elsewhere in Britain.[5]
Wages in the West Country cloth industry were below rates in
Yorkshire throughout the nineteenth century.[6] The police

1. Ibid. 27 Oct., 10 Nov. 1849. 'Ireland was not the only place in the British
   Isles where the potato prevented a population from starving.' R. Molland,
   op. cit., p. 84. Molland notes that comparisons between labourers in Wiltshire and those elsewhere were 'nearly always to the disadvantage of
   Wiltshire' (pp. 80–1). B. Kerr has said much the same of Dorset labourers,
   'The Dorset Agricultural Labourer, 1750–1850', *Proc. Dorset Natural
   History and Archaeological Society*, lxxxiv (1962), 166.
2. J. H. Clapham, *An Economic History of Modern Britain* (Cambridge,
   1952), ii. 293–4. For some notes on Girdlestone's activities see below,
   pp. 39–40, 45–6, 253 n. 3.
3. Table 1–4.
4. Ibid.; *Second Report on Wages . . . Agricultural Labourers*, pp. 151, 158–9.
5. This is not surprising; farm labourers' wages are almost certainly the best
   single guide to the general wage level in an area. For notes on their reliability and on wages in other occupations see above, p. 4 and the appendix
   to this chapter.
6. J. de L. Mann, *The Cloth Industry in the West of England from 1640 to 1880*
   (Oxford, 1971), p. 250; see also below, pp. 116–17.

forces of the region were noted for their poor pay; constabulary pay in the south-west as a whole compared unfavourably with that in each of the other regions of England and Wales.[1] Building wages in Taunton, Dorchester, and St. Austell were between half and two-thirds of the London rate.[2] Employers in larger and more flourishing centres like Exeter, Plymouth, Bristol, and Swindon paid a little more, but these were not high-wage towns.[3] Plymouth dockers received considerably less than dockers in London and the north[4] and when minimum rates came into operation in the tailoring industry in 1909 Swindon was one of the few centres where men's rates were sufficiently low to be affected.[5] Shortly before this miners in Somerset and the Forest of Dean opposed the Miners' Federation campaign for a national minimum wage because they believed that many local pits would close if forced to pay rates nearer the national average.[6] Somerset miners were by far the lowest paid in Britain;[7] those in the Forest of Dean, nearer to south Wales, fared somewhat better but their pay too was considerably less than average; mine wages in the Forest of Dean

---

1. J. P. Martin and G. Wilson, *The Police: A Study in Manpower* (1969), p. 19; G. H. Wood, wage collection, loc. cit.; Table 1–8.
2. See above, pp. 10–11, and Table 1–5 which shows building wages for several towns in the region.
3. Craftsmen's (C) and Labourers' (L) Wages per Hour (pence)

| | 1886 | | 1897 | | 1906 | |
| | C | L | C | L | C | L |
|---|---|---|---|---|---|---|
| London | 9 | 6 | 9 | 6 | $10\frac{1}{2}$ | 7 |
| Bristol | 6 | 4 | $7\frac{1}{2}$ | $4\frac{1}{2}$ | 9 | 6 |
| Exeter | $5\frac{1}{2}$ | $3\frac{1}{2}$ | 6 | $3\frac{3}{4}$ | $7\frac{1}{2}$ | 5 |
| Plymouth | 6 | 4 | 6 | $3\frac{3}{4}$ | 8 | 5 |
| Swindon | 6 | — | — | — | 7 | — |

*Sources:* Table 1–5; F. W. Lawrence, *Local Variations in Wages* (1899), pp. 12–13; Operative Bricklayers' Society, Annual Reports.
4. *R.C. on Labour, Secretary's Report*, pp. 144–5, para. 168–9.
5. The legal minimum was a consequence of the Trade Boards Act of 1909. The main influence of the act in the tailoring industry was to raise women's wages. R. H. Tawney, *Minimum Rates in the Tailoring Industry* (1915), pp. 80–1.
6. H. S. Jevons, *The British Coal Trade* (1915), p. 80. See also below, p. 198.
7. In Northumberland and Durham and several other fields wages were 50 per cent or more above Somerset rates. See Table 1–7, and accompanying note.

were usually above those in Somerset but as low as those of any
other field in Britain.[1]

## III

R EGION  T HREE  (Rural South-east—see Map 1)

Region Three, comprising East Anglia and the south-east
with the exception of London and the Home Counties, had
much in common with the south-west; both were low-wage
regions. They differed, however, in one respect: whereas the
position of the south-west improved slowly throughout the
period, the standing of Region Three deteriorated. The exact
position in Region Three varied according to occupation; in
general terms, at the beginning of the period wages were near
average, by 1914 they were among the lowest in Britain.[2]

Farm wages are again the best guide to the general pattern.
The mid-century *Morning Chronicle* investigation showed that
wages in parts of the region were similar to, or only slightly
above, prevailing rates in the south-west. Labourers' wages in
Hampshire and west Sussex were no higher than in counties
to the west—most received between 7s. and 8s.; some, in the
New Forest area for example, received a little more, but others
were paid as little as 6s.[3] Suffolk and south Cambridgeshire
present a similarly dismal picture; bread and potatoes and 7s.
to 8s. a week; 7s. was the more usual rate in Suffolk.[4] In
Norfolk and the Fens, however, wages were higher: 'the condition of labour in the fenlands... presents a marked contrast to
the southern portion of the county of Cambridge.'[5] This

1. Ibid. See also *Coal Industry Commission*, P.P. 1919, XI, minutes of evidence
   para. 7407: 'The wages of the Forest of Dean miners were admittedly low,
   and perhaps, with the exception of Somerset, the lowest in the whole
   Kingdom prior to the war?—Yes.' Evidence of Sir Francis Brain on behalf
   of the colliery owners of the Forest of Dean.
2. Although Region Three's position in the rank order of regions worsened
   over time, this decline took place against a background of diminishing
   regional differentials, see below, p. 58.
3. *M.C.* 26 Jan. 1850.
4. Ibid. 5 Dec. 1849; 18 Oct. 1850. When the *Morning Chronicle* investigated
   the area in December 1849 the farmers of Cavendish and Clare were contemplating a reduction to 6s.
5. *M.C.* 18 Oct. 1850.

distinction between the Fens and the south of Cambridgeshire
held good throughout the period and, while it would be an
over-simplification to represent the distinction between the
low-wage south and the north and Midlands by a single line on
a map, if such a line were drawn it would pass through Cambridgeshire. A. Wilson Fox made a distinction between wage
levels in the north and south of Cambridgeshire when he gave
evidence to the R.C. on Agricultural Depression[1] and one of
the less important consequences of the minor revolution in
transport effected by the bicycle was that some labourers
living on the low-wage clays increased their standard of living,
and helped to erode wage differentials, by cycling to jobs on the
Fens.[2] Norfolk's advantage over counties to the south was less
enduring but in 1850 wages in south Norfolk exceeded wages in
Suffolk by 1s. a week, while wages in north Norfolk were 2s.
greater than those in Suffolk.[3] Wages in Buckinghamshire and
Oxfordshire were similar to those in north Norfolk, 9s. to
10s. a week; in Berkshire, Bedfordshire, and Hertfordshire 8s.
was the more usual rate, although towards the south of Hertfordshire, approaching London, they rose to as much as 12s.[4]

More comprehensive figures are available for 1867–70 and
there is less doubt about treatment of payments in kind. At
that time farm earnings in the rural south-east as a whole
were near the British average.[5] Labourers were better paid than
those in Wales and most of Scotland, they retained their
earlier advantage over the south-west, and were not yet at a
disadvantage compared with labourers in the Midlands.[6] But if

1. 'Wages in Cambridgeshire vary more than in any other county I know,
   because when you get up to the North you get the men paid very nearly
   as much as they are in Lincolnshire, and when you get down South you
   get them paid very much on the same scale as they are paid in Suffolk.'
   R.C. on Agricultural Depression, P.P. 1896, XVII, minutes 61258-60, 61288.
2. Wages and Conditions of Employment in Agriculture, P.P. 1919, IX, General
   Report, p. 63. See also below, p. 19 n. 4.
3. M.C. 5, 26 Dec. 1849.
4. M.C. 27 Oct. 1849; 5 Apr., 18 Oct. 1850.
5. Earnings in most counties are shown in Table 1–3; regional averages are
   shown in Table 1–4.
6. Ibid. Regional boundaries are shown on Map 1. The average for Region 3 in
   1867–70 was calculated without figures for Suffolk and Huntingdonshire—
   had they been included the regional average would probably have been
   less. According to Clifford, meat was still a great luxury in Suffolk in the

England alone is considered, earnings in the rural south-east
were below the average and the place of the region in the national
wage hierarchy was far inferior to that described a century
earlier by Arthur Young.[1] Further deterioration occurred
between 1870 and the end of the century as earnings in the
region rose less rapidly than in other low-wage regions. In 1898
earnings were only just above those in the south-west and had
fallen below those of the Midlands, Wales, and central and
northern Scotland.[2] This trend continued in the following
decade; by 1907 the region had fallen another two percentage
points below average and had become the lowest-wage region
in Britain.[3] Within the region the greatest relative decline had
occurred in East Anglia. In the 1890s a contemporary was able
to contrast conditions in Norfolk with those in Northumberland
as examples of the worst and best that a labourer might endure.
At that time wages in Suffolk were probably the lowest in
England and only Caithness and Orkney and Shetland denied
the county the distinction of being the worst-paid in Britain.[4]

The picture that emerges from a study of farm earnings in
the region is generally reproduced by the examination of wages

1870s (F. Clifford, *The Agricultural Lock-out of 1874* [Edinburgh and London, 1875], p. 183). See also the letter from the Norfolk migrant to Sheffield,
written in 1873 and reproduced in L. M. Springall, *Labouring Life in
Norfolk Villages, 1834–1914* (1936), p. 144: '... instead of working with
bread and cheese, and sometimes with bread and nothing with it, we get a
thumping bit of beef ... we have had more beef this week than we had in
three months at Acle.'
1. When Young wrote wages in the region were among the highest in England;
wages in Norfolk were then a third more than those in the West Riding.
By contrast, in 1867–70 West Riding wages were one fifth above those in
Norfolk. Young's findings are summarized in A. L. Bowley, *Wages in the
U.K. in the Nineteenth Century* (Cambridge, 1900), endtable Col. 1; earnings
in 1867–70 are shown in Tables 1–3 and 1–4. For more details of regional
changes in the century before 1850 see Caird, op. cit., pp. 512–13.
2. Table 1–4.
3. Ibid.
4. Table 1–3. 'Norfolk is generally accounted the exact opposite of Northumberland in all that regards the well being of the peasant ...', P. A.
Graham, *The Rural Exodus* (1892), p. 7. According to G. E. Evans, gypsies,
who fraternized with the 'Red Vanners' of the Land Restoration League
and assumed they had something to sell, drew their attention to Suffolk's
low wages and poor trade and recommended that they go instead to the
fenlands. G. E. Evans, *Ask the Fellows who Cut the Hay* (1965 edn.), p. 116.
On wages in East Anglia see also C. S. Orwin and B. I. Felton, 'A Century of

in other occupations. The building trades are a rather less satisfactory basis than agriculture for regional generalizations[1] but, if the figures in Table 1-6 can be accepted as reasonably representative, the position in building was much as in agriculture with wages in Region Three (represented by Chichester, Oxford, and Norwich) below the national average in 1886 and further below average in 1906.[2] At the latter date carpenters' and building labourers' wages in Region Three shared the next to last places in the regional wage table with parts of rural Scotland,[3] and wages in towns like Carnarvon, Hawick, and Peterhead were not significantly lower than those in Chichester, Oxford, and Norwich.[4] The rural constabulary in Region Three were relatively better placed than farm labourers; in 1870 they received 3 per cent above the national average.[5] But at no time were they well paid and in the second half of the period they suffered the same decline relative to other areas that has been noted in agriculture and the building trades.[6] There is a great deal of more fragmentary evidence which suggests that this description could well be applied to other occupations in the region.[7]

Wages and Earnings in Agriculture', *J.R.Ag.S.*, xcii (1931), 248. 'Essex, Norfolk and Suffolk had sunk to the position of the counties of lowest wages.'

1. See below, pp. 67, 71.
2. Tables 1-5 and 1-6.
3. Table 1-6. The south-west (Region 2) occupied last place.
4. In each case wages were 30-40 per cent below London rates. Table 1-5.
5. Tables 1-4 and 1-8. This margin is no greater than might arise from shortcomings in the statistics, but it appears to be confirmed by the position at other dates.
6. Table 1-8. By 1906 the south-east shared the foot of the regional table with parts of rural Scotland and the south-west. After 1890 the region's position, relative to the national average, was unchanged. Martin and Wilson (op. cit., p. 20) note that regional differentials diminished in the 1890s to the advantage of the low-wage areas. Regional differentials in county police pay were less marked than in most occupations. For notes on police pay see above, p. 5 and below, pp. 75-6.
7. See e.g. A. E. Musson, *The Typographical Association* (1954), pp. 191-2, on printers' wages; Tawney, op. cit., pp. 80-1, 85-6, on wages in the tailoring trades; *R.C. on Labour, Secretary's Report*, pp. 144-5, para. 168-9, on dockers' wages in the south-coast ports; H. Bosanquet (ed.), *Social Conditions in Provincial Towns* (1912), especially the chapters on Oxford and Cambridge.

# IV

REGION FOUR (South Wales—see Map 1)

By 1914 south Wales, like London, was an enclave of high
wages in an area where pay was considerably lower. The region
also demonstrates the difficulties which arise from the necessity
of defining regions according to county boundaries. Carmarthen
and Pembroke might reasonably have been included in either
Region Four or Region Five; in the event they appear in
Region Four with the result that the region has major wage
variations within its boundary. Consequently the regional
averages shown in Tables 1–4, 1–6, and 1–8 in the appendix to
this chapter require considerable qualification. A third characteristic of wages in south Wales was the improvement that
occurred relative to other regions between 1850 and 1914. It
was scarcely a high-wage area in 1850; between then and 1914
wages rose faster than they did in Britain as a whole and an
increasing proportion of the region came to enjoy better than
average earnings.

At the beginning of the period farm labourers in the Vale of
Glamorgan received between 10s. and 13s.[1] The latter sum,
although some way short of rates in Northumberland and
Durham,[2] was at the time a fairly good wage. However, 10s.
was probably not much above average, and to the west of
Glamorgan wages were as low as those in the worst-paid parts
of southern England: 'not often more than 6s. in the upper, and
7s. per week in the lower country'.[3] The prevalence of peasant
farming in this part of Britain makes farm wages a less certain
guide to over-all earnings than elsewhere, but the broad
picture in 1850 was probably much as these figures suggest.
Dodd cites evidence that the general wage level in south-west

1. C. S. Read, 'On the Farming of South Wales', *J.R.Ag.S.* ix (1849), 154.
2. See above, p. 14.
3. Read, op. cit., p. 148. A. H. John gives similar rates for 1846, 1s. a day in
   Pembroke, 2s. in Glamorgan, *The Industrial Development of South Wales,
   1750–1850* (Cardiff, 1950), pp. 80–1.

2

Wales was as low as anywhere in the south of Britain[1] and the contrast in farm earnings between the east and the west of the region was paralleled by a similar differential in the earnings of miners. Wages in Pembroke were lower than those on the coalfield to the east,[2] and even in the east miners' earnings were below those on the major English fields.[3]

There is no convincing evidence of improvement in the region's relative position during the following twenty years. In 1870 average farm earnings were below every region except the south-west of England,[4] although the average continued to mask large differentials within the region. Labourers in Pembroke and Carmarthen were among the worst-paid in Britain whereas those in Monmouth and Glamorgan received wages near the national average and some of them, almost certainly, considerably more.[5] In the thirty years after 1870 wages rose rapidly; by 1898 farm wages in the region as a whole were near the national average and in Glamorgan they exceeded the average by some 10 per cent.[6] Glamorgan rates were still below those of several counties in the north of England and parts of Scotland but they were considerably above rates in the

---

1. A. H. Dodd, *The Industrial Revolution in North Wales* (Cardiff, 1933), p. 347. See also R. Giffen on low agricultural wages at the time of the Rebecca riots, 'Further Notes on the Progress of the Working Classes in the Last Half Century', *J.R.S.S.*, xlix (1886), 52.
2. According to Morris and Williams, Pembroke miners in 1841 earned about half the rate in the east. J. H. Morris and L. J. Williams, *The South Wales Coal Industry, 1841–75* (Cardiff, 1958), p. 220.
3. The margin of disadvantage is not easily established. Miners' earnings are especially difficult to handle (see below, pp. 71–4) and in south Wales there is the additional problem of varying rates in pits producing 'sea-coal' and those associated with the iron works. According to E. W. Evans, earnings were 'substantially lower' than in other coalfields 'for at least some thirty years before 1890', *The Miners of South Wales* (Cardiff, 1961), p. 214. Dodd gives some figures for 1850 which show south Wales clearly (although hardly 'substantially') below Northumberland, Durham, Staffordshire, and Lancashire (op. cit., p. 343). See also A. H. John, op. cit., p. 86. For details of mine earnings in various parts of the region around the middle of the century see *M.C.* 21 and 27 Mar. 1850; Morris and Williams, op. cit., *passim*; A. Dalziel, *The Colliers' Strike in South Wales* (Cardiff, 1872), p. 9 and *passim*.
4. Table 1–4.
5. Table 1–3. See also *Commission on the Employment of Children, Young Persons and Women in Agriculture, Third Report*, P.P. 1870, XIII, p. 18.
6. Tables 1–3, 1–4.

south of England.[1] So much was this the case that farm labourers from Wiltshire, Somerset, Devon, Herefordshire, and Gloucestershire had been attracted into the Vale of Glamorgan and largely replaced indigenous labour. By 1919 the farm labouring population throughout the whole county was 'in all probability overwhelmingly English' . . . 'Welshmen . . . are not such fools as to work on the farms when they can obtain higher wages for fewer hours in the works and collieries.' [2]

There was a similar long-term relative improvement in mining and building wages.[3] Rowe's figures show that by 1888 hewers in south Wales received near the national average, and by 1914 6 per cent more than average.[4] It would be unwise to place much emphasis on the precise percentages calculated from Rowe's figures for single years[5] but some considerable improvement over the whole period is beyond doubt. A similar improvement is visible in the earnings of south Wales mine labourers between 1888 and 1914, although at both dates their earnings compared less favourably than south Wales hewers' earnings with rates in other coalfields.[6] Building wages, on the

1. Tables 1–3, 1–4.
2. *R.C. on Labour* (The Agricultural Labourer: Wales), P.P. 1893–4, XXXVI, p. 8; *Wages and Conditions of Employment in Agriculture* (Vol. ii), P.P. 1919, IX, p. 452.
3. This trend is not apparent in police wages. These show the usual pattern of variation within the region—Glamorganshire paid the highest rate followed by Monmouthshire, Carmarthenshire, and Pembrokeshire—but the average of wages in the four counties throughout the period fluctuated about a level somewhat above the national average. Parts of this region, and parts of Region Five, were affected by the 'Rebecca' unrest and the pay of the local constabulary may have been influenced by the need to secure more-able recruits than sufficed elsewhere, see below, p. 76. Table 1–8 and the G. H. Wood unpublished collection of wage statistics (Library of the Royal Statistical Society).
4. Table 1–7, also above, p. 22 n. 3.
5. Rowe's figure for 1914 probably underestimates relative wages in south Wales over the period 1900–14. At that time the better-paid of the Welsh hewers were almost certainly among the highest paid in Britain. See below, p. 153 n. 1 and Jevons, op. cit., p. 120.
6. Table 1–7. Wage differentials between skilled and unskilled mineworkers seem to have been especially marked in South Wales. The region was noted also for exceptional variations in hewers' earnings. South Wales, in spite of its proportion of well-paid hewers, probably gained more from the 1912 Minimum Wage Act than any major field. B. Thomas, 'Studies in Labour Supply and Labout Costs', Ph.D. thesis, University of London (1931), pp. 180–1; J. W. F. Rowe, *Wages in the Coal Industry* (1923), pp. 105–7.

evidence of Cardiff and Newport, followed a similar pattern. Craftsmen's rates were near average in the 1880s and moderately high by 1906.[1] At the latter date carpenters received 9d. per hour in Cardiff and 8½d. in Newport. Cardiff was on a par with Leicester, Nottingham, and Hull, a halfpenny below Manchester and other major centres in the north, and three-halfpence below London.[2] In this trade, too, unskilled wages compared less favourably with other areas; builders' labourers received less than the average rate in 1886 but near the average twenty years later.[3]

The most characteristic feature of wages in south Wales was long-term improvement relative to rates elsewhere. By the end of the period the moderately well-paid building craftsmen of Newport and Cardiff were probably representative of a great many occupations on and south of the main coalfield as far west as the border between Glamorgan and Carmarthen. However, another distinguishing feature of wages in the region, marked local variations, had not disappeared. To the west and north of the main coalfield wages were not above the national average even at the end of the period.[4] A further characteristic of wages in south Wales may have been an unusually wide differential for skill; as we have seen, unskilled labour in the coal and building trades, even in the better-paid areas, received little more than the national average at the end of the period and less than average in the 1880s.

# V

REGION FIVE (Rural Wales and Herefordshire—see Map 1)

The course of wages in this region had some features in common with the pattern in south Wales, particularly with the

1. Table 1–6.
2. Table 1–5. Newport craftsmen received little more than half of the London rate in 1860; in 1906 they received 80 per cent of the London rate.
3. Table 1–6.
4. According to the figures in Tables 1–3 and 1–5 farm labourers in Pembroke-shire were paid some 5 per cent less than average in 1907, Abergavenny building labourers were paid 16 per cent below average in 1906.

more rural parts of that region. In both regions wages were below the national average in 1850 but rose faster than the average in the next sixty years; wages in Region Five, however, rose neither as fast nor as far as those in south Wales.

The evidence relating to wages in this area is sparser than in any other part of England and Wales, particularly for the early part of the period, but there can be no doubt that wages at that time were well below average. The counties of Region Five, together with Pembrokeshire and Carmarthenshire in Region Four, comprised possibly the worst-paid part of England and Wales: 'In the middle of the nineteenth century it was stated that wages in north Wales and the western counties of South Wales were lower than in any other part of south Britain.'[1] Flint and Denbigh miners, like those in Pembroke, received between half and three-quarters of the rates paid in the south Wales field and much less than most English miners.[2]

There is, however, reason to believe that improvement, relative to other areas, was under way by 1870: 'It would appear that the average condition of the agricultural labourer in Wales is superior to what is met with in many of the southern counties of England, though not equal to the state of things in the northern and eastern districts.'[3] This statement may be slightly optimistic but it is not wildly misleading, for by 1870 farm wages were a little above those in the south-west of England (Region Two); and in only two of the ten counties in Region Five were wages as low as the average rate in south-

1. Dodd, op. cit., p. 347. On farm labourers' wages in Cardiganshire in 1846, 'one of the most poverty stricken districts', see S.C. on Railway Labourers, P.P. 1846, XIII, evidence para. 1744–5. In mid-nineteenth-century Liverpool there were complaints that Welsh migrants were prepared to undercut normal wages: 'The Welsh can live where other people would starve.' M.C. 16 Sept. 1850.

2. Dodd, op. cit., p. 343, and see above, p. 22 n. 2. For a further unfavourable comparison between earnings in north Wales and in England and Scotland see E. Rogers, 'The History of Trade Unionism in the Coal Mining Industry of North Wales', Trans. Denbighshire Historical Society, xv (1966), 157; on the differential between miners' wages in Wrexham and south Lancashire in the 1830s see T. C. Barker and J. R. Harris, A Merseyside Town in the Industrial Revolution, St Helens 1750–1900 (1959), p. 275.

3. Employment of Women, Children, etc. in Agriculture, p. 18.

west Wales.[1] There may be further evidence of recent improvement in the fact that the rural constabulary was not worse paid than average in 1860, but there is no earlier evidence with which this position can be compared and it seems likely that, as in south Wales, police wages followed a pattern in some respects peculiar to themselves.[2] Miners' wages in this region were still well below the national average in 1862. According to Rogers they were then some two-thirds of rates in Yorkshire, north Staffordshire, and the north-east, but his estimate is too vague to make any useful comparison with the equally vague accounts of relative earnings in 1850.[3]

There is firmer evidence of relative improvement between 1870 and the end of the century. The miners of north Wales were still among the worst-paid in Britain in 1888—of all the fields for which figures are available only Somerset paid less[4]—but the margin of disadvantage was narrower than it had been twenty or thirty years previously. Hewers were paid half to three-quarters of the rate in high-wage districts in the 1850s and 1860s, but by 1888 they received some 86 per cent of the average rate and about 75 per cent of the highest rates in Britain.[5] Farm wages, likewise, were below the national average at the end of the century but to a smaller extent than in 1870. By 1898 farm earnings in Region Five were above those in the south-east and East Anglia as well as the south-west.[6] Within

1. Earnings of around 11s. 6d. were paid in Anglesey, Cardiganshire, Pembrokeshire, and Carmarthenshire. Within Region 5 the average ranged between 11s. 6d. and 13s. 6d.; the national average was then 14s. 3½d. Tables 1–3, 1–4.
2. Table 1–8 and see above, p. 23 n. 3. Police wages appear to have compared more favourably with rates elsewhere than most wages in Wales in the early part of the period and to have failed to share in the subsequent improvement in relative position. In Region 5 they were at, or near, average over the whole period from 1860 to 1906.
3. E. Rogers, 'The History of Trade Unionism in the Coal Mining Industry of North Wales', *Trans. Denbighshire Historical Society*, xvii (1968), 151.
4. Table 1–7.
5. Ibid., and see above, p. 25. According to Rowe's figures the gap between mine labourers' earnings in north Wales in 1888 and earnings in the best-paid districts was somewhat wider than the hewers' differential; none of his individual figures will bear much scrutiny, although together with the probably even cruder estimates of Dodd and Rogers they are sufficient to indicate the main trend and approximate proportions. See notes on miners' earnings below pp. 71–4.
6. Table 1–4. Regional boundaries are shown on Map 1.

the region farm earnings were highest in Carnarvonshire,
Flintshire, and Denbighshire.[1] Between 1888 and the end of the
period miners' relative earnings improved again. They moved
some 5 to 8 per cent closer to the national average, well above
the level in Somerset, above the Forest of Dean, and not far
behind Cumberland, Cannock Chase, and south Staffordshire.[2]
Even so, wages in the north Wales coalfield remained well
below the national average.

The general pattern of wages in the region, relative to other
areas, is reasonably clear; it was characterized by steady improvement although in 1914 most wages remained below
average.[3] Progress consisted in the transition from a very low-
wage region at the beginning of the period to a moderately low-
wage region at its end. No single time series can accurately
portray this transition but farm labourers' earnings are probably
the best single guide; in 1867–70, 1898, and 1907 they were 9,
6, and 3 per cent respectively below the national average.[4]

# VI

REGION SIX (Midlands—see Map 1)

Wages in the midland counties were above average but
clearly below the level in the north of England. There were
considerable variations within the region: to the south and
south-east the Midlands merged into the rural south-east
(Region 3), to the west lay rural Wales (Region 5), another
area distinguished by low earnings, yet immediately to the
north were the high-wage counties where modern industrialism
had appeared first and progressed furthest. Midland wages
reflected this variety of peripheral conditions. In some of the

1. Table 1–3. By 1898 Flint earnings reached the national average.
2. Table 1–7.
3. Evidence from the building trades in this region is too scanty to show long-
   term changes in relative wages; wages in Carnarvon and Hereford were well
   below average in 1906. Table 1–5.
4. Table 1–4.

more rural parts of Warwickshire, Worcestershire, and Leicestershire market conditions were hardly distinguishable from those prevalent in the rural south. Elsewhere, in Birmingham, Nottingham, and most of Derbyshire, conditions were not dissimilar to those in Lancashire and the West Riding.

As a transitional area between north and south the Midlands warrant more attention than would be generally appropriate in a survey of regional differentials. Farm earnings are again the best single indicator of relative wages; it should be noted, however, that farm wages in the Midlands compared less favourably with other areas than did urban wages; industrial towns in the Midlands showed the greatest affinity with conditions to the north, while rural areas, particularly in the south Midlands, had most in common with southern England and rural Wales.[1] In the late 1860s farm wages, in the region as a whole, were near the national average; they were above rates in Wales and the south-west, roughly on a par with rates in the rural south-east, but well below rates in the north of England.[2] At the end of the century farm wages were a little above the national average; by this time the midland farm workers were better off than those in the rural south-east as well as those in Wales and the south-west, and the differential between northern regions and the Midlands had contracted in the previous thirty years. The position was substantially the same in 1907, save that south Wales by then had drawn level with the Midlands.[3]

The relationship between farm wages in different parts of the region was fairly consistent throughout the period; they rose from south to north, and from west Shropshire and east Leicestershire towards the centre.[4] Derbyshire and Nottinghamshire labourers were paid the most; average farm wages in Derbyshire were 15 to 20 per cent above the Worcestershire rate and between 8 and 15 per cent above the rate in the

---

1. For notes on agricultural wages see above, p. 4 below, pp. 65–6.
2. Table 1–4.
3. Ibid.
4. Table 1–3.

Midlands as a whole. The order of the other countries is less
clear but Staffordshire was probably in third place behind
Derbyshire and Nottinghamshire, and Worcestershire labourers
were probably the least well paid in the Midlands.[1] Local
variations can be illustrated by material from the *Second
Report on the Wages, Earnings and Conditions of Employment of
Agricultural Labourers in the U.K.* Wages fell steeply on the
southern perimeter of the industrial Midlands; within Warwickshire, along a line from the Birmingham area south-south-
west towards Oxford, cash payments fell from 18*s.* to 12*s.* in
less than 40 miles:

| Rural districts | Farm labourer's weekly cash wage, winter 1903[2] |
|---|---|
| Castle Bromwich (War.) | 17*s.*–18*s.* |
| Solihull (War.) | 15*s.*–16*s.* |
| Warwick (War.) | 15*s.* |
| Stratford-on-Avon (War.) | 13*s.* |
| Brailes (War.) | 12*s.* |

In the south of the county, near the border with Gloucestershire and Oxfordshire, farm wages (12*s.* to 13*s.*) were as low as
almost anywhere in England;[3] and it seems probable that
wages here had been well below average for several decades—
in the late 1860s, for example, labourers in Oxfordshire and
Gloucestershire were paid considerably less than the Warwickshire average, and in Joseph Ashby's Tysoe, close to the
Oxford border, the labourers' wage 'would not buy bread for a
family, let alone any meat'.[4] The general situation in the area
south of Birmingham was similar to those described earlier in
Cambridgeshire and on the edge of the London area: in each
case the gradient of the wage contours marks the transition
from one major wage area to another.[5]

1. Ibid.
2. *Source: Second Report on Wages ... Agricultural Labourers*, p. 155. These
   figures make no allowance for payments in kind but as the average value of
   such payments in Warwickshire was only 2*s.* their inclusion would not
   significantly alter the general pattern. Ibid., p. 28.
3. *Second Report on Wages ... Agricultural Labourers*, pp. 151–9. This inquiry
   showed only one rural district with cash wages less than 11*s.* (Dorchester
   in Dorset).
4. Table 1–3; M. K. Ashby, *Joseph Ashby of Tysoe, 1859–1919* (Cambridge,
   1961), p. 36. On conditions in Tysoe in the early 1890s see ibid., pp. 158–9.
5. See above, pp. 10–11, 17–18.

North from Birmingham along a line through Staffordshire to the Derbyshire-Cheshire border wages were considerably higher; at first they fell slightly, to around 15s. in mid-Staffordshire; they then rose again towards the Potteries:

| Rural District | Farm labourers' weekly cash wage, winter 1903[1] |
|---|---|
| Walsall (Staffs.) | 17s. to 18s. |
| Lichfield (Staffs.) | 16s. to 18s. |
| Stafford (Staffs.) | 15s. to 16s. |
| Uttoxeter (Staffs.) | 14s. to 16s. |
| Cheadle (Staffs.) | 16s. to 17s. |
| Stoke-on-Trent (Staffs.) | 18s. |
| Leek (Staffs.) | 15s. to 18s. |
| Chapel-en-le-Frith (Derbys.) | 19s. to 21s. |

To the east and west of south Staffordshire, across Shropshire towards central Wales and across Leicestershire towards Rutland, wages fell slightly but, again, the wage contours were far more widely spaced than to the south of Birmingham:

| Rural district | Farm labourers' weekly cash wage, winter 1903[2] |
|---|---|
| Forden (Montgomery) | 14s. |
| Atcham (Salop) | 15s. |
| Wellington (Salop) | 14s. |
| Shifnal (Salop) | 15s. |
| Cannock (Staffs.) | 15s. to 16s. |
| Lichfield (Staffs.) | 16s. to 18s. |
| Market Bosworth (Leices.) | 17s. |
| Blaby (Leices.) | 16s. |
| Billesdon (Leices.) | 15s. |
| Oakham (Rutland) | 14s. |

By 1903 Leicestershire wage rates were clearly above the level found in the south-east of England, no district paid less than 14s.; this, however, was no less clearly below wage levels in the north Midlands, the lowest return in Derbyshire was 17s.[3]

Less need be said about wages in other trades. Table 1–8 shows that the rural constabulary in the Midlands occupied a position in the regional wage table similar to agriculture. At

1. *Source*: as in p. 29 n. 2, 3 above, q.v.; payments in kind averaged 2s. 5d. in Staffordshire and 1s. 11d. in Derbyshire.
2. *Source;* ibid.; payments in kind averaged 1s. in Montgomery, 3s. 4d. in Shropshire, 2s. 5d. in Staffordshire, 1s. 7d. in Leicestershire and Rutland.
3. Ibid., pp. 153–4. In Leicestershire the highest returns were for Hinckley, Market Bosworth, Ashby-de-la-Zouch, Barrow-upon-Soar, and Castle Donnington—all these districts were on, or near, the Leicestershire coalfield.

each of seven dates between 1860 and 1906 their wages exceeded the national average for the rural constabulary by between 3 and 6 per cent; differentials among the seven midland counties were less marked than in farm wages, but the rank orders of farm and police wages were almost identical.[1] Wages in mining are less easily summarized because there were at least five separate coalfields in the region, developed at different times, worked by different methods, and serving different markets. Fragmentary evidence for parts of Staffordshire at the beginning of the period shows that earnings varied between the south Staffordshire and north Staffordshire fields, between one district and another within these fields, and according to whether 'thick coal' or 'thin coal' was worked. However, most Staffordshire men were paid as much as miners on other major fields and were better paid than those in south Wales and the minor fields.[2] More detailed information is available for 1888 and 1914; as always with mine wages considerable reserve is required in their interpretation but a few tentative observations may be made without placing unreasonable burden on the evidence.[3] Hewers in Nottinghamshire and Derbyshire, in common with farm labourers and policemen in these counties, received more than the national average and more than most other midland miners; D. H. Lawrence's Nottinghamshire miners were among the more fortunate members of a relatively well-paid occupation. On the west midland fields, north and south Staffordshire and Cannock Chase, earnings were near average in 1888[4] but by 1914 in south Staffordshire and Cannock Chase had fallen below average. In Warwickshire, however, earnings rose rapidly

1. Table 1–8 and, for county rates, G. H. Wood Collection.
2. *Returns of Wages published between 1830 and 1886*, P.P. 1887, LXXXIX, pp. 25–6; Dodd, op. cit., p. 343, and see above, pp. 22, 26.
3. See Table 1–7 and accompanying notes on which the following observations are based. Rowe cast especial doubt on his estimates for south Staffordshire and Cannock Chase and in particular on the differential between hewers' and labourers' wages in these fields. For more details of midland wages in 1888 and 1914 see B. R. Mitchell, 'The Economic Development of the Inland Coalfields 1870–1914', Ph.D. thesis, University of Cambridge (1955), p. 208.
4. This may indicate some relative decline from the position in 1850.

and by 1914 were among the highest in the Midlands.[1]
This variety of experience is not easily covered by any single
generalization: the least unsatisfactory description is that the
midland miners, like the farm labourers and policemen, were
paid rates near or somewhat above the national average.

Building wages illustrate the disparity between relative wages
in urban and rural occupations mentioned earlier.[2] In 1886 and
1906, the two dates for which an index of building wages has
been calculated, labourers and craftsmen in Birmingham,
Nottingham, and Leicester were relatively well paid and the
Midlands, represented by these towns, was one of the two
highest-wage regions in Britain—a considerably better position
than it occupied in the table of farm wages.[3] Before 1880
builders' wages in Birmingham were a little below those in
Manchester and rather more below wages in London. By 1906
Birmingham men had achieved parity with Manchester and
received much the same as those in Leeds, Newcastle, and
Glasgow; they were still a little behind London but, compared
with many places, Birmingham was a high-wage centre.[4]
The question of representativeness is particularly important
in the building trades because in Table 1–6 each region is
represented by just two or three towns. By 1906 Nottingham
and Leicester rates were similar to those in Birmingham,[5]
but in the more rural parts of the region wages were
considerably lower. Craftsmen's wages in Shrewsbury and
Stratford-upon-Avon in 1906, for example, were 10 to 35 per
cent below the Birmingham rate; they were roughly on a
par with craftsmen's wages in Exeter and Dover and not much

1. Table 1–7 and see J. W. F. Rowe, *Wages in the Coal Industry*, p. 79. The
   Leicestershire miners, according to Rowe's figures, although only some
   twenty miles distant, failed to share Warwickshire's relative improvement.
   It is interesting to note the great contrast between unskilled mine earnings
   in the north of Warwickshire and the earnings of farm labourers in south
   Warwickshire. In 1903 the farm labourers received as little as 12s. to 13s.
   a week, they were unlikely to have had more than a shilling or so more
   by 1914, and at that time six days unskilled mine work in north Warwickshire paid around 37s. Ibid.; above, p. 29, below, p. 72, and A. L. Bowley,
   *Prices and Wages in the United Kingdom, 1914–20*, p. 171.
2. See above, p. 28.
3. Tables 1–4, 1–5, 1–6.
4. Table 1–5; see also A. Briggs in *V.C.H. Warwickshire*, vii (1964), 224–5.
5. Table 1–5.

higher than those in Taunton and Chichester.[1] The dangers inherent in averages have been mentioned several times; the 'average midland farm labourer' and the 'average midland building worker' were both conceived in the statistical appendix to this chapter, but we may be fairly sure that the Stratford-upon-Avon farmworker was closer to the first than his bricklayer neighbour to the second because most midland building workers were employed in the larger towns. We may be reasonably confident, also, that even if rates in Birmingham, Nottingham, and Leicester were above the regional average, building wages in the region as a whole compared more favourably than farm wages with rates elsewhere in Britain.

For Birmingham itself building wages are probably a fairly reliable guide to the general level of wages. A detailed account of earnings in the city's multitudinous metal trades would afford material for at least one monograph,[2] and at least one more could be written on other features of wages in the city: on differentials for sex and skill;[3] on relative wage levels in Birmingham and the Black Country; and on the nail makers and others who formed a low-paid sector analogous to London's East End.[4] But space, and a regard for proportion, confine our attention to the major features and, as any of the more comprehensive wage surveys of the kind increasingly available after 1890 confirm, the overwhelming characteristic of wages in Birmingham was that they compared well with those in

---

1. Table 1–5 and sources, T, U, and W below, p. 66.
2. For a general account of labour in these trades see G. C. Allen, *The Industrial Development of Birmingham and the Black Country, 1860–1927* (1929).
3. Both appear to have been wider than average: Table A–3; see also D. E. C. Eversley in *V.C.H. Warwickshire*, vii (1964), 136; G. C. Allen, op. cit., p. 158; E. Cadbury, M. C. Matheson, and G. Shann, *Women's Work and Wages* (1906), p. 119.
4. Sweating and outwork were a part of the local scene but they do not modify descriptions of Birmingham as a high-wage centre to the extent that similar descriptions of London are qualified by unskilled earnings in the East End. Sweating and outwork were less a feature of Birmingham than of the Black Country where wage rates were generally below the level in Birmingham, particularly in the last quarter of the century. On these points see Allen, op. cit., pp. 158, 212, 226–7, 263–4, 272, and B. M. D. Smith in *V.C.H. Warwickshire* vii (1964), 183.

most other centres.[1] Much the same can be said of the relationship between wages in the building trades and other occupations
in Nottingham. In the mid-nineteenth century the city was
regarded as 'the Manchester of the Midlands'; it was a pushing
and prosperous town with 'an abundance of employment for
labourers, bricklayers, and brickmakers'; all of these, and most
of the lace makers, were well paid.[2] Leicester's relative
position, however, was less favourable at the beginning of the
period than it became after 1880. Even in 1886 building wages
in Leicester were slightly below Nottingham rates[3] and in 1850
the differential between the general wage level in the two
centres may have been considerable because Leicester was
considerably the less prosperous. At that time its staple trade,
hosiery, was 'antiquated and overcrowded . . .',[4] 'employment
was irregular and wages were low.'[5] Not long after this the

1. Birmingham was noted for its skill, its long-term prosperity, and for wages
   greater 'than fall to the lot of labouring men in general', see Smith and
   Briggs in *V.C.H. Warwickshire*, vii. 109, 224–5. The level of building wages
   suggests that Birmingham compared rather less well with London and
   Manchester before 1880 than after; in the 1890s brass workers were moving
   to London attracted by high wages and in the middle of the century
   Birmingham's lower wages were instrumental in allowing the city to capture
   a part of Sheffield's trade in edge tools and other metal goods; however,
   both London and Sheffield were high-wage centres. B. M. D. Smith, ibid.,
   p. 178, and Allen, op. cit., pp. 67, 73.
2. R. A. Church, *Economic and Social Change in a Midland Town: Victorian
   Nottingham, 1815–1900* (1966), pp. 228–9, 295. In 1850 wages in the
   hosiery trade were depressed but they rose rapidly soon after. Ibid.,
   Ch. x. For more details on lace wages in 1850 see *M.C.* 10 Jan. 1850. In
   1860 Mundella's employees received between 25s. and 40s. and in 1865,
   when farm labourers in Britain earned between 9s. and 20s., half of Nottingham's lace makers received above 25s. and a third received in the region of
   35s.; in 1906, when average male earnings in Britain were about 30s.,
   average earnings in the lace trade were about 40s. Church, op. cit., pp. 269,
   295, 304–5; H. A. Clegg, A. Fox, and A. F. Thompson, *A History of British
   Trade Unions Since 1889*, i (Oxford, 1964), 482; also Table 1–3. On wages
   in the Nottingham and Derby lace trade in 1906 see G. H. Wood, *The
   History of Wages in the Cotton Trade* (1910), p. 83. As in most high-wage
   centres there were exceptions to the general rule, notably the handframe
   knitters who clung to pre-machine methods in a steam age and paid dearly
   for the privilege. A remnant of this class survived into the twentieth
   century knitting underwear for soldiers and the very finest silk stockings;
   for this they received as little as 7s. a week. F. A. Wells, *The British
   Hosiery Trade* (1935), pp. 186–7; Church, op. cit., pp. 279–80.
3. Table 1–5.
4. C. Ashworth in *V.C.H. Leicestershire*, iv (1958), 308.
5. R. A. McKinley and C. T. Smith in ibid., iv. 259–60.

town's fortunes improved; by 1868 the Leicester 'lean stockinger' had disappeared and the following decades were characterized by prosperity and expansion[1] and also, no doubt, by a gradual improvement in relative wages so that by 1900 Leicester could be counted a high-wage centre. The variety in wages among and within these three towns by no means exhausts the range of wage patterns found in the Midlands. In small towns on the southern and western fringes of the region, wages in other occupations doubtless compared no better with Birmingham rates than the building trades;[2] and there were probably other and more idiosyncratic patterns— in Coventry, for example, whose staple trade collapsed at about the time Leicester's was beginning to improve.[3] However, there is little doubt that most men in Birmingham, Nottingham, and Leicester received rates well above the national average for their particular occupations and that in the other, more rural, occupations which have been examined most midland wages were not below the national average. The best single description of wages in the region as a whole is that, compared with other areas, wages were 'middling-high': town wages were nearer 'high' than 'middling' while rural and mine wages, particularly in the south Midlands, were not much above the national average.

# VII

REGION SEVEN (Lincs., Rutland, E. and N. Ridings—see Map 1)

Far less comment is necessary on Region Seven, a somewhat untidy collection of counties too northerly to be included in Region Three (rural south-east) and too rural for inclusion with

---

1. Ibid., iv. 269, 275.
2. See above, pp. 32–3.
3. On labour in Coventry see J. M. Prest, *The Industrial Revolution in Coventry* (Oxford, 1960). Prest has few details of wages outside the silk trade but it would be surprising if the general level of wages was unaffected by the collapse of the town's staple.

Regions Six (Midlands) or Eight (Lancs., Cheshire, and the
W. Riding). Wages here were moderately high; in most cases
somewhere between the national average and rates in the
highest-wage areas. In this respect the region had much in
common with the Midlands (Region Six), although wages in
rural occupations in Region Seven probably compared more
favourably than urban wages with rates elsewhere, whereas in
the Midlands the opposite was the case.[1]

In the late 1840s farm labourers in East Yorkshire were said
to be among the best-paid in England and accounts of 1848 and
1849 put their wages at 2s. to 2s. 6d. a day.[2] Twenty years later
farm earnings in the region were some 20 per cent above the
national average and 50 per cent above rates in the lowest-wage
counties;[3] they were still above average at the end of the period,
although the margin of advantage had been reduced.[4] The same
general pattern can be seen in the index of county constabulary
pay.[5] Building wages, on the evidence of rates in Hull, Lincoln,
and Scarborough, compared less favourably than farm wages
with rates elsewhere, but not to an extent that seriously
qualifies the pattern described above.[6] Craftsmen's wages were
slightly below average in 1886 and 1906 but their labourers' pay
was above average at both dates and the craftsmen's disadvantage would probably disappear if Middlesbrough were
included in the index.[7]

Within the region wages were almost certainly highest in the
vicinity of Middlesbrough where building rates in 1906 were the
same as in Birmingham and Manchester and not much below

1. Farm wages were higher in Region 7 than Region 6 but the opposite was
   true of building wages. Tables 1–4 and 1–6.
2. J. A. Sheppard, 'East Yorkshire's Agricultural Labour Force in the mid-
   Nineteenth Century', *Agricultural History Review*, ix (1961), 47; C. S. Read,
   op. cit., p. 148. 2s. 6d. a day was an exceptionally high rate at this time,
   see above, p. 14 and below p. 39 n. 2.
3. Tables 1–3 and 1–4. These figures are the average of wages in Lincolnshire
   and the East and North Ridings; no figure is available for Rutland at this
   date.
4. Ibid.
5. Table 1–8. Wages were consistently above average and by a greater margin
   at the beginning of the period than in the early twentieth century.
6. Table 1–6.
7. Tables 1–5, 1–6.

rates in London.[1] Hull rates were somewhat below Middlesbrough's, but above those in Lincoln to the south.[2] A similar
tendency for wages to increase from south to north within the
region is suggested by the farm wages shown in Table 1–3: in
1898 labourers were paid 17s. 2d., near the national average, in
Rutland, 17s. 9d. in Lincolnshire, and 18s. 6d. and 18s. 8d. in
the East and North Ridings respectively.[3]

## VIII

REGION EIGHT (Lancs., Cheshire, and the West Riding—
see Map 1)

Wages in Lancashire, Cheshire, and the West Riding have
already been mentioned sufficiently to indicate their general
level. They were high by contemporary standards; almost
invariably above average and in many occupations among the
highest in Britain. There were exceptions to this statement, as
there are exceptions to any generalization about the labour
market in this period: for example, the remnants of the handloom weavers like the 'handful of miserable old men' discovered by the investigator of the *Morning Chronicle* in Ashton-
under-Lyne in 1849, the 'low Irish' of Liverpool, Huddersfield,
and elsewhere 'pigging themselves on the floors of garrets and
cellars',[4] cotton workers during the 'famine', and similar cases—
but these groups were not typical.

Manchester freetraders were more aware of regional differentials and local advantages than most of their contemporaries;
at the time of the corn law agitation one commented: 'the
further people were removed from the manufacturing districts,
the worse was their condition.' [5] Twenty years later David
Chadwick, treasurer of Salford, made favourable comparisons
between local agricultural earnings and those in districts 'where
there is no competition for employments connected with

---

1. Table 1–5. See also the detailed account of farm wages by rural districts in
   *Second Report on the Wages . . . of Agricultural Labourers*, pp. 152, 154, 156.
2. Table 1–5.
3. Tables 1–3, 1–4.
4. *M.C.* 8 Nov., 3 Dec. 1849. The Ashton-under-Lyne handloom weavers
   earned less than 5s. a week; average wages in a local mill were 22s. 5d.
5. Quoted in A. Briggs, *Victorian Cities* (1963), p. 118.

manufacturers'.[1] Not all contemporaries were so perceptive; many were preoccupied with chronological fluctuations in local prosperity and thus failed to appreciate even greater spatial variations. When local dignitaries doubted the ability of Lancashire ratepayers to meet the cost of relief during the 'cotton famine' it was necessary for *The Times* to mention that far higher poor rates were commonplace in the rural south.[2] But most of the comment and surveys which include realistic comparisons of the north-west and other areas are tinged with optimism. One commentator on conditions during the 'famine' suggested that Lancashire suffered unduly because good living in normal times had left the operatives ill prepared to make the most of reduced incomes,[3] and the *Morning Chronicle* survey, which was more thorough than any in the middle decades of the century, noted conditions in Manchester with approval. It found the cotton workers well shod and seldom in want of a meat dinner; 'their general appearance is that of unostentatious comfort'; reports on the Yorkshire woollen district in the same survey were hardly less favourable.[4] At St. Helens, according to Barker and Harris, 'many of the local workmen were well-paid',[5] and Pollard has noted 'exceptionally high' earnings at Sheffield in the 'fifties and 'sixties—high enough for the better-paid Sheffield workers to acquire a reputation as prodigious, and discriminating, meat eaters: 'in good times the operatives insist on having the prime joints.' [6] Of course there were periodic hard times in Sheffield,[7] as in the rest of Region

1. D. Chadwick, 'On the rate of wages in Manchester and Salford, and the Manufacturing Districts of Lancashire, 1839–59', *J.R.S.S.*, xxiii (1860), 18.
2. W. O. Henderson, *The Lancashire Cotton Famine, 1861–1865* (Manchester, 1934), pp. 56–7. These were bad years in the cotton towns but Wessex rates were twice Lancashire's and five times as high in some parishes.
3. Ibid., p. 101.
4. *M.C.* 22 Oct., 29 Nov., 3, 6, and 10 Dec. 1849.
5. Barker and Harris, op. cit., pp. 275–7, 284–9, 375, 453.
6. S. Pollard, 'Wages and Earnings in the Sheffield Trades, 1851–1914', *Yks. Bull.*, vi (1954), 59; idem, *A History of Labour in Sheffield* (Liverpool, 1959), p. 25.
7. Times were less good in Sheffield after 1875 and some of the town's wage differentials over other areas were lost; even so, in 1878 the American consul was complaining that the 'ignorant poor' of the city scorned cheap American meat. High wages and the local preference for the more expensive cuts of meat were noted again in the early twentieth century. Pollard, *Labour in Sheffield*, pp. 107, 180, 229; idem, 'Wages and Earnings', p. 59.

Eight, and by no means all the labour forces was well off even in the best years. But any comparison between conditions here and elsewhere in Britain suggests that much of what has been written of the 'industrial north' in the nineteenth century has been unduly influenced by the experience of exceptional groups like the handloom weavers and by romantic contemporary notions of Arcadias recently lost or still existent. Compared with other areas, and particularly with the rural south of England, the chief characteristic of labour in the industrial north was its high wages and long term prosperity.[1] The quantitative evidence that follows defines the region's advantage more precisely but in no way alters this overall impression.

In 1849, when the average farm labourer's wage in England was about 10s.,[2] labourers in the area 10 miles around Manchester were paid 15s., and those between 10 and 20 miles from Manchester a shilling less. Around Sheffield wages ranged between 12s. and 15s.[3] Twenty years later average earnings in Region Eight as a whole were just over 17s.; that is, 20 per cent above the national average and some 40 per cent more than the level of wages in the lowest-wage region.[4] It is hardly surprising, therefore, that Lancashire and Yorkshire were prominent among the destinations of farm labourers sent north by Canon Girdlestone:

1. For some comment on relative conditions in Lancashire and elsewhere in the early part of the century see J. D. Marshall: 'The Lancashire farm-workers . . . received, in the early decades of the century, money wages which were among the highest in the kingdom.' 'The Lancashire Rural Labourer in the Early Nineteenth Century', *Trans. Lancashire and Cheshire Antiquarian Society*, lxxi (1961), 97. On wages and conditions at Platts works in Oldham near the end of the century see de Rousiers, op. cit., pp. 332–9. For a short account of conditions at the same works in the 1840s, including references to high wages and plentiful diet, see T. Wood, *Autobiography* (1956).
2. There is insufficient evidence of Welsh and Scottish wages and of payment in kind to be sure of the national average in 1850. The figures given above are impressions based on evidence in the *M.C.* survey and elsewhere. Bowley gives 9s. 7d. as the average English cash wage in 1851 with Lancashire and the West Riding the best-paid counties. A. L. Bowley, *Wages in the U.K.*, endtable.
3. Chadwick, op. cit., p. 19; *M.C.* 15 Feb. 1850.
4. Table 1–4.

. . . In the year 1867 I migrated into different parts of the North of England several hundred families of labourers from the county of Devon. I did it on strictly politico-economical principles, that is to say, I sent the supply where there was the demand.

To what part of the north of England did you send them? (Sir Charles Wentworth Dilke).

I sent them to Lancashire and Yorkshire in large numbers, and likewise to Northumberland and other counties.[1]

Farm earnings were still distinctly above average in 1898 and 1907 although now by a smaller margin (8 per cent in each case) and the advantage over the lowest-paid region was down to 19 per cent by 1907.[2] County differentials were wider than this and district differentials wider still. In January 1903 the highest wage in the rural districts of Lancashire was 22s., the lowest 18s. In Essex and Warwickshire, by contrast, farm labourers in some districts received only 11s. and the highest returns from Norfolk and Suffolk were only 14s.[3] Within Region Eight farm earnings throughout most of Lancashire and the West Riding were slightly above those in Cheshire; in 1903 the lowest rates in the region were recorded near the Shropshire and Welsh border and in the most easterly parts of the West Riding.[4]

The over-all position in agriculture was that wages in the region were well above the national average although never clearly the highest in Britain.[5] Rural constabularly wages in Region Eight also compared favourably with wages in other areas; in fact, policemen in the region were at most dates the best-paid in Britain.[6] In building, the relative position was very much as in agriculture; at the two dates for which indices have been calculated, 1886 and 1906, wages in Manchester, Preston, and Bradford were between 6 per cent and 15 per cent above

1. Evidence before the *R.C. on the Housing of the Working Classes*, P.P. 1884–5, XXX, para. 17074–5.
2. Table 1–4.
3. *Second Report on the Wages . . . of Agricultural Labourers*, pp. 152, 155–6. These figures show cash wages; payments in kind were lower in Lancashire than in the other counties mentioned (ibid., p. 28) but in no case by more than 1s. 5d.
4. Ibid., pp. 152–3 and Table 1–3.
5. They may have occupied this position in 1850, see above, p. 39 n. 2.
6. Table 1–8.

the national average, about equal to the average in Region Ten and a little below the averages in Regions One and Six.[1] Most building workers in Region Eight were paid less than London rates but not significantly below the prevailing rates in any other areas. In the official inquiry of 1886 London bricklayers' wages are shown as 9d. and rates of 8d. or more were returned by 34 other centres; of these, 24 were in Region Eight.[2] In the official inquiry of 1906 the London rate was $10\frac{1}{2}d.$; 24 centres paid 10d. and 18 of these were in Region Eight.[3]

Evidence of miners' wages is scarcer and less reliable. Several sources put the earnings of Lancashire hewers at or near 20s. in 1849–50; if these and similar figures can be trusted, then earnings in Lancashire were near, or a little below, those in Staffordshire and the north-east and above rates in south Wales and the minor coalfields.[4] For 1888 there is more evidence of miners' earnings in Lancashire but there is little of value for either the west or south Yorkshire fields before 1914.[5] The 1888 figures suggest that miners in Lancashire, both skilled and un-skilled, were better paid than most miners elsewhere and that the hewer's position, relative to other fields, was at least as favourable as it had been in 1850.[6] Between 1888 and 1914,

1. Region 10 is represented by South Shields and Sunderland, Region 1 by London and Dover, Region 6 by Birmingham, Leicester, and Nottingham. Tables 1–5, 1–6.
2. *Wages of the Manual Labouring Classes*, P.P. 1893–4, LXXXIIIii, pp. 176–215. Of the remaining 10 returns, one came from near London, the rest from the Midlands (Region 6), Northumberland and Durham (Region 10), and central Scotland (Region 12).
3. *Earnings and Hours Inquiry III*, P.P. 1910, LXXXIV, pp. 160–70.
4. Dodd, op. cit., pp. 343–4; Chadwick, op. cit., p. 28; *Returns of Wages published between 1830 and 1886*, P.P. 1887, LXXXIX, p. 134. For notes on mine wages see the appendix to this chapter.
5. J. W. F. Rowe, who calculated earnings in 1888 for most coalfields, was unable to estimate earnings in Yorkshire (*Wages in the Coal Industry*, pp. 62, 85, and see below pp. 71–4). B. R. Mitchell gives some tentative figures for these fields in 1888 which suggest that hewers on the West Yorkshire field were paid less than those in Lancashire but that Yorkshire mine labourers were at least as well paid as those in Lancashire; his figures for hewers in south Yorkshire at this date are too vague to be of value (University of Cambridge Ph.D. thesis, p. 208). In 1876 the editor of the *Beehive* wrote to Thomas Brassey: 'In the coal trade the highest wages are earned in Northumberland and Yorkshire' (T. Brassey, *Lectures on the Labour Question* (1878, 3rd edn.), p. 180).
6. Table 1–7.

however, Lancashire seems to have lost ground, for at the latter date earnings were no more than average. West Yorkshire was not much better placed at this time, but in south Yorkshire earnings were among the highest in Britain.[1]

How much weight should be attached to the calculations of mine wages is difficult to estimate. Even if the figures for Lancashire and West Yorkshire miners are not misleading, which they may be,[2] they are certainly not representative of wages in other occupations in the region as a whole which were still well above average in the early twentieth century although the margin of advantage by then was not as great as it had been in the third quarter of the nineteenth century.[3] In most occupations, and over the period as a whole, these three northern counties were an area of distinctly high wages. Wages were a little below London rates in most occupations and in some they compared unfavourably with rates in Northumberland and Durham and parts of Scotland, but there were not many cases where the margin of disadvantage was substantial and in most cases wages were well above the British average.[4]

1. Table 1–7.
2. Miners' earnings fluctuated violently; any single reading of relative wage levels may be unrepresentative. For notes on mine wages see below, pp. 71–4.
3. In addition to the evidence on farm, police, and building wages above, see figures of earnings in other trades in, e.g. *Fifteenth Abstract of Labour Statistics*, P.P. 1912–13, CVII.
4. It might be supposed that no survey of wages in this area would be complete without some mention of textile earnings and a word of explanation seems in order. Three considerations argued against detailed consideration of earnings in the cotton and wool trades. First, the incredible complexity of the wage data. On this point see G. H. Wood, *The History of Wages in the Cotton Trade*, p. 1; A. L. Bowley, 'Wages in the Worsted and Woollen Manufactures of the West Riding of Yorkshire', *J.R.S.S.*, lxv (1902), 102–3. Second, for most of the period employment was concentrated in Lancashire and the West Riding to an extent that makes these trades peculiarly unsuitable as a basis for regional comparisons (see above. p. 4). Third, a large proportion of the labour force was female and women's earnings concern us only indirectly. Female earnings are considered in Ch. 3—in most cases earnings in Region 8 compared favourably with textile earnings elsewhere in Britain. A cursory examination of the evidence used in Ch. 3 suggests that male earnings in the Lancashire cotton trades were above those in the Yorkshire wool trades but that both groups were well paid relative to men in similar occupations elsewhere in Britain. See also above, p. 15, and below, pp. 115–17.

# IX

REGION NINE (Cumberland and Westmorland—see Map 1)
North of Lancashire wages were lower; but Cumberland and
Westmorland were rural counties for the most part, so some
fall in this direction is hardly surprising. The more remarkable
fact is that wages closely approached the levels in Lancashire;
there is no evidence here of a steep decline similar to those
noted in rural regions south of Birmingham and around
London.[1] J. D. Marshall drew attention to this feature in his
article on rural labour in the early nineteenth century; he
found labourers in remote parts of Westmorland earning nearly
as much as those within a few miles of Liverpool and Manchester.[2] At the beginning of the period, when the average of
farm labourers' earnings in England was about 10s.,[3] the prevailing rate in Cumberland and Westmorland was 12s.[4] In
1867–70 farm earnings were second only to those in Region Ten
(Northumberland and Durham); they were nearly 30 per cent
above the national average, and were nearly 50 per cent above
rates in south Wales (Region Four). Later figures suggest that
the region was losing ground by the end of the century although earnings remained high. In 1898 it was third among the
thirteen regions and earnings were 9 per cent above average;
in 1907 it was in fifth position with earnings 5 per cent above
average.[5]

The pay of the county constabulary in Cumberland and
Westmorland compared rather less well than farm wages with

1. See above, pp. 10–11, 29.
2. J. D. Marshall, op. cit., p. 98. For a comparison of wages in the rural
districts of Lancashire, Cumberland, and Westmorland in 1903 see *Second
Report on Wages . . . of Agricultural Labourers*, p. 152.
3. See above, p. 39 n. 2.
4. *M.C.* 19 Jan. 1850; for a general comment on the favourable position of
farm labourers in this area see the issue for 5 Jan. 1850. Bowley showed
Cumberland wages in 1851 as 13s. when the English average was 9s. 7d.;
he showed only two counties with wages above the level in Cumberland.
Wages in Westmorland were not shown at this date (A. L. Bowley, *Wages
in the U.K.*, endtable).
5. Table 1–4.

pay for similar work in other areas but tends to confirm the impression of above-average wages.[1] When we turn to building and mining, however, similar comparisons are far less favourable. In 1888 and 1906 building wages in Carlisle were above most rates in the rural south but certainly not better than average.[2] This modifies first impressions although this point must be qualified because throughout the country there was a correlation between building wages and city size and if Carlisle is compared only with towns of similar size it emerges more favourably from the comparison.[3] Miners' wages introduce a more weighty qualification to the position suggested by farm earnings. No figures have been discovered for the beginning of the period, when farm wages compared most favourably with rates elsewhere, but there is little doubt that the level of mine earnings in 1888 and in 1914 was decidedly mediocre, being average at best and almost certainly below rates in the north-east and other major coalfields.[4]

On this evidence it is difficult to sum up the relative wage level in Cumberland and Westmorland in a single generalization. At times, and in some occupations, wages were well above average and no examples of really low wages have been discovered; but it seems probable that wages were far more above average in the early decades of the period than later, and that farm wages were more clearly above average than wages in the coal and building trades.

# X

REGION TEN (Northumberland and Durham—see Map 1)

The position in Northumberland and Durham was less ambiguous. These counties have already been mentioned

1. Table 1–8.
2. Tables 1–5, 1–6. At the dates shown in Table 1–5 Workington rates compared more favourably than Carlisle rates with the national average. Operative Bricklayers' Society, Annual Reports.
3. Table 1–6; see also below, p. 71.
4. Table 1–7.

several times and for this reason their wages can be described briefly. Throughout the whole period, and in each occupation for which figures have been collected, the area was characterized by high wages. It was especially true of agriculture. In Northumberland, good food and good wages, 'much better than in most of the southern counties', were noted by Caird in his mid-century tour.[1] The *Morning Chronicle* investigator was similarly impressed: '. . . the standard of comfort is considerably higher, and the means of enjoyment less stinted, than in most parts of the south and west.'[2] At that time most day labourers were paid 2s. 6d.; this did not necessarily give them 15s. a week but they could be fairly sure of receiving substantially more than the majority of English labourers,[3] and there were probably considerable numbers whose earnings fell little short of this figure. Around Newcastle hinds, hired by the year or half-year, received between 14s. and 15s. plus a cottage, potatoes, and fuel; there could have been few farm workers elsewhere as well placed as these.[4] A Durham labourer, interviewed during the course of the *Morning Chronicle* survey, said his wages were 15s. He must have been particularly aware of regional wage variations because he had come to Durham from Essex. His wages in Durham allowed him meat every day whereas in Essex at this time there were a great many labourers who earned less than half 15s. and seldom tasted meat.[5] A trickle of similar comment from informed contemporaries indicates that Region Ten maintained its advantage over most other areas until the First World War. In the 1860s Girdlestone sent

1. Caird, op. cit., pp. 378, 388–9.
2. *M.C.* 5 Jan. 1850; see also similar comment in the issue for 16 Jan. 1850.
3. Ibid. 9 Jan. 1850; the average wage in England at this time was about 10s. (see above, p. 39 n. 2). There is some confusion as to the most representative wage in Durham and Northumberland. Caird put it at 11s., below the rate in Yorkshire, Lancashire, Cheshire, and Cumberland (Caird, op. cit., p. 480), but the *Morning Chronicle* survey gives the impression that Durham and Northumberland labourers were as well off as any. The two sources also disagree on the state of labourers' housing in Northumberland. Caird, op. cit., p. 389; *M.C.* 9 Jan. 1850.
4. *M.C.* 16 Jan. 1850.
5. *M.C.* 26 Dec. 1849, 9 Jan. 1850, and see above, p. 10.

labourers to Northumberland and Durham as well as to Lancashire and Yorkshire.[1] Kebbel's work on farm labour in the 'seventies and 'eighties includes favourable comments on conditions in Northumberland[2] and in the previous decade P. A. Graham found Northumberland labourers, 'better off . . . than elsewhere', their condition the 'exact opposite' of labourers in Norfolk,[3] a sentiment which was echoed by A. Wilson Fox when he described conditions in the Glendale district as 'nearly all that an Eastern Counties labourer ever hoped for in his wildest dreams'.[4] There is more prosaic testimony to local conditions in Tables 1–3 and 1–4. At each of three dates for which indices of farm labourers' earnings have been compiled (1867–70, 1898, and 1907), earnings in Region Ten were the highest of Britain's thirteen regions.

The wages of miners, policemen, and building workers in Northumberland and Durham compared rather less favourably with wages in similar occupations elsewhere than did farm labourers wages, but none fared badly and most were very well paid. According to Dodd and the *Morning Chronicle*, miners earned in the region of 3s. 6d. to 4s. a day in 1849–50; this was probably more than earnings elsewhere.[5] In 1888 and 1914 mine wages were still among the highest in Britain although the north-eastern miners were not obviously the best-paid and it seems likely that certain grades of labour in parts of the coal-field received distinctly less than similar grades in other fields.[6]

1. See above, pp. 39–40.
2. T. E. Kebbel, *The Agricultural Labourer* (1893), p. 2.
3. P. A. Graham, op. cit., pp. 4, 7.
4. *R.C. on Labour, The Agricultural Labourer, England. A. Summary Report*, 1893–4, XXXV, p. 25.
5. Dodd, op. cit., p. 343; *M.C.* 20 Dec., 31 Dec. 1849 and see above, pp. 22 n. 3, 41 n. 5. For an interesting, and favourable, account of the diet of north-eastern miners and their house-furnishings see, *M.C.* 24 Dec. 1849.
6. Table 1–7. The notes which accompany this table show clearly that the figures are too tentative to bear much weight but it is worth mentioning that they show shift earnings and were it possible to show hourly rates the north-eastern hewers would stand in a more favourable position because the north-east was well known for its short working day. The provisions of the Eight Hours Act which shortened working hours on most fields were resisted in the north-east where hewers had long enjoyed a seven-hour shift (see below, pp. 337–8).

Police constables' pay was always above average,[1] and the wages
of building workers occupied a similar position near the top of
the regional wage hierarchy—in Newcastle, for example,
building wages, although below London rates, were on a par
with Manchester, Birmingham, and the other high-wage
centres.[2]

## XI

REGION ELEVEN (South Scotland—see Map 1)

Wage material for counties north of the border is less plentiful, less precise, and, because so many surveys were confined to
England or England and Wales, often not comparable with
material for the rest of Britain. Fortunately county earnings in
agriculture are available, or can be calculated, for each of the
three dates at which indices of regional earnings in England and
Wales have been compiled.

Table 1–4 shows the level of farm labourers' earnings in
south Scotland in 1867–70, 1898, and 1907. Despite the lack of
industrial development within its boundaries earnings were not
low. In 1867–70 they were 5 per cent above the British average;
they were higher than wages in the rest of Scotland, the English
Midlands, Wales, and most of southern England.[3] However,
they were clearly below rates in the north of England; the
broad tendency for wages to increase northwards from the
southern parts of East Anglia and the south Midlands seems to
have ended in Lancashire on the west of the Pennines and in
Durham on the east.[4] In 1898 and in 1907 farm earnings in the

1. Table 1–8. The north-east was second of the thirteen regions at 4 of the 6
   dates shown.
2. Table 1–5. Table 1–5 also shows the level of wages in Sunderland, South
   Shields, and Durham relative to rates in other cities.
3. Tables 1–3, 1–4. 'National' here, as elsewhere, refers to the whole of Britain.
4. In the late 1860s, according to the figures in Table 1–4, farm earnings in the
   four most northerly English counties were some 25 per cent above those in
   the seven counties of southern Scotland. This figure, and others which
   compare farm wages north and south of the border, should be treated with
   more than usual reservation. First, because payment in kind was far more
   extensive in Scotland and, second, because the status of the 'agricultural

region were again some 5 or 6 per cent above the British average—the 1907 position represented an improvement from sixth to fourth position in the regional wage table and a considerable reduction in the differential between south Scotland and the north of England.[1] Within the region wages tended to be higher in the east; Wigtownshire labourers were probably the worst-paid during the period as a whole and those of Selkirk the highest-paid. In 1907 labourers' earnings exceeded 20s. a week in three counties of southern Scotland—Roxburgh, Selkirk, and Berwick; only five English counties reached this level.[2]

There are few figures of farm wages before 1867 sufficiently reliable for this investigation, but it seems likely, from the work of Purdy, Bowley, and Wood on chronological variations, that the relative position of the region was less favourable at that time. 'Earnings of Scotch agricultural labourers . . . increased very much'[3] in the two decades before 1870. Earlier in the century they were well below English levels; Purdy noticed a substantial rise from the mid-1830s and the rate of increase in money wages after 1830 was greater than in any of the several occupations covered by Wood and Bowley in their survey at the end of the nineteenth century.[4] At the time of the union, and for some time after, England was far richer than Scotland; the beginning of this study overlaps with the end of the long period during which the disparity between the two economies was shrinking rapidly.

---

labourer' there (and in parts of the English border counties, particularly Northumberland) was slightly inferior to that of his namesake south of the border, while the status of the Scottish 'ploughman' was somewhat above that of the English labourer. Except where stated, farm wages in this chapter refer to agricultural labourers and may therefore underestimate relative wage levels north of the border. On these points see below, p. 65.

1. Table 1–4.
2. Table 1–3.
3. *Employment of Children, Young Persons, and Women in Agriculture*, P.P. 1870, XIII, Fourth Report, p. 23.
4. F. Purdy, 'On the Earnings of Agricultural Labourers in Scotland and Ireland', *J.R.S.S.*, xxv (1862) (tables on pp. 439 and 465); G. H. Wood, *Wages in the Cotton Trade*, p. 147; *idem*, *A Glance at Wages and Prices since the Industrial Revolution* (Manchester, 1900), p. 7; G. Houston, 'Farm Wages in Central Scotland from 1814 to 1870', *J.R.S.S.*, Ser. A, cxviii (1955), 227.

Evidence of earnings in occupations other than agriculture is less good but suggests that non-agricultural wages in the region compared with wages elsewhere less favourably than did farm wages. Police pay appears to have risen rapidly between 1860 and 1890 but was never better than average, although it might compare rather more favourably with other regions if variations in the provision of free housing could be taken into account.[1] Building wages in Hawick were near or below average in both 1886 and in 1906, although here again the comparison may be biased against the region because Hawick was an extremely small town and building wages, in all regions, tended to correlate with town size.[2] Much the same could be said of wages in other towns and other occupations—building and printing wages in Galashiels, engineering wages in Annan and Dumfries[3]—in each case earnings were below average but compared not unfavourably with wages in towns of similar size, especially those in the south of England.[4]

1. Table 1–8 and accompanying notes.
2. Table 1–6. There is an obvious similarity here with the position in Carlisle (see above, p. 44). Hawick wages compared well with towns of similar size in the south of England and with some much larger towns. Norwich for example was seven times as populous (in 1911) yet in 1886 and 1906 its building workers were rather less well paid than Hawick's. Table 1–5. See also below, p. 71.
3. *Inquiry into Working Class Rents and Retail Prices*, P.P. 1913, LXVI, p. 34; *Standard Time Rates of Wages*, P.P. 1910, LXXXIV, pp. 54–5.
4. The woollen and hosiery trades provided considerable employment in parts of this region but textile wages are not discussed in detail for the reasons given above (p. 42 n. 4). Bremner commented very favourably on conditions in Galashiels in the 1860s: '. . . squalid poverty is totally unknown . . . the scale of dietary is more costly than that of Scotch operatives generally' (D. Bremner, *The Industries of Scotland* (Edinburgh, 1869), p. 193). In 1890, according to a recent study, wages in the Border wool trades were not inferior to those in Yorkshire, C. Gulvin, 'Wages and Conditions in the Border Woollen Industry about 1890', *Trans. Hawick Archaeological Society* (1967), pp. 44–5. In 1906 they were still roughly on a par with the West Riding and above rates in the West Country. These generalizations, however, may give a slightly over-favourable impression of men's wages in the Scottish industry because it seems that female wages compared the more favourably with the West Riding and elsewhere (Bremner, op. cit., p. 171; de Rousiers, op. cit., pp. 307, 313). The average wages of all full-time men in 1906 was, in Yorkshire, 27s. 3d.; in the west of England 21s. 9d.; and in Roxburgh, Selkirk, and Peebles 27s. 7d. (*Earnings and Hours Enquiry. I. Textile Trades*, P.P. 1909, LXXX, p. xli). However, the value of these figures is limited because different regions served different markets and the occupational structure in the border industry was not identical with those elsewhere. [cont.]

It is difficult to generalize about wage levels from the evidence above. The rural south of Scotland, like Cumberland and Westmorland, was a fairly high-wage region in the sense that agriculture was the staple economic activity and farm wages were high, but it lacked substantial industrial centres of the kind in which urban wages were usually high and well-paid occupations commonplace.

# XII

REGION TWELVE (Central Scotland—see Map 1)

The central lowlands included the bulk of Scotland's population and an even larger proportion of its industrial workers. The economic history of this region was quite unlike that of the southern border counties but in one respect their wage patterns were similar; both were characterized by a rapid rise in wages and improvement relative to other regions by the end of the period.

This trend was more pronounced in the central lowlands than in the border counties and can be seen most clearly in agriculture. In the late 1860s farm earnings in central Scotland were near the British average. They were well below rates in the north of England and, surprisingly, below the border counties (Region Eleven) as well.[1] Further, there is every indication that the position relative to rates in England was even less favourable at the beginning of our period.[2] By the end of the century the position had greatly improved; relative

---

Hawick and Dumfries were the main hosiery centres in Region 11. Bremner claimed that the Hawick stocking knitters in 1868 were 'better paid than their brethren in the midland counties of England' (op. cit., p. 180); in 1890, however, the advantage was clearly with the Midlands (F. A. Wells, *The British Hosiery Trade* (1935), p. 198). In 1906 average full-time male earnings were 34s. 7d. in Nottingham, 31s. 7d. in Leicester, and 28s. 7d. in Scotland (*Earnings and Hours Enquiry. I.* p. lxiii).

1. Table 1–4.
2. See above, p. 48.

wages had risen more than in any other region except south
Wales (Region Four). Farm earnings were 12 per cent above the
national average in 1898 and were higher than in every region
except Region Ten (Northumberland and Durham).[1] This
advantage was maintained, although not increased, in the
next decade: in 1907 there were five counties in the region
where farm labourers' average earnings were a pound a week
or more, as many as there were in the whole of England.[2]
There was a similar improvement in the earnings of the county
constabulary in central Scotland between 1850 and 1914. At
the beginning of the period earnings were less than in every
region in England and Wales;[3] after 1880 they were always
above average.[4] The same pattern is discernible, although less
distinctly, in the wages of building craftsmen: near to average
in 1886 and among the high-wage regions by the early twentieth
century.[5] Glasgow carpenters were paid $7\frac{1}{2}d.$ per hour in 1886
which was similar to wages in moderately large cities south of
the border but below those in London, Birmingham, Manchester, and Newcastle.[6] By 1906 they received $9\frac{1}{2}d.$ per hour,
still below the London rate but the same as carpenters' rates in
Birmingham, Manchester, and Newcastle.[7]

1. Table 1–4.
2. Tables 1–3 and 1–4. The five English counties were Derbyshire, Durham,
   Middlesex, Northumberland, and the West Riding.
3. Table 1–8. But see the note on police housing above, p. 49, which may have
   some bearing on relative wages in parts of Region 12.
4. Ibid.
5. Table 1–6.
6. Table 1–5.
7. Ibid. Unskilled building wages appear to have followed a rather different
   pattern: in 1886 they compared more favourably with other regions than
   skilled wages but in 1906 the position was reversed (Table 1–6). In most
   towns of central Scotland other than Glasgow the differential between
   building craftsmen's and labourers' wages in 1886 was less than average.
   But in 1906, according to the figures in Table 1–5, the differential in
   Glasgow, Edinburgh, and Greenock was wider than average. This feature
   was also noted by the *Inquiry into Working Class Rents and Retail Prices*,
   P.P. 1913, LXVI, p. xii. Why unskilled wages in that part of Scotland in
   1886 were so high *vis-à-vis* skilled wages, for how long they had been at that
   level, why Glasgow was an exception to this feature, and why the differential widened in the following twenty years, are all interesting questions. A
   close study of the building cycle, the movement of Irish into Scotland, and
   the movement of Scots overseas might provide a partial explanation.

Evidence of miners' wages comes mainly from Lanarkshire and relates chiefly to the second half of the period.[1] It suggests a different pattern from the one just described for farm and building workers. In 1914, as in 1888, hewers in Lanarkshire earned no more than the national average for hewers; if anything, their relative position had been better at the earlier date. At both dates their earnings were above those in Somerset, north Wales, and the Forest of Dean but below those in most of the other major fields.[2] Miners were by no means the only exception to the tendency for wages to improve over time relative to other areas but there is little doubt that improvement was the chief characteristic in central Scotland.[3] It can be seen again in the heavy-metal industries: shipbuilding, engineering, and the making of iron and steel. Cheap labour

1. Earnings probably varied little between the different Scottish fields. In 1886 Lanarkshire hewers were better paid than those in east Scotland and Ayrshire but the reverse may have been true of mine labourers' wages. East Scotland was noted for relative stability of earnings. Rowe, *Wages in the Coal Industry*, pp. 144–5; Bremner, op. cit., p. 22; A. J. Youngson Brown, 'The Scots Coal Industry 1854–86', D.Litt. thesis, University of Aberdeen (1952), pp. 226–8. There is a considerable amount of wage material on the first thirty years of the period, perhaps more than for any other mining area, but much of it is vague and some of it contradictory. See e.g. Bowley, *Wages in the U.K.*, Ch. XIII; J. Strang, 'On the Money Rate of Wages of Labour in Glasgow and the West of Scotland', *J.R.S.S.*, xx (1857); A. J. Youngson Brown, op. cit., pp. 226–7, 309–10; G. H. Wood Collection; Webb Collection in the British Library of Political and Economic Science (T.U. reports MSS. Miners); Bremner, op. cit., pp. 21–2; A. Slaven, 'Earnings and Productivity in the Scottish Coalmining Industry during the Nineteenth Century', in P. L. Payne (ed.), *Studies in Scottish Business History* (1967).
2. Table 1–7. Rowe points out that the rise in unskilled earnings in Lanarkshire between 1888 and 1914 was probably much less than shown in this table. The probable increase was of the order of 80 per cent, not 105 per cent. This adjustment would leave Lanarkshire earnings in 1888 and 1914 as 96 and 93 per cent respectively of the British average in the case of skilled wages, and 103 and 99 per cent in the case of unskilled wages (Rowe, *Wages in the Coal Industry*, p. 85). R. Page Arnot considers that mine earnings in Scotland were below average in the 1880s and in 1911 (*A History of the Scottish Miners* (1955), pp. 72, 121).
3. Unskilled building wages may have been another (see above, p. 51 n. 7). A less surprising divergence from the general pattern was cotton. The Scottish trade was already in difficulties in the 1850s; between then and the First World War Lancashire's advantage was at least maintained and probably increased (Wood, *Wages in the Cotton Trade*, pp. 71–4, 96–101, 119). This area compared more favourably with English centres in the other textile trades (D. J. Robertson in A. K. Cairncross (ed.), *The Scottish Economy* (Cambridge, 1954), p. 167).

was counted one of the advantages of the Scottish iron industry in the first half of the century and considered to be among the reasons for the phenomenal expansion of the Clyde shipyards after 1840.[1] After 1850 labour became less cheap but wages in most Scottish industries were still not high in 1880; the exact position varied from one occupation and one industry to another with the over-all level somewhat below the United Kingdom average.[2] By 1906, however, earnings had risen to near average in the engineering trades and above average in the shipbuilding and iron and steel industries.[3]

Despite the exceptions mentioned, the main features of relative wage levels in central Scotland are clear enough. In 1850 it was a low-wage region, half-way through the period wages were near the national average, by the early twentieth century it was one of the four highest-wage regions in Britain.

# XIII

REGION THIRTEEN (Northern Scotland—see Map 1)

Region Thirteen, that part of Scotland north of the central lowland counties, in 1851 supported a little over a million people; that is 38 per cent of the population of Scotland and 5 per cent of the British population. In this investigation the area presents more problems than most because wage material is particularly sketchy and because money wages accounted for a smaller proportion of total earnings here than anywhere in Britain. Many men were self-employed and, even at the end of the period, farm workers to the north of Glen More still commonly received between a quarter and a half of their

---

1. 'Local labour was both highly skilled and relatively cheap' (A. K. Cairncross in R. Miller and J. Tivy (eds.), *The Glasgow Region* (Glasgow, 1958), p. 223). See also R. H. Campbell, *Scotland since 1707; The Rise of an Industrial Society* (Oxford, 1965), p. 119.
2. D. J. Robertson in Cairncross (ed.), *The Scottish Economy*, pp. 150–1.
3. Ibid., p. 153.

earnings in kind.[1] In addition, the borders of the region, dictated by the statistical material which was collected on a county basis, coincide only roughly with 'economic regions'. The north, the west, and the islands were sufficiently homogeneous to meet the not very exacting standards necessary if the whole of Britain is divided into only thirteen regions, but much of the south and east, parts of Aberdeen, Angus, Perthshire, Kincardine, and Kinross, could have been included in either Region Twelve or Region Thirteen. All this makes generalizations about the whole region more than usually hazardous, unless they are qualified with a note to the effect that any characteristic was likely to be found in varying intensities. Crofting and payment in kind, for example, were most common in the north and west of the region; earnings were lowest in the same areas and highest in the south-east.

In the late 1860s north Scotland was one of the lowest-wage regions in Britain. Farm earnings were 8 per cent below average, slightly above those in Wales and the English West Country but below those in the other nine regions.[2] Within the region, earnings in the seven crofting counties, taken alone, were some 15 per cent below the national figure for farm workers while earnings in the three highest-wage counties within the region were in each case a little above the national average.[3] Thirty years later earnings had improved relative to the national average and were now 6 per cent below average; but north Scotland still occupied tenth place in the regional wage table.[4] This slight improvement continued in the next decade. In 1907 earnings were 4 per cent below average.[5] In five counties, all in the south-east of the region, farm earnings were above the British average and labourers in Angus and Kinross could

1. *Second Report on Wages . . . Agricultural Labourers*, p. 94. Crofters and cottars 'constitute the labouring portion of the community in the Highlands and Islands' (F. Purdy, 'On the Earnings of Agricultural Labourers in Scotland and Ireland', p. 426).
2. Table 1–4.
3. Tables 1–3, 1–4. The crofting counties are those designated thus by the Crofters Holdings (Scotland) Act of 1886, viz.: Argyll, Caithness, Inverness, Orkney, Ross and Cromarty, Shetlands, Sutherland.
4. Ibid. It was equal with rural Wales, and now above the rural south-east as well as south-west England; but south Wales had gone ahead after 1870.
5. Ibid.

consider themselves well paid, but earnings in the seven crofting counties were again below the average of all other regions and the labourers of Orkney, Shetland, and Caithness were the worst-paid in Britain.[1]

Although farm earnings were still low in 1907 the figures in Table 1–4 show that this region had shared in the greater than average increase in farm earnings which was a feature of nineteenth-century Scotland.[2] The earnings of the rural constabulary followed the same pattern. They were 10 per cent below the national average in 1860 and only 3 per cent below in 1906.[3]

Building wages too were distinctly low.[4] The shortcomings of building wages as a guide to regional variations have already been mentioned;[5] the figures for Region Thirteen in Table 1–6 are based on wages in Perth, Aberdeen, Elgin, and Inverness.[6] Only one of these towns was in a crofting county and it could perhaps be argued that the index slightly exaggerates the level of building wages in the region. On the other hand, and perhaps balancing this point, Dundee, the largest town in the region, was not included in the index. In 1906 carpenters and labourers in

1. Tables 1–3, 1–4. In this respect they followed, at some distance, the labourers of Oxfordshire and Norfolk.
2. See above, pp. 48, 50. For more detailed observations on parts of the region see Houston, op. cit., pp. 227–8, and R. Molland and G. Evans: '. . . farm wages in the north-east of Scotland seem to have risen substantially over those thirty years, whereas for Britain they remained about the same . . .' 'Scottish Farm Wages from 1870 to 1900', *J.R.S.S.*, Ser. A, cxiii (1950), 226.
   The faster than average rise in farm earnings seems to have been experienced by the crofting and non-crofting counties although not in equal measures:

|  | 1867–70 | 1907 |
|---|---|---|
| Farm Earnings G.B. | 100 | 100 |
| Region 13 | 92 | 96 |
| Region 13 (crofting counties only) | 86 | 87 |
| Region 13 (non-crofting counties only) | 97 | 101 |

   Source: Tables 1–3, 1–4.
3. Table 1–8. Within the region, police earnings were highest in the south and east—in 1860 the seven crofting counties paid 11 per cent less than average and the rest of the region 9 per cent less than average; in 1906, when pay in the non-crofting counties was near the national average, it was 7 per cent less in the crofting counties and Sutherland and Shetland returned the lowest county figures in Britain. Ibid. and G. H. Wood Collection.
4. Table 1–6.
5. See above, p. 49 and section III of the appendix to this chapter.
6. Table 1–6.

Dundee were paid almost as much as those in Glasgow.[1] The Tayside shipbuilders and engineers were similarly placed relative to shipbuilders and engineers in Glasgow and they enjoyed a margin of advantage over men in these occupations in Aberdeen.[2] Angus, of course, was one of those counties which might have been included in either central Scotland (Region Twelve) or in northern Scotland (Region Thirteen) and Dundee belongs emphatically to that part of Angus which had most in common with the central lowlands. Earnings there and elsewhere in the less inhospitable parts of the coastal counties between the Tay and the Moray Firth were an exception to the generalization that Region Thirteen was one of Britain's lowest-wage areas.[3] Elsewhere the generalization held good throughout the period.

## XIV

In one sense the pattern that has been described is exceedingly complex. Within the main framework of regional differentials there were several subsidiary patterns. There was, first, a profusion of local variations. Some of these marked the dividing line between major wage regions such as those around the Birmingham and London areas, but a great many more owed their survival to the strength of custom. Second, there was the 'city-size wage differential' within each region. Third, there was a certain amount of inconsistency among regional variations in different occupations—in Cumberland for example where, relative to what they might obtain elsewhere, farm labourers were much better paid than miners.

Each of these minor patterns is interesting in its own way and their influence has been noted wherever they significantly affected the broad regional pattern. But the investigator who seeks to describe and explain regional variation in the whole of Britain must be prepared to sacrifice some of the finer points or

---

1. Table 1–5.
2. S. G. E. Lythe, 'Shipbuilding at Dundee down to 1914', *Scottish Journal of Political Economy*, ix (1962) 230; Robertson in Cairncross (ed.), *The Scottish Economy*, pp. 151, 163–4.
3. See, in particular, county agricultural earnings in Table 1–3.

risk losing the over-all pattern in a confusion of local detail. For this reason the foregoing account has concentrated on the broad regional variations—in Bowley's words: 'when we only want a telescopic effect it is of no use to work under a microscope.' [1] And from this more distant vantage point the view is clearer and the pattern less cluttered. Wide disparities between relative wages in different occupations were exceptional, and once the ambiguities which arise from the necessity to work with county units have been removed the general level of wages in most areas is readily apparent. Further, there were remarkably few changes of substance in the rank order of regions. All were affected by marginal changes, but if we consider them in just two groups—high-wage regions and low-wage regions—most remained in the same category throughout the period. Only two areas changed status dramatically, south Wales and central Scotland; two others, south Scotland and the rural south-east of England, were affected to a lesser extent; and in each of these cases change took the form of simple one-way movement either up or down the regional wage table. Reduced to fundamentals, there were two high-wage areas in 1850; first London, and, second, the northern counties of England and parts of the Midlands as far south as Birmingham. In 1914 the position was similar except that these two areas had been joined by south Wales and the northern high-wage areas by then extended to central Scotland. All this suggests a system in which market forces offered steady compensation to the low-wage regions or constant advantages to the rest of Britain, or possibly a combination of the two.

A great many indications of the size of differentials and the way they changed over the period have been given above: in this respect variation between different occupations was important and generalization is difficult. It is not surprising, for example, to find that regional differentials in engine-drivers' pay were far less than in occupations which were locally confined, or that the pay of the county constabulary, determined in part by Whitehall, varied less from county to county than the pay of farm labourers who each made their own

1. A. L. Bowley, *Economic Journal*, viii (1898), 479.

bargain.[1] Similarly, the size of the differential was a function
of area: the larger the area the more variety it contained and
the more averages conceal. In agriculture, for example, towards
the end of the period farm labourers in the highest-wage region
received, on average, some 27 per cent more than those in the
lowest-wage region; those in the highest-wage county received
nearly 60 per cent more than those in the lowest; and in parts
of Northumberland, Durham, and Lancashire wages were more
than twice the level in parts of Oxfordshire, Dorset, Essex, and
other southern counties.[2]

Clearly, any measurement of the size of differentials will be
fairly specific to the occupations and areas involved. But there
is one generalization which may be made with confidence about
most differentials—they were less wide at the end of the period
than in 1850. There are, of course, a great many ways of
measuring deviation from average, each likely to give a slightly
different answer; the figures below illustrate the general trend
by showing the range of regional variations in those occupations
considered in the appendix to this chapter:[3]

TABLE 1–1

*Percentage (of G. B. average) by which Maximum Regional Wage
Exceeded Minimum Regional Wage*

| Agriculture | | Building (carpenters) | | Building (labourers) | |
|---|---|---|---|---|---|
| *1867–70* | *1907* | *1886* | *1906* | *1886* | *1906* |
| 44 | 28 | 39 | 24 | 37 | 32 |
| Mine hewers | | Mine labourers | | Police | |
| *1888* | *1914* | *1888* | *1914* | *1860* | *1906* |
| 44 | 51 | 49 | 40 | 20 | 19 |

Source: Tables 1–4, 1–6, 1–7, 1–8.

1. J. W. F. Rowe, *Wages in Practice and Theory* (1928), pp. 75–6; section V
   of the appendix to this chapter.
2. Tables 1–3, 1–4; *Second Report on Wages . . . Agricultural Labourers*, pp.
   151–9.
3. Apart from showing the reduction in differentials over the period there are
   two other interesting points in these figures. Coal hewers' differentials seem
   actually to have widened a little between 1888 and 1914, and in 1886 the
   differential for carpenters was greater than that for building labourers
   whereas the opposite might have been expected because the carpenters
   were more skilled, better educated, more unionized, and, presumably,
   more mobile. Given the reservations on miners' wages stated in the appendix to this chapter it would be unwise to make much of movements in
   differentials in that industry.

It is worth looking at farm and building wages more closely both as a check on the long-run trends in the size of differentials and in the hope of discovering an indication of the rate at which differentials narrowed through the period:

TABLE 1–2

*Agricultural Labourers' Wage Differentials, 1867–1907*

|  | 1867–70 | 1898 | 1907 |
|---|---|---|---|
| Number of regions (13) where earnings within 5 per cent of national average | 4 | 4 | 8 |
| Number of counties (86)* where earnings within 5 per cent of national average | 26 | 29 | 30 |
| Number of regions (13) where earnings within 10 per cent of national average | 6 | 11 | 11 |
| Number of counties (86)* where earnings within 10 per cent of national average | 50 | 55 | 60 |

Source: Tables 1–3 and 1–4.

* No figures are available of earnings in 1867–70 in Huntingdonshire, Suffolk, Rutland, and Bute. It has been assumed, on the evidence of earnings in contiguous counties, that in Huntingdon and Suffolk at this time earnings were within 5 per cent of the national average, that in Rutland they were between 5 and 10 per cent of the national average, and that in Bute earnings were more than 10 per cent below average.

Table 1–2 shows again the tendency of differentials to decline over time but it is equivocal on the question of whether decline occurred more rapidly in the thirty years after 1867 or in the decade after 1898. The standard deviation of county earnings from their mean was 14 per cent in 1867–70, 10 per cent in 1898, and 9 per cent in 1907, which suggests that differentials eroded at a similar rate in the two periods.[1] A similar exercise on bricklayers' wages in 21 English and Welsh towns[2] in 1886, 1900, and 1913 produced standard deviations of 14·5 per cent, 10·7 per cent, and 10·8 per cent, which suggests a rather different pattern—viz. more rapid erosion of differentials between 1886 and 1900 than in the following 13 years.[3]

1. Allowance must be made for the fact that the time-span between the first and second dates was rather more than three times that between the second and third.
2. Those towns shown for Regions 1–10 on pp. 68–9 below, with the exception of Chichester and Dorchester for which insufficient material is available. Sources: T, U, and W(below, p. 66) and, for 1913, *Standard Time Rates of Wages*, P.P. 1914, LXXX, pp. 2–24.
3. The standard deviation of labourers' wages in 1886 was 14·5 per cent which throws some doubt on the relationship between skilled and unskilled differentials at that date suggested above, p. 58 n. 3.

Given the variety of interpretations suggested by different measures applied to single occupations, and by similar measures applied to different occupations, it seems wisest to regard each of these measures as specific to itself[1] and, while noting the strong evidence that differentials were reduced, to eschew generalization about the speed of erosion. Some reduction in differentials over the period is exactly what might have been expected given their magnitude in 1850. But, as was noted earlier, even after 1900 there were many examples of men earning only half as much as others obtained for similar work elsewhere in Britain and what is remarkable about differentials is not that they were reduced but that they persisted so tenaciously.

1. There is some further evidence of even more diversity than has been shown here. The rate of erosion of local differentials in each occupation may, and probably did, follow a different course from the rate of erosion of regional differentials (see below, p. 336) and police differentials may have widened in the third quarter of the century. J. P. Martin and G. Wilson, *The Police*, pp. 19–20.

# APPENDIX TO CHAPTER ONE

## I

Wages are described in detail in Chapter One. The relative level in each region varied slightly according to occupation. There were also, in most occupations, marked variations within regional boundaries mainly as a consequence of the necessity to work with county units. Any single index of regional wages, therefore, would obscure a certain amount and could be misleading, and for these reasons no such index has been calculated. The material used most often in Chapter One is set out below with notes on sources and reliability; as indicators of regional wage levels these figures should only be used in conjunction with the notes and the more detailed analysis in Chapter One.

## II

AGRICULTURAL LABOURERS

Table 1–3    Earnings by county 1867–70, 1898, 1907
Table 1–4    Earnings by region 1867–70, 1898, 1907
*Sources:*
Most figures are from Bowley, *Wages in the United Kingdom in the Nineteenth Century*, endtable; *Reports on Wages and Earnings of Agricultural Labourers*, P.P. 1900, LXXXII, pp. 28–9, 58, 73–4; *Earnings and Hours Inquiry. V. Agriculture*, P.P. 1910, LXXXIV, pp. xvii, xxi, xxiv. In addition the following sources have been used, mainly to make good omissions in Bowley and the reports of 1900 and 1910: *Commission on the Employment of Children, Young Persons and Women in Agriculture*, P.P. 1867–8, XVII, 1868–9, XIII, 1870 XIII; *Returns of Wages published between 1830 and 1886*, P.P. 1887, LXXXIX, pp. 411–19; *R.C. on Labour: The Agricultural Labourer*, P.P. 1893–4, XXXVI, XXXVIIii; *Report on the Wages and Earnings of Agricultural Labourers*, P.P. 1900, LXXXII; A. L. Bowley, 'The Statistics of Wages in the United Kingdom during the last Hundred Years', Pts. I and II, *J.R.S.S.*, lxi (1898) and lxii (1899). In a few cases, mainly for Welsh and Scottish counties in 1867–70, the figure in Table 1–3 is an estimate based upon earnings in contiguous counties.

## TABLE 1–3
### Agricultural Labourers' Weekly Earnings: Counties

| County | Region | 1867–70 | 1898 | 1907 |
|---|---|---|---|---|
| Kent | 1 | 17s. | 19s. 10d. | 18s. 10d. |
| Middlesex | 1 | 17s. 3d. | 19s. 5d. | 20s. 3d. |
| Surrey | 1 | 17s. 6d. | 19s. | 18s. 9d. |
| Essex | 1 | 14s. 3d. | 15s. 6d. | 16s. 4d. |
| Cornwall | 2 | 12s. 6d. | 16s. 7d. | 17s. 7d. |
| Devon | 2 | 12s. 6d. | 16s. 4d. | 17s. 9d. |
| Somerset | 2 | 12s. 3d. | 15s. 10d. | 17s. 3d. |
| Gloucester | 2 | 12s. 9d. | 15s. 1d. | 16s. 3d. |
| Wiltshire | 2 | 13s. | 15s. | 16s. |
| Dorset | 2 | 11s. 6d. | 14s. 9d. | 16s. 1d. |
| Bedfordshire | 3 | 14s. 3d. | 16s. 2d. | 16s. 3d. |
| Berkshire | 3 | 13s. 6d. | 15s. 1d. | 16s. 8d. |
| Buckingham | 3 | 14s. 3d. | 15s. 2d. | 16s. 11d. |
| Cambridge | 3 | 14s. 3d. | 16s. 5d. | 16s. 3d. |
| Hampshire | 3 | 14s. | 16s. 7d. | 17s. 5d. |
| Hertfordshire | 3 | 13s. 6d. | 16s. 1d. | 16s. 10d. |
| Huntingdon | 3 | — | 15s. 4d. | 16s. 2d. |
| Norfolk | 3 | 14s. 9d. | 14s. 9d. | 15s. 4d. |
| Northampton | 3 | 15s. 3d. | 16s. 8d. | 16s. 9d. |
| Oxford | 3 | 13s. 6d. | 14s. 8d. | 14s. 11d. |
| Suffolk | 3 | — | 14s. 5d. | 15s. 9d. |
| Sussex | 3 | 16s. 6d. | 17s. 10d. | 17s. 9d. |
| Carmarthen | 4 | 11s. 6d. | 16s. 7d. | 18s. 1d. |
| Glamorgan | 4 | 14s. | 19s. 1d. | 19s. 3d. |
| Monmouth | 4 | 13s. 6d. | 16s. 8d. | 18s. 1d. |
| Pembroke | 4 | 11s. 6d. | 15s. 10d. | 17s. 3d. |
| Hereford | 5 | 12s. 9d. | 15s. 10d. | 17s. 1d. |
| Anglesey | 5 | 11s. 6d. | 15s. 6d. | 17s. 6d. |
| Carnarvon | 5 | 13s. 6d. | 17s. 2d. | 18s. 7d. |
| Flintshire | 5 | 13s. 6d. | 17s. 3d. | 18s. 10d. |
| Denbigh | 5 | 13s. 6d. | 16s. 9d. | 18s. 1d. |
| Merioneth | 5 | 13s. 6d. | 16s. 5d. | 18s. 2d. |
| Radnor | 5 | 13s. 6d. | 15s. 6d. | 16s. 8d. |
| Cardigan | 5 | 11s. 6d. | 14s. 9d. | 16s. 6d. |
| Brecknock | 5 | 13s. 6d. | 16s. 8d. | 18s. 9d. |
| Montgomery | 5 | 13s. 6d. | 15s. 5d. | 16s. 7d. |
| Derbyshire | 6 | 15s. 6d. | 19s. 11d. | 20s. 5d. |
| Leicestershire | 6 | 13s. 6d. | 17s. 2d. | 18s. 9d. |
| Nottinghamshire | 6 | 15s. | 19s. 2d. | 19s. 5d. |
| Shropshire | 6 | 12s. 3d. | 17s. 5d. | 18s. |
| Staffordshire | 6 | 14s. | 17s. 11d. | 18s. 8d. |
| Warwickshire | 6 | 15s. | 16s. 2d. | 17s. 2d. |
| Worcestershire | 6 | 13s. 6d. | 17s. 1d. | 16s. 3d. |

## TABLE 1-3
*Agricultural Labourers' Weekly Earnings: Counties (contd.)*

| County | Region | 1867–70 | 1898 | 1907 |
|---|---|---|---|---|
| Lincoln | 7 | 16s. 3d. | 17s. 9d. | 19s. 5d. |
| Rutland | 7 | — | 17s. 2d. | 17s. |
| Yorks. E. Riding | 7 | 17s. 6d. | 18s. 6d. | 19s. 3d. |
| Yorks. N. Riding | 7 | 17s. 6d. | 18s. 8d. | 19s. 7d. |
| Cheshire | 8 | 16s. | 18s. | 19s. |
| Lancashire | 8 | 17s. 9d. | 19s. 4d. | 19s. 10d. |
| Yorks. W. Riding | 8 | 17s. 6d. | 18s. 7d. | 20s. |
| Cumberland | 9 | 18s. 6d. | 18s. 9d. | 19s. 3d. |
| Westmorland | 9 | 18s. 6d. | 18s. 9d. | 19s. 1d. |
| Northumberland | 10 | 17s. 6d. | 20s. 2d. | 21s. 2d. |
| Durham | 10 | 20s. | 20s. 9d. | 21s. 9d. |
| Berwick | 11 | 14s. | 18s. 6d. | 20s. 4d. |
| Dumfries | 11 | 16s. 6d. | 17s. | 18s. 1d. |
| Kirkcudbright | 11 | 16s. 6d | 16s. 11d. | 17s. 10d. |
| Peebles | 11 | 15s. | 19s. 2d. | 19s. 11d. |
| Roxburgh | 11 | 14s. | 18s. 8d. | 20s. 3d. |
| Selkirk | 11 | 16s. 6d. | 19s. | 20s. 8d. |
| Wigtown | 11 | 12s. 6d. | 16s. 11d. | 18s. 2d. |
| Clackmannan | 12 | 12s. | 18s. 2d. | 21s. 4d. |
| Ayrshire | 12 | 12s. | 18s. 5d. | 19s. |
| Dunbarton | 12 | 16s. 6d. | 20s. 3d. | 19s. 7d. |
| Fife | 12 | 14s. | 18s. 2d. | 20s. 7d. |
| Lanark | 12 | 15s. | 20s. 2d. | 21s. 1d. |
| Renfrew | 12 | 15s. 6d. | 20s. 8d. | 19s. 11d. |
| Stirling | 12 | 15s. | 20s. 3d. | 21s. 1d. |
| Edinburgh | 12 | 14s. 6d. | 19s. 3d. | 20s. 8d. |
| Haddington | 12 | 14s. | 18s. 6d. | 19s. 7d. |
| Linlithgow | 12 | 14s. 6d. | 19s. 4d. | 19s. 5d. |
| Aberdeen | 13 | 13s. | 16s. 6d. | 18s. 3d. |
| Angus | 13 | 14s. | 18s. 9d. | 19s. 11d. |
| Banffshire | 13 | 15s. | 16s. 10d. | 17s. 6d. |
| Buteshire | 13 | — | 16s. 5d. | 17s. 10d. |
| Caithness | 13 | 13s. | 13s. 5d. | 14s. 2d. |
| Argyll | 13 | 9s. | 16s. 5d. | 17s. 10d. |
| Inverness | 13 | 13s. | 16s. | 17s. 1d. |
| Kincardine | 13 | 12s. | 18s. 1d. | 18s. 3d. |
| Kinross | 13 | 14s. | 18s. 2d. | 19s. 8d. |
| Elgin | 13 | 15s. | 15s. 8d. | 18s. |
| Nairnshire | 13 | 15s. | 15s. 4d. | 17s. 2d. |
| Orkney and Shetland | 13 | 13s. | 13s. 5d. | 13s. 10d. |
| Perth | 13 | 13s. 6d. | 17s. 3d. | 19s. 2d. |
| Ross and Cromarty | 13 | 13s. | 15s. 11d. | 16s. 9d. |
| Sutherland | 13 | 12s. | 15s. 10d. | 17s. 9d. |

## Table 1-4
### Agricultural Labourers' Earnings: Regions[1]

| Region | Earnings per week | | | Index when G.B. = 100 | | |
|---|---|---|---|---|---|---|
| | 1867–70 | 1898 | 1907 | 1867–70 | 1898 | 1907 |
| 1 London and Home Counties | 16s. 6d. | 18s. 5d. | 18s. 6½d. | 115 | 107 | 102 |
| 2 South-west | 12s. 5d. | 15s. 7d. | 16s. 10d. | 87 | 91 | 92 |
| 3 Rural south-east | 14s. 4½d. | 15s. 9d. | 16s. 5d. | 101 | 92 | 90 |
| 4 South Wales | 12s. 7½d. | 17s. ½d. | 18s. 2d. | 88 | 99 | 100 |
| 5 Rural Wales and Herefordshire | 13s. | 16s. 1½d. | 17s. 8d. | 91 | 94 | 97 |
| 6 Midlands | 14s. 1d. | 17s. 10d. | 18s. 4½d. | 99 | 104 | 101 |
| 7 Lincs, Rutland, E. and N. Riding | 17s. 1d. | 18s. | 18s. 10d. | 120 | 105 | 103 |
| 8 Lancs, Cheshire, W. Riding | 17s. 1d. | 18s. 8d. | 19s. 7d. | 120 | 108 | 108 |
| 9 Cumberland and Westmorland | 18s. 6d. | 18s. 9d. | 19s. 2d. | 129 | 109 | 105 |
| 10 Northumberland and Durham | 18s. 9d. | 20s. 5½d. | 21s. 5½d. | 131 | 119 | 118 |
| 11 South Scotland | 15s. | 18s. | 19s. 4d. | 105 | 105 | 106 |
| 12 Central Scotland | 14s. 3½d. | 19s. 4d. | 20s. 2½d. | 100 | 112 | 111 |
| 13 Northern Scotland | 13s. 2d. | 16s. 3d. | 17s. 6½d. | 92 | 94 | 96 |
| G.B. Average | 14s. 3½d. | 17s. 2½d. | 18s. 2½d. | 100 | 100 | 100 |

1. In each case the regional average is the unweighted average of the counties in the region. The average for Britain is the unweighted average of all the counties. Bowley found that weighting gave results practically identical to the arithmetic average, *J.R.S.S.*, (1898), 710. For regions see Map 1.

The advantages of farm wages as a guide to relative wage levels in different areas were discussed in the introduction to Chapter One where it was suggested that they are probably the most useful single guide. There are difficulties, however. In an occupation as widespread as agriculture it is difficult to distinguish market boundaries. Wages were usually given by counties, but county boundaries were seldom market boundaries and in some areas, particularly on the approaches to London, rates changed rapidly over short distances. There were other, less predictable, variations; from farm to farm and parish to parish often for no good reason other than that the differential had existed for as long as anyone could remember.[1] Additional problems arise from differences in the working day and working conditions which varied between regions according to soil, climate, and custom. Some labourers were hired for the day, some for six months or longer; the latter often 'lived in', others found their own accommodation or occupied a tied cottage. Some men were paid mainly in cash, others mainly in kind. Each of these cases presents difficulties— variations in work most of all because in much of Scotland the horseman (or ploughman) and not the ordinary labourer (or orraman) was the most representative farm worker. The status of the English labourer was between these two. For the sake of consistency the figures used for Scotland in Tables 1–3 and 1–4 are those of ordinary farm labourers and probably slightly underestimate the relative position of earnings in Scottish counties.[2]

Fortunately, most of these problems were encountered, tackled, and, as near as could be, resolved by contemporary investigators.[3] There is no absolute shortage of wage evidence for most occupations in the period 1850–1914, but for the greater part it consists of piecemeal references to different dates and areas collected by different authorities each using their own method. Evidence of this nature is not nearly as well adapted for regional comparison as that in the far less numerous surveys conducted by a single investigator or a close-knit team, and it is in this respect especially that agriculture is

---

1. In late-nineteenth-century Warwickshire Joseph Ashby noted wage differences of 2s. a week, almost 20 per cent, in adjacent villages without any difference in demand or supply. M. K. Ashby, *Joseph Ashby of Tysoe*, p. 159.

2. On those distinctions see, *Report on the Wages and Earnings of Agricultural Labourers*, P.P. 1900, LXXXII, pp. 108–9; Bowley, *Wages in the United Kingdom in the Nineteenth Century*, p. 55; A. K. Cairncross (ed.), *The Scottish Economy*, p. 161.

3. All the figures in Tables 1–3 and 1–4 are for total earnings including payment in kind.

distinguished—it was more frequently and more thoroughly investigated than any other nineteenth-century occupation. It would be unwise to place much weight on any single figure in Table 1–3 and it should be borne in mind that the highest and lowest rates are concealed in the averages,[1] but taken together, and with the qualifications made here and in Chapter One, Tables 1–3 and 1–4 are as reliable a guide to regional wage variations in any one occupation as can be obtained without very extensive work on the contemporary sources. In this inquiry whenever a single index of county or regional wage has been required for statistical analysis Tables 1–3 and 1–4 have been used.

# III

BUILDING CRAFTSMEN AND LABOURERS

Table 1–5  Craftsmen and Labourers' Wages, 1860, 1886, 1906.
Table 1–6  Index of Carpenters' and Labourers' Wages 1886, 1906.
*Sources:*

In Table 1–5 several figures are the results of averaging two or more sources or, in the case of labourers, of rates paid to different labourers; bricklayers' labourers, for example, were sometimes paid a little more or less than carpenters' labourers.

> Source T—*Wages of the Manual Labour Classes*, P.P. 1893–4, LXXXIIIii, pp. 176–220.
> Source U—*Earnings and Hours Inquiry III*, P.P. 1910, LXXXIV, pp. 160–73.
> Source W—*Operative Bricklayers' Society*, Annual Reports.
> Source X—G. H. Wood unpublished wage statistics, library of the Royal Statistical Society, and library of the Department of Employment and Productivity.
> Source Y—*Returns of Wages published between 1830 and 1886*, P.P. 1887, LXXXIX, pp. 36–8, 354–86.
> Source Z—A. L. Bowley, 'The Statistics of Wages in the U.K. during the last One Hundred Years', Pts VI–VIII, *J.R.S.S.*, lxiii, lxiv (1900, 1901).
> B—Bricklayers' Wage Rate.
> C—Carpenters' Wage Rate.

---

1. Details of intra-county variations are given in Chapter One.

Table 1–6 is based upon figures in Table 1–5. The figure for Great Britain is the average of the sum of the regional averages. The regional averages are calculated from carpenters' and labourers' rates in the following towns:

Region 1. London, Dover; labourers in 1906–London, Folkestone.
Region 2. Bristol, Dorchester, Exeter, Taunton.
Region 3. Chichester, Norwich, Oxford.
Region 4. Cardiff, Newport.
Region 5. —
Region 6. Birmingham, Leicester, Nottingham.
Region 7. Hull, Lincoln, Scarborough.
Region 8. Bradford, Manchester, Preston.
Region 9. Carlisle.
Region 10. South Shields, Sunderland.
Region 11. Hawick.
Region 12. Edinburgh, Glasgow, Greenock, Stirling.
Region 13. Aberdeen, Inverness, Perth; labourers in 1906–Aberdeen, Elgin, Perth.

A. L. Bowley drew attention to wages in the building trades as more representative than most of general wage trends;[1] as a guide to regional differentials they are a close second to farm wages. Although more were employed in agriculture, building shared the advantages of geographical ubiquity and relative immunity to technical change. In some respects building wages are more easily handled: 'brick-layer' and 'builders' labourer' are less equivocal descriptions than 'farm labourer'; considered together they provide a useful bonus by way of indicating the differential for skill; and whereas in agriculture local markets merged imperceptibly one into the other, the markets for building labour normally extended to the town boundary and within towns one rate prevailed in each trade.[2] For these reasons the figures in Table 1–5 are especially useful; they reflect actual rates in separate towns far more accurately than Table 1–3 reflects rates in separate counties and the labourer's wage is a good guide to the relative level of all unskilled wages in any town.[3] As a guide to regional variations, however, Table 1–6 is much inferior to Table 1–4

1. Bowley, *Wages in the United Kingdom in the Nineteenth Century*, pp. 58–9.
2. J. W. F. Rowe, *Wages in Practice and Theory*, pp. 5, 25, 65–7, 126.
3. Building labourers, in fact, were usually paid a little more than general unskilled labourers but the amount by which their pay exceeded unskilled labourers' pay is unlikely to have varied much from one town to another. Bowley, *Wages in the United Kingdom in the Nineteenth Century*, pp. 58–9.

TABLE 1–5 *Building Craftsmen and Labourers' Wage per Hour (pence): Towns*

| Town | Region | 1860 | | | 1886 | | | 1906 | | |
|---|---|---|---|---|---|---|---|---|---|---|
| | | Craftsman | Labourer | Source | Craftsman | Labourer | Source | Craftsman | Labourer | Source |
| London | 1 | B. 6¾ | 4 | X | C. 9 | 6 | T | C. 10½ | 7 | U,X |
| Canterbury | 1 | | | | C. 6½ | 3¾ | T | B. 7½ | | W |
| Dover | 1 | | | | C. 7½ | 4¾ | T | C. 8 | | |
| Folkestone | 1 | | | | | | | | 5¾ | U |
| Halstead | 1 | | | | B. 6 | | W | B. 6 | | W |
| Bristol | 2 | C. 5¼ | | Y | C. 6 | 4 | T | C. 9 | 6 | U |
| Dorchester | 2 | | | | C. 5 | 3¾ | T | C. 6 | 4 | U |
| Exeter | 2 | | | | C. 5½ | 3½ | T | C. 7½ | 5 | U |
| Plymouth | 2 | | | | C. 6 | 4 | T | B. 8 | 5 | W,X |
| St. Austell | 2 | | | | | | | C. 5 | 4 | U |
| Taunton | 2 | | | | C. 5 | 3¾ | T | C. 7 | 4 | U |
| Chichester | 3 | | | | C. 6 | 4 | T | C. 7 | 4¾ | U |
| Norwich | 3 | | | | C. 6¾ | 3¾ | T | C. 8 | 5 | U |
| Oxford | 3 | | | | C. 7½ | 4 | T | C. 8 | 5½ | U |
| Southampton | 3 | | | | C. 6½ | 4 | X | C. 8 | 5 | X |
| Winchester | 3 | | | | C. 6 | 3¾ | T | B. 8 | | W |
| Abergavenny | 4 | | | | | | | C. 7 | 4¾ | U |
| Cardiff | 4 | | | | C. 7½ | 4½ | T | C. 9 | 5½ | U |
| Newport | 4 | C. 3½ | | X | C. 6½ | 4 | T | C. 8½ | 5½ | U |
| Carnarvon | 5 | | | | | | | C. 7 | 5 | U |
| Hereford | 5 | | | | B. 6 | | X | C. 7 | 4½ | U |
| Birmingham | 6 | B. 5 | 3¼ | X | C. 8 | 5 | T | C. 9½ | 6½ | U |
| Leicester | 6 | | | | C. 7½ | 5¼ | T | C. 9 | 6¾ | U |
| Nottingham | 6 | | | | C. 8 | 5½ | T | C. 9 | 6½ | U |
| Shrewsbury | 6 | | | | C. 6¼ | 4 | T | B. 8 | 5½ | U,W |

| | | | | | | | | | |
|---|---|---|---|---|---|---|---|---|---|
| Hull | 7 | | | | C. 7 | 5½ | T | C. 9 | 6½ | U |
| Lincoln | 7 | | | | C. 6¾ | 4¼ | T | C. 8 | 5¾ | U |
| Middlesbrough | 7 | | | | C. 7 | | X | B. 9½ | 6½ | U, W |
| Scarborough | 7 | | | | C. 7 | 5 | T | C. 8 | 6 | U |
| Bradford | 8 | | | | C. 7 | 4¾ | T | C. 8½ | 6¼ | U |
| Leeds | 8 | C. 5 | | X | C. 7½ | 5 | T, X | B. 9½ | 6½ | W, X |
| Manchester | 8 | B. 7 | | X | C. 8 | 5½ | T | C. 9½ | 6¼ | U |
| Preston | 8 | | | | C. 7½ | 5½ | T | C. 9 | 6 | U |
| Huddersfield | 8 | C. 5 | | X | C. 6¾ | 5¼ | T | C. 8½ | 6 | X |
| Carlisle | 9 | | | | C. 6½ | 4½ | T | C. 8 | 5¼ | U |
| Workington | 9 | | | | B. 7½ | | W | B. 9 | | W |
| Durham | 10 | | | | C. 6¾ | 4½ | T | C. 9 | 6 | U |
| Newcastle | 10 | B. 5½ | | X, Y | C. 8 | | X | C. 9½ | 6¼ | U |
| South Shields | 10 | | | | C. 8 | 5 | T | C. 9½ | 6¼ | U |
| Sunderland | 10 | | | | C. 7½ | 4½ | T | C. 9¼ | 6¼ | U |
| Dumfries | 11 | | | | | | | C. 7½ | 5¼ | U |
| Galashiels | 11 | | | | C. 6½ | 5 | T | | | |
| Hawick | 11 | | | | C. 7 | 4 | T | C. 8 | 5½ | U |
| Edinburgh | 12 | | | | C. 6½ | 5 | T | C. 9 | 5½ | U |
| Glasgow | 12 | C. 5 | 3½ | X, Z | C. 7½ | 4¾ | T | C. 9½ | 5¾ | U |
| Greenock | 12 | | | | C. 7 | 5 | T | C. 9 | 5½ | U |
| Stirling | 12 | | | | C. 6 | 4¼ | T | C. 8 | 6 | U |
| Aberdeen | 13 | | | | C. 6 | 4½ | T | C. 8 | 5 | U |
| Dundee | 13 | | | | C. 7 | | X | C. 9 | 5½ | U, X |
| Elgin | 13 | | | | | | | C. 7 | 4¾ | U |
| Inverness | 13 | | | | C. 5½ | 3½ | T | C. 7½ | | U |
| Oban | 13 | | | | | | | C. 8 | 4¾ | U |
| Perth | 13 | | | | C. 6½ | 4¾ | T | C. 8 | 5½ | U |
| Peterhead | 13 | | | | | | | C. 6½ | 5 | U |

For notes and abbreviations see text.

TABLE 1–6 *Carpenters' and Labourers' Wages for a Nine-Hour Day: Regions*

| Region | Carpenters 1886 | | Carpenters 1906 | | Labourers 1886 | | Labourers 1906 | |
|---|---|---|---|---|---|---|---|---|
| | Per 9 hours | When GB 1886 = 100 | Per 9 hours | When GB 1906 = 100 | Per 9 hours | When GB 1886 = 100 | Per 9 hours | When GB 1906 = 100 |
| 1 London and Home Counties | 6s. 2d. | 117 | 6s. 11d. | 109 | 4s. | 117 | 4s. 10d. | 114 |
| 2 South-west | 4s. 1d. | 78 | 5s. 6d. | 87 | 2s. 9d. | 80 | 3s. 7d. | 84 |
| 3 Rural south-east | 5s. 1d. | 97 | 5s. 9d. | 91 | 3s. | 88 | 3s. 10d. | 90 |
| 4 South Wales | 5s. 3d. | 100 | 6s. 7d. | 104 | 3s. 2d. | 93 | 4s. 2d. | 98 |
| 5 Rural Wales and Herefordshire | — | — | — | — | — | — | — | — |
| 6 Midlands | 5s. 11d. | 113 | 6s. 11d. | 109 | 3s. 11d. | 115 | 4s. 11d. | 116 |
| 7 Lincs, Rutland, E. and N. Riding | 5s. 2d. | 98 | 6s. 3d. | 99 | 3s. 9d. | 110 | 4s. 6d. | 106 |
| 8 Lancs, Cheshire, W. Riding | 5s. 7d. | 106 | 6s. 9d. | 107 | 3s. 11d. | 115 | 4s. 6d. | 106 |
| 9 Cumberland and Westmorland | 4s. 11d. | 94 | 6s. | 95 | 3s. 5d. | 100 | 4s. | 94 |
| 10 Northumberland and Durham | 5s. 10d. | 111 | 7s. | 111 | 3s. 7d. | 105 | 4s. 8d. | 110 |
| 11 South Scotland | 5s. 3d. | 100 | 6s. | 95 | 3s. | 88 | 4s. 2d. | 98 |
| 12 Central Scotland | 5s. 1d. | 97 | 6s. 8d. | 105 | 3s. 7d. | 105 | 4s. 3d. | 100 |
| 13 Northern Scotland | 4s. 6d. | 86 | 5s. 11d. | 93 | 3s. 2d. | 93 | 3s. 10d. | 90 |
| G.B. av. | 5s. 3d. | 100 | 6s. 4d. | 100 | 3s. 5d. | 100 | 4s. 3d. | 100 |

because the distinctiveness of local markets for building labour introduces a large measure of unreality into averages formed from rates in a small number of towns within a large region. There is the further complication that building wages were in part a function of town size, so that if they are used as a guide to other wage levels ideally only towns of similar size should be compared.[1] For these reasons Table 1–6 should be handled with greater circumspection than Table 1–5.

Only towns for which carpenters' and labourers' wages were available in 1886 and 1906 have been included in Table 1–6 and none suitable were found to represent Region 5. The towns in Table 1–5 were selected to illustrate wage variations between and within regions. Wage rates are available for a great many towns not shown in the tables[2] and some of these are used in Chapter One although it should be noted that most material is for the years after 1875—over the period as a whole farm wages are better recorded. Reliable figures for the third quarter of the century could probably be found in local records but in the present survey their absence is no great handicap.

# IV

## Coal Miners

Table 1–7   Wages per day of Hewers (H) and Labourers (L) 1888, 1914.

*Sources:* J. W. F. Rowe, *Wages in the Coal Industry,* pp. 75, 82, 85. Rowe indicates that some of his figures are more reliable than others. Those marked † in the table 'should probably be about 65 per cent', that marked # 'about 80 per cent'. These adjustments will affect the other figures shown for the same fields. The figure for Great Britain is a weighted average. All the figures are subject to considerable qualification (see notes below).

In 1850 mining was a sizeable and rapidly growing occupation which offered employment in a number of fairly well-defined areas. For these reasons the industry merits consideration; but as a guide to regional wage variations it has severe limitations. One obvious

1. F. W. Lawrence, *Local Variations in Wages,* p. 9.
2. In the sources cited and elsewhere. For surveys of local rates in 1897, 1905, and 1912 see Lawrence, op. cit., pp. 12–13; *B. of T. Inquiry into Working-Class Rents and Retail Prices,* P.P. 1913, LXVI, pp. 114–19.

TABLE 1–7  *Coal Hewers and Labourers: Wages per Day*

| | Wages 1888 | | Wages 1914 | | Per cent increase | | Index 1888 | | Index 1914 | |
|---|---|---|---|---|---|---|---|---|---|---|
| | H | L | H | L | H | L | H | L | H | L |
| Northumberland | 5s. 1d. | 3s. 4d. | 9s. 1d. | 6s. | 79 | 80 | 107 | 108 | 103 | 104 |
| Durham | 5s. | 3s. 9d. | 8s. 11d. | 5s. 9d. | 80 | 54 | 105 | 122 | 101 | 99 |
| Cumberland | 4s. 5d. | 3s. 2d. | 8s. 2d. | 5s. 8d. | 85 | 79 | 93 | 103 | 92 | 98 |
| Lancashire | 5s. 2d. | 3s. 4d. | 8s. 7d. | 5s. 10d. | 66 | 75† | 109 | 108 | 97 | 101 |
| N. Wales | 4s. 1d. | 2s. 8d. | 8s. | 5s. 5d. | 98 | 103 | 86 | 86 | 91 | 94 |
| Notts and Derby | 5s. 4d. | 3s. 5d. | 9s. 10d. | 5s. 8d. | 84 | 66 | 112 | 111 | 111 | 98 |
| N. Staffs | 4s. 10d. | 3s. | 9s. 1d. | 5s. 7d. | 88 | 86 | 102 | 97 | 103 | 96 |
| S. Staffs | 4s. 6d. | 3s. 4d. | 7s. 1d. | 5s. 10d. | 57† | 75† | 95 | 108 | 80 | 101 |
| Cannock Chase | 5s. | 3s. | 8s. 6d. | 5s. 7d. | 70† | 86† | 105 | 97 | 96 | 96 |
| Warwickshire | 5s. | 3s. | 10s. 1d. | 6s. 2d. | 102 | 106 | 105 | 97 | 114 | 106 |
| Leicestershire | 4s. 3d. | 3s. 6d. | 7s. | 5s. 10d. | 65 | 66 | 89 | 114 | 79 | 101 |
| Somerset | 3s. 3d. | 2s. 3d. | 5s. 9d. | 4s. 4d. | 77 | 94 | 68 | 73 | 65 | 75 |
| Forest of Dean | 4s. 6d. | 2s. 10d. | 6s. 9d. | 4s. 6d. | 51 | 59 | 95 | 92 | 76 | 78 |
| S. Wales | 4s. 10d. | 2s. 10d. | 9s. 4d. | 5s. 9d. | 93 | 103 | 102 | 92 | 106 | 99 |
| Lanarkshire | 4s. 7d. | 3s. 2d. | 8s. 3d. | 6s. 6d. | 80 | 105# | 96 | 103 | 93 | 112 |
| W. Yorkshire | — | — | 8s. 11d. | 6s. 3d. | — | — | — | — | 101 | 108 |
| S. Yorkshire | — | — | 10s. 3d. | 6s. 8d. | — | — | — | — | 116 | 115 |
| G.B. | 4s. 9d. | 3s. 1d. | 8s. 10d. | 5s. 9½d. | 86 | 88 | 100 | 100 | 100 | 100 |

For notes and abbreviations see text.

disadvantage is the large areas of Britain where mining was not important. More serious than this is the nature of the evidence—wage statistics in this industry are far more intractable than those for either building or agriculture. Table 1–7 shows what are probably the most reliable figures of mine wages available, yet they are almost certainly less reliable than the figures in Tables 1–3 to 1–6. Even so, dubious as they are more figures of the same type as those shown in Table 1–7 would be welcome because there were very few large-scale surveys of coal wages and in this industry more than anywhere else isolated observations must be treated with great suspicion. Nineteenth-century inquiries were concerned most with mine safety, truck, and the employment of women and children—wages were relatively ignored.[1] The first major wage survey was in 1886 and none followed until shortly before the First World War.

The miner's daily routine in each locality changed little over the period, technical developments present few problems; but geology and custom imposed a bewildering variety of working methods between different coalfields, in different pits, and often within the same pit. Had the miner been paid by the hour, day, or week this would present no great difficulty but most miners were paid piece-rates—there was no standard wage. How much a man earned depended on the piece-rate, his output, and the 'consideration'. Piece-rate lists catered for a variety of geological conditions and for subsidiary tasks like timbering and maintenance. As a consequence they were enormously complex and in most areas there was a different list for each pit. Output was a function of the miner's strength and application, how long he worked, random factors like the presence of gas and, again, geology. The 'consideration' was an allowance paid for work carried on in 'abnormal' places and compensation for other difficulties beyond the miner's control. 'Considerations' reduced the possible range of earnings, but anything approaching standard earnings would have been as surprising as a handicap race in which all the runners finish together. Earnings varied widely, the pay of any one man might be wildly unrepresentative, and there was a great scatter on either side of the 'typical' rates shown in Table 1–7. There are other difficulties too: on some fields a variation of the sub-contract system where hewers had to pay an assistant from their own earnings; dramatic changes in earnings as piece-rates were adjusted to changes in the price of coal;

1. This was probably because pay was not high among the coalfield problems. By the standards of the time most miners were relatively well paid.

some payment in kind; sundry deductions from pay for candles, explosives, and similar items; and difficulties which arise from the fact that coal is not a homogeneous commodity—export coal prices fluctuated more than prices in the home market and in the winter when the fields cutting household coal were busiest those serving the Baltic had their slack season.[1]

Changes in piece-rates were caused mainly by movements in the price of coal and these are recorded for most coalfields since 1871.[2] These changes were usually effective throughout a whole coalfield and sometimes in several fields together. On their own the percentage changes are of no assistance in calculating 'average' rates, but they show the direction and rate of change in earnings and given the availability of 'average' wage rates for one date in the nineteenth century and again for the early twentieth century they offer, or seem to offer, a means of calculating 'average' rates over a considerable number of years. In practice they are less useful. Rowe tested their accuracy by calculating 'nominal' wages in 1914 from percentage changes on 'actual' wage figures collected in 1886. In each of several coalfields he examined the 'calculated' wage for 1914 was below the 'actual' wage.[3] As they stand the figures, although often used,[4] seriously underestimate the rise in earnings. Rowe concluded that the 'basis' from which percentage changes were calculated must have been altered at various times between 1888 and 1914 and the changes not recorded.[5] The difference between 'actual' wages in 1914 and 'nominal' wages as calculated from recorded percentage changes in the 'basis' rates varied from one field to another—on average it was around 25 per cent of the rate in 1888.

1. These notes are intended as no more than an outline of the problems involved. For more detailed accounts see Rowe, *Wages in the Coal Industry;* H. S. Jevons, *The British Coal Trade;* Bowley, *Wages in the United Kingdom in the Nineteenth Century,* section XIII; B. R. Mitchell, 'The Economic Development of the Inland Coalfields, 1870–1914' pp. 192–223; A. J. Youngson Brown, 'The Scots Coal Industry 1854–1886', pp. 219–28. Jevons contains a reproduction of a south Wales price-list (pp. 340–2) but some of his wage figures are unreliable—Rowe is much the better source.
2. In official papers and by private investigators. See e.g. *Seventeenth Annual Abstract of Labour Statistics,* P.P. 1914–16, LXI, pp. 70–1. The G. H. Wood Collection has more extensive material than the official returns.
3. Rowe, *Wages in the Coal Industry,* pp. 72–3, *passim.*
4. By, among others, B. R. Mitchell and P. Deane, *Abstract of British Historical Statistics* (Cambridge, 1962), pp. 348–50. Mitchell and Deane show an increase of 53 per cent in coal wages between 1888 and 1914; according to Rowe (*Wages in the Coal Industry,* p. 82) the increase was between 70 and 88 per cent.
5. Rowe, *Wages in the Coal Industry,* Chs. 3 and 4.

## V

POLICE CONSTABLES (County)

Table 1-8    Index of County Constabulary Wages by Region, 1860-1906.

*Source:* G. H. Wood unpublished collection of wage statistics, Library of the Royal Statistical Society.

TABLE 1-8

*Index of County Constabulary Wages by Region, 1860-1906*

At each date the figures shown represent the regional wage as a proportion of the national average wage. The national wage is the average of the wage rate in each country.

| Region | 1860 | 1870 | 1880 | 1890 | 1900 | 1906 |
|---|---|---|---|---|---|---|
| 1 London and Home Counties | 105 | 106 | 102 | 103 | 100 | 98 |
| 2 South-west | 100 | 97 | 93 | 91 | 92 | 93 |
| 3 Rural south-east | 104 | 103 | 98 | 97 | 96 | 97 |
| 4 South Wales | 107 | 103 | 102 | 101 | 106 | 103 |
| 5 Rural Wales and Herefordshire | 100 | 101 | 100 | 99 | 97 | 100 |
| 6 Midlands | 104 | 104 | 106 | 103 | 104 | 103 |
| 7 Lincs., Rutland, E and N. Riding | 107 | 106 | 108 | 105 | 104 | 101 |
| 8 Lancs, Cheshire, W. Riding | 110 | 112 | 114 | 111 | 114 | 112 |
| 9 Cumberland and Westmorland | 102 | 107 | 109 | 106 | 108 | 104 |
| 10 Northumberland and Durham | 105 | 105 | 112 | 109 | 111 | 109 |
| 11 South Scotland | 95 | 95 | 97 | 99 | 99 | 97 |
| 12 Central Scotland | 98 | 95 | 102 | 105 | 103 | 104 |
| 13 Northern Scotland | 90 | 95 | 93 | 97 | 97 | 97 |
| GB | 100 | 100 | 100 | 100 | 100 | 100 |

The main reason for the appearance of Table 1-8 in this appendix is the detailed record of constables' pay in the G. H. Wood wage collection; he shows minimum, maximum, and mean rates for each county for every year between 1857 and 1906. But there are few other reasons for using these figures. The county constabulary can hardly be considered a major employer and by the middle of the century, long before most other occupations were similarly affected, wages were determined in London.[1] Whenever wages are determined

1. J. P. Martin and G. Wilson, *The Police: A Study in Manpower*, pp. 9, 15, 18.

in one centre regional variations are more apparent; they seem more anomalous and are more likely to be eradicated.[1] Variations between counties were greater than those shown in Table 1–8 because the regional figures are calculated from the mean average of several counties, but county rates had to fall within minimum and maximum rates laid down by the Home Office. Boroughs were free of this restriction and pay between towns varied more than between counties.[2] There is evidence that some authorities attached especial importance to securing good recruits and some regions may have occupied a different place on the list had each authority employed men of similar calibre[3] It seems likely too that south Scotland (Region 11) would compare more favourably with other areas if it were possible to take into account variations in the provision of subsidized accommodation.[4] With these provisos Table 1–8, although it greatly underestimate the range of differentials, may be considered a useful supplementary guide to the rank order of pay in the rural parts of each region.

1. These points are discussed at greater length in Ch. 9.
2. Martin and Wilson, op. cit., pp. 15, 17–18.
3. Ibid., p. 20 and see above, pp. 23, 26.
4. *Return of Rates of Wages paid by Local Authorities and Private Companies,* P.P. 1892, LXVIII, p. xiii.

# 2

## THE COST OF LIVING

### I

THE first question suggested by the regional differences in wages described in Chapter One is the extent to which they were compensated by variations in the cost of living. An answer to this question requires evidence of regional prices, in particular the price of those items which were most important in wage earners' budgets: food, fuel, and accommodation. But such evidence is not readily available. There was no systematic investigation of regional retail prices until the Board of Trade inquiries into urban cost of living in the early twentieth century,[1] and price historians, like wage historians, have concentrated on chronological changes in the national average.

Three price relationships are relevant here: the differentials between high- and low-wage rural areas, between town and country, and between high- and low-wage urban areas. They will be examined in this order. None of these relationships have received much attention from historians, although there is sufficient piecemeal evidence to make commonplace the belief that rural labourers who contemplated town life could expect at least part of their enhanced wage to be offset by higher prices. But how great a part? Contemporaries certainly had no clear idea. The majority of those whose evidence is most trustworthy considered that the town advantage, while less in real terms than in money terms, was nevertheless substantial.[2] But there

---

1. *Board of Trade Inquiry into Working Class Rents, Housing and Retail Prices*, P.P. 1908, CVII; *Board of Trade Inquiry into Working-Class Rents and Retail Prices*, P.P. 1913, LXVI (subsequently referred to as the *First* and *Second B. of T. Cost-of-Living Inquiries*).
2. See e.g. H. L. Smith in C. Booth, *Life and Labour*, 1st Ser., iii. 137; A. L. Bowley, 'Rural Population in England and Wales', p. 617.

were many who thought the attractions of towns largely
illusory.[1] And we are little wiser today—Professor Checkland
has lent weight to the opinions of the latter group while Pro-
fessors Chambers and Mingay have generalized in terms of farm
labourers in the late nineteenth century having received some
two-thirds of the average industrial real wage.[2]

From a theoretical standpoint it seems highly improbable that
prices varied from one area to another by an amount sufficient
to offset wage differentials. A situation where money wages
vary and real wages are uniform implies that men are more
mobile than things that they purchase, which is unlikely,
except in the case of housing. Also, we know that beneath the
regional wage pattern there was a micro-pattern with features
scarcely less remarkable; farm earnings sometimes varied by
as much as 20 per cent in neighbouring villages and it is scarcely
conceivable that prices varied by similar proportions. We know,
too, that consumption varied with money wages which would
have been impossible had high wages been offset by high prices;
Chapter One contains several references to the contrast between
southern labourers, who ate much bread and seldom tasted
meat, and their more fortunate counterparts in the north.[3]

1. See e.g. P. M. Roxby, who argued that the average rural worker was
   'fully as well off as the moderately skilled town artisan'—quoted in J.
   Saville, *Rural Depopulation in England and Wales 1851–1951* (1957), p. 18.
   For a comment on the relationship between the real and money wages of
   farm labourers in different areas see Fay's observation on Bowley's paper
   in the *J.R.S.S.*, 1914. Fay suggested that the whole of the advantages of
   higher wages in the north might be 'swallowed up in house rent' (ibid.,
   p. 649).
2. S. G. Checkland, *The Rise of Industrial Society in England, 1815–1885*
   (1964), pp. 243–4; J. D. Chambers and G. E. Mingay, *The Agricultural
   Revolution* (1966), p. 197.
3. Most of the references in Ch. 1 were for the first half of the period. By 1900
   real wages had risen in all areas but the same yardsticks suggest the continued advantage of the high-wage counties:

| Weekly Expenditure of Agricultural Labourer's Families in 1902 | High-Wage Counties | | Low-Wage Counties | |
|---|---|---|---|---|
| | Northern Counties | Midland Counties | Eastern Counties | Southern and South-western Counties |
| On Bread and Flour | 2s. 10¾d. | 3s. ¾d. | 3s. 10d. | 3s. 10¼d. |
| On Meat | 5s. 2½d. | 4s. 9¾d. | 3s. 2d. | 3s. 5½d. |

Source: *Memoranda, Statistical Tables and Charts on British and Foreign
Trade and Industrial Conditions*, P.P. 1903, LXVII, p. 211.

Clearly wage and price levels were not entirely inter-dependent, but the question of to what extent variations in one were offset by variations in the other remains. This is an interesting question, and not only within the confines of the present inquiry. Spatial variations in the standard of living are related to chronological changes and scarcely less worthy of attention. In certain cases, for example, the study of industrialization and its effect on labour, spatial variations may be the more pertinent consideration. Moreover, most investigations of living standards use price evidence and the question of how far price and rent data for one centre may be used as evidence of a general pattern, or combined with data from different areas to measure chronological change, can only be answered when more is known about regional prices. In this chapter it is argued that spacial differences in wages were not much offset by spacial differences in the cost of living.

II

We can begin by considering the least complicated case—the cost of living of rural workers in regions of different wage levels.[1] Most agricultural inquiries gave some attention to labourers' housing; from these and other sources information on rural rents is readily obtainable. The prevailing level of rent in any area, like the prevailing wage rate, was qualified by numerous but insignificant exceptions. Thus a report of the 1860s noted that cottage rents varied between £1 and £6 per annum but, 'as a general rule, they are not let for less than 50s. or more than £4.'[2] There were also local variations in rural rents on the outskirts of towns and in colliery districts where cottages might be occupied with equal convenience by rural or

---

1. Payments in kind can be ignored here. Most calculations of rural earnings in Ch. 1 include payments in kind.
2. *Commission on the Employment of Children, Young Persons, and Women in Agriculture*, P.P. 1868–9, XIII, p. 69.

urban workers.[1] We shall assume that these patterns occurred
everywhere and concentrate upon the rents paid by the majority
of rural labourers in each area. These were remarkably
uniform. The *Morning Chronicle* inquiry of 1849–50 found
cottages in East Anglia rented at between 63*s.* and £7 per
annum; in the East Riding, where earnings were considerably
higher, the range was between £3 and £6 and Caird noted
similar rates in Lancashire.[2] After 1860 impressions can be based
on better evidence. The 1867 Report on the *Employment of
Children, Young Persons, and Women in Agriculture* has details
of rents in most counties;[3] they were perhaps a little higher in
high-wage areas and a little lower elsewhere, but the ordinary
range of rents, between 1*s.* and 1*s.* 6*d.* a week, was similar
throughout the country: 'between the several counties there is
not a marked difference to be observed in the maximum and
minimum rents.' [4] That this pattern still held at the end of the
century is indicated by evidence in the *R.C. on Labour*, which
concluded: '. . . rents of estate or farm cottages vary very little
as between districts of high and low earnings.' [5] Another
characteristic of rural rents was their remarkable uniformity
over time—most were still between 1*s.* and 2*s.* in 1904.[6]

There is little worthwhile evidence on the cost of food in
rural areas before 1860. Several sources, notably the 1849–50
*Morning Chronicle* investigation, include references to prices
but in the context of broader inquiries and usually without

1. In Cornwall for example both rents and wages were relatively high around
   the mines. *M.C.* 14 Nov. 1849. See also M. K. Ashby, *Joseph Ashby of
   Tysoe*, p. 159.
2. *M.C.* 5 Dec. 1849; 28 Oct. 1850; J. A. Sheppard, 'East Yorkshire's Agricultural Labour Force in the mid-Nineteenth Century', p. 47; Caird, op.
   cit., p. 284.
3. For a useful summary of the rent data in this report see the *Royal Commission on Labour*, P.P. 1893–4, XXXVIIii, Section 1-A. Memorandum on the
   Reports and Proceedings of the Children's Employment Commission, 1862,
   and the Commission on the Employment of Children, Young Persons, and
   Women in Agriculture, 1867, pp. 30–2, 45–51.
4. Ibid., pp. 30–1. County agricultural earnings at this time ranged between
   9*s.* and 20*s.* a week. Table 1–3.
5. *R.C. on Labour*, P.P. 1893–4, XXXVIIii, General Report, p. 120.
6. *Second Report on Wages . . . of Agricultural Labourers*, p. 6. On this point,
   and on cottage rents generally, see A. Wilson Fox, 'Agricultural Wages in
   England and Wales during the last Fifty Years', *J.R.S.S.*, lxvi (1903), 306.

commenting on the quality of the goods in question.[1] For 1860–1, however, we have figures for five English counties and three counties in Scotland. On this evidence, which is shown in Table 2–1, none of the counties was at a marked advantage or disadvantage.

The 1867 *Commission on the Employment of Children, Young Persons, and Women in Agriculture* included a few rural prices; they are insufficient to provide more than a very rough impression but lend no support to the thesis that higher prices offset earnings in high-wage areas.[2] We are back on firmer ground in the 1890s with the *Royal Commission on Labour* which provides probably the best single source for the study of nineteenth-century rural prices. Table 2–2 summarizes the evidence for seven frequently purchased commodities in counties selected to represent a variety of geographical and economic conditions. Prices were not identical, but in the majority of cases differences were insignificant having regard to the variety of qualities involved and the tendency for butter prices to fluctuate seasonally. The variations follow no discernible pattern and no county was clearly either dearer or cheaper than the others.

After the turn of the century evidence is comparatively abundant. There are detailed accounts of prices in a Bedfordshire village in 1903, at Corsley, Wiltshire, in 1906–7, and the immediate pre-war period is partly covered by scattered references in government publications.[3] None of these sources suggest food prices were higher in high-wage than in low-wage counties. For comparative purposes the most useful of the material for these years is in Rowntree and Kendall's survey of 1912–13 from which the figures in Table 2–3 have been extracted.[4] The prices there represent the average of those shown in 42 budgets collected between August 1912 and

1. Prices varied greatly according to quality and in some cases, butter and milk for example, with the season.
2. Those figures are summarized in the *R.C. on Labour*, P.P. 1893–4, XXXVIIii Section 1-A, pp. 51–4.
3. H. H. Mann, 'Life in an Agricultural Village in England', *Sociological Papers*, i (1904), 166; M. F. Davies, *Life in an English Village* (1909), Ch. XIV; *Financial Results of the Occupation of Agricultural Land and the Cost of Living of Rural Workers*, P.P. 1919, VIII; *Wages and Conditions of Employment in Agriculture*, P.P. 1919, IX.
4. B. S. Rowntree and M. Kendall, *How the Labourer Lives* (1913), Ch. III.

TABLE 2-1 *Farm Labourers' Earnings (1867–70) and Retail Prices in Rural Areas (1860–1)*

| | Bread 4 lb. | Flour 7 lb. | Butter lb. | Tea oz. | Sugar lb. | Earnings (1867–70) |
|---|---|---|---|---|---|---|
| Kent | 8d. | 1s. 4d. | 11d. | 2½d. | 4½d. | 17s. |
| Norfolk | 7d. | 1s. 2d. | 1s. | 3d. | 4½d. | 14s. 9d. |
| Devon | 7½d. | 1s. 5½d. | 1s. | 3d. | 5d. | 12s. 6d. |
| Warwickshire | 7d. | 1s. 2d. | 1s. 2d. | 3½d. | 5d. | 15s. |
| Orkney | 6d. (second quality) | 1s. (second quality) | 8d. | 3d. | 5d. | 13s. |
| Perthshire | 7½d. | 1s. 9d. | 1s.–1s. 2d. | 2½d.–3d. | 5d.–6d. | 13s. 6d. |
| Argyllshire | 7d. | 11½d.–1s. 4½d. | 1s. 1d. | 3d.–3¼d. | 5d.–6d. | 9s. |
| Cumberland | — | 1s. 1d. | — | 2¾d.–3d. | 5½d. | 18s. 6d. |

*Sources*: F. Purdy, 'On the Earnings of Agricultural Labourers in England and Wales, 1860', *J.R.S.S.*, xxiv (1861), 367; *idem*, 'On the Earnings of Agricultural Labourers in Scotland and Ireland', pp. 473–4; *R.C. on Labour*, P.P. 1893–4, XXXV, reports by A. Wilson Fox, p. 158. Earnings are taken from Table 1–3.

TABLE 2-2  *Farm Labourers' Earnings (1898) and Retail Prices in Rural Areas (1892–3)*

| | Bread 4 lb. | Tea 4 oz | Sugar 1 lb. | Bacon 1 lb. | Butter 1 lb. | Flour 7lb | Cheese 1 lb. | Earnings (1898) |
|---|---|---|---|---|---|---|---|---|
| Cornwall | 4½d.–5d. | 6d. | — | — | 1s. 8d. | 1s. ½d. | 8d. | 16s. 7d. |
| Kent | 5¾d. | 6d. | — | — | 1s. 4d. | — | 7d. | 19s. 10d. |
| Norfolk | — | 4d.–5½d. | 2d. | 8d. | 1s.–1s. 2d. | 9½d. | 6½d. | 14s. 9d. |
| Bedfordshire | 5d. | 6d. | 3d. | — | 1s. 2d. | — | 8d. | 16s. 2d. |
| Leicestershire | 4d. | 5d. | 2d. | 6d.–7d. | 1s.–1s. 2d.* 1s. 6d.** | 9d | 7d.–8d. | 17s. 2d. |
| Nottinghamshire | 4½d. | 5d. | 2½d. | 6d.–8d. | 1s. 4d. | 9d. | 6d.–9d. | 19s. 2d. |
| Lancashire | — | 7½d. | 2½d. | 8d. | 1s. 6d.** | 10d. | — | 19s. 4d. |
| Cumberland | — | 5½d.–7½d. | 2½d. | — | — | 8d.–9d. | — | 18s. 9d. |

*Sources*: R.C. on Labour, P.P. 1893–4, XXXV, district reports; Table 1–3.

\* summer

\*\* winter

February 1913.[1] The table requires little comment; labourers paid comparable prices for provisions regardless of their earnings; the differences between counties are no greater than the differences between prices paid by different families in the same county.[2]

There is little that can be said of the remaining items of expenditure, other than fuel, beyond the fact that there is no reason to suppose their prices varied significantly in different areas nor is there any evidence that this might have been the case. Fuel prices are of some interest; first, because coal accounted for a larger proportion of rural incomes than might be expected. A Norfolk labourer's budget in 1873 shows 1s. 9d. of the 12s. he spent was for fuel, 1s. 3d. for rent.[3] Budgets in the *Report of the Commission on the Employment of Children etc.* . . . . *in Agriculture* show that fuel generally accounted for a sum equivalent to two-thirds or more of rent,[4] and this seems to have been the pattern in later years.[5] The other point of interest about coal was that its price, unlike the price of other goods examined, varied in different parts of the country. This is not really surprising since no significant item in the labourers' budget was so dear to move or so restricted in origin. The general effect of variations in coal prices was to reinforce the advantages of high-wage counties. Edward Stanhope, an assistant commissioner on the 1867 inquiry, for example, noted that, 'As I went north the greatest difference to be noted in the condition of the agricultural population was the increased comfort afforded to them by the greater cheapness of fuel.'[6]

1. Some items have been ignored; one Leicestershire family, for example, with a curiously expensive taste in tea and a family in the North Riding which paid dearly for tea in order to accumulate trading stamps. Rowntree and Kendall, op. cit., pp. 214–5, 236, 253, 258–9.
2. This difference presumably arose from price changes in the course of the six-month period, from variation in the quality of provisions, and from small variations in prices from one village to the next according to the amount of retail competition.
3. L. M. Springall, *Labouring Life in Norfolk Villages, 1893–1914*, p. 138.
4. Summarized in *R.C. on Labour*, P.P. 1893–4, XXXVIIii, Section 1-A. .pp. 51–4.
5. *R.C. on Labour*, P.P. 1893–4, XXXV (most references are in the appendices to the district reports); Rowntree and Kendall, op. cit., Ch. III.
6. *Employment of Children, etc. in Agriculture* (Appendix to second report), P.P. 1868–9, XIII, p. 28.

TABLE 2–3 *Farm Labourers' Earnings (1907) and Retail Prices in Rural Areas (1912–13)*

| | Bread 4 lb. | Butter lb. | Margarine lb. | Sugar lb. | Tea 4 oz. | Flour 7 lb. | Bacon lb. | Cheese lb. | Earnings (1907) |
|---|---|---|---|---|---|---|---|---|---|
| Oxfordshire | 5½*d*. | 1*s*. 3*d*. | 6*d*. | 2*d*. | 4½*d*. | 11*d*. | 8*d*. | — | 14*s*. 11*d*. |
| Berkshire | 5½*d*. | 1*s*. 2½*d*. | 6*d*. | 2*d*. | 4¼*d*. | 11*d*. | 8*d*. | 9*d*. | 16*s*. 8*d*. |
| Essex | 6*d*. | 1*s*. | 7¾*d*. | 2*d*. | 4½*d*. | 11*d*. | 7¾*d*. | 9*d*. | 16*d*. 4*d*. |
| Leicestershire | 5¾*d*. | 1*s*. 3*d*. | 6*d*. | 2*d*. | 4¼*d*. | 11½*d*. | 10*d*. | 9*d*. | 18*s*. 9*d*. |
| Yorks. E.R. | — | 1*s*. 4*d*. | 5½*d*. | 2¼*d*. | 4¼*d*. | 10½*d*. | — | — | 19*s*. 3*d*. |
| Yorks. W.R. | — | 1*s*. | 8*d*. | 2½*d*. | 5*d*. | 10½*d*. | 10*d*. | 8½*d*. | 20*s*. |
| Yorks. N.R. | — | 1*s*. 2½*d*. | 6*d*. | 2¼*d*. | 4½*d*. | 10¼*d*. | 10*d*. | 9½*d*. | 19*s*. 7*d*. |

*Sources:* B. S. Rowntree and M. Kendall, *How the Labourer Lives* (1963); Table 1–3.

Another investigator suggested that cheap coal was responsible for the comparatively modest rise in mortality in the northern counties during the severe winter of 1864,[1] and coal prices have been cited as one reason for regional variations in diet—home baking made the northern labourer less dependent upon village shops which probably reinforced his initial advantage of cheaper coal.[2] The 1905 and 1912 cost-of-living inquiries both remarked on higher coal prices in the south: the lowest prices were found in 'towns situated in the midst of colliery districts; the highest prices obtained in Dover, Croydon, Portsmouth, Sheerness, Southampton, Taunton, Chatham and Swindon, all of which are situated in the Southern Counties remote from the important areas of supply.'[3]

This evidence is not so precise that it is necessary to delve deeply into the weights appropriate to rent, food, and fuel. Food ranked far above rent in the rural budget and fuel, as we have seen, was in most cases rather less important than rent. Cottage rents of between 1s. and 2s. could seldom have accounted for more than 12 per cent of a family budget, and this proportion was likely only in low-wage areas at the beginning of the period. In the 1860s a Dorset man, whose circumstances were recorded in an official inquiry, supported a wife and four children on 11s. a week. Of this he spent 1s. on rent, 6s. 10d. on food, and 9d. on fuel. At the same time a Berkshire man, who earned 13s. and had similar commitments but some help from other members of his family, paid 1s. 4d. in rent, 1s. 1d. on fuel, and 11s. 9½d. for food, half of it bread.[4] We might, therefore, bear in mind a very approximate ratio between expenditure

1. *Employment of Children, etc. in Agriculture*, P.P. 1867–8, XVII, p. xiv.
2. P. Mathias, *Retailing Revolution* (1967), p. 19. Home brewing, too, survived longest in the north and Midlands. William Cobbett was bemoaning the eclipse of home brewing in parts of the south as early as 1821. (*Rural Rides*, 1967 ed., p. 68). For references to the prevalence of home baking in the north see, among others, J. Burnett, *Plenty and Want* (1966), p. 122; *Second B. of T. Cost-of-Living Inquiry*, p. xxxiv; on prices in village shops see section IV of this chapter.
3. *First B. of T. Cost-of-Living Inquiry*, p. xxiv; *Second B. of T. Cost-of-Living Inquiry*, p. xxxv. For details of coal prices see pp. 98–101 of the second inquiry. These inquiries were concerned with the towns, but there is no reason to suspect that southern villages fared better than southern towns.
4. *R.C. on Labour*, pp. 1893–4, XXXVIIii, section 1-A, pp. 51–2.

on rent and food, at the time when the relative importance of rural rent was greatest, of between 1:7 and 1:10[1]—and no evidence was found of significant variations in food prices. With expenditure on rent and fuel of similar importance and, in broad terms, compensating marginal advantages in rent and fuel for low-wage areas and high-wage areas respectively, we can conclude that the cost of living of rural workers did not vary significantly in different parts of the country: differences in real wages paralleled differences in money wages.

## III

What we now know of rents and prices in rural areas will throw some light on the second of the three relationships to be investigated, viz. the extent by which price variations offset the margin between agricultural and town earnings. It is impossible to be precise about the money differential since it varied between occupations and areas, over time, and according to age. J. R. Bellerby has suggested that industrial wages were about double agricultural wages before 1914 and that this margin was not much affected by differences in retail prices.[2] But some authorities have put forward conflicting opinions[3] and Bellerby's figures, which were compiled as part of an exercise quite different from the present investigation, cannot

1. Urban rents were higher, both in real terms and as a proportion of income. According to Booth's figures 20 per cent is a reasonable guide to the proportion of working-class expenditure on rent in London towards the end of the century. C. Booth, *Life and Labour*, 1st Ser., i. 135. The 1884–5 housing inquiry suggests that in central London at that time rents took an even larger share of income—*R.C. on the Housing of the Working Classes*, P.P. 1884–5, XXX, p. 17. In other towns rents occupied a less prominent position (ibid., p. 17). The 1913 cost-of-living inquiry gave food and fuel a weight four times that of rent (*Second B. of T. Cost-of-Living Inquiry*, p. xxi). By that time of course there was a substantial margin available for less essential items. As a general guide we can accept that in the second half of the century food accounted for some 60 to 75 per cent of working-class expenditure- (Mathias, op. cit., p. 16) with the exact proportion varying over time, between regions and occupations, and according to individual circumstances and preferences.
2. J. R. Bellerby, 'Distribution of Farm Income in the U.K., 1867–1938', *Procs. of the Agricultural Economics Society*, x (1953), 135.
3. See above, pp. 77–8.

be accepted without further inquiry; they make no distinction between high- and low-wage regions and the cost-of-living adjustment appears to omit rents and to be based entirely on a calculation of the margin in 1904.[1] Further, many urban occupations were not immediately open to rural labourers and Bellerby's calculations are based upon average industrial earnings. The 'operative differential', that is the gap between farm earnings and what an agricultural labourer could reasonably hope to obtain in a town, was clearly smaller than the gap between farm earnings and what he might aspire to receive after several years and further training. One point worth noting at the outset is that the existence of wide regional variations in rural real incomes suggests that, in testing the conflicting opinions as to how far the town workers' money wage advantage was nullified by higher cost of living, we may be fairly sure that the lowest-paid agricultural labourers could secure a substantial increase in real wages by moving to a town. There is one other point which is beyond dispute: rural rents were low and remarkably stable[2] but in towns population grew rapidly, land prices were high, and rents were much higher than in the country. High rents, in fact, were the crucial element in variations in the cost of living between town and country.

It is possible to estimate very approximately the burden of higher town rents.[3] The gap between town and country rents, as might be expected from the contrasting demographic

1. Bellerby, op. cit., p. 134.
2. See above, p. 80.
3. Assessing the quality of accommodation received for average rents raises especially difficult problems and will not be tackled here, although the results of such inquiry would probably not be as favourable to rural life as might be expected. A. L. Bowley considered that while migrants usually paid more rent in urban areas it was often a case of his being obliged to pay for accommodation superior to that in rural districts ('Rural Population in England and Wales', p. 617). When accommodation was scarce in rural areas the availability of town housing, even at higher rents, might be counted among the urban attractions. See e.g. *Report on the Decline in the Agricultural Population of Great Britain, 1881–1906*, P.P. 1906, XCVI, p. 15. Low rents in rural areas were one reason for bad housing—the prevailing level of rent gave a poor return on capital invested in new cottages and the stock of accommodation in the towns tended to be newer than that in the country. There is much discussion of this point in the report on the *Housing of the Working Classes*. Rural landlords were no less negligent, the rural labourers' wives were prolific and their cottages cramped; concern

experience of the two areas, was less in 1850 than in 1914. Rural rents were little higher in 1900 than they had been 50 years earlier but in Sheffield, for example, an artisan's cottage of a kind which could be rented for 2s. 6d. a week at mid-century, cost between 3s. 9d. and 4s. 6d. in 1905.[1] At the earlier of these dates the gap between rural rents and rents in provincial towns was not wide. In the early 1840s urban cottages in Cheshire, Staffordshire, Derbyshire, and Lancashire were let at between 1s. 3d and 3s. 6d. a week, little more than the run of rural rents,[2] and in 1850 when farm labourers in the East Riding paid £3 to £6 per annum in rent,[3] labourers in Sheffield probably paid about £5 or £6[4] which suggests that migrants to the town were likely to find accommodation for no more than an additional shilling a week. Unskilled labourers in Sheffield at this time earned about 18s. a week whereas farm workers in the vicinity of the town, who were better paid than most farm workers, received between 12s. and 15s.[5] Some very simple calculations will show that unless food and fuel were much more expensive in the town migrants to Sheffield from rural Yorkshire or parts of East Anglia (to take the first of several hypothetical migrations which will be used to illustrate the likely effect of prices on differentials in money wage) could afford the high rent and remain well in pocket.[6] Other urban rents noted

---

about the moral consequences of overcrowding was a recurring theme in contemporary inquiries. In favour of rural conditions, however, it may be said that multiple occupation was an urban phenomenon and few rural families lived entirely in one room. Some urban workers were accommodated at low rent, but these were exceptions. Coal miners in the north-east enjoyed free accommodation and railwaymen at Crewe, beneficiaries of company paternalism, were housed well and cheaply. *M.C.* 20 Dec. 1849; Rowe, *Wages in the Coal Industry*, p. 84; W. H. Chaloner, *The Social and Economic Development of Crewe 1780–1923* (Manchester, 1950), p. 49.

1. S. Pollard, *A History of Labour in Sheffield*, p. 20; Table 2–4.
2. *Sanitary Conditions of the Labouring Population*, P.P. (H. of L.) 1842, XXVI, p. 400 and see above, p. 80.
3. See above, p. 80.
4. This figure assumes the labourer paid rather less than the rent of an artisan's cottage (see above, this page). The *Morning Chronicle* investigation (15 Feb. 1850) reported rents in the town between 1s. 6d. and 3s. 6d.
5. *Returns of Wages published 1830–86*, P.P. 1887, LXXXIX, p. 158, and above, p. 39.
6. A letter from a Norfolk labourer who went to the city in 1873, quoted above, p. 18 n.6., gives an insight into the progress of one such migrant.

by the 1849–50 *Morning Chronicle* investigation suggest that in provincial towns rents for accommodation of a kind likely to be occupied by unskilled labourers were between 1s. and 2s. a week higher than rural rents,[1] a far smaller difference than the difference between rural and urban wages.

This situation can be compared with the position in 1884 by using evidence from the *Royal Commission on the Housing of the Working Classes*. The Hackney medical officer of health considered that the usual rent for two small rooms in Hackney was 4s. 6d. to 5s. a week; London building labourers at that time received between 24s. and 27s. a week.[2] The same report also contains evidence of conditions in rural areas. In Steeple Bumstead (Essex), a typical low-wage area near the capital, a man, his wife, and eight children shared a cramped three-roomed cottage with no garden or water supply, other than a pit at the side of the road,[3] for 4 guineas per annum. At this time farm labourers in that part of Essex were paid 11s. a week.[4] The rent is representative of rural cottages although most had better amenities. If a farm labourer left this part of Essex for unskilled work in Hackney he could expect to pay an additional 3s. to 3s 6d. a week in rent but his cash earnings

1. In Middleton comfortable accommodation rented for £6–£7 p.a. (26 Nov. 1849); 2s. 3d. a week secured a 'decent cottage' at Saddleworth where the general run of rent was about 3s. 3d.; a substantial terrace house in Ashton-under-Lyne cost 3s. 6d. (29, 8 Nov. 1849); in Leicester 'better class' houses went for between 2s. 3d. and 2s. 6d., others for as little as 1s. 6d. (21 Jan. 1850); good accommodation cost between 2s. 6d. and 3s. a week in the Potteries and rather less than this in the south Wales iron and coal centres (28 Jan., 21 and 27 Mar., 8 Apr. 1850). Manchester was more expensive than the other examples, very poor accommodation cost only 1s. a week but this was almost certainly inferior to most rural accommodation; the majority of cotton workers paid between 3s and 4s. 6d. (25 Oct. 1849). London rents were higher still but the evidence from this source is too vague to permit generalizations about rent in the capital. Figures in G. Stedman Jones (*Outcast London*, p. 216) show working-class rents in St. George's-in-the-East between 3s. 3d. and 4s. 2d. a week in 1848.
2. *Housing of the Working Classes*, Evidence para. 9747–9. Builders' labourers in London received 24s. 8d. to 27s. in 1886, painters 31s. 8d. to 35s. 8d. (*Wages of the Manual Labour Classes*, P.P. 1893–4, LXXXIIIii, p. 130). Police constables began at £62 p.a. plus a clothing and coal allowance (*Sums Received and Expended for the Purposes of the Metropolitan Police*, P.P. 1886, LIII, p. 17).
3. *Housing of the Working Classes*, evidence, para. 15209–32.
4. Ibid. Report, p. 26; evidence, para, 15234.

would more than double, from 11s. to about 24s. His net gain, assuming that food and other prices were identical in town and country, was of the order of 10s. a week; that is his real income would almost double despite a tripling of rent.

Provincial rents at this time were well below those in London. In Newcastle, where accommodation was more expensive than in most provincial towns, two rooms cost between 3s. and 5s. a week, that is, about 1s. 6d. to 3s. above rural rents.[1] Newcastle labourers earned about 21s. a week and farm workers in the surrounding countryside about 16s. to 18s.[2] In this case a migrating farm labourer would face an increase of 1s 6d. or more in rent which would take a substantial part of any gain in wages obtained by leaving the land for an unskilled job in the town. Whereas the Essex labourer could hope almost to double his real earnings by moving to London, or indeed to Newcastle, the north-eastern labourer, it seems, was likely to gain no more than between 10 and 20 per cent. Of course he might enter a better-paid job than labouring; police constables in Newcastle, for example, started at 24s. a week.[3] Town employment also offered shorter hours and a greater prospect of advancement so the total margin, even in this case, was perhaps greater than 10 to 20 per cent. The north-eastern farm labourer was among the best-paid in Britain and Newcastle rents among the highest outside London. Most migrants in the 1880s, therefore, stood to gain more by moving from country to town than the north-eastern labourer in the case just described. In Edinburgh working-class rents were between 1s. and 4s. a week, not a lot more than rural rents. A 'back to back' in Sheffield could be rented for 3s. or 3s. 6d. a week; and in Liverpool two rooms and an attic cost 2s. 6d.[4] Two-roomed houses in Bristol could be rented for only 1s. 6d. to 2s. 6d.; some rents in Bristol were higher than this but these at least were not

1. *Housing of the Working Classes*, Report, p. 17; evidence para. 7392, 7611–2, 8366–9, 8431–3.
2. *Wages of the Manual Labour Classes*, pp. 213–14. For farm wages see Table 1–3.
3. *Reports of Inspectors of Constabulary*, P.P. 1886, XXXIV, p. 175.
4. *Housing of Working Classes*, evidence para. 13583; evidence for Scotland P.P. 1884–5, XXXI, para. 18602; Pollard, op. cit., p. 102.

far above rural levels.[1] A little later, in 1897, F. W. Lawrence collected figures of rents in nine provincial towns—they varied little from town to town and averaged 5s. to 5s. 6d. or about 3s. 6d. more than most rural rents.[2] These, however, were the rents paid by trade union artisans and the usual margin over rural rents for labourers' accommodation at this time was probably about 1s. 6d. to 2s. a week; that is rents in the larger provincial towns were approximately double rural rents, whereas in London, as in 1884, they were approximately three times as high.[3]

TABLE 2–4

*Rents for Accommodation of Three Rooms, 1905*[4]

| Birmingham | 3s. 6d.–5s. | Newcastle | 5s. 3d.–6s. 6d. |
|---|---|---|---|
| Bristol* | 4s.–5s. | Sheffield | 3s. 9d.–4s. 6d. |
| Leeds | 3s. 6d.–4s. 6d. | Taunton* | 3s. 6d.–4s. 6d. |
| Manchester | 4s. 6d.–5s. 6d. | London | 6s.–9s. |

* Bristol and Taunton figures are for 4 rooms; rents for 3 rooms in these towns were not shown.

The general pattern of urban rents in 1905 is shown in Table 2–4. In large provincial towns rents were about 4s. 9d. a week for three rooms (rather less in southern towns like Bristol and Taunton) and in London the same number of rooms cost approximately 7s. 6d. These levels were some 3s. and 5s. 9d. higher than rural rents at the same date.[5] For purposes of comparison Suffolk and the West Riding can be taken as examples of low- and high-wage counties. In 1907 agricultural labourers received 15s. 9d. per week in Suffolk;[6] unskilled labour was paid around 30s. in London and between 26s. and 30s. in

1. *Housing of the Working Classes*, Report p. 23, evidence para, 6777, 6828, 7285.
2. F. W. Lawrence, *Local Variations in Wages*, p. 82.
3. An 1893 paper referred to a survey of 30,000 working-class London families: the head of the house earned an average of 24s. 6½d. and the average rent paid was 6s. 2d. H. Higgs, 'Workmen's Budgets', *J.R.S.S.*, lvi (1893), 256. See also P. de Rousiers, *The Labour Question in Britain*, p. 355.
4. *First B. of T. Cost-of-Living Inquiry*, pp. xiv, 6–7, 86, 117, 259, 301, 322, 411, 465.
5. See above, p. 80.
6. Table 1–3.

the large industrial cities.[1] These rates would give a Suffolk migrant a money gain of between 10s. and 14s. and a net gain, after paying higher rent, of approximately 7s. to 9s. That is, if we again ignore possible variations in other prices, his real income rose by some 45–60 per cent. West Riding agricultural labourers were paid 20s. a week at this time and stood to gain less from migration than the lower-paid Suffolk labourers. In the case of the northern labourers an enhanced money wage of 6s. to 10s. would be reduced by higher rents to between 3s. and 5s.; a real rise of some 15–25 per cent.

These figures, and those for the 1850s and 1880s, are intended not as an index of regional rent but merely to advance discussion from the stage where contradictory statements can be made with equal confidence. The position was that rents were far higher in the towns; in some cases they might have accounted for as much as half a migrant's enhanced earnings, but, unless there were substantial numbers of farm labourers foolish enough to move from the rural north to low-wage southern towns like Taunton or Dorchester, there could have been few cases where rents entirely offset higher town earnings. Migrants from low-wage rural districts could pay three times as much for rent in towns and be left with a handsome increase in real income. Moreover, the figures used above probably underestimate gains from migration since the calculations are based on the earnings of building labourers in towns. Many town jobs offered better wages than those paid to building labourers and some migrants, helped by relatives and friends in the town, moved to such jobs immediately.[2] Another reason for suggesting that the 'operative differential' was perhaps greater than

1. Building labourers' wages 1905: London 29s. 2d., Birmingham 27s. 7d. to 31s. 6d., Leeds 26s. 10d. to 28s. 10½d. *First B. of T. Cost-of-Living Inquiry*, p. 612.
2. In these cases their gain might be very substantial indeed. Essex farm labourers, for example, earned 15s. 9d. in 1907 (Table 1–3), London building labourers were paid 29s. 2d. in 1905, but painters received about 36s. and carpenters 43s. 9d. (*First B. of T. Cost-of-Living Inquiry*, p. 27). On this point see also Booth, *Life and Labour*, 1st Ser., iii. 131–4. There was in London a sizeable low-wage sector (see Ch. 1, above, pp. 11–14)— but rural migrants formed little part of it, 'the major part of London poverty and distress is home made, and not imported from outside' (ibid., pp. 90, 120–1, 142).

indicated above is the fact that the rural-urban differential in youths' wages was exceptionally large; money gains of up to 700 per cent were not unusual in this category and young people were likely to be well represented among migrants.[1]

# IV

It was assumed in section III that rent was the sole cause of the difference in cost of living between town and country. This assumption will now be tested.

In addition to low rent the rural labourer enjoyed a miscellany of other advantages; various payments in kind, the cottage garden, perhaps an allotment, free firewood, and, according to some accounts, opportunities for poaching. In addition it might be supposed that purchased food was likely to be cheapest before it bore the cost of carriage to town markets. Of these items poaching and payments in kind can be ignored, the former because the risk was great and penalties severe to an extent that poaching was probably less a general advantage in rural areas than opportunities for petty thieving in towns, the latter because their value is included in most of the figures that have been used for comparative purposes. Allotments, when available, were worth (in 1904) 3d. to 6d. a week.[2] Firewood was more easily obtained in the country, although not everywhere and not to the extent that prevented coal being an important item in rural budgets,[3] and this

1. Booth, *Life and Labour*, 1st Ser., iii. 133, 138; J. Heads, 'The Internal Migration of Population in England and Wales 1851–1911', M.Sc. thesis, University of Cambridge (1955), p. 186.
2. H. H. Mann, 'Life in an Agricultural Village in England', pp. 170–1. Some labourers hired men to cultivate their land and by various means could accumulate a much greater income than Mann suggests—some lost money by similar means. See J. Ashby and B. King, 'Statistics of some Midland Villages', *Economic Journal*, iii (1893), 11–18.
3. In many areas its collection was a privilege not a right. An Oxfordshire family found it necessary to buy faggots (Rowntree and Kendall, op. cit., p. 263); see also G. E. Evans, *Ask the Fellows who Cut the Hay*, p. 59, and, for expenditure on fuel, above, pp. 84, 86.

advantage was probably offset by dearer coal.[1] By far the most important item in most working-class budgets was food, and unless this came from the labourer's garden it was almost certainly no cheaper in the country.[2] The garden, in fact, was the only important compensating rural advantage for low wages. The 42 families surveyed by Rowntree and Kendall in 1912 obtained rather less than one twelfth of their food in this way which suggests the garden was worth about 1s. a week.[3]

But the greater part of the countryman's food came from the village shop[4] whose prices were frequently higher than prices in the towns. To assume the contrary, that town prices reflected the cost of transport from the country, overlooks changing sources of foodstuffs in the nineteenth century and implies a less developed system of distribution than existed by that time. Even in the eighteenth century proximity to food sources was no guarantee of cheapness: 'The price of bread and butchers' meat are generally the same or very nearly the same throughout the greater part of the united kingdom . . . fully as cheap or cheaper in great towns than in the remoter parts of the country . . .' [5] A recent study of retail trade in the first half of the nineteenth century noted a similar uniformity in urban prices, particularly food prices, in different parts of the country,[6] and we know that the same was true of food prices in different rural areas after 1850.[7] The large towns, London most of all, provided a sure market. Goods went first to these centres and were then distributed over surrounding areas; farmers preferred to send produce in bulk to urban markets and

---

1. D. J. Davies, 'The Condition of the Rual Population in England and Wales, 1870–1928', Ph.D. thesis, University of Wales (1931), p. 197. Country villages, unless in mining areas, received their coal from the town and had to bear the cost this entailed.
2. On rural budgets see above, pp. 86–7.
3. Rowntree and Kendall, op. cit., p. 307. Rural families' expenditure on food averaged 13s. 6½d. in 1902. *Memoranda etc. on British and Foreign Trade and Industrial Conditions*, P.P. 1903, LXVII, p. 210.
4. This is not true of single labourers in those areas where 'living in' remained prevalent. See below, pp. 280, 332.
5. A. Smith, *The Wealth of Nations*, ed. E. Cannan, i. 76. See also Gilboy, *Wages in Eighteenth Century England*, p. 40.
6. D. G. Alexander, *Retailing in England during the Industrial Revolution* (1970), pp. 38–40.
7. See above, pp. 80–4.

many were reluctant to meet the trifling requirements of their labourers.[1]

But there were other influences, probably no less powerful than distribution, which worked to the advantage of towns. Before the railways were built wholesale meat prices were 2d. per lb higher in London than in the country: the railways removed this disadvantage; 30 years later the advantage was moving to the town and in 1882 Philip Armour claimed that he could supply the towns with boneless corned beef at half the price of fresh meat.[2] Less and less of the nation's food was provided by the British farmer; as imports rose prices fell and the main source of cheap food became the ports.[3] This was especially the case for lower-working-class Britain because in response to competition the British farmer turned to the artisan and middle-class market. By the 1880s the ill-paid farm labourers who produced food for the more affluent of the urban classes were themselves probably more dependent on imported food than most workers; artisans in Sheffield may have scorned imported meat but for many farm labourers meat of any kind, other than bacon, was a rare treat until imports became freely available.[4] Further, most of Britain's gain was imported and the farm labourer spent a greater proportion of his income on bread than other workers,[5] and even at the end of the period

---

1. Alexander, op. cit., p. 41; Burnett, op cit., p. 124. Fruit was often available in large towns when it could not easily be purchased in the country, A. Torode in T. C. Barker, J. C. McKenzie and J. Yudkin (eds), *Our Changing Fare* (1966), p. 117. The pattern described affected different goods at different times; milk, bulky as well as perishable, was affected later than most: London's milk was expensive well into the second half of the century. Fish provides a somewhat similar example; before 1840 it was scarce and expensive in inland towns and rural districts. But the railway was a remarkable leveller: it reduced fish prices by three-quarters or more in Manchester, and increased sales tenfold in Birmingham. G. Dodd, *The Food of London* (1856), pp. 298–9; Alexander, op. cit., p. 17; E. H. Whetham, 'The London Milk Trade, 1860–1900', *Ec.H.R.*, 2nd Ser., xvii (1964).
2. Barker, McKenzie, and Yudkin, op. cit., pp. 77, 81.
3. In the years 1910–14 Britain imported four-fifths of its wheat, three-quarters of its butter, and over two-fifths of its meat. S. B. Saul, *Studies in British Overseas Trade, 1870–1914* (Liverpool, 1960), p. 29.
4. See above, pp. 38, 78 and D. J. Davies, 'The Condition of the Rural Population in England and Wales, 1870–1928', p. 195.
5. *Memoranda etc. on British and Foreign Trade and Industrial Conditions*, P.P. 1903, LXVII, pp. 211–12. See also above p. 78 and Ch. 5, *passim*.

he spent as much on imported margarine as on butter.[1]

The urbanization of wholesale distribution and the growth of imports go some way to explain lower prices and a greater choice of goods in urban centres. In this light it is not surprising that a witness before the 1884–5 housing inquiry suggested that cheap food was one of the attractions of living in central London and a partial compensation for high rents.[2] M. F. Davies found that prices in the Wiltshire village of Corsley were higher than those in York and F. W. Lawrence in 1897 described a general pattern where prices were lowest in large towns and increased towards the smaller and more remote places.[3] But there was a third influence responsible for the urban advantage—differences in retailing. Whereas the village shop enjoyed something akin to monopoly power, town prices reflected greater competition among retailers. When the paying-out time of farm labourers in a Kentish village was changed from Saturday evening to Saturday morning their wives, who now had time to shop further afield, deserted the village store for the better and cheaper shops of Maidstone some six miles distant.[4] According to F. E. Green village shops often sold goods which had proved unsaleable in the towns, and it is significant that when competition reached the villages it came from the horse-drawn mobile shops belonging to urban retailers which toured neighbouring districts and undercut village prices.[5]

---

1. See the budgets in Rowntree and Kendall, op. cit., Ch. III. Most of the butter, cheese, and eggs consumed by the working classes was imported (*Second B. of T. Cost-of-Living Inquiry*, pp. xxxiii). The urban poor, also, probably consumed more margarine than butter ('How the Casual Labourer Lives', *Liverpool Economic and Statistical Society* (1909), xxi).
2. *Housing of the Working Classes*, P.P. 1884–5, XXX, evidence, para. 2035, 3936–9.
3. M. F. Davies, op. cit., p. 140; Lawrence, op. cit., pp. 47–8.
4. *Employment of Women and Children in Agriculture*, P.P. 1843, XII, pp. 140–1.
5. D. J. Davies, op. cit., p. 97; T. E. Kebbel, *The Agricultural Labourer*, p. 57. On this theme see also, among others, J. Burnett, op. cit., p. 146; L. M. Springall, op. cit., p. 137; J. Blackman, 'The Development of the Retail Grocery Trade in the Nineteenth Century', *Business History*, ix (1967), 111; Mathias, op. cit., p. 83; and the *Morning Chronicle* for 26 Dec. 1849 on the price of groceries in Norwich and surrounding rural areas.

Not long after 1850 these urban advantages were powerfully reinforced by changes in the structure of retailing, in particular by economies of scale derived from vertical integration and multiple branches. The co-operatives pioneered both developments but Sainsburys, Liptons, and the rest were not far behind.[1] Their influence was overwhelmingly in urban markets; the co-operatives largely in the industrial north, the multiple stores throughout the country but most of all in those towns where the co-operative movement made least progress.[2] In so far as it is possible to distinguish between competition in quality and competition in price the co-operatives perhaps gave greater attention to quality and the multiples to prices, but neither sold the lowest-quality goods and both were renowned for low prices.[3] Rowntree found prices in co-operatives 5 per cent lower than most prices in York. A desire to reduce the price of food was the chief reason for establishing a co-operative store in Crewe, and co-operative prices were the yardstick by which the multiples judged their efficiency.[4] Also, of course, co-operative dividends were a form of price reduction.[5] Together, the multiples and co-operatives exercised a significant influence on retailing efficiency and the urban cost of living.[6] They rarely granted credit,[7] a major handicap in competing for the custom of the poorest wage earners, and they seldom dominated a town's retail trade, but their standards controlled those of their competitors; in country areas this control was seldom operative.[8] A report of 1919 noted the development of co-operative retailing in rural areas, but progress occurred slowly and even

1. The Toad Lane store opened in 1844, Sainsbury's commenced in 1869, two years later Thomas Lipton opened his first store in Glasgow.
2. Mathias, op. cit., pp. x, 5; Clapham, *An Economic History of Modern Britain*, ii. 308; J. B. Jefferys, *Retail Trading in Britain, 1850–1950* (Cambridge, 1954), p. 157.
3. Jefferys, op. cit., pp. 17, 57–8; Mathias, op. cit., p. 53. Lipton's first London store cut prices by up to 50 per cent—his entry to the tea trade was marked by even greater reductions. Ibid., pp. 98, 101.
4. B. S. Rowntree, *Poverty. A Study of Town Life* (1908 edn.), p. 135. Chaloner, op. cit., p. 250; Mathias, op. cit., pp. 66, 83.
5. In the late nineteenth century and early twentieth century they returned, on average, about 2*s*. 6*d*. for each pound spent. Clapham, op. cit., iii. 250.
6. Mathias, op. cit., p. x.
7. Ibid., p. 47; J. Burnett, op. cit., p. 110.
8. They held some 25–30 per cent of the grocery and provision trade in 1910. Jefferys, op. cit., p. 163.

had the movement been more widespread country villages would still have lacked certain urban economies of scale.[1] The co-operatives and the multiples held a share of retailing outside the grocery and provision trade; their hold here was less substantial although it was probably sufficient to affect the price of certain articles.[2] This influence, together with the greater competition between shops of any kind in urban areas and the fact that most manufactured goods originated in the town, was probably sufficient to ensure that the prices of manufactured goods also were lower in the town than in the country.[3] London was noted for its numerous second-hand markets and 'unequalled opportunities . . . of securing at low rates every article consumed, worn, or used in the home'.[4] With regard to travelling expenses, however, the towns were at a disadvantage. Significant expenditure on travel was probably unusual outside London; even there most working men preferred to live where they could walk to work and return home for lunch, and the few wage earners who commuted were probably compensated by lower rents.[5] However, in London and the other large towns casual labourers, building workers, and others whose place of work was not constant were probably involved in some travelling expense which was not compensated by lower rent.[6]

1. D. J. Davies, op. cit., p. 197. Many mining villages had co-operative stores long before 1900 but their prices, although they probably compared favourably with those in rural areas, were higher than town prices because turnover was not sufficient to warrant the installation of the freezing chamber necessary to benefit fully from imported dairy produce and meat. de Rousiers, op. cit., pp. 179, 181, 294–5. On this theme see also *Memoranda etc on British and Foreign Trade and Industrial Conditions*, 1903, LXVII, p. 212, and J. Ashby and B. King, 'Statistics of some Midland Villages', p. 201.
2. For exact proportions see Jefferys, op. cit., p. 18.
3. For complaints of dear clothing in village shops see, *Wages and Conditions of Employment in Agriculture*, P.P. 1919, IX, p. 280.
4. *Housing of the Working Classes*, para. 2022–4; Booth, *Life and Labour*, 2nd Ser., i. 125.
5. E. J. Hobsbawm in R. Glass (ed.) *London: Aspects of Change* (1964), pp. 7–9; see also H. J. Dyos, 'The suburban Development of Greater London south of the Thames', Ph.D. thesis, University of London (1952), pp. 133, 147; H. Rees, 'The North-Eastern Expansion of London since 1770,' M.Sc. thesis, University of London (1945), p. 73.
6. For evidence on the London building trades see Booth, *Life and Labour*, 2nd Ser., i. 125.

In all, it seems likely that town prices were lower for almost all articles. The burden of high prices upon the rural poor was perhaps no less than that which the truck system imposed upon some early industrial workers and was certainly more persistent—but both are difficult to quantify. In her study of Corsley, M. F. Davies compared village prices with those in York. There was more retail competition in Corsley than most villages but food prices exceeded those in York by an amount sufficient to offset the village advantage with respect to garden produce.[1] The 1843 report on the *Employment of Women and Children in Agriculture* spoke of prices in rural shops between 10 and 25 per cent above town prices.[2] These figures, together with Rowntree and Kendall's calculation that gardens supplied about one twelfth of rural food,[3] suggest that we may not be far out if we regard the value of lower food prices in the towns and the value of cottage gardens as approximately equal. If we make the further assumption that travelling expenses in towns were offset by lower prices for items other than food, rent is left as the residual and best single indicator of cost-of-living differentials between town and country. Admittedly some of the assumptions made are of fairly major proportions but more rigorous measurement is unlikely to affect the broad conclusions and might well produce no better answers because circumstances varied so much from one case to the next. Countless individuals must have experienced a pattern quite different from that suggested above. Many farm labourers, for example, lived within walking distance of urban markets, some had no gardens, and gardens in town houses were not unusual. With these limitations in mind the conclusions of section III, where rent was assumed to be the only significant variable, can now be accepted.

# V

The relationship between the cost of living and wage variations in different rural areas and between town and country

1. M. F. Davies, op. cit., pp. 140, 192.
2. *Employment of Women and Children in Agriculture*, P.P. 1843, XII, p. 141.
3. See above, p. 95.

have been examined. It now remains to be seen whether variations in wages from town to town were offset by variation in prices from town to town. Table 2–5 shows building wages in London, a high-wage provincial town, and a low-wage town in the south of England.[1]

TABLE 2–5

*Building Wages. Average Hourly Rate in Taunton, Manchester, and London*

|  | 1886 | | 1906 | |
|---|---|---|---|---|
|  | Craftsmen | Labourers | Craftsmen | Labourers |
| Taunton | 5d. | 3¾d. | 7d. | 4d. |
| Manchester | 8d. | 5½d. | 9½d. | 6¼d. |
| London | 9d. | 6d. | 10½d. | 7d. |

*Source:* Table 1–5.

From what was said in section III it might seem likely that the cost of living, or at least rent, rose according to town size. Was this the case, and, if it was, how far did higher rents offset higher wages? These questions are partly answered in sections III and IV of this chapter. Food prices were similar in different rural areas and cheaper in towns than in the country. The causes of lower food prices in the towns, greater retail competition and better access to both imported and home-produced foodstuffs, suggest that food prices correlated negatively with town size; that is, as Lawrence indicated, we should expect food prices to rise from greater to lesser towns.[2] The price of coal was affected by distance from colliery and by town size. Here London was at a disadvantage compared to the large northern cities, but there is no reason to expect that small towns generally enjoyed an advantage over large towns in this respect.[3] Nor is there anything else in the earlier evidence, other

1. For details of town wages see Ch. 1.
2. See above, p. 97. However, there was little sign of this in the evidence of those towns examined in the 1912 cost-of-living inquiry. Prices in towns of population between 14,000 and 50,000 were less than 1 per cent above those in London. *Second B. of T. Cost-of-Living Inquiry*, p. xxxviii.
3. Fuel was a much less important item in urban budgets than either food or rent. See above, pp. 84–7.

than travelling costs for some workers, to raise suspicions that
high urban wages and high prices were found together. The
two Board of Trade inquiries substantiate this impression. They
found that town prices were relatively uniform, with only rents
varying much from one town to another; if London is excluded
even this variation was not substantial: 'If we exclude London,
the variation in rents in England and Wales is not very great,
and prices are on the whole singularly uniform, with the result
that for equal accommodation and equal provision of food and
fuel the necessary expenditure would not differ very much from
one town to another.' [1]

TABLE 2–6

*Building Wages (average hourly rates) and Rents, Taunton,
Manchester, and London*

| | Wages 1886 | | Rent 1884–5 | Wages 1906 | | Rent 1905 |
|---|---|---|---|---|---|---|
| | Crafts-men | Labourer | 2 rooms | Crafts-men | Labourer | 4 rooms |
| Taunton | 5d. | 3¾d. | 2s. | 7d. | 4d. | 4s. |
| Manchester | 8d. | 5½d. | 3s. 6d. | 9½d. | 6¼d. | 5s. 6d. |
| London | 9d. | 6d. | 4s. 9d. (Hackney) | 10½d. | 7d. | 9s. |

Wages are from Table 2–5. Rents in 1884–5 are from the inquiry into
the *Housing of the Working Classes*, P.P. 1884–5, XXX. Neither Taunton
nor Manchester was mentioned in this inquiry and rents in these towns are
estimated from information on rents in rural areas and Bristol (for Taunton)
and from rents in Liverpool, Sheffield, and Newcastle (for Manchester). All
the 1905 rents are from the *First B. of T. Cost-of-Living Inquiry*, pp. xiv,
301, 465.

Table 2–6 combines the figures of wages shown in Table 2–5
with average rents in the same towns. That some correlation
existed between rent and wages is obvious, and probably helps
to explain the 'city-size wage differential' noted earlier,[2] but a
few simple calculations show that higher rent in most cases

1. *First B. of T. Cost-of-Living Inquiry*, p. vii; 'There appears to be no close
   correlation between local variations in rents and retail prices and the level
   of wages. . .' (*Second B. of T. Cost-of-Living Inquiry*, p. xii).
2. See above, p. 56.

offset no more than a small proportion of money wage variations between towns. It seems however, on the evidence of
Manchester and London, that rents in the capital were sufficiently high to make substantial inroads upon its higher money
wages compared with the large provincial cities.[1] A craftsman
who moved from Taunton to Manchester in the 1880s could expect to pay 1s. 6d. more in rent; he could make good this increase
by six hours work at Manchester rates and at the end of a 56-hour
week he would be 12s. 6d. in pocket: his money wage would rise
by 60 per cent; higher rent reduced this to 53 per cent. The
same calculations show that a labourer stood to make a gain of
similar proportions: 10 hours work offset his enhanced rent
and his net gain at the end of the week would be about 6s. 6d.
A move from Taunton to London at the same date brought
even higher money wages but it also brought more than a
doubling in rent. In this case the craftsman's 'break-even
point' came after 8 hours work, the labourer's after 14 hours.
At the end of the week, and having paid their London rent, both
would be substantially in pocket, 15s. 11d. (68 per cent) and
7s. 9d. (44 per cent) for the craftsman and labourer respectively.
A move from Manchester to London was less profitable. A week's
work left the craftsman a net gain of only 3s. 5d., and the
labourer, who probably paid out half his extra income in rent,
less than half this.

The same calculations using the figures for 1905–6 show a
similar pattern. A day's work in Manchester earned the
craftsmen sufficiently more than in Taunton to pay the difference
in rent; in London the break-even point came towards the end
of the second day, and at the end of a 50-hour week and having
paid his enhanced rent, a craftsman would find himself some
8s. 11d. better off in Manchester, and 9s. 7d. better off in
London—that is, with net gains of 30 and 33 per cent respectively after money wage increases of 35 and 50 per cent. In

1. The level of rent in London relative to rents elsewhere in Britain varied
over time and according to which part of London is considered. It seems
likely that many London workers, especially those that lived near to the
centre, offset some of the burden of London rent by enduring poorer accommodation than that commonly rented by their social equals in provincial
cities. On the general subject of housing in and near the centre of London
see, G. Stedman Jones, op. cit., Part II.

this case London's wage advantage over Manchester was almost entirely offset by higher rent.

It would be easy to read too much into these calculations—different dates, cities, and occupations would each produce a different set of answers; also of course there were small variations in the price of food and coal.[1] But there is no reason to suspect that other examples would produce answers significantly, if at all, less favourable to the high-wage centres and in each of the cases examined the wage differential between high- and low-wage towns, although partly offset by rent variations, remained substantial after discounting the influence of prices.

# VI

The evidence can now be viewed as a whole. It indicates a remarkable similarity in the cost of living in various parts of Britain and offers little to support those like Fay who believed that the attractions of towns were largely illusory.[2] At a time when economic life was characterized by regional diversities, when generalizations about wages, population, and the standard of living can easily be meaningless unless qualified by regional accounts, prices of commodities were similar throughout the country. Rent varied more than any other item of expenditure and was the main cause of regional variation in the cost of living; food prices also varied but to a smaller extent. These differentials introduce some modifications into the wage pattern described in Chapter One but few of any significance and none of the main features are eradicated. Variations in food prices, in fact, favoured the high-wage areas and food accounted for the greater part of working-class budgets. If

1. However, on the whole these favoured the larger towns and helped to offset rent variations. In 1912, for example, Manchester rents exceeded Taunton's by a third but food and fuel were cheaper to an extent sufficient to equalize the cost of rent, food, and fuel combined (*Second B. of T. Cost-of-Living Inquiry*, pp. xxvi, xxxvi–vii, l). On the other hand, travelling costs were more likely to be incurred in large cities like Manchester and London (see above, p. 99).
2. See above, p. 78 n. 1.

there was insufficient migration to erode wage variations it was obviously not because real incomes were everywhere similar, although what the majority of wage earners thought the real wage pattern to be, and what it was, were not necessarily the same. Market knowledge was far from perfect but whether the distinction between money and real wages was underestimated or exaggerated, whether it stimulated or retarded migration, is difficult to say. According to some writers labour was unaware of price variations[1] but it is difficult to believe that this was generally the case. It seems more likely that the weight of advice to would-be migrants inclined towards emphasizing the expense of living in the high-wage centres.[2] Joseph Ashby, who should have known, was emphatic on this point: 'the country labourer is well aware of the increased expense of town life.'[3] The situation was probably not quite what either of these views suggests; the most likely position was that, against a background of imperfect knowledge, most rural inhabitants exaggerated the extra expense of town life while many, particularly young people, either underestimated it or assessed it correctly. The first group stayed where they were, the latter moved. Those who migrated may sometimes have discovered their real gains to be less than expected, but their gains, nevertheless, were likely to have been substantial and higher prices very seldom could have tipped the scales between gain and loss.

1. See R. H. Hooker, 'On the Relation between Wages and the Numbers Employed in the Coal Mining Industry', *J.R.S.S.*, lvii (1894), 633–4. H. L. Smith was of a similar opinion and Brinley Thomas saw no reason to modify Hooker's view. Booth, *Life and Labour*, 1st Ser., iii. 74, 137; B. Thomas, 'The Migration of Labour into the Glamorganshire Coalfield', *Economica*, x (1930), 291.
2. On this point see below, pp. 274–5
3. J. Ashby and B. King, op. cit., p. 197.

# FAMILY EARNINGS

## I

IT WAS shown in Chapter Two that the regional wage variations described in Chapter One were not compensated by regional differences in the cost of living. But were they offset by differences in family earnings? This study is concerned to explain differentials in the wage rates of adult males, but in many families their income was supplemented by the earnings of wives and children.[1] Variations in real wages of the order described earlier offered substantial rewards to migrants from low-wage areas, but the family often operated as a unit and where there was more than one bread-winner there was more than the man's wage to consider; if women's and adolescents' work was unobtainable or very badly paid in areas where men's wages were high then migration was less likely.[2] It is necessary, therefore, to examine the pattern of family earnings to see whether they varied significantly, and, in particular, whether they varied inversely to the pattern of men's wages.

Females accounted for a sizeable part of the labour force; of those aged ten and over about one third were occupied, equivalent to about 30 per cent of the total labour force,[3] that is, not

1. At the turn of the century the average household contained two wage earners whose income amounted to about one and a half men's wage packets. E. H. Phelps Brown, *The Growth of British Industrial Relations* (1959), p. 19 (subsequently referred to as Phelps Brown, *Industrial Relations*).
2. The point can be illustrated from two studies of mobility in the inter-war years. Compared with other regions, and especially with the coalfields, labour in the north-west textile region was immobile. Extensive family employment was one of the main causes of immobility. B. Thomas, 'The Influx of Labour into the Midlands, 1920–37', *Economica* N.S. v (1938), 416; J. Jewkes and H. Campion, 'The Mobility of Labour in the Cotton Industry', *Economic Journal*, xxxviii (1928), 135–7.
3. The proportion fell slowly after 1871 but varied very little over the period. Mitchell and Deane, op cit. p. 60.

much below the high rate which has prevailed in Britain since the Second World War.[1] Children were less important, although their contribution was not insignificant in the first half of the period; of those aged ten to fifteen, 28 per cent were employed in 1851 and 14 per cent in 1911.[2] But family earnings had far less influence on labour mobility and male earnings than these high proportions might suggest. Women worked fewer hours than men and were paid less per hour, so that although they accounted for around 30 per cent of the labour force they received a considerably smaller part of the nation's wage packet. And for a working wife the net advantage was usually a great deal less than her modest wage. Someone had to mind her children; whoever did was usually paid, and even close relatives expected meals.[3] Additional working clothes might be required, and precious pence might be lost by inefficient spending—working wives were said to be poor cooks and ready customers for easily prepared and expensive groceries.[4] Such were these disadvantages that some writers have come near to discounting the earnings of wives entirely.[5]

Just as important for this inquiry was the proportion of women whose work entailed living away from home, because in these cases their contribution to the family budget was unaffected when the head of the family moved. A Suffolk-born

1. Of all females aged 15 and over, 34·5 per cent were occupied in 1901 and 37·5 per cent in 1961. Very few non-communist countries had a higher proportion of occupied women than Britain in 1961. See B. L. Hutchins, 'Statistics of Women's Life and Employment', *J.R.S.S.*, lxxii (1909), 215 and reports and tables in *The Times*, 3 May 1967, p. 27; 1 Sept. 1969, p. 3.
2. See Table 3–3. In addition, of course, an unknown number earned small sums for odd jobs out of school hours.
3. The survey conducted by the *Morning Chronicle* in 1849–50 described 3s. a week as a high average for women in the rural districts of Berkshire, Buckinghamshire, Oxfordshire, and Wiltshire. Out of this sum the baby-sitter took between 8d. and 1s. plus food (*M.C.* 27 Oct. 1849).
4. See G. E. and K. R. Fussell, *The English Countrywoman* (1953), pp. 198–9, 202; I. Pinchbeck, *Women Workers and the Industrial Revolution, 1750–1850* (1930), p. 99; S. G. Checkland, *The Rise of Industrial Society in England, 1815–1885*, p. 236.
5. G. E. and K. R. Fussell, op. cit., pp. 198, 202; Checkland, op. cit., p. 236. There were, of course, other social costs not relevant to this discussion: there is food for thought in the decline of infantile mortality rates in Lancashire textile towns during the cotton famine. M. Hewitt, *Wives and Mothers in Victorian Industry* (1958), pp. 177–8.

domestic servant in London could send money to Birmingham as easily as to Beccles. Not all domestic servants lived away from home of course, but many did and so did many shop assistants, and throughout the period domestic service employed almost half of all female workers.[1] The women whose earnings were most likely to influence male mobility were working wives who probably accounted for less than 20 per cent of female employees, or about 5 per cent of the total labour force.[2] There is the further point that married men are in any case almost always under-represented among migrant groups and young single men, those most likely to respond to wage differentials, were not much concerned with the potential earnings of women and children.[3] For these various reasons it seems unlikely that the pattern of family earnings will throw much light on male wage differentials. However, we need to examine the position in rather more detail because, despite these points, if women and adolescents were paid markedly higher rates in areas where men's wages were low, or if activity rates (the employed proportion of the total population) varied significantly, and inversely to men's earnings, then family earnings will provide at least a partial explanation of the male wage pattern. Family earnings are examined in section II of this chapter and activity rates in section III—it is argued

---

1. Mitchell and Deane, op. cit., p. 60. Migration rates of young females exceeded those of young men. J. Saville, *Rural Depopulation in England and Wales, 1851–1951*, Ch. 1, section 4, Ch. 3, sections 2 and 3; *Census of England and Wales for 1891 and 1901, General Reports*, P.P. 1893–4, CVI, p. 40; 1904, CVIII, p. 135; R. V. Lennard, *Economic Notes on English Agricultural Wages* (1914), pp. 34–6.

2. Exact figures are not available. The Lancashire cotton industry was noted as an employer of married women; in 1901 one quarter of its female workers were married. *Statistics of Employment of Women and Girls*, P.P. 1894, LXXXIii, p. 25; M. Hewitt, op. cit., pp. 17–18. See also J. C. Dunlop, 'The Fertility of Marriage in Scotland', *J.R.S.S.*, lxxvii (1914), 282; *Royal Commission on Labour: Summary of Evidence and Appendices*, P.P. 1894, XXXV, p. 507; Phelps Brown, *Industrial Relations* p. 68.

3. On the composition of migrant groups generally and in nineteenth- and early twentieth-century England, see D. S. Thomas *Migration Differentials* (New York 1938) p. 162; D. J. Davies, 'The Condition of the Rural Population in England and Wales, 1870–1928', p. 81.

that neither do much to explain spatial variations in men's wages.

## II

Women and adolescents in London enjoyed advantages over their provincial counterparts broadly comparable to the advantages of London males over provincial males. There is no evidence which suggests that a man moving to London from a low-wage district need have contemplated lower earnings for other members of his family, provided they could find employment. A casual reading of Mayhew, parts of the Booth survey, and some of the late nineteenth-century inquiries into sweated labour might convey a different impression, but only because these dealt mainly with the worst-paid of the East End sweated trades. These trades have received highly disproportionate attention; their female workers correspond to that exceptional group of ill-paid males which was mentioned earlier.[1] The two groups had more in common than low wages; they were largely confined to the same districts and many households included members of each group. The worst-placed of all were the wives, widows, and daughters of what Beatrice Webb called 'the irregularly employed and . . . purely parasitic population of East London'—the drunken, the work-shy, and the simply unfortunate of whom the East End had far more than its share.[2] Low pay was far from their only problem and often not the most pressing. Mayhew touched the conscience of his middle-class readers most effectively by his description of 15 poor needlewomen reduced to supplementing their earnings by prostitution. These, who were interviewed by Mayhew, with two *Morning Chronicle* reporters hidden behind a screen

1. See above, pp. 11–14, and below, pp. 312–19.
2. C. Booth, *Life and Labour*, 1st Ser., iv. 62. On the relationship between these two groups see also Ch. IX by C. E. Collet in the same volume; her article 'Women's Work in Leeds', *Economic Journal*, i (1891), 468–9; above, p. 12, and below, pp. 313–14.

'so as not to wound the modesty of the women', illustrate this point as clearly as any example. A careful reading of the *Morning Chronicle* suggests that their plight, although doubtless due in part to low wages, was as much a consequence of specific personal misfortune which would have placed an undue burden upon even moderately high wages. Eight of the women admitted to prostitution for little worse than living with a man out of wedlock; over half of the total were encumbered with illegitimate offspring, four were widows, two had been cast out by their fathers at a tender age, and three were orphans, one of whom was sufficiently careless to confound her plight with six illegitimate children.[1] Some East End women were very badly paid, particularly those who worked at home.[2] Employees in workshops were generally better off but some of these were sufficiently ill-paid to benefit from minimum wage legislation[3] and it seems likely that London had a greater proportion of women than men whose earnings failed to compare favourably with earnings in the rest of Britain. For this reason they comprise a rather more weighty qualification to generalizations about high London wages—but both groups were exceptional.

The greater part of those women in London whose earnings compared unfavourably with other centres worked in the clothing trades, but even in these trades many women were well paid by contemporary standards. At the same time as Beatrice Webb was recording women in the East End earning under 2*d.* per hour there were others in the West End earning a pound a week, which was more than a male labourer could hope for in many provincial centres.[4] The 1906 wage census, in fact, showed that women's earnings in London were distinctly above the U.K. average in almost every branch of the clothing trade

1. *M.C.* 23 Nov. 1849. For further details of the relative importance of the level of earnings among East End social problems see below, pp. 315–19.
2. Clara Collet discovered matchbox makers working for a penny an hour in 1888. Booth, *Life and Labour*, 1st Ser., iv. 281.
3. R. H. Tawney, *Minimum Rates in the Tailoring Industry*, pp. 69–70, 108.
4. Booth, *Life and Labour*, 1st Ser., iv. 63, 152; C.H. d'E. Leppington, 'Side Lights of the Sweating Commission', *Westminster Review*, CXXXVI (1891), 279; and Table 1–5.

except ready-made tailoring:

## TABLE 3-1

*Average Full-Time Earnings of Women over 18, 1906*[1]

|  |  | U.K. | U.K. excluding London | London |
|---|---|---|---|---|
| Dress, millinery, etc. | Workshop | 13s. 10d. | 12s. 9d. | 16s. 9d. |
|  | Factory | 15s. 5d. | 14s. 9d. | 16s. 7d. |
| Shirts, blouses, underclothing, etc. |  | 13s. 4d. | 12s. 7d. | 15s. 10d. |
| Bespoke tailoring |  | 14s. 2d. | 13s. 10d. | 16s. 2d. |
| Ready-made tailoring |  | 12s. 11d. | — | 11s. 11d. |

Shop assistants in the capital were also relatively well paid; in 1913 they earned 10 to 25 per cent above provincial rates.[2] Of eleven grades of indoor servants, in the mid-nineties earnings in London were clearly above average in every case but one.[3] The wages of women in the London printing trades were also higher than the average earnings of women in these trades.[4] There is less evidence on young persons' wages but H. L. Smith, in the Booth survey, considered that the earnings of boys in London were 'relatively high' and it seems likely that they compared with rates elsewhere at least as well as the earnings of London men and women compared with provincial rates.[5]

Not far from London men's wages were a great deal lower and the non-metropolitan part of the area south of a line from the Wash to the Bristol Channel comprised the most significant low-wage area in Britain. In the north and the industrial Midlands, on the other hand, and in south Wales and central

1. D. M. Barton, 'The Course of Women's Wages', *J.R.S.S.*, lxxxii (1919), 530.
2. Their advantage was greater than that enjoyed by the capital's male assistants over other towns. Ibid., p. 524.
3. D. M. Barton, op. cit., p. 515.
4. See below, p. 112, and see women's rates for shirtmaking in 1906 in *Report of the War Cabinet Committee on Women in Industry*, P.P. 1919, XXXI, p. 51.
5. 'London and the great towns are the paradise of boys' labour' (Booth, *Life and Labour*, 1st ser., iii, 138–9, and see below, p. 125, n. 1). The figures of women's and boy's earnings in London refer only to the second half of the period; there is no evidence that women's wages accelerated much faster than provincial rates in previous decades but the London market for boys' labour at that time may have been less buoyant than it was by the 1880s. On this point see G. Stedman Jones, op. cit., pp. 71–2.

Scotland after 1880, men's wages were generally high.[1] Much the same might be said of women's and children's rates in the same areas: 'Speaking broadly . . . in the south, south-east and south-west of England, women's labour is relatively cheap; in the north, north-east and north-west it is relatively dear.' [2] In the printing trades, in the autumn of 1918, London women received nearly 70 per cent above rates in some of the smaller East Anglian towns like Lynn, Beccles, and Bungay, and more than half as much again as those in Norwich, Ipswich, Colchester, and Cambridge; and earnings in each of these towns compared unfavourably with earnings in the north and Midlands.[3] In the 1906 wage census the lowest returns in the ready-made tailoring trade were from Norwich and Bristol; of the centres shown the highest rates were paid in Manchester and Leeds,[4] and when this trade was made subject to minimum wage legislation a few years later the districts most affected were in the west of England and the eastern counties—those least affected were in the north.[5]

A similar relationship can be seen in rural areas; in broad terms women and children were paid most where men's earnings were highest and least where they were lowest. In 1906 female agricultural workers in Lancashire were reported to be able to earn up to 20s. a week and those in Wiltshire and Berkshire only 9s. to 12s., a sum which was said to correspond with the far lower earnings of men in these counties.[6] These figures probably refer to maximum female earnings and are not representative but the relative position of female earnings in

1. See Ch. 1 above.
2. Tawney, op. cit., p. 71.
3. Barton, op. cit., 528.
4. *Earnings and Hours Inquiry, II, Clothing Trades*, P.P. 1909, LXXX, p. xl; Barton, loc. cit. 530.
5. Only 6 of 95 tailoring concerns in the north had to increase their rates: in London and the south 41 out of 56 were affected. Elsewhere, Leicester and Nottingham were cited as towns where women's wages were scarcely affected by the establishment of minimum rates in the box-making industry. R. H. Tawney, op. cit., pp. 69–70, 108; M. E. Bulkley, *Minimum Rates in the Boxmaking Industry* (1915), p. 89; *Report of the War Cabinet Committee on Women in Industry*, P.P. 1919, XXXI, p. 51 (subsequently referred to as *War Cabinet Committee on Women*).
6. *War Cabinet Committee on Women*, p. 60.

the two areas and the implied proportionality between male and female earnings in each area is quite clear. It is significant, too, that the Agricultural Wages Board in 1918 fixed a standard legal minimum for females in all counties except Yorkshire, Cumberland, and Westmorland where the minimum was 20 per cent higher.[1] That female wages were relatively high in areas where male wages were relatively high is suggested also by evidence in the *Royal Commission on Labour*. Women in the Glendale Union, Northumberland, were paid 1s. 4d. to 1s. 6d. a day, in the Swaffham district of Norfolk they were paid 1s.; male labourers were paid 17s. a week in Glendale and 12s. a week in Swaffham.[2]

M. F. Davies gave some details of other rural earnings at the beginning of the twentieth century in her study of the Wiltshire village of Corsley. Domestic glove manufacture survived in Corsley and paid up to 7s. 6d. a week, although most women in the industry earned considerably less than this amount; few married women in the gloving trade earned more than 2s. 6d. a week. The chief female occupations in the village were taking in washing and 'charring', and the average wage was about 6s.[3] Wives' earnings, of course, are the most significant for this inquiry[4] and it seems likely that by 1900 most wives in rural areas earned very little; few of those in the families investigated by Rowntree and Kendall added more than a shilling or two to the family budget and there is nothing in their survey which suggests that women in southern villages were able to offset the low wages of their husbands.[5] Employment was probably more readily available in country towns than in villages and wages a little higher; at Oxford, for example, in

1. Barton, op. cit., p. 521. Wartime inflation had in any case significantly reduced the proportionate importance of many regional differentials; for details of male labourers' wage rates at this time, including rates set by the Agricultural Wages Board, see A. L. Bowley, *Prices and Wages in the United Kingdom 1914–20*, pp. 171–2. See also below, p. 358.
2. P.P. 1893–4, XXXVIIii, pp. 61–2.
3. M. F. Davies, *Life in an English Village* (1909), pp. 124–30. The average for the village includes the value of food and was for an average of four days' employment, outworkers in the Colchester clothing trades were paid a similar rate. C. Black (ed.) *Married Women's Work* (1915), p. 241.
4. See above, p. 108
5. B. S. Rowntree and M. Kendall, *How the Labourer Lives*, p. 333.

1911 the general run of female earnings in the clothing factories, for shop assistants, and at the Clarendon Press, was 10s.[1] But neither 6s. at Corsley nor 10s. at Oxford was as much as the average of women's wages in Britain at this time.[2]

Most of this evidence of women's and children's wages comes from the second half of the period; there is less evidence for the 1850s and 1860s but sufficient to suggest strongly that their relative level in different regions shared much in common with the regional pattern of male earnings. Sundry references in the 1843 *Report on the Employment of Women and Children in Agriculture* have been conveniently summarized by Hasbach and by Pinchbeck. They show farm earnings varying according to task and season as well as between counties; the average was about 9d. per day and those areas where the rate was usually a little below this, like Norfolk, Suffolk, and the south-west, and those where the rate was usually somewhat higher, like Northumberland, Yorkshire, and Lincoln, were those where men's wages also were below or above the national average.[3] There is more information on female farm wages in the *Morning Chronicle* survey of 1849–50, although this was collected in a very unsystematic fashion; it records women earning from as little as 6d. a day in the West Country and East Anglia to 10d. or more in Northumberland and Kent.[4] Both these sources have

1. Cleaners in Oxford could earn 2s. or 2s. 6d. a day but their employment was greviously subject to the seasonal demand pattern of the university population. C. V. Butler in H. Bosanquet (ed.), *Social Conditions in Provincial Towns*, pp. 63–4.

2. The average was about 12s. to 14s. a week. *War Cabinet Committee on Women*, pp. 67–8; E. Rathbone in V. Gollancz (ed.) *The Making of Women* (1918), p. 203; Phelps Brown *Industrial Relations*, p. 221; H. A. Clegg, A. Fox, and A. F. Thompson, *A History of British Trade Unions since 1889*, i. 482. On male wages in Wiltshire, Oxford, and the rural south generally see Ch. 1.

3. W. Hasbach, *A History of the English Agricultural Labourer* (1908 edn.), pp. 226–7; I. Pinchbeck, *Women Workers and the Industrial Revolution*, pp. 95–6.

4. *M.C.*, 10, 17 Nov.; 5 Dec. 1849; 16, 30 Jan. 1850. Women's work in agriculture was irregular and uncertain and these daily rates are no guide to annual earnings. A survey of 241 labourers' wives in Norfolk and Suffolk in 1837 recorded average earnings of just over 1s. a week (Pinchbeck, op. cit., p. 96). The *M.C.* (27 Oct. 1849) considered 3s. a high weekly average in Wiltshire, Berkshire, Buckinghamshire, and Oxfordshire and A. Wilson Fox calculated that a wife and up to four children might together earn between 2s. and 5s. a week in the period 1840–70, the wife alone about

evidence on children's earnings in agriculture; these present special problems because they varied so much according to the child's age and the figures shown are too ambiguous to suggest any broad regional variations—but there is certainly no suggestion of distinctly higher rates in areas where men were badly paid.[1] One feature that does emerge clearly from the *Morning Chronicle* survey and from other evidence on earnings in the middle decades of the century is that a large proportion of women and children in the great mining and manufacturing centres of the north, the Midlands, and south Wales were relatively well paid. Most women in the Lancashire and West Riding textile centres, in the lace, hosiery, and silk mills of Nottingham and Derby, in the Birmingham and Sheffield metal trades, and in south Wales iron and copper works earned between 6*s*. and 9*s*. a week.[2] This was far above the 3*s*. to 4*s*. a woman could normally hope to earn in agriculture or domestic industry and it was as much or more than the pay of many male agricultural labourers in the low-wage south.

The cotton workers were always the most numerous and best-paid of the female textile workers. In 1886, when the average of women's wages in the industries covered by the official wage census was 12*s*. 8*d*. a week, the average for cotton operatives was 15*s*. 3*d*. and they headed the list with regard to both wages and numbers employed.[3] In the minor textile

---

3*s*. 6*d*. in domestic industry. 'Agricultural Wages in England and Wales during the Last Fifty Years', p. 301. The *Morning Chronicle* survey suggests that women and children in Northumberland and Durham, where men's wages were among the highest in Britain, could earn a great deal more than the national averages given by Wilson Fox, *M.C.*, 9 and 16 Jan. 1850.

1. *M.C.*, see e.g. the issues of 27 Oct., 1 and 26 Dec. 1849; 9 and 30 Jan., 18 Oct. 1850; Hasbach, op. cit., pp. 227–8.

2. *M.C.* 29 Oct., 8, 22, and 29 Nov., 3, 6, 10 Dec. 1849; 10, 17, 21 Jan., 18, 21, Mar., 8 Apr., 14 June, 4 Nov. 1850; A. L. Bowley, 'Wages in the Worsted and Woollen Manufacture of the West Riding of Yorkshire', *J.R.S.S.*, lxv (1902), 110–11, 116; *Returns of Wages*, P.P. 1887, LXXXIX, pp. 1–22, 47–134; R. A. Church, *Victorian Nottingham*, pp. 266–8; F. A. Wells, *The British Hosiery Trade* (1935), p. 148. On wages in a variety of non-textile occupations in south Wales, north Wales, Birmingham, and Sheffield see Pinchbeck, op. cit., p. 280, and A. H. Dodd, *The Industrial Revolution in North Wales*, pp. 363–4.

3. G. H. Wood in B. L. Hutchins and A. Harrison, *A History of Factory Legislation* (1903), p. 261.

trades the level of women's wages followed the same general rule of lower wages at a distance from Lancashire.[1] Young people in the cotton mills were also well paid, and the high level of family earnings in Lancashire was common knowledge among informed observers.[2] These advantages were well maintained in the following twenty years; the wage census of 1906 shows that the average wage of women in the cotton trade was 18s. 8d. which was more than the average of male farm labourers in every southern county except those bordering London.[3] The female cotton workers, well paid, well organized, and well protected, were a no less representative and far more enduring consequence of the industrial revolution than the much lamented handloom weavers.

Across the Pennines, the Yorkshire wool operatives were better paid than most women but not as well paid as the cotton workers.[4] However, they illustrate more clearly the general coincidence of relative wage levels for men and women because both wage censuses include figures for the West Country as well as Yorkshire. In 1886 the average wage for women and girls (taken together) in the northern woollen manufacturing districts was 13s. 2d. a week; in the west of England it was 10s. 8d.; men and boys in the West Country were at a similar disadvantage.[5] A few years later a survey described women's wages in the factories of Trowbridge and Stroud as about two-thirds of the Yorkshire rate,[6] and the 1906 census again showed the West

---

1. *Wages in the Minor Textile Trades*, P.P. 1890, LXVIII, p. ix.
2. Lads and boys averaged 9s. 4d., girls 6s. 10d. *Wages in the Principal Textile Trades*, P.P. 1889, LXX, p. xxv. On family earnings in Lancashire see T. Brassey, *Lectures on the Labour Question*, p. 253; W. Smart, *Women's Wages* (Glasgow, 1892), p. 23; P. de Rousiers, *The Labour Question in Britain*, 332.
3. *Earnings and Hours Inquiry: Textile Trades*, P.P. 1909, LXXX, p. xvi; Table 1–3. 40 per cent of the female cotton operatives earned £1 or more—this was as much as urban labourers in several towns. The worst-paid farm labourers earned less than the cotton industry paid lads and boys—see *Earnings and Hours Inquiry: Textile Trades*, p. xvi; Table 1–5; Phelps Brown, *Industrial Relations*, p. 24; *Second Report on Wages . . . of Agricultural Labourers*, pp. 154–9.
4. This was not least because they were less well organized. On the relative strength of women's trade unionism in the two trades see H. A. Clegg, A. Fox, and A. F. Thompson, op. cit., pp. 29–30, 34, 120–1.
5. *Statistics of Employment of Women and Girls*, P.P. 1894, LXXXIii, pp. 52, 66.
6. A. A. Bulley and M. Whitley, *Women's Work* (1894), pp. 105–6.

Country at a disadvantage.[1] A similar pattern can be seen in the lace and silk trades[2] and towards the end of the century earnings in the Essex crape trade were said to be lower than women's earnings in any other factory employment.[3]

This survey has been restricted to testing the hypothesis that the level of women's and young persons' wages varied from one area to another in a manner likely to have offset variations in men's earnings.[4] The major characteristics are not in doubt: regional variations in the wages of women and young people failed to compensate for regional variations in men's wages. On the contrary, there was a generally positive correlation between the two variables. This conclusion is really not very surprising for two reasons. First, all wages in an area would be affected by the over-all level of demand for labour in that area. Second, the differentials between the earnings of men, women, and

1. *Earnings and Hours Inquiry: Textile Trades*, P.P. 1909, LXXX, pp. xli, 83–102, 105–12.
2. On lace see *Wages in the Minor Textile Trades*, pp. 47–51. Menders, for example, were paid 12s. 8d. in Nottingham, 9s. 5d. elsewhere in Nottinghamshire and in Derbyshire, 8s. 8d. in Ayrshire, Lanark, and Stirling, and 7s. 9d. in Somerset.
3. Bulley and Whitley, op. cit., p. 106. See also *R.C. on Labour, The Employment of Women*, P.P. 1893–4, XXXVIIi, p. 135. In the 1906 census female power-loom weavers, working full-time and on piece-rates, are shown to have averaged 14s. 10d. in Congleton, Macclesfield, and Leek, 14s. in Lancashire and Yorkshire, and 10s. 11d. in the eastern counties (*Earnings and Hours Inquiry: Textile Trades*, p. 152).
4. There is considerably less evidence on which a more comprehensive survey of family earnings might be based than exists for men's wages. Local variations in women's wages and in activity rates are not considered in this chapter although they were sometimes substantial; they must have exercised an influence upon migration, marriage, and the birthrate, and might well repay investigation. Leigh in Lancashire is an interesting example of the way these local variables could influence economic activity. It was no less a textile town than nearby Bolton, but unlike most of Lancashire concentrated upon silk rather than cotton. The Lancashire silk industry never recovered the level of prosperity it enjoyed in 1860 and by the end of the century Leigh was a rarity among Lancashire towns with an abundance of relatively cheap female labour. These characteristics may help to explain why Courtaulds chose Leigh when they began operating in the traditional textile district for the first time in 1898. In 1906 the average earnings of female silk workers over 18 was 9s. 9d. a week in the Eastern Counties and 12s. 4d. in Lancashire and Yorkshire (in Lancashire the trade was concentrated at Leigh); the average in the Lancashire and Yorkshire cotton trade was 18s. 7d. On these various points see *V.C.H. Lancashire*, ii (1908), 395; *Earnings and Hours Inquiry I. Textile Trades*, P.P. 1909, LXXX, pp. 31 149–50.

young people were strongly influenced by custom. Women's wages were determined, in large part, by consideration of what most people believed they ought to earn and this was usually measured as a customary proportion of the male rate. Tradition was reinforced by the especially close links between the wages of men and boys; boys graduated to full men's wages in a number of well-defined stages so that in any one area their rate, relative to the boys' rate in other areas, was likely to be similar to the relative level of the men's rate. Similarly the pay of girls was in part determined by what boys received and by women's rates.

## III

It has been shown that spatial variations in earnings of women and adolescents had much in common with spatial variations in men's earnings: but if activity rates in different regions varied sufficiently (and inversely to wages) then it is still possible that family earnings may have compensated for variations in men's wages. The position in the cotton towns where high wages were combined with a high activity rate[1] casts doubt on the hypothesis, as does the only inquiry on this subject, Lawrence's survey of 1897.[2] However, the possibility exists and requires some investigation.

A precise and realistic account of women's and children's employment in different areas is more elusive than a cursory examination of the occupational census might suggest. The returns are least specific on the numbers and definition of domestic servants and part-time workers, and both categories included a large proportion of working women. Another difficulty arises with the wives and daughters of farmers, certain

1. See below, pp. 124, and above, pp. 37–42, 115–16.
2. Lawrence found no evidence to suggest that the artisan was willing to accept a lower wage in those towns where he could obtain employment for his wife and daughters. F. W. Lawrence, *Local Variations in Wages*, p. 51. Some contemporaries, however, held other views, see e.g. H. S. Jevons, *The British Coal Trade*, p. 70.

craftsmen, and small tradesmen—these were counted in some censuses and not in others. Further, at no time in the period is it possible to distinguish working wives from the unmarried. Fortunately, a certain amount of incomplete but serviceable quantitative evidence is available which, together with some literary evidence, is sufficient to illustrate the salient features.[1]

Another difficulty in the interpretation of female employment statistics is that, while low activity rates were often a consequence of low demand for women's labour, supply also was a variable. Some men everywhere, and in some places a majority of men, attached great importance to keeping their wives in the home; the first category included many artisans,[2] the second much of Wales.[3] In these cases women's work was regarded as poor compensation for low male earnings and the family might well have preferred to move to a higher-wage area even when this involved a drop in family earnings. For this reason even statistics far more suited to our purpose than those of the kind shown in the appendix to this chapter would need to be interpreted with a considerable degree of latitude.

1. The proportions of women, girls, and children returned as occupied in north and south Wales and the various counties of England in 1851 and 1911 are shown in the appendix to this chapter. However, they offer no more than a crude, inconsistent, and often misleading guide to the size of the group which concerns us here—viz. wives and children who both worked for wages and lived at home (see above, pp. 107–8).

2. The attitude of artisans to women's work is well illustrated in a comment by Henry Broadhurst, secretary of the T.U.C., in 1875. He considered that one of the functions of trade unions was '. . . to bring about a condition . . . where wives would be in their proper sphere at home'—quoted by H. A. Turner, *Trade Union Growth, Structure and Policy* (1962), p. 185. See also Lawrence, op. cit., pp. 82–3; S. Pollard, *A History of Labour in Sheffield*, p. 210; Booth, *Life and Labour*, 2nd Ser., i. 365.

3. See e.g. *R.C. on Labour: Summary of Evidence and Appendices*, P.P. 1894, XXXV, p. 507. Newcastle would probably also qualify for inclusion in the second category: men there resented their wives working, they felt it 'undignified and out of order' (*Women's Industrial Council. Married Women's Work*, ed. C. Black (1915), p. 195). Similar attitudes were found over large parts of the rural south (see below, p. 120 n. 1), although opinions varied even within a county; there were parts of Worcester where, even at the end of the century, married women who abstained from fieldwork were considered indolent (C. Black, op. cit., p. 233). For an account of attitudes in various parts of rural Kent see D. W. Harvey, 'Aspects of Agricultural and Rural Change in Kent, 1800–1900', Ph.D. thesis, University of Cambridge (1961), pp. 224–5, 243.

There were two types of areas where circumstances might lend support to the hypothesis that the level of employment among women and children offset differentials in men's earnings. One of these was the low-wage rural south of England in the first 15 or 20 years of the period when considerable numbers of women and children worked on the land.[1] In addition, at that time the south retained much of its domestic industry; the pay was poor but it enabled women and children to add something to family incomes.[2] The south's misfortune, particularly after the introduction of the new poor law in 1834,[3] was that male wages were so low that any ill-paid employment for their wives and children was accepted gladly.[4] But conditions in the rural south lend little real support to the hypothesis that family earnings may have offered compensation for regional variations in men's earnings. There are two reasons for this. First, female activity rates in the south were not outstandingly high; they were high compared with most rural areas elsewhere in England and Wales and low-activity areas like the coalfields and centres of heavy industry, but even in the 1850s and 1860s they were probably equalled or exceeded by rates in rural Scotland, in the textile centres of the north and north Midlands, in the Potteries, in Birmingham, and in London.[5] This left a great many migration opportunities where the southern labourers could reasonably hope for a net gain in family earnings. Second, family

1. There is some evidence that rural labourers in this area should be counted among those who were inclined to keep their wives at home when they could. The diminishing number of women engaged in farm work after 1870 was considered due in part to higher wages for men. See below, p. 121; Hasbach, op. cit., Ch. 4; A. Wilson Fox, 'Agricultural Wages in England and Wales during the last Fifty Years', p. 298; J. A. Sheppard, 'East Yorkshire's Agricultural Labour Force in the mid-Nineteenth Century', p. 47.
2. Hasbach, op. cit., pp. 262, 267. See also above, p. 107 n. 3, and below, p. 121.
3. Hasbach, op. cit., pp. 224–5; Pinchbeck, op. cit., pp. 84–6; C. S. Orwin and B. I. Felton, 'A Century of Wages and Earnings in Agriculture', p. 241.
4. See e.g. A. Wilson Fox, op. cit., p. 297; Pinchbeck, op. cit., p. 102; Hasbach, op. cit., p. 230.
5. London, the textile areas, and rural Scotland are discussed below. There are some references to activity rates in Birmingham in G. C. Allen, *Birmingham and the Black Country*, pp. 167–8, 441, including the observation that in 1856 it has as high a proportion of juvenile labour as anywhere in the country. See also B. M. D. Smith in *V.C.H. Warwickshire*, vii, 176–7, and J. D. Marshall, 'The Lancashire Rural Labourer in the early Nineteenth Century', p. 108.

earnings in the rural south were so low that any advantage the region possessed in activity rates was unlikely to go far towards reducing differentials in male earnings. Four shillings is probably a generous estimate of the average gross earnings of wives and children in the 1850s,[1] and this was no more, and in many cases less, than the margin between farm labourers' wages in the north and south.[2] Miners and urban workers in the north and Midlands enjoyed an even greater wage advantage over the rural south, and the north and Midlands offered ample well-paid work for boys. Finally, and this is perhaps the most telling confirmation of the failure of family employment to compensate for low male earnings, there is the evidence of the poor relief returns and what we know of diet in the area.[3]

Whatever residual compensations the rural south may have enjoyed at the beginning of the period were not enduring. As men's wages rose some women and children opted to stay at home; others were affected by the decline of domestic industry, by the Gangs Act of 1867, and the Education Acts of 1870 and 1876.[4] The decline in the number of women and children employed on the land was not restricted to the south: by the early 'eighties there were many districts where their labour was confined to hay-making and harvest and twenty years later Wilson Fox reported that women were not employed in ordinary field work in any English county except Northumberland and Durham.[5] However, the decline was probably greatest in the

1. Net earnings were less than this and the advantage of the south in this respect over other areas was smaller still because few families anywhere relied entirely on the husband's wage. See above, pp. 106-7, 114-15.
2. See Ch. 1, above.
3. Expenditure on poor relief was extraordinarily high, and so was the consumption of bread. Both points are discussed above, p. 78 and below, pp. 148, 204-15.
4. On the decline of family employment in the south see A. Wilson Fox, op. cit., p. 298; Orwin and Felton, op. cit., p. 244; Hasbach, op. cit., pp. 256-7, 267-71; L. Davidoff, 'The Employment of Married Women in England 1850-1950', M. A. thesis, University of London (1956), p. 207; J. Saville, *Rural Depopulation in England and Wales, 1851-1951, passim.* The interesting question of whether family income in the rural south possibly fell between 1860 and 1880, despite higher real wages for men, was raised by Hasbach at the end of the nineteenth century but has never been answered.
5. *Second Report on Wages . . . Agricultural Labourers,* p. 12. See also J. Ashby and B. King, 'Statistics of some Midland Villages', p. 8.

south; a report in 1870 noted that the greatest number of
working females were 'in those counties where the agricultural
labourer's position was the best'.[1]

The high-wage county of Northumberland employed a greater
proportion of females in agriculture than any other English
county; in 1871 women in Northumberland accounted for 22
per cent of the agricultural labour force when the average for
England and Wales was only 3·4 per cent.[2] The high level in
Northumberland was in part a consequence of its proximity to
Scotland where females were much more extensively employed
than in England and Wales. Scotland was affected by the
decline of family employment on the land but remained considerably more dependent on women's labour than the rest of
Britain. In 1891 women accounted for 18 per cent of the farm
labour force in Scotland,[3] and those migrant farmers who introduced the Scottish system to East Anglia in the 'agricultural
depression' were a source of considerable interest and comment.[4]
For most of the period male wages in south and central Scotland
were relatively high[5] and the situation there underlines the
absence of any general inverse correlation between men's
wages and activity rates in agriculture. In fact, it seems likely
that by 1870 in areas where men's wages were high total
family earnings exceeded total family earnings in low-wage
areas by more than the difference in men's wages—partly
because women and children's wage rates were roughly proportional to men's and partly because more women worked in
high-wage areas, particularly in Scotland.[6] Moreover, the

1. *R.C. on Labour. The Agricultural Labourer. Misc. Memoranda etc.*, P.P.
   1893–4, XXXVIIii, p. 9. The 1871 census returns suggest that the relationship was less close than this statement implies but there was some measure
   of correlation and there is no doubt that activity rates were not generally
   higher in low-wage areas (ibid., pp. 39–40, Tables II, IV).
2. *R.C. on Labour. The Agricultural Labourer. Misc. Memoranda etc*, p. 40,
   Table V. See also *Report on the Wages and Earnings of Agricultural Labourers*, P.P. 1900, LXXXII, p. 18.
3. *R.C. on Labour. The Agricultural Labourer. Misc. Memoranda etc.*, pp.
   165, 313.
4. See e.g. *R.C. on the Agricultural Depression*, P.P. 1894, XVIi, Report by
   R. Hunter Pringle, pp. 45–6; 1894, XVIii, evidence para. 31956–7.
5. Sections XI and XII of Ch. 1, above.
6. The case for a generally positive relationship between men's wages and
   family earnings in rural areas, however, is no more than tentative. One

scarcity of family employment in most rural areas by the last quarter of the century is also contrary to the hypothesis that family employment was most widespread where men's wages were low because average farm wages were considerably less than average wages in urban areas.[1]

The second category of areas where the level of activity rates was not inconsistent with a situation in which they might be regarded as compensating for the level of men's earnings was the mining and heavy-engineering districts. Most of these were distinguished by high wages for men and low female activity rates. In 1891, when the average proportion of females occupied in England and Wales was 34·4 per cent, the average in Middlesbrough was 19·3 per cent, in St. Helens it was 22 per cent, and in Sunderland 21·9 per cent. Newcastle (28·7 per cent), Merthyr Tydfil (28·3 per cent), and some of the larger ports like Liverpool (31·9 per cent) and Hull (26·8 per cent) also returned figures of female employment well below the national average.[2] These examples, however, lend less weight to the hypothesis that high male wages compensated for lack of family employment than might at first appear. The disadvantage of these areas was limited to low activity rates for women and girls; there was

---

complication is the pattern of child employment after 1870 which seems to have been quite different to the pattern of women's employment and often its reverse (*R.C. on Labour. The Agricultural Labourer. Misc. Memoranda etc.*, pp. 44–5, 259, 291). Another is the question of the extent to which varying rates of female employment on the land simply reflected the availability of alternative employment in domestic service and elsewhere. But there can be little doubt that family earnings provided no general and significant compensation for differences in men's wages.

1. The paucity of employment opportunities in rural areas by the last quarter of the century is well established. In 1891, in England and Wales, 34·4 per cent of all females aged 10 years and over were occupied; in the urban sanitary districts of over 50,000 population the proportion was 37·1 per cent (*Statistics of Employment of Women and Girls*, p. 78). See also Saville, op. cit., pp. 14, 30–5, 96; Davidoff, op. cit., pp. 207–8; Booth, *Life and Labour*, 1st Ser., iii. 138–9, and above, p. 113.

2. All these figures are taken from *Statistics of Employment of Women and Girls*, pp. 78–102. For more detailed accounts of the low proportion of females occupied in some of these towns see T. C. Barker and J. R. Harris, *A Merseyside Town in the Industrial Revolution, St. Helens 1750–1900*, pp. 278–9, 321; J. Bellamy, 'Occupations in Kingston upon Hull, 1841–1948' *Yks. Bull.*, iv (1952), 37–42; A. Harrison, *Women's Industries in Liverpool* (Liverpool, 1904); S. Pollard, *A History of Labour in Sheffield*, p. 210.

plenty of work for boys and their wages were correspondingly
higher than the wages of boys in areas where men were badly
paid.[1] Second, there is a point which was raised earlier: many
married women remained at home from choice and the wives of
well-paid miners, engineers, and metal workers were likely to be
over-represented among these.[2] Further, not all the mining and
heavy-industrial areas lacked female employment: considerable parts of the Lancashire and West Riding textile districts
stand on coalfields and according to one report miners' wives
accounted for a large proportion of the married women in the
Lancashire mills;[3] the Potteries was another area with a
mixture of heavy and light industry which provided employment for both sexes. In addition there is the fact that the level
of men's wages in towns like Newcastle and Middlesbrough
contrasted most favourably with the level in the rural south
and for much of the period activity rates there were also well
below average.[4] Similarly, if we were to accept that low family
earnings were important in explaining high male wages in the

1. See section II of this chapter. In 1849–50 lads of 16 were paid 9s. in the
   Swansea copper works and boys of unspecified age a similar sum in the coal
   trade near Manchester. *M.C.* 14 June 1850; see also *Returns of Wages
   published between 1830 and 1886*, p. 134. Few farm labourers in the low-
   wage south received as much as this. de Rousiers described lads of 12 earning
   12s. to 15s. on the Lothian coalfield in the 1890s when average earnings of
   adult farm labourers in the rural south were about 16s. to 17s. (de Rousiers,
   op. cit., pp. 124–6; Table 1–4).
2. See above, p. 119. An investigator for the *R.C. on the Employment of
   Children, Young Persons, and Women in Agriculture* (1867), mindful of
   south Wales, 'where the large wages given to men obviated all necessity
   for women to work', found it remarkable that the wives of well-paid
   Scottish miners should be content to labour in the fields for 1s. or 1s. 6d. a
   day (*R.C. on Labour. The Agricultural Labourer. Misc. Memoranda etc.*,
   p. 255); see also Phelps Brown, *Industrial Relations*, p. 40. However, the
   wives of miners in Lancashire and the West Riding argue against generalization and there is no way of telling to what extent miners in south Wales
   and elsewhere were making a virtue of necessity. Attitudes probably
   varied from one coalfield to another just as in the first half of the century
   women and children were extensively employed in some areas and scarcely
   at all in others. With respect to south Wales, and the widespread belief that
   women's employment was unusual there, it is interesting to note that the
   *Morning Chronicle* survey of 1849–50 discovered considerable numbers of
   females in the iron mills, at pit heads, and in the Swansea copper works—
   most were engaged in heavy manual labour (*M.C.* 18, 21, Mar. and 14
   June 1850).
3. *R.C. on Labour, Summary of Evidence and Appendices*, P.P. 1894, XXXV,
   p. 507.
4. See above, p. 121.

mining and metal centres we should expect to find that men's wages in towns like London, Birmingham, and Manchester, where female activity rates were above average, were substantially less than in towns like Newcastle and Middlesbrough and also below rates in the rural south. In fact, of course, men's wages in London, Birmingham, and Manchester were among the highest in the country and far above those in the rural south.[1] In short, the position in the mining and heavy-engineering districts can scarcely be used as evidence that activity rates were an important element in explaining general differentials in men's wages because other areas combined the two variables in so many different ways.

This evidence, considered together with the generally positive relationship between wage rates for men and those for women and children, leaves no doubt that family earnings, like variations in the cost of living, do little to explain regional variations in men's wages. Doubtless there were some men reluctant to move to the coalfields and to towns like Sheffield and Middlesbrough because these areas offered few opportunities

---

1. *1891 Proportion of occupied females aged 10 years and over*

| England and Wales | 34·4 | Manchester | 42·4 |
| Leeds | 38·0 | Nottingham | 45·5 |
| London | 38·4 | Leicester | 48·2 |
| Birmingham | 40·4 | Bradford | 49·1 |

*Statistics of Employment of Women and Girls*, pp. 82–98.

On men's wages in these areas see Chapter 1 above. The level of activity rates in these areas can be seen also in the appendix to this chapter. The figures shown there must be used with care (see above, pp. 118–19) but high activity rates are readily apparent in London, Lancashire, Yorkshire, Nottingham, and Leicestershire. London was not remarkable for the number of working children but it employed well above the average proportion of females; in 1911 it was second only to Leicestershire in this respect. The Booth survey earlier drew attention to high earnings for boys and plentiful female employment in the capital: 'The difference of wage between the county and the town would seen still greater if we took the family rather than the individual as our unit' (Booth, *Life and Labour*, 1st Ser., iii. 138–9). The textile areas were remarkable for the proportion of both women and children employed (Tables 3–2 and 3–3). Cotton towns were the stronghold of the half-time system, and were also noted for the high proportion of wives among the female employees (Phelps Brown, *Industrial Relations*, pp. 58–9, 68). In 1891 when the proportion of girls aged 10–15 at work in England and Wales was 16·3 per cent there were eleven large towns where the proportion was over 30 per cent, all of these were in Lancashire and the West Riding (*R.C. on Labour, Statistics of Employment of Women and Girls*, pp. 18–19).

for working women just as there were probably some farm labourers in the south in the 1850s and 1860s who were reconciled to low earnings by the work of their wives and children, and in such cases activity rates had some effect on migration and thus on men's wages. But cases like this were not significant because in the main, and for most of the period, areas where men's wages were low were distinguished neither by high activity rates nor high family earnings, while many other areas combined high wages for men with better than average opportunities for women and young people.

TABLE 3–2  *Occupied Females (Age 15 and over): Counties*

| 1851 | Female activity rate (%) | 1851 | Female activity rate (%) | 1911 | Female activity rate (%) | 1911 | Female activity rate (%) |
|---|---|---|---|---|---|---|---|
| Bedfordshire | 57 | Oxfordshire | 37 | Leicestershire | 45 | Dorset | 33 |
| Buckinghamshire | 48 | Herefordshire | 36 | London | 44 | Kent | 33 |
| Lancashire | 47 | N. Riding | 35 | Lancashire | 43 | Norfolk | 33 |
| Leicestershire | 47 | Sussex | 35 | Warwickshire | 41 | Rutland | 33 |
| Nottinghamshire | 46 | E. Riding | 34 | Bedfordshire | 40 | Buckinghamshire | 32 |
| Somerset | 45 | Norfolk | 34 | Nottinghamshire | 39 | Cumberland | 32 |
| Gloucestershire | 44 | North Wales | 34 | Sussex | 39 | Hampshire | 32 |
| Warwickshire | 44 | South Wales | 34 | Cheshire | 38 | Cambridgeshire | 31 |
| Cheshire | 43 | Surrey | 34 | Gloucestershire | 38 | E. Riding | 31 |
| London | 43 | Cornwall | 33 | Somerset | 38 | Essex | 31 |
| Worcestershire | 43 | Hampshire | 33 | Surrey | 38 | North Wales | 31 |
| Derbyshire | 41 | Shropshire | 33 | Westmorland | 38 | Shropshire | 31 |
| Devon | 41 | Essex | 32 | Worcestershire | 38 | Suffolk | 31 |
| Hertfordshire | 41 | Lincolnshire | 32 | ***England and Wales | 36 | Wiltshire | 30 |
| Westmorland | 41 | Staffordshire | 32 | Hertfordshire | 36 | Cornwall | 29 |
| Cumberland | 40 | Suffolk | 32 | Middlesex | 36 | Derbyshire | 29 |
| W. Riding | 40 | Cambridgeshire | 31 | Oxfordshire | 36 | Huntingdonshire | 28 |
| Dorset | 39 | Kent | 31 | W. Riding | 36 | N. Riding | 28 |
| ***England and Wales | 39 | Northumberland | 31 | Berkshire | 35 | South Wales | 27 |
| Northamptonshire | 39 | Rutland | 31 | Devon | 35 | Lincolnshire | 26 |
| Wiltshire | 39 | Huntingdonshire | 30 | Northamptonshire | 35 | Northumberland | 26 |
| Berkshire | 37 | Monmouthshire | 28 | Herefordshire | 34 | Monmouthshire | 22 |
| Middlesex | 37 | Durham | 25 | Staffordshire | 34 | Durham | 21 |

*Source:* D. V. Glass in L. Hogben (ed.), *Political Arithmetic* (1938), pp. 201–2.

TABLE 3-3  Occupied Children: Counties

| 1851 | Child activity rate (%) (Age 10–15) | 1851 | Child activity rate (%) (Age 10–15) | 1911 | Child activity rate (%) (Age 10–15) | 1911 | Child activity rate (%) (Age 10–15) |
|---|---|---|---|---|---|---|---|
| Bedfordshire | 50 | Essex | 25 | W. Riding | 25 | Wiltshire | 13 |
| W. Riding | 44 | Shropshire | 25 | Northamptonshire | 24 | Devon | 12 |
| Northamptonshire | 40 | Gloucestershire | 23 | Lancashire | 23 | Herefordshire | 12 |
| Buckinghamshire | 39 | Herefordshire | 23 | Leicestershire | 20 | Norfolk | 12 |
| Lancashire | 39 | Norfolk | 23 | Huntingdonshire | 19 | Westmorland | 12 |
| Nottinghamshire | 39 | Cambridgeshire | 22 | Nottinghamshire | 19 | Berkshire | 11 |
| Derbyshire | 38 | Durham | 22 | Derbyshire | 18 | Dorset | 11 |
| Leicestershire | 38 | E. Riding | 22 | Bedfordshire | 17 | E. Riding | 11 |
| Warwickshire | 35 | Hampshire | 22 | Staffordshire | 17 | Hertfordshire | 11 |
| Staffordshire | 35 | Suffolk | 22 | Somerset | 16 | Shropshire | 11 |
| Cheshire | 34 | Sussex | 22 | Buckinghamshire | 15 | Essex | 10 |
| Hertfordshire | 34 | N. Riding | 20 | Cambridgeshire | 15 | Hampshire | 10 |
| Cornwall | 32 | Cumberland | 19 | Cheshire | 15 | London | 10 |
| Worcestershire | 32 | Lincolnshire | 19 | Oxfordshire | 15 | Northumberland | 10 |
| Huntingdonshire | 29 | Rutland | 19 | Suffolk | 15 | N. Riding | 10 |
| Somerset | 29 | Surrey | 19 | Warwickshire | 15 | Sussex | 10 |
| Wiltshire | 29 | Kent | 18 | ***England and Wales | 14 | Cornwall | 9 |
| Devon | 28 | Northumberland | 18 | Rutland | 14 | Durham | 9 |
| ***England and Wales | 28 | Westmorland | 18 | Worcestershire | 14 | Cumberland | 8 |
| Monmouthshire | 27 | London | 17 | Gloucestershire | 13 | Kent | 8 |
| Oxfordshire | 26 | Dorset | 14 | Lincolnshire | 13 | Middlesex | 8 |
| Berkshire | 25 | Middlesex | 13 | Monmouthshire | 13 | Surrey | 8 |

Source: D. V. Glass in L. Hogben (ed.), Political Arithmetic (1938), p. 210.

# 4

## DEMAND FOR LABOUR

CHAPTERS Two and Three have removed some uncertainties
about the nature of regional wage variations but done little to
explain them: variations in demand for labour should prove a
more fruitful field of inquiry. Few would dispute that the
transformation of the regional wage pattern in the century
before 1850[1] was mainly a consequence of the industrial
revolution which displaced the south from its traditional pre-
eminence and concentrated economic growth and demand for
labour in the north and Midlands. Structural changes continued
after 1850 and it seems likely that their size and momentum
may have been prominent among the forces which maintained
different wage rates in different parts of the country. It is
difficult, however, on the basis of published evidence, to go far
beyond generalizations of this nature. The major variations in
demand, such as the rapid expansion of the south Wales coalfield after 1880 or the Teeside iron boom which began in the
1850s, are well known, but we lack quantitative and comprehensive studies of the kind familiar to students of American
economic history.[2] There is no shortage of local and regional
history, but few accounts permit more than impressionistic
comparisons of one region with another, and by concentrating
upon one area they leave little choice but to distinguish the
locally significant by contrasting it with the 'general pattern' or
'national average', a compound of regional experiences which
may not have existed in any single part of Britain. This
chapter is based upon a number of occupational indices which
go a little way towards making good one part of the deficiency.

1. See above, p. 19.
2. The best example is H. S. Perloff, E. S. Dunn, E. E. Lampard, and R. F.
   Muth, *Regions, Resources and Economic Growth* (Baltimore, Md., 1960).

They provide a means of testing the relationship between demand and wage levels in different regions and allow some insight into the nature and speed of structural change, the relative importance of changes in the labour requirements of different sectors, and the degree of variation between regional economies and the 'national average'.

The indices are based upon the decennial occupational census. They show, for Britain and for each region, the importance of employment in thirteen different occupational categories selected to include representatives from most of the major employment sectors.[1] For the sake of clarity only a summary of the position at the beginning and end of the period is given in the text: details of the census categories covered by the tables, together with some of the numerous caveats and qualifications which attend any attempt to make use of the occupational census, are shown in the appendix to this chapter.[2] Except where cited otherwise all subsequent references to the occupational structure are based upon evidence in the occupational census. The indices themselves have several limitations which should be kept in mind in the following discussion. First, they show employment in the same 'regions' whose wage levels were described in Chapter One. What was said there of the short-comings of these 'regions'—the variety within them and the difficulties created by the need to represent regional boundaries by a single line which must also coincide with a county boundary—applies also to Tables 4-1 to 4-13 in this chapter. Second, there are problems arising from the fact that the level of demand for labour is a nebulous concept which cannot be accurately represented by any index. Tables 4-1 to 4-13, which purport to show 'demand for labour', might more correctly be described as indicators of the structure of employment and the rate of change in employment. Considered alone the level of demand would indicate little of value: what matters is the

1. Viz. agriculture; mining; craftsmen; the major and minor textile trades, including some in which domestic or workshop production was predominant in 1850; the main categories of non-textile manufacturing industry; 'new' industries; transport; commerce; and domestic service. For details see the appendix to this chapter.
2. For more detailed tables, which contain figures from each census between 1851 and 1911, see my dissertation, 'Regional Wage Variations in Britain, 1850–1914', Ph.D. thesis, University of London (1971), pp. 471–96.

relationship between demand and supply. To meet this problem employment is shown relative to population. But this device raises the possibility, unlikely though it is, that uniformly rapid expansion of employment across the whole range of occupations might have occurred at the same time as substantial migration to a region and consequently the growth in employment would not be reflected in figures showing numbers employed as a proportion of population. There is also a problem of specification; changes in employment might arise from changes in supply as well as changes in demand and their separate effects cannot be distinguished. For example, it is suggested below (p. 140 n. 2) that increased employment in domestic service, far from being conducive to higher wages, was sometimes a reflection of poverty and the lack of more remunerative employment. For these various reasons the figures in Tables 4–1 to 4–13 should be regarded not as precise indications of the relative level of demand for labour in different areas, no index could show this, but rather as a serviceable guide to the more important employment trends which were likely to influence wage rates. Where the tables, considered alone, are likely to mislead this is indicated in the text; in addition the tables are supplemented by evidence of poor relief expenditure, migration flows, absolute numbers employed, and sundry other indicators of the likely level of demand for labour in different areas.

# I

REGION ONE (London and Home Counties—see Map 1)

Table 4–1 shows employment in major occupational categories for Region One and for Britain as a whole at the beginning and end of the period under investigation. The national figures contain some points of interest. They show, for example, that in 1851 domestic service provided employment for as many as wool and cotton manufacture combined and in 1911 for as many as were employed in cotton manufacture and agriculture. They show too the enormous expansion

TABLE 4–1

*Numbers Occupied per 1,000 population: Region One (London and Home Counties)*

| | Britain | | | Region 1 | | |
|---|---|---|---|---|---|---|
| Occupation category | 1851 | 1911 | Change | 1851 | 1911 | Change |
| 1. Metals | 21 | 33 | +12 | 12 | 16 | +4 |
| 2. Domestic Service | 48 | 45 | −3 | 72 | 61 | −11 |
| 3. Wool | 14 | 7 | −7 | 1 | — | −1 |
| 4. Cotton etc. | 34 | 19 | −15 | 1 | — | −1 |
| 5. Silk, Straw, Gloves, Hats, Stockings | 15 | 4 | −11 | 11 | 1 | −10 |
| 6. Mines and Quarries | 16 | 27 | +11 | — | — | — |
| 7. Shoemakers, Millers, Tailors, Saddlers, Carpenters | 32 | 20 | −12 | 35 | 20 | −15 |
| 8. Railways | 3 | 12 | +9 | 2 | 10 | +8 |
| 9. Chemicals, Pottery, Glass, Paper | 4 | 6 | +2 | 3 | 5 | +2 |
| 10. Coachbuilding, Ship-building | 2 | 4 | +2 | 3 | 2 | −1 |
| 11. 'New' Industries (Cars, Cycles, Electrical) | — | 5 | +5 | — | 7 | +7 |
| 12. Commerce | 3 | 22 | +19 | 7 | 36 | +29 |
| 13. Agriculture | 85 | 26 | −59 | 40 | 11 | −29 |

*Source:* Census of Occupations. For details of occupations included in these categories, see the appendix to this chapter.

of commercial employment. Over the period commercial employment increased more rapidly than employment in any of the other sectors shown in the table—an expansion more than equal to the total increase in demand from the various metal-working trades, shipyards and coachbuilding, chemical, pottery, glass, and paper manufacture. Of those sectors whose share in the national labour force declined, agriculture was by far the most important. The difference between the proportion of the labour force which would have been occupied on the land in 1911 had agriculture maintained its mid-nineteenth-century importance, and the proportion it actually employed, is equivalent to the accumulated expansion of employment in the commerce, metal, mining, railway, car, cycle, and electrical categories. It seems unlikely that there could have been many parts of rural Britain where agriculture's diminishing labour requirements failed to exercise a considerably greater influence on demand for labour than either reduced employment opportunities for craftsmen or the decay of rural industry.

More specifically, Table 4–1 helps to explain certain of the wage features in the London and Home Counties region which were described earlier. The great diversity between earnings in London and those in rural areas near the capital is easier to understand given the dominance of agriculture in those sectors where demand for labour was falling. The region as a whole was affected less than most regions by agricultural contraction, but those parts of it more than fifteen miles from Westminster probably suffered more than Britain as a whole. Further, for most of the period the rural areas experienced very little compensation from the region's commercial and industrial expansion. In short, the low-wage parts of this region were characterized by an unfavourable employment pattern while the higher-wage parts were characterized by a pattern which compared favourably with the national average and was far more conducive to high earnings.

London's share of commercial and industrial expansion helps to explain how the capital maintained its position as the highest-wage centre in Britain throughout the period despite its small stake in the staple industries whose expansion occupies the centre-stage in most accounts of nineteenth-century economic history. The figures suggest that London's disadvantage in this respect was most marked in the century after 1760 and was nearing its end by 1870.[1] In those years wages in areas where the staple industries were expanding rose rapidly; they rose faster than average and faster than London wages.[2] In the second half of the nineteenth century, however, expansion in the manufacturing sector decelerated; Marshall noted in 1890 that those set free from agriculture were no longer going to manufacturing and that the manufacturing proportion of the population had not increased between 1851 and

1. This point is most apparent in comparisons between employment in Region 1 and employment in Lancashire, Cheshire, and the West Riding (Region 8).
2. In 1750 London paid clearly the highest wages in Britain—in the third quarter of the nineteenth century there was little margin between London and the best-paid parts of industrial Britain. See above, pp. 7, 103–4.

1881.[1] Britain was entering the mature phase of industrialization; as she did so trade, transport, and other service industries
became the most buoyant sectors and London benefited increasingly from providing the rest of Britain, and the rest of
the world, with professional, commercial, and administrative
services.[2] Its commercial dominance is suggested in Table 4–1;
by 1911 the importance of commercial employment in Region
One as a whole was about twice the national average and five
times as great as it was in 1851. And London's share of commercial expansion was probably paralleled by an impressive
share of similar expansion in printing, retailing, food manufacture, and the other service trades and light consumer
industries which depended heavily upon the home market and
made up the more palatable parts of what Charles Wilson has
called 'the curate's egg economy'.[3] Table 4–1 gives little indication of London's share in these trades (other than in commerce
and the car, cycle, and electrical trades) but London had
always been more dependent on the home market than other
industrial areas, not least upon its own numerous and well-
paid inhabitants,[4] and its trades were better placed than most
to benefit from rising real incomes at home.[5] In short, by 1880
demand for labour in London was as buoyant as it was almost
anywhere in Britain and it seems likely that this improvement
in its position, relative to other industrial areas, slowed the

1. A. Marshall, *Principles of Economics* (1890), i. 337.
2. For a general account of these changes see P. Deane and W. A. Cole,
   *British Economic Growth, 1688–1959* (Cambridge, 1962), Ch. IV.
3. C. Wilson, 'Economy and Society in Late Victorian Britain', *Ec.H.R.*, 2nd
   Ser., xviii (1965), 198.
4. See E. A. Wrigley, 'London's Importance 1650–1750', *Past and Present*,
   xxxvii (July, 1967), 60.
5. It is interesting, too, to note the region's above-average share of employment in the car, cycle, and electrical trades in 1911, another sign that
   although London had played a minor part in the initial stages of the first
   industrial revolution it was likely to participate fully in the second. In
   these trades, which were selected to represent the 'new' industries, the
   concentration of employment in the London and Home Counties region
   was 40 per cent above the national average. The 1921 returns show that by
   then 37·4 per cent of all electrical engineering workers in England and
   Wales were employed in London. P. G. Hall, *The Industries of London
   since 1861*, p. 148. On London's extraordinary prosperity during the
   Edwardian boom see A. J. Taylor in S. Nowell-Smith, (ed.) *Edwardian
   England 1901–14* (1964), pp. 132–3.

relative decline of London wages and allowed the capital to remain the highest-wage centre in Britain until the end of our period. Too much concern for the basic industries leads to a failure to appreciate the extent to which London was regaining its traditional pre-eminence in the same way that it has led to over-gloomy impressions of the state of British industry and enterprise.

By 1890 the contrast between buoyant demand for labour in London and the far less happy position in the rural parts of Region One was beginning to diminish. One of the service trades which grew rapidly at this time was the provision of holidays and excursions and this development helped to distribute London's wealth along the Kent and Essex coasts.[1] Bricklayers' wages in Margate were only 1d. per hour below London rates in 1890 and 2d. above rates in Halstead which was nearer London but further removed from its influence.[2] Between 1901 and 1911 the long decline in farm employment was temporarily halted[3] and there were signs, too, that parts of the Home Counties were beginning to enjoy a share of industrial expansion. The main developments came after the war, but the first stages of a modification of the predominantly low-wage character of the rural south had begun by 1900.[4] In this respect

1. Charles Booth noted 'a very remarkable increase in the population of sea side resorts all round the coast' in the 1881 Census, 'Occupations of the People of the United Kingdom 1801–81', *J.R.S.S.*, xlix (1886), 332.
2. Source W above, p. 66; Table 1–5.
3. This relief was shared by other areas but has never been satisfactorily explained. In Britain as a whole farm employment actually increased slightly between 1901 and 1911. The increase probably owed something to a change in Britain's terms of trade. It was also, in part, a consequence of the Boer War; according to Lord Eversley some 20,000 should be added to the 1901 census figures for England and Wales to offset the effect of the war. But this adjustment, although it may account for most of the increase in employment, leaves much to be explained. Lord Eversley, 'The Decline in Number of Agricultural Labourers in Great Britain', *J.R.S.S.*, lxx (1907), 272.
4. Wage rates illustrate the decline and recovery of the rural south as clearly as most indices.
   *Agricultural Labourers' Wage*

   |            | 1767–70  | 1851     | 1914      | 1950            |
   |------------|----------|----------|-----------|-----------------|
   | Essex      | 7s. 9d.  | 8s       | 14s. 8d.  | 94s. (minimum)  |
   | Lancashire | 6s. 6d.  | 13s. 6d. | 20s. 5d.  | 94s. (minimum)  |

   *Sources:* A. L. Bowley, *Wages in the United Kingdon*, endtable; *idem, Prices and Wages in the U.K. 1914–20*, pp. 175–6; *Time Rates of Wages and Hours* (1950), H.M.S.O., p. 1.

Chelmsford, which like many southern towns was hardly affected by the 'industrial revolution', was fairly typical. In 1898 the Marconi Company established its first factory in a disused Chelmsford silk mill and, together with Crompton's (another electrical company) and Hoffman's (ballbearings), gave the town a sure stake in twentieth-century developments.[1]

Tables 4–1 and the occupational census threw some light on another feature which was noted in Chapter One—a substantial sector of 'less well-paid' workers in the capital, particularly in the East End.[2] Many of those whose plight was noted by Mayhew depended upon the 'silk, straw, gloves, hats, and stockings' group of occupations and their distress was doubtless due in part to a decline in demand for their services. There were some 25,000 silkworkers in Region One in 1851, 21,000 in London; by 1911 free trade and competition from within the country had reduced their number to 3,000; half of these were in Essex and the bulk of them employed in one firm. The makers of hats and footwear were similarly affected.[3] In the clothing trade, which was probably the largest single employer in the East End, the long-term trend was a slow rise in absolute numbers, an increase of about 20 per cent between 1861 and 1921, but a slow decline in relative importance.[4] In each of these cases employment trends, like wages, were noticeably less favourable than the over-all pattern in the capital. One of the causes of reduced demand for labour in these trades was competition from factories elsewhere in Britain—to this extent the 'depressed' sector of the London labour force may be considered to have been still paying the price for London's failure to share in the first 'industrial revolution'.[5]

1. M. R. H. Innes, 'Chelmsford: The Evolution of a County Town', M.A. thesis, University of London (1951), pp. 273, 423–4, 429. See also below, pp. 140–1, 146.
2. On wages in these trades see above, pp. 11–14, 109–11, and below, pp. 315–18.
3. In the region as a whole there were 61,000 making hats, bonnets, caps, and footwear in 1851, only 41,000 in 1911.
4. Hall, op. cit., pp. 38–9. Between 1851 and 1921 London's population rose from 2·5 to 4·5 millions. Mitchell and Deane, op. cit., pp. 20–2.
5. This partial explanation of London's 'depressed sector' should be placed in the context of other influences which worked mainly from the supply side of the market, see above, pp. 12, 109, and below, pp. 313–14. There is a case for regarding the East End problem as due as much to low average earnings,

## II

REGION TWO (South-west—see Map 1)

Table 4–2 shows employment trends in the south-west between 1851 and 1911 and helps to explain why wages there were so far below average at the beginning of the period and remained below average despite other market forces which, presumably, worked mainly towards the erosion of differentials. When Caird toured Wiltshire in 1850 he noted that hand-threshing of barley continued; this was partly in order to provide labourers with work rather than have them go on the parish.[1] A contemporary survey of Dorset noted 'sufficient hands in the county to perform even the extra work of harvest time without importing labour . . .' and two decades later Canon Girdlestone was engaged in what amounted to a one-man campaign to erode regional wage differentials by redeploying labour according to what he called 'politico-economical principles': this consisted in reducing the supply of labour in Devon.[2] An official report published at about the same time had this to say of conditions in Wiltshire: 'the labour market has of late years been, and is now, overstocked and . . . wages in that county have consequently been low.'[3]

---

the consequence of short-time or temporary low piece-rates, as to absolutely low wages. Many of Mayhew's cases certainly fall into this category (*M.C.* 20, 23 Nov. 1849; see also below, pp. 313, 317, and above, pp. 12–13) and in so far as this was the case distress might be regarded as partly a consequence of the capricious nature of demand for labour in the East End trades. For detailed accounts of London's 'depressed trades' see Hall, op. cit., and G. Stedman Jones, op. cit.

1. J. Caird, *English Agriculture in 1850–51*, p. 84. Caird gave Wiltshire as an example of a county where farm wages were the same in 1770 as in 1850. In the same period wages in Lancashire and the West Riding had doubled (ibid., p. 513). Despite hand-threshing and similar attempts to absorb surplus labour (see e.g. Molland in *V.C.H. Wiltshire*, iv. 81–3) expenditure on poor relief in the south-west was high. County poor rate expenditure, which may be used as a rough guide to the relationship between demand. and supply of labour, is discussed below, p. 148 n. 1.

2. *M.C.* 28 Nov. 1849 and see above, pp. 15, 39–40, 45–6

3. *Report on the Employment of Women and Children (1867)*, quoted in *V.C.H. Wiltshire*, iv. 80.

These and similar remarks confirm what Table 4–2 and the occupational census show more thoroughly if less eloquently: the labour force of the southwest was deployed in a manner which resulted in wages there receiving less than average stimulus from expansionary trends in the economy and more than average restraint from sectors which failed to maintain their share of the labour force.

TABLE 4–2

*Numbers Occupied per 1,000 population:*
*Region Two (South-west)*

| | Britain | | | Region 2 | | |
|---|---|---|---|---|---|---|
| Occupation Category | 1851 | 1911 | Change | 1851 | 1911 | Change |
| 1. Metals | 21 | 33 | +12 | 11 | 16 | +5 |
| 2. Domestic Service | 48 | 45 | −3 | 49 | 58 | +9 |
| 3. Wool | 14 | 7 | −7 | 12 | 3 | −9 |
| 4. Cotton etc. | 34 | 19 | −15 | 5 | 2 | −3 |
| 5. Silk, Straw, Gloves, Hats, Stockings | 15 | 4 | −11 | 11 | 3 | −8 |
| 6. Mines and Quarries | 16 | 27 | +11 | 21 | 11 | −10 |
| 7. Shoemakers, Millers, Tailors, Saddlers, Carpenters | 32 | 20 | −12 | 35 | 24 | −11 |
| 8. Railways | 3 | 12 | +9 | 1 | 10 | +9 |
| 9. Chemicals, Pottery, Glass, Paper | 4 | 6 | +2 | 1 | 4 | +3 |
| 10. Coachbuilding, Ship-building | 2 | 4 | +2 | 2 | 3 | +1 |
| 11. 'New' Industries (Cars, Cycles, Electrical) | — | 5 | +5 | — | 2 | +2 |
| 12. Commerce | 3 | 22 | +19 | 2 | 14 | +12 |
| 13. Agriculture | 85 | 26 | −59 | 117 | 49 | −68 |

*Source:* Census of Occupations. For details of occupations included in these categories, see the appendix to this chapter.

Of the three occupational categories in Table 4–2 which expanded most rapidly in Britain as a whole—commerce, metals, and mining—the south-west in 1851 was under-represented in two. In the third, mining, the position was worse because, at a time when mining exercised a powerful upward pressure on wages over considerable parts of Britain, in the south-west its importance fell.[1] But of all the declining sectors, agriculture was by far the most important. Although the West Country was more dependent on domestic industry than most regions in 1850 the decline of the West Country woollen and lace industries in the face of competition from Yorkshire and Nottinghamshire, the contraction of Somerset glove making, the decline of sundry other workers in clothing and textiles, of bootmakers, millers, saddlers, and other craftsmen, together amounted to considerably less than the contraction of agriculture.[2] Villages were particularly affected by the decline in crafts and domestic industries since a great many displaced village craftsmen probably found similar work in local towns; but in 1911 the region as a whole had scarcely fewer carpenters, saddlers, or harness makers than 60 years earlier and, of the craft occupations analysed, only boot and shoemakers declined in large numbers while the number of tailors (perhaps surprisingly in view of the development of the ready-made garment industry) increased from 16,000 in 1851 to 22,000 in 1911.[3] In fact, the decline in craft and textile employment (Table 4–2 categories 3, 4, 5, and 7), although greater

1. The decline of West Country tin and copper mining was most rapid in the 1860s at the same time as a marked, and probably connected, worsening in the region's share of employment in the 'metals' category. Devon and Cornwall supplied over half the world's copper in the 1850s but after 1862 employment fell rapidly. W. G. Hoskins, *Devon* (1954), pp. 138–9. Expansion of coal mining in the region was quantitatively insignificant but the more rapid expansion of mining in Gloucester, together with proximity to south Wales, helps to explain the differential between miner's wages in the Somerset and Forest of Dean fields (see above, pp. 16–17).

| Coalminers (male) | *1851* | *1881* | *1911* |
|---|---|---|---|
| Somerset | 5,200 | 5,100 | 5,300 |
| Gloucestershire | 2,000 | 3,900 | 8,200 |

2. The list refers to categories 3, 4, 5, and 7 in Table 4–2.
3. The number of millers was nearly halved over the period: milling was becoming concentrated in the large ports, but there were only 5,300 millers in the south-west region in 1851. Shipbuilding, surprisingly, retained its relative importance throughout the period, probably because vessels built in the south-west were too small to be much affected by the developments that put the Clyde, Tees, and Tyne at an advantage in the construction of larger vessels. For details of the decline of rural employment in the south-west see J. Saville, *Rural Depopulation in England and Wales 1851–1951*, pp. 8–30, 206–13; Hoskins, op. cit., p. 243; A. H. Shorter, 'The Historical Geography of Manufacturing Industry in the South-west of England in the Nineteenth Century', M.A. thesis, University of Manchester (1948), pp. 23–8.

than in several other areas, was not above the national average; the more important influences in explaining low wages in the region seem to have been the dearth of expanding occupations and the decline of employment in mining and agriculture.[1] When other things are equal high wages will be found in places with a more than proportionate share of rapidly growing occupations and a dependence on labour from outside the area. Expanding sectors must offer wages sufficient to overcome labour's inertia and the cost of moving; this rate will obviously be higher than the rate necessary to retain a man once he is engaged. Employers in areas with a more than proportionate share of declining occupations, on the other hand, will feel less necessity to raise wages to maintain an adequate labour force and, because declining trades have less scope to meet increased labour costs from profits or prices, will also feel more pressure to keep wages low. Despite one or two exceptions to the general pattern, such as the railway works at Swindon, there is no doubt that the south-west was clearly in the second of these two categories.[2]

One other feature of the occupational structure in the region deserves attention. Near the end of the period there were signs of general improvement in the employment situation, a feature

1. The statement refers to the period 1851–1911. In the first half of the century the relative importance of declining employment in domestic industries was probably greater and that of declining employment in agriculture considerably less. The conclusion for the period 1851–1911 could itself be qualified in several respects; a given number of redundant tin or copper miners, for example, probably exercised a less unfavourable influence on local wage rates than the same number of redundant farm labourers because the miners were more likely to migrate.
2. The 14,000 employed in the G.W.R. works in 1905 (*V.C.H. Wiltshire*, iv. 215) were only about two-thirds of the number by which farm employment in 1911 in Wiltshire alone fell short of the number employed in 1851. It should be noted that one of the few other sectors where employment in the south-west compared not unfavourably with the national average, domestic service (see Table 4–2), has little significance. Domestic service employed mainly females and its expansion was unlikely to have much effect on the general wage level in the region; indeed, expansion may have represented more an increase in supply than in demand, a reflection of poverty and of declining employment opportunities for women in agriculture and domestic industry (see above, pp. 113, 121). The proportion of domestic servants in Ireland increased rapidly after 1841; 'The only explanation that suggests itself is that servants are more numerous where poverty makes service cheap' (C. Booth, 'Occupations of the People of the United Kingdom, 1801–81', p. 343).

the south-west shared with the rural parts of Region One (London and Home Counties),[1] and, as we shall see, with the rural south-east. A large part of this improvement came from the easing in the rate of agricultural contraction[2] but this was part of a broader influence which affected a wide range of employment in the rural south. Several occupations which had been in decline throughout the second half of the nineteenth century were by 1900 holding their own; the Devon lace industry, for example, after a minor mid-century revival, said to be due to Queen Victoria's patronage and the stimulating influence of the Great Exhibition,[3] returned a diminished number at each census until 1891. The south-western woollen industry is another example; it employed some 27,000 in 1851 and only 8,000 by 1901, but in the following decade the labour force fell by fewer than 500 persons.[4] The most likely explanation of this phenomenon is some combination of general economic buoyancy after 1896 which relieved pressure on high-cost areas, agricultural recovery, the revivifying effect of electric power upon small concerns far from the coalfields, and the fact that many survivors of the long decline in southern industry enjoyed advantages arising from market imperfections or more than usually enterprising management.[5]

# III

REGION THREE (Rural south-east—see Map 1)

It was shown in Chapter One that wages in Region Three were below average; in the first part of the period they were among the lowest in England and after 1880 they were among the lowest in Britain. It was to be expected that in the century

1. See above, pp. 135–6.
2. See above, p. 135.
3. Hoskins, op. cit., p. 141.
4. The occupational census shows similar patterns among silk makers, millers, shipbuilders, paper makers, and glovers.
5. See, among others, Phelps Brown, *Industrial Relations*, pp. 9–11; A. K. Cairncross, *Home and Foreign Investment 1870–1913* (Cambridge, 1953), pp. 75–7.

after 1750 wage rates in the north of England would overhaul those in the south and East Anglia, and clearly the pattern of demand for labour in that period is a large part of the explanation. The maintenance of this differential throughout the second half of the nineteenth century and up to the First World War, and the contrast between this region and areas like north Wales, the south-west, and the upland parts of Scotland, where wages advanced more rapidly, is more remarkable. To what extent was the situation after 1850 a consequence of employment trends?

Table 4–3 shows that the more expansive trends in the national labour market were not much in evidence in the rural south-east. It contains little coal and its iron ore was still hardly disturbed in 1914. Commercial employment expanded rapidly, but less rapidly than in the country as a whole.[1] In the range of occupations grouped together as 'workers in metals'[2] the pattern was similar: expansion, but to a point in 1911 where they still accounted for a far smaller proportion of the labour force than in Britain as a whole. Employment in the metal trades in 1911 was only about two-thirds as important as it had been in the national labour force in 1851. In 1871 'workers in metal' were no more numerous in Region Three than workers whose main raw material was straw, and the latter group outnumbered those in the 'commerce' category by four to one.[3] Of the occupational groups analysed only one expanded faster than average—domestic service. Unfortunately, as was shown earlier, expansion here is by no means a sure indicator of prosperity and a buoyant demand for labour.[4] In 1851 this group accounted for about 46 jobs per 1,000 population, a figure which itself can tell us a great deal about employment in the region;

1. In this respect the rural south-east was affected to about the same extent as the south-west, south Wales, and northern Scotland and rather more than rural Wales and Cumberland and Westmorland.
2. Workers in iron and steel mills, engine and machine workers, engineers, fitters, tool makers, and others. For details of occupational categories used in Table 4–3 see the appendix to this chapter.
3. In 1911 the 'metals' and 'commerce' categories accounted for a rather smaller share of employment in Region Three than they did in northern Scotland.
4. See above, p. 140 n. 2.

## TABLE 4-3
### Numbers occupied per 1,000 population:
### Region Three (Rural south-east)

| Occupation category | Britain | | | Region 3 | | |
|---|---|---|---|---|---|---|
| | 1851 | 1911 | Change | 1851 | 1911 | Change |
| 1. Metals | 21 | 33 | +12 | 8 | 14 | +6 |
| 2. Domestic Service | 48 | 45 | −3 | 46 | 65 | +19 |
| 3. Wool | 14 | 7 | −7 | 1 | — | −1 |
| 4. Cotton etc. | 34 | 19 | −15 | 11 | — | −11 |
| 5. Silk, Straw, Gloves, Hats, Stockings | 15 | 4 | −11 | 17 | 4 | −13 |
| 6. Mines and Quarries | 16 | 27 | +11 | — | 1 | +1 |
| 7. Shoemakers, Millers, Tailors, Saddlers, Carpenters | 32 | 20 | −12 | 36 | 29 | −7 |
| 8. Railways | 3 | 12 | +9 | 3 | 11 | +8 |
| 9. Chemicals, Pottery, Glass, Paper | 4 | 6 | +2 | 1 | 2 | +1 |
| 10. Coachbuilding, Shipbuilding | 2 | 4 | +2 | 2 | 4 | +2 |
| 11. 'New' Industries (Cars, Cycles, Electrical) | — | 5 | +5 | — | 3 | +3 |
| 12. Commerce | 3 | 22 | +19 | 1 | 13 | +12 |
| 13. Agriculture | 85 | 26 | −59 | 149 | 57 | −92 |

*Source:* Census of Occupations. For details of occupations included in these categories, see the appendix to this chapter.

all those working in the 'metal' trades, in commerce, on the railways, building boats and coaches, and making chemicals, glass, paper, and pottery (categories 1, 8, 9, 10, 12 in Table 4-3) amounted to only one third the number of domestic servants. Add to this the fact that for each domestic servant there were three workers in agriculture and we have a salutary reminder of the shortcomings of generalized accounts of industrialization in Britain which focus attention on the areas of transition. No less interesting, particularly in the context of seeking explanations for the continuation of low wages in the region, is the fact that in 1911, after a further sixty years of industrialization, those workers in Categories 1, 8, 9, 10, 12—all occupations associated with a post-industrial economy—still amounted to only two-thirds the number in domestic service. Here was an area which was pre-industrial in 1760, pre-industrial in 1850, and in most respects still pre-industrial in 1911.

To this rather dismal account must be added the existence of several declining industries. The number of workers in the group of occupations that has been collected under Category 5 (Table 4–3) fell by the equivalent of 13 workers per 1,000 population between 1851 and 1911, in absolute terms a loss of 30,000 jobs.[1] Region Three was probably more affected than any other by decline in this group;[2] losses were greatest among the silk and straw workers, especially the latter. Some indication of the importance of straw plaiting and hat manufacture in the region has already been given. In 1851 workers in straw outnumbered those engaged in building and running railways by 4 to 1.[3] The eventual decline of the straw trade and its essentially pre-industrial nature have caused its economic history to be almost overlooked. Its history, and influence on the labour market, were paralleled in a host of similar trades— in lace and silk manufacture, in making gloves, hats, umbrellas, pins, needles, buttons, nets, and similar items. Southern England had more than its share of these trades but few of the factories which were to replace them and for this reason the straw industry merits closer study. It was already well established in the south-east at the end of the seventeenth century, especially in Bedfordshire, a county noted for the excellence of its straw.[4] It employed mainly women and children[5] and the census returns show employment growing until 1871. Earnings fluctuated a great deal; Freeman generalizes in terms of a level about half of that paid to farm labourers but this obscures a

1. This decline was concentrated in the 30 years after 1880.
2. The average for Britain is very much affected by the decline of these trades in Regions Six and Eight (the Midlands, Lancashire, Cheshire, and the West Riding). But, unlike Region Three, these areas had ample compensation in the expansion of other employment sectors.
3. In England and Wales as a whole the two groups employed similar numbers—here is a genuine contender for that overworked label 'neglected'.
4. J. G. Dony, *A History of the Straw Hat Industry* (Luton, 1942), Ch. 2; C. Freeman, *Luton and the Hat Industry* (Luton, 1953), p. 9.
5. A fact which goes a long way to explain the position of Bedfordshire, Buckinghamshire, and Hertfordshire near the top of the tables showing the proportion of employed women and children in 1851 (above, pp. 127–8) and the opinion of a mid-century investigator that Bedfordshire and Hertfordshire were the most ignorant counties in England (*M.C.* 5 Apr. 1850).

long-term decline throughout the century.[1] Work was done at home and, as in many of London's East End trades, it tended to be irregular and very susceptible to changes in fashion: 'an increase of only two inches in the size of the ridiculously small bonnets worn in the middle of the century would have required twice as much plait.' [2] After 1870 the villain of the piece, foreign competition in the shape of cheap Chinese plait, began to make serious inroads; in twenty years Region Three lost 25,000 workers. This affected wages: in the early nineteenth century wages were not far short of what a man could earn on the land; in 1850 they were still high enough to afford a substantial supplement to family incomes; but by 1893, it was said, plaiters 'could not earn twopence if they worked at it all day'.[3] After 1890 the oriental onslaught was reinforced by the arrival of Japanese plait, and by 1901 most of the industry's much reduced labour force was in the factories and workshops of Luton. This sort of pattern, which was repeated in other domestic industries, had an obvious effect on wage rates in the region.[4]

In one case, the manufacture of boots and shoes, Region Three benefited from this pattern; a large part of the transformed industry was located in Northamptonshire and Norfolk.[5]

1. Freeman, op. cit., p. 13.
2. Dony, op. cit., p. 68.
3. Dony, op. cit., p. 92; Pinchbeck, op. cit., pp. 219–21; M.C. 5 Apr. 1850.
4. There were nearly 62,000 lace makers in England and Wales in 1851, half of these in Region 3; by 1911 the number in England and Wales had fallen by about a third, the number in Region 3 by over 90 per cent to less than 2,000. Silk manufacture employed 11,000 in Region 3 in 1851 (almost half of this total were in Norfolk) but only 2,000 by 1911. For an account of the transfer of the Long Crendon (Bucks.) needle trade to the Redditch area see, G. C. Allen, *Birmingham and the Black Country*, pp. 81–2.
5. In 1851 each village had its cobbler and production was mainly for the local market although there was already some concentration in Northants. By 1881 the proportion of footwear workers in Northants was 10 times the average of England and Wales and by 1911 it was 20 times the average. In Norfolk the density was about 3½ times the average in England and Wales. Elsewhere, other than in Staffordshire, Gloucestershire, Somerset, and Leicestershire, production had declined to near insignificance. Proportions calculated from the occupational census, various figures in C. Day, 'The Distribution of Industrial Occupations in England, 1841–61', *Trans. Connecticut Academy of Arts and Sciences*, xxviii (1927), and P. R. Mounfield, 'The Location of Footwear Manufacture in England and Wales', Ph.D. thesis, University of Nottingham (1962).

In addition, there are slight but definite signs of an over-all improvement in the area's fortunes after 1900 similar to that noted in the Home Counties and the south-west.[1] But neither the footwear industry nor the beginning of general revival had more than a limited and local effect on wage differentials before the First World War and there were few other employment trends likely to hasten, rather than retard, erosion of the wage differential between Region Three and more fortunate areas.[2] The footwear case illustrates this point. In 1910 workers in Northampton's boot and shoe factories were paid as much as those in London, Leeds, or Manchester.[3] The wages of North-ampton building workers might be taken to indicate some sign of a tighter labour market there than elsewhere in the region but, relative to wages in the same trade elsewhere, they were less well paid than the Northampton footwear workers.[4] Farm wages in the county as a whole, one stage further from North-ampton's factories, seem to have been unaffected by their development.[5] The occupational statistics suggest that the limited influence of developments in the footwear trade is not surprising because between 1881 and 1911 the number it employed in Northamptonshire barely changed. Output rose

1. See above, pp. 135–6, 140–1. In Region 3 there was a loss of some 184,000 jobs on the land between 1851 and 1901 but a gain of 14,000 between 1901 and 1911.

2. There were some; the fishing industry, for example, which provided additional employment in Norfolk and Suffolk. But there were fewer than 8,000 fishermen in the region in 1881 and after 1891 expansion ceased. Elsewhere on the coast the developing seaside holiday industry provided some stimulus to the labour market.

3. *Boot and Shoe Operatives' Minimum Weekly Rate of Wages, 1910*

|  | Clickers | Pressmen |
|---|---|---|
| Leeds | 30s. | 26s.–28s. |
| London | 30s. | 27s. |
| Manchester | 26s. | 26s. |
| Northampton | 30s. | 26s.–28s. |

Source: *Standard Time Rates of Wages in the U.K., 1910*, P.P. 1910, LXXXIV, p. 104.

4. In 1906 rates compared well with most towns in Region 3 but were 25 per cent below London rates and between 10 and 20 per cent below rates in Manchester and Leeds. Sources U, W, and X in Table 1–5.

5. *Farm Labourers' Average*

| Weekly Earnings | 1867–70 | 1898 | 1907 |
|---|---|---|---|
| Northamptonshire | 15s. 3d. | 16s. 8d. | 16s. 9d. |
| Region Three | 14s. 4½d. | 15s. 9d. | 16s. 5d. |
| Britain | 14s. 3½d. | 17s. 2½d. | 18s. 2½d. |

Source: Tables 1–3, 1–4.

much faster than employment: high wages within the factories should be regarded as due more to higher productivity than increased demand for labour and, because so few workers were affected, the rate of wages in the factories was unlikely to have had much influence on other wage rates in the area. In the same period, between 1881 and 1911, Northamptonshire lost 3,000 jobs in the lace industry and 7,000 in agriculture. What was true of Northamptonshire was true in the region—any relief afforded by those few parts of the regional economy where employment trends were favourable was quite insufficient to offset the decline of agriculture and domestic industries. Between 1851 and 1911 expansion in all the occupations included under the headings 'metals', commerce, boot and shoe manufacture, railways, cars, cycles, and electricity together increased demand for labour by approximately 160,000 jobs. Against this, demand for workers in straw, silk, and lace fell by 56,000 and the agricultural labour force by about 170,000. Two points are clear from these figures. First, that demand for labour in the sectors where we would expect growth to occur was expanding more slowly than the rate of decline in agriculture and domestic industry. Second, that in this region where domestic industry was probably of greater importance than anywhere else in Britain its decline, although significant, was less important than the reduction of the farm labour force— a point which is underlined by the far higher proportion of males in the latter category.

The over-all impression is that the rural south-east was an economic backwater. The pre-industrial world that was lost in the middle of the nineteenth century was lost only in the more dynamic parts of Britain. Focus upon these, and upon economic aggregates, hides the essential continuity which characterized large parts of Britain through the 'industrial revolution' and into the twentieth century. Or, if the 'industrial revolution' is interpreted in a broader sense as involving a revolution not only in industry but in each part of the economy, the south-east, East Anglia,[1] and the south-west are best understood as

1. On the situation in East Anglia before 1850 see D. C. Coleman, 'Growth and Decay during the Industrial Revolution: The Case of East Anglia', *Scandinavian Economic History Review*, x (1962).

parts of the economy by-passed by the more positive aspects of change but showing all too clearly evidence of the demographic revolution, of the influence of factories upon domestic industry, and of transport improvements which brought cheap overseas food to compete with the produce of local labour. The immediate consequence of all this was over-population, high poor rates, and low wages.[1]

There is a final point on the relationship between wages and demand for labour in this region. In an indirect way the pattern of demand helps to explain the relative decline in wage rates compared with those in rural areas like the south-west (Region Two) where the general level of demand for labour was not noticeably more buoyant than in Region Three. Demand for labour is a derived demand and agriculture in Region Three was particularly affected by overseas competition for the British grain market. The consequences of this competition upon prices and farm incomes in different parts of Britain in the second half of the century have been adequately recorded; it would

---

1. The *Morning Chronicle* correspondent noted the 'enormous poor rate' of mid-century Norwich; in 1848 almost a quarter of the city was on relief (*M.C.* 12, 15 Dec. 1849). Caird showed poor relief expenditure per head of population in various counties; Norfolk rates were over twice rates in Lancashire and Durham (Caird, op. cit., pp. 514–15). The general pattern of high rates in the rural south and low rates in the mining and manufacturing counties continued until the First World War—returns are available for most years, see e.g. *Statement of the Amount Expended for In-maintenance and Out-door Relief in England and Wales*, P.P. 1887, LXX. Poor rates may be regarded as a rough and ready guide to the relationship between demand and supply of labour in each county although it would be unwise to attach much weight to individual figures without careful investigation because part of the distress relieved by the rates had only tenuous connections with the state of the labour market; moreover poor rates varied not only according to need but also according to the amount of supplementary relief available from private charity and from self-help arrangements such as friendly societies. They also varied according to the generosity of the local authorities. Leeds and Winchester, for example, in the middle of the century were noted as generous authorities and, in addition to raising the amount paid to relieve local distress, a reputation for open-handedness attracted tramps. London, which provided charity hospitals and other institutions on a scale not practicable elsewhere, had such a reputation—and high poor rates. The London 'Houses of Refuge' were a great attraction to the nation's unemployed and unemployable; professional vagrants came to town 'as regularly as noblemen every winter' (*M.C.* 11, 25 Jan. 1850; see also H. L. Smith in C. Booth, *Life and Labour*, 1st Ser., iii. 75).

be surprising if wages were not also affected and the wage pattern described in Chapter One suggests they were. Similarly, the relative decline of wages in Norfolk and Suffolk within Region Three was probably in part a consequence of their particularly heavy dependence upon grain.[1]

# IV

REGION FOUR (South Wales—see Map 1)

Table 4–4 shows a very different employment pattern from that just examined; and the contrast between the course of wages in Regions Three and Four was equally great. In 1851 wages in south Wales were moderately low: by 1911 they were distinctly above average—the employment pattern shown in Table 4–4 is broadly compatible with this long-term improvement.

Employment trends in south Wales were dominated by the expansion of mining.[2] In 1851 there were more men working on the land than taking coal from beneath it, a decade later the position was reversed, and by 1911 mining employed seven times the number in agriculture. Over the period as a whole the mines provided eight additional jobs for each one lost in agriculture.[3] There were, in addition, considerable numbers

---

1. On these various points see above p. 19; C. S. Orwin and B. I. Felton, 'A Century of Wages and Earnings in Agriculture', p. 246; and the graphs facing p. 48 in *Wages and Earnings of Agricultural Labourers*, P.P. 1900, LXXXII. In arable areas the connection between grain prices and wages may have been further reinforced by customary influences upon wages—at one time it was believed that a day's wage was worth a peck of wheat and that the labourer should always get the same sized loaf. In parts of Suffolk labourers were still paid on the basis of a bushel of wheat plus 2s. 6d. a week in the 1830s. F. Clifford, 'The Labour Bill in Farming', *J.R.Ag.S.*, 2nd Ser. xi (1875), 73; Wilson Fox, op. cit., pp. 280–2.

2. This was especially true after 1880.

3. Table 4–4 which shows the number occupied as a proportion of population fails to bring out the contrast in absolute numbers employed. Rising population meant that agriculture would have needed to employ an additional 100,000 men by 1911 in order to retain its 1851 share of the labour force—in fact it employed 21,000 fewer in 1911 than in 1851.

employed in the various 'metal' trades although after 1871 employment in this sector rose less rapidly than elsewhere.[1] Perhaps a greater advantage to the region, although a negative one, was that in 1850 craft and cottage occupations of a type that elsewhere declined in the second half of the century were not important.

TABLE 4–4

*Numbers Occupied per 1,000 Population:*
*Region Four (South Wales)*

| Occupation category | Britain | | | Region 4 | | |
|---|---|---|---|---|---|---|
| | 1851 | 1911 | Change | 1851 | 1911 | Change |
| 1. Metals | 21 | 33 | +12 | 44 | 39 | −5 |
| 2. Domestic Service | 48 | 45 | −3 | 35 | 31 | −4 |
| 3. Wool | 14 | 7 | −7 | 3 | 1 | −2 |
| 4. Cotton etc. | 34 | 19 | −15 | — | — | — |
| 5. Silk, Straw, Gloves, Hats, Stockings | 15 | 4 | −11 | 2 | — | −2 |
| 6. Mines and Quarries | 16 | 27 | +11 | 69 | 119 | +50 |
| 7. Shoemakers, Millers, Tailors, Saddlers, Carpenters | 32 | 20 | −12 | 29 | 12 | −17 |
| 8. Railways | 3 | 12 | +9 | 3 | 15 | +12 |
| 9. Chemicals, Pottery, Glass, Paper | 4 | 6 | +2 | 2 | 1 | −1 |
| 10. Coachbuilding, Ship-building | 2 | 4 | +2 | 2 | 3 | +1 |
| 11. 'New' Industries (Cars, Cycles, Electrical) | — | 5 | +5 | — | 2 | +2 |
| 12. Commerce | 3 | 22 | +19 | 2 | 14 | +12 |
| 13. Agriculture | 85 | 26 | −59 | 86 | 17 | −69 |

*Source:* Census of Occupations. For details of occupations included in these categories, see the appendix to this chapter.

1. After 1873 the basic metal industries expanded less fast than the metal manufacturing trades, and other areas were expanding faster than south Wales even in the basic sector (Mitchell and Deane, op. cit., pp. 132–3). South Wales manufacturers supplied a large part of the domestic market for iron railway lines but they were slow to change to the production of steel lines. A little later, in 1891, the McKinley tariff dealt a crushing blow to the tinplate trade; before the tariff the United States took three-fifths of British output. G. R. Hawke, *Railways and Economic Growth in England and Wales, 1840–70* (Oxford, 1970), pp. 234–5; A. J. Taylor, in S. Nowell-Smith (ed.) *Edwardian England 1901–14*, p. 115. For a detailed account of events in the tinplate industry see, W. E. Minchinton, *The British Tinplate Industry* (Oxford, 1957), Ch. 2.

Until 1850 most coal mined in south Wales was consumed locally, either in domestic hearths or in the ironworks; these demands made slight inroads on the region's reserves. But in the second half of the century expansion occurred at a faster rate than in any other major field. Growth was seldom seriously interrupted; the label 'Great Depression' is less easily attached to south Wales than any other region.[1] This expansion gave rise to a greater demand for labour than could be met locally and the need to attract men from elsewhere had an obvious influence on wages.[2] Miners' wages were affected most but expansion was more than sufficient to influence the general level of wages throughout the mining districts. The stimulus was also felt in areas like west Pembrokeshire where local employment trends were considerably less favourable.[3] Towards the end of the 1880s the productivity of labour in the mines began to fall, but this had no adverse influence upon wages because the fall in physical output was offset by higher coal prices and the value of output per man continued to rise until

1. In 1854 south Wales accounted for 13 per cent of all coal mined; by 1911 it accounted for 18 per cent of a much enlarged total. The leading sectors of the regional economy were heavily dependent upon overseas demand and their fortunes were often contrary to those of trades more dependent on the home market. B. Thomas (ed.), *The Welsh Economy* (Cardiff, 1962), pp. 15–16; Mitchell and Deane, op. cit., pp. 115–16.

2. On migration trends see below Ch. 7. There were other signs of buoyant demand for labour; owners found difficulty in recruiting sufficient men to operate a double shift and the introduction of the 'discharge note' was partly a consequence of labour scarcity and the need to retain existing employees. H. S. Jevons, *The British Coal Trade*, pp. 758–9; J. H. Morris and L. J. Williams, 'The Discharge Note in the South Wales Coal Industry, 1841–1898', *Ec.H.R.*, 2nd Ser., x (1957), 286. In the early seventies expansion was so hectic that 'inexperienced plough-boys and shoe-makers' were being put straight on to cutting coal. The Amalgamated Association of Mineworkers declined to support plans for a regular apprenticeship scheme on the grounds that this was a problem peculiar to south Wales (J. H. Morris and L. J. Williams, *The South Wales Coal Industry*, p. 236).

3. The close association between expansion and wage rates can also be seen within the coalfield; wages were lowest in the established mining areas near the ironworks and highest in areas most recently developed: ' . . for the labour we had to get people from all parts; we took any who would come . . and we were of course obliged to pay a very high rate of wages in order to induce them to live in an uncivilized part of the country.' Evidence to *R.C. on Trade Unions 1867–8* quoted in Morris and Williams, *The South Wales Coal Industry*, p. 221; see also. A. Dalziel, *The Colliers' Strike in South Wales*, p. 11.

the early twentieth century.[1] In fact, here and on the other coalfields the combination of falling physical productivity and rising and price-inelastic demand meant that the expansion of coal output had a far greater effect upon demand for labour and wages than increases in output of similar proportion in other industries.[2]

One other feature shown by the occupational statistics is worth mentioning: the small extent to which south Wales depended on industries other than coal mining and the basic metal trades.[3] It supplied the world with rails but produced few locomotives; no chemical industry developed to use the local fuel; few were employed in making glass, paper, pottery, cars, cycles, or electrical goods, and commercial employment was no more important in 1911 than it was in the south-west or northern Scotland (Regions Two and Thirteen). At that time, however, there were few signs that south Wales was soon to pay dearly for this concentration; wages were well above average and their relative position was compatible with existing employment trends and those of the previous sixty years. In fact, given the enormous stimulus from mining expansion perhaps the more remarkable thing is that wages in the region failed to rise above average earlier and more decisively. The most likely reason for this is the proximity of low-wage counties (in Regions Two, Three, and Five) where employment trends were far less favourable. While demand for labour was greater than could be met in the immediate area it was not overwhelming when measured against manpower reserves in the wider vicinity; in these areas wages were so low that for most of the period employers in south Wales could

1. W. Ashworth, 'Changes in the Industrial Structure, 1870–1914', *Yks. Bull.*, xvii (1965), 67. This point is of special importance because labour accounted for well over half the cost of coal output; this relationship necessitated a close link between the price of coal and wages and also helps to explain the high rate of expansion of employment in south Wales because south Wales coal commanded the highest price of all (Jevons, op. cit., p. 121). The close relationship between wages and prices was also the main cause of greater wage fluctuations in the export coalfields of which south Wales was the most important (Rowe, *Wages in the Coal Industry*, pp. 47, 119–20).
2. On this point see above, pp. 146–7, and below, pp. 202.
3. In each of the other industries for which statistics have been collected south Wales employed fewer in 1911 than the national average.

offer substantial inducements and still pay less than rates in London and the industrial north.[1]

# V

REGION FIVE (Rural Wales and Herefordshire—see Map 1)

Table 4–5 shows that the pattern of employment in north and central Wales and Herefordshire had more in common with the pattern in southern England than that in the coalfield area of south Wales. Most of the occupations which were expanding and exerting upward pressure on wages were seriously under-represented. In 1851 the proportion employed in the 'metal' trades was less than two-thirds of the British average and in 1911, by which time these trades had increased their share of the British labour force by half, their relative importance in Region Five had scarcely altered. The region was equally backward in commerce and the various manufacturing industries included under categories 9 and 11 in Table 4–5; there was only one other region where employment in the metal trades occupied a smaller proportion of the labour force in 1911 and none had a smaller proportion in commercial employment.

Of those occupations analysed the only expanding sector which brought more than average advantage to rural Wales was mining and quarrying.[2] There was one other mitigating

1. This suggested explanation conflicts with that advanced by Jevons. He was presumably unaware of relative wages in the second half of the nineteenth century and, noting the high level of mine wages in 1915, suggested that part of the explanation was that 'the geographical position of South Wales makes it more isolated from large centres of population than any of the English coalfields' (Jevons, op. cit., p. 121). A further reason why wages failed to advance more rapidly is suggested below, p. 331 n. 3

2. Domestic service cannot be considered in this category (see above, p. 140 n. 2). Quarrying accounted for an unusually large share of the mining and quarrying employment category in Region 5. After 1900 demand for quarrymen fell away with the end of the building boom and the introduction of tiles and foreign slate into markets once served by north Wales. But these developments were offset by increasing demand for coalminers in Flint and Denbighshire (V. C. Davies, 'Some Geographical Aspects of the Depopulation of Rural Wales since 1841', Ph.D. thesis, University of London (1955), p. 116).

## Table 4–5
### Numbers Occupied per 1,000 Population:
### Region Five (Rural Wales and Herefordshire)

| Occupation category | Britain | | | Region 5 | | |
|---|---|---|---|---|---|---|
| | 1851 | 1911 | Change | 1851 | 1911 | Change |
| 1. Metals | 21 | 33 | +12 | 12 | 13 | +1 |
| 2. Domestic Service | 48 | 45 | −3 | 38 | 57 | +19 |
| 3. Wool | 14 | 7 | −7 | 10 | 1 | −9 |
| 4. Cotton etc. | 34 | 19 | −15 | — | — | — |
| 5. Silk, Straw, Gloves, Hats, Stockings | 15 | 4 | −11 | 3 | — | −3 |
| 6. Mines and Quarries | 16 | 27 | +11 | 34 | 47 | +13 |
| 7. Shoemakers, Millers, Tailors, Saddlers, Carpenters | 32 | 20 | −12 | 31 | 16 | −15 |
| 8. Railways | 3 | 12 | +9 | 1 | 10 | +9 |
| 9. Chemicals, Pottery, Glass, Paper | 4 | 6 | +2 | — | 1 | +1 |
| 10. Coachbuilding, Ship-building | 2 | 4 | +2 | 1 | 1 | — |
| 11. 'New' Industries (Cars, Cycles, Electrical) | — | 5 | +5 | — | 1 | +1 |
| 12. Commerce | 3 | 22 | +19 | 1 | 9 | +8 |
| 13. Agriculture | 85 | 26 | −59 | 159 | 83 | −76 |

*Source:* Census of Occupations. For details of occupations included in these categories, see the appendix to this chapter.

feature: like south Wales the region was fortunate in not being burdened at the start of the period by large numbers in decaying craft and cottage trades.[1] But the over-all position is quite clear from Table 4–5; Region Five was one of those unfortunate areas which benefited only marginally from nineteenth-century developments. Population grew rapidly and the number in agriculture fell—but industrial and commercial expansion occurred elsewhere. This situation helps considerably to explain the persistence of low wages. At the same time, expansion of mining and quarrying, a small initial dependence on craft and cottage trades, and the fact that farming here was

1. For this reason declining employment in Region 5 was more completely dominated by agriculture than it was in Regions 2 and 3 (the south-west and the rural south-east—see above, pp. 139–40, 147). The Region was not entirely unaffected by the decline of small-scale industry: it had 7,000 woollen workers in 1851, and by 1911 competition from the West Riding had reduced their number to fewer than 1,500.

not much affected by foreign competition in grain[1] may help explain why wages were 'very low' at the beginning of the period but not worse than 'moderately low' by 1914.[2]

# VI

REGION SIX (Midlands—see Map 1)

The pattern of wages in the Midlands was particularly intricate. For the most part earnings were above average but the relative level varied both according to occupation and within the region; wages were highest in Nottinghamshire, Derbyshire, and Birmingham and lowest in the rural parts of Warwickshire and Worcestershire.

The deployment of the labour force in 1851 indicates a region fairly well abreast of economic developments; the various 'metal' trades were more important than in any other region[3] and the same can be said of employment in the manufacture of chemicals, pottery, glass, and paper (Category 9 in Table 4–6).[4] Coalmining, another expanding occupation, was well represented and the region enjoyed a considerably less than average dependence upon agriculture, the sector where demand for labour fell most. There was one exception to this promising pattern; in 1851 the Midlands employed a greater proportion in silk, straw, glove, hat, and hosiery manufacture (Category 5, Table 4–6) than any other region, and the relative importance of this group in the national labour force fell steadily throughout

---

1. See above, pp. 148–9.
2. See above p. 27.
3. The relative importance of the 'metal' trades was two and a half times the national average and more than six times their importance in the rural south-east (Region 3). Not all workers in this group were well paid; the plight of the Black Country nailers was mentioned earlier (see above, p. 33), but economic development required a rapid increase in the number making and manufacturing metal and for the most part their wages were high.
4. This position was due mainly to the number of Staffordshire pottery workers but the manufacture of glass and chemicals provided considerable employment.

the period.[1] Elsewhere, however, employment trends remained generally favourable to high wages. More than twice the number of metal workers were employed in the region by 1911 and more than three times as many miners.[2] The extent of industrial

TABLE 4–6

*Numbers Occupied per 1,000 Population:
Region Six (Midlands)*

| Occupation category | Britain | | | Region 6 | | |
|---|---|---|---|---|---|---|
| | 1851 | 1911 | Change | 1851 | 1911 | Change |
| 1. Metals | 21 | 33 | +12 | 52 | 61 | +9 |
| 2. Domestic Service | 48 | 45 | −3 | 44 | 36 | −8 |
| 3. Wool | 14 | 7 | −7 | 4 | 2 | −2 |
| 4. Cotton etc. | 34 | 19 | −15 | 18 | 12 | −6 |
| 5. Silk, Straw, Gloves, Hats, Stockings | 15 | 4 | −11 | 45 | 12 | −33 |
| 6. Mines and Quarries | 16 | 27 | +11 | 26 | 40 | +14 |
| 7. Shoemakers, Millers, Tailors, Saddlers, Carpenters | 32 | 20 | −12 | 31 | 23 | −8 |
| 8. Railways | 3 | 12 | +9 | 3 | 13 | +10 |
| 9. Chemicals, Pottery, Glass, Paper | 4 | 6 | +2 | 14 | 16 | +2 |
| 10. Coachbuilding, Ship-building | 2 | 4 | +2 | 1 | 1 | — |
| 11. 'New' Industries (Cars, Cycles, Electrical) | — | 5 | +5 | — | 12 | +12 |
| 12. Commerce | 3 | 22 | +19 | 2 | 19 | +17 |
| 13. Agriculture | 85 | 26 | −59 | 78 | 22 | −56 |

*Source:* Census of Occupations. For details of occupations included in these categories, see the appendix to this chapter.

development at the beginning of the period was such that, in contrast to the pattern noted in Regions Two, Three, and Five (the south-west, the rural south-east, rural Wales and Herefordshire), the fall in farm employment between 1851 and 1911

1. By 1901 some 52,000 fewer midland workers were employed in these trades. Straw workers and hatters accounted for only 3,000 of this loss, not enough to have more than a local impact on wages. The loss of 5,000 glovers (mainly in Nottinghamshire and Worcestershire) was hardly more significant. The main fall in demand was in silk and hosiery. Silk employment fell by 28,000 between 1851 and 1901 (mainly in Warwickshire) and hosiery by 14,000 (mainly in Leicestershire and Nottinghamshire).
2. Employment in the 'metal' trades expanded 17 per cent faster than population, a rate sufficient for the Midlands to retain the highest density of metal workers even though other regions were experiencing more rapid expansion.

was not a serious influence on the labour market; expansion
in the 'metal' trades alone accounted for double the 76,000
lost farm jobs.[1] Most impressive of all, both as an indicator of
demand for labour at the time and as a guide to the region's
fortune in the 1920s and 1930s, is the amount of labour employed in the 'new' industries. The makers and menders of
cars, cycles, and electrical goods totalled 57,000 in 1911, more
than a quarter of the British total.[2] The general impression is a
region where demand for labour was more pressing than was
general throughout the country except in parts of the industrial north—in all a situation consistent with moderately high
wages,[3] and it seems not unreasonable to assume that employment trends are among the more important of the influences
which determined this wage level.

But what of variations within the Midlands? Wages in this
region were analysed in some detail and it seems worthwhile
to examine briefly whether or not the broad correlation between
wages and demand in the region as a whole was repeated within
the region. The long-run demand for labour in Birmingham was
certainly consistent with the level of wages there. The city contained none of the ailing midland textile trades and very few
of those 'metal' occupations whose tardy growth caused midland expansion in the 'metals' sector as a whole to lag below
average. There were wide fluctuations in demand for some of
Birmingham's miscellaneous products, particularly for arms

1. If to 'metals' are added the requirements of mining, the pottery industry,
   and the 'new' industry group, the expansion in demand amounted to five
   times the number that left agriculture. The fall in the number employed
   in the silk, glove, hosiery, and nail trades amounted to about four-fifths
   of the loss in agriculture. These changes in absolute numbers are not
   apparent in Table 4–6 which shows numbers employed as a proportion of
   population.
2. The indirect impact of this development upon the labour requirements of
   existing industries—the providers of saddles, car seats, electric wire and
   fittings, springs, locks, tubes, and the rest—may have been as great as the
   direct impact.
3. Region 8 (Lancs., Cheshire, and the West Riding) and Region 10 (Northumberland and Durham) had a far smaller proportion of their labour force in
   agriculture (see below, pp. 165, 171); falling labour requirements in the silk,
   hosiery, and nail trades, and the less than average growth in 'metal'
   occupations also distinguish demand for labour in the Midlands from the
   pattern in the highest-wage areas.

and jewellery of various kinds, and wages fluctuated with demand, but the diversity of metal products was itself a source of strength—not least because it facilitated a speedy contraction of recruitment into dying trades.[1] Birmingham was noted for enterprise; it had supplied swords to both sides during the 1745 rebellion and in 1815 speedily converted redundant gun barrels into gas piping.[2] Its adaptability, and the broad basis of its prosperity, enabled the city quickly to shrug off depression in individual trades and every year some new development made fresh demands of its labour force. Railway construction had an obvious and lasting effect; even more important was the town's development as an engineering centre after 1880 when the metal trades turned increasingly to mechanical methods. By 1890 cycle and electrical manufacturers were significant employers and in 1896 a Birmingham company produced the first British car. Less obvious than these developments, but also significant, was a multitude of smaller windfalls such as the greatly enlarged demand for watercocks following the mid-century public health acts.[3]

The industrial structure of the Black Country, to the north and west of Birmingham, was quite different. Employment there depended mainly upon mining, iron making, and the manufacture of heavy metal products; demand for labour was less buoyant and wages considerably lower.[4] The hand-nail trade with its low wages and permanent over-supply of labour illustrates in a greatly exaggerated form both the differences between Birmingham and the Black Country and the relationship between wages and demand for labour.[5] The contrast between the two areas was most obvious during the 'Great

1. Allen, *Birmingham and the Black Country*, pp. 441–2. There is an obvious and important contrast in this respect between Birmingham and areas with little alternative employment to agriculture.
2. D. E. C. Eversley, *V. C. H. Warwickshire*, vii. 90; Allen, *Birmingham and the Black Country*, p. 91.
3. Ibid., pp. 34, 292–3; B. M. D. Smith in *V. C. H. Warwickshire*, vii. 198.
4. Allen, *Birmingham and the Black Country*, pp. 29, 57, 226, and see above, pp. 31, 33.
5. Over 19,000 worked at this trade in 1861; by 1914 foreign competition and the factory-made nail reduced their number to less than a thousand. Allen, *Birmingham and the Black Country*, pp. 157, 273, 459.

Depression'. This label may or may not be appropriate for Britain as a whole; it was certainly inappropriate for Birmingham[1] and it has already been noted that it requires stronger modification than the conventional inverted commas when applied to south Wales, but for the Black Country it was entirely appropriate. With antiquated plant and local raw materials already showing signs of exhaustion, the Black Country by 1873 had reached a stage analogous to Britain's place in the world economy in 1920. Its iron industry was far from flourishing even in the 1850s; while over-all demand remained high it enjoyed a mild prosperity, but the onset of more rigorous conditions after 1873 exposed its weaknesses[2] and it was the Black Country iron and nail industries that were largely responsible for the less than average expansion in the midland 'metal' trades. Unlike south Wales, whose iron industry was similarly, although less seriously, affected at about the same time, the Black Country found no compensation in mining. Coal producers in any case depended heavily on the iron trade for their markets, but the mine owners also had difficulties of their own and between 1865 and 1913, while the number of miners in Britain more than trebled, employment in that part of the south Staffordshire field south of the Great Bentley Fault fell by 15,000 jobs.[3]

South of Birmingham, in the more rural parts of Worcestershire and Warwickshire, demand for labour was indistinguishable from the general pattern in southern England. The same

1. 'Notwithstanding the general slackness of the country's trade; Birmingham not only looked busy, but was busy' (ibid., p. 226).
2. Cheap steel and the premium on coastal sites added to the area's handicaps. Several companies and many skilled workers moved out of the region (ibid., pp. 86, 233–4, 288).

| Pig Iron Output (Thousand Tons) | Britain | South Staffordshire |
|---|---|---|
| 1854 | 3,070 | 744 |
| 1873 | 6,566 | 673 |
| 1886 | 7,010 | 294 |
| 1894 | 7,427 | 333 |

Source: Mitchell and Deane, op. cit., pp. 131–2.
3. Allen, Birmingham and the Black Country, pp. 85–6, 194, 281; Mitchell and Deane, op. cit., pp. 118–19. The Great Bentley Fault, just north of Wolverhampton and Walsall, coincides approximately with the northern boundary of the Black Country.

may be said of the level of wages in the area.[1] The situation in
Coventry is particularly interesting because it illustrates in
dramatic fashion several themes which are applicable to much
of southern England. The city's fortunes changes twice in our
period. In 1850 it was a textile centre of the old type enjoying
a near monopoly in the manufacture of plain silk ribbons;
it was still not much affected by free trade and had only
recently, and reluctantly, become acquainted with steam
power.[2] Coventry, in fact, was one of the few surviving centres
of a once prosperous southern industry. In 1860 the silk trade
was thrown open: in the following year a national relief fund
was necessary to alleviate hardship in the city and the 1871
census returned 9,000 fewer Warwickshire silk workers than a
decade earlier.[3] Free trade had placed Coventry firmly among
the majority of towns in the south—characterized by low
wages, a shortage of employment, and the struggle to escape
the consequences of carrying a pre-industrial economy too far
into the nineteenth century. By 1890, however, the city's
fortunes were on the mend and the 'lean years of unemployment and under-employment' ending.[4] The new prosperity was
less precarious and more closely linked to the fortunes of
Birmingham—what had happened, in effect, was that Coventry
dispensed with the classical 'industrial revolution' of coal and
steam and graduated from a pre-industrial to a twentieth-
century industrial society in the short space of forty years.
Cycle-making led the recovery at first and was followed by car
production in the late 'nineties.[5] In 1905 Courtaulds opened a
plant for the manufacture of artificial fibres, another distinctly twentieth-century activity.[6] By this time wages were

1. Only 40 miles south of Birmingham wages were as low as almost anywhere
   in Britain, see above, p. 29.
2. J. M. Prest, *The Industrial Revolution in Coventry*, pp. 48–9, 93, 120.
3. Ibid., p. 128. There were 22,000 silk workers in Warwickshire in 1861,
   13,000 in 1871, and fewer than 6,000 in 1891.
4. Prest, op. cit., p. x.
5. There were over 4,000 cycle makers in Coventry in 1891, 7,000 making
   cars by 1911; and, as in Birmingham, the car industry brought with it a
   host of other well-paid jobs in a variety of ancillary trades. Allen, *Birmingham and the Black Country*, pp. 293, 296, 298.
6. On Courtaulds see, D. C. Coleman, *Courtaulds: An Economic and Social
   History* (Oxford, 1969), ii, Ch. 2.

not far below rates in Birmingham, Nottingham, and the large
northern towns.[1] In this respect, and again in an exaggerated
form, Coventry illustrates the extension of prosperity south-
wards by the end of the century, a trend noticed above in
Regions One, Two, and Three—its experience was Chelmsford's
writ large[2].

A broad correlation between demand and wages is also
evident to the north of Birmingham. Wages fell least steeply
in that direction and further north rose to levels well above the
regional average; employment trends followed a similar pattern.
In contrast to the situation in the Black Country, demand for
labour in those parts of the south Staffordshire coalfield north
of Wolverhampton, and in the Cannock Chase and North
Staffordshire fields, continued to rise after 1873; and although
north Staffordshire was certainly not one of the more prosperous
iron-making centres it nevertheless fared better than south
Staffordshire.[3] Nottingham and Derbyshire, the most northerly
and highest-wage midland counties, benefited from most of the
expansive trends in the national economy and had few declining occupations of significance other than agriculture. The
most potent expansive influence in these two counties was coalmining; between 1851 and 1911 mine employment increased
tenfold accounting for some 85,000 additional well-paid jobs.[4]
The various 'metal' trades were not here as important as they
were in Staffordshire and Warwickshire, but they expanded

---

1. See e.g. fitters' rates in 1910, *Standard Time Rates in the U.K.*, P.P. 1910,
LXXXIV, pp. 34–54. In 1906 carpenters received 9*d.* per hour in Coventry
and Nottingham, 9½*d.* in Birmingham and Manchester, 8*d.* in Norwich and
Oxford (Table 1–5 and Source U on p. 66 above.) Farm labourers in the
vicinity of Coventry received about 15*s.* to 18*s.* in 1903; this was well above
the general level in the south of England although still below levels in the
north and north Midlands (*Second Report on Wages . . . Agricultural
Labourers*, pp. 151–9). The association of above-average increase in employment and wages on the Warwickshire coalfield is also worth noting; there
were 4,200 employed in 1891, 15,200 by 1911, a rate of increase nearly twice
that in Britain as a whole. On wages in this field see also above, pp. 31–2.
2. See above, p. 136.
3. Allen, *Birmingham and the Black Country*, pp. 191–4, 236–7; Rowe, *Wages
in the Coal Industry*, p. 22; Mitchell and Deane, op. cit., pp. 131–2.
4. This was equivalent to over four times the loss in agriculture. The size of
this expansion also puts into perspective the importance of other declining
sectors in Nottinghamshire and Derbyshire—the loss of 2,000 jobs in
Derbyshire lead mines, for example.

faster, and Nottinghamshire and Derbyshire had no declining sectors comparable to the Black Country nailers.[1] The manufacture of textile machinery,[2] and Derby's railway workshops, gave the north Midlands an early and substantial stake in the engineering trades and, although it benefited less than Birmingham and Coventry, the area secured a disproportionate share of the newer industries which became important after 1890.[3] Even in textiles, one of the least expansive parts of the north midland economy, there is an obvious contrast between Nottingham and Derby and centres like Coventry or the lace districts of Buckinghamshire where there were no alternative occupations to absorb redundant workers.[4]

# VII

REGION SEVEN (Lincs., Rutland, E. and N. Ridings—see Map 1)

The broad correlation between relative wages and demand for labour in the Midland region as a whole, and in districts within

1. Iron output increased by more than four times in Nottinghamshire and Derbyshire between 1854 and 1914; in south Staffordshire output fell. Mitchell and Deane, op. cit., pp. 131–3.
2. In 1886 every lace machine at work in Germany had been made in Nottingham (R. A. Church, *Economic and Social Change in a Victorian Town: Victorian Nottingham*, 1815–1900, p. 245).
3. Raleigh's opened their first factory at Nottingham in 1896, Boots and Players gave the town a useful stake in the pharmaceutical and tobacco trades, and in 1908 Derby's flourishing and diverse engineering industries were enriched by the arrival of Rolls Royce (K. C. Edwards (ed.), *Nottingham and its Region* (Nottingham, 1966), pp. 410, 461). Derby's broad-based industrial prosperity was noted by the *Morning Chronicle* correspondent in 1850: 'the industrial resources of the place are fortunately so varied, that although one branch of its trade may occasionally be in a languishing condition, the town, as a whole, enjoys to a high degree a general and continuous degree of prosperity'—a comment which was no less applicable to Derby at any time in the following century. *M.C.* 17 Jan. 1850.
4. Although textile employment failed to expand in Nottinghamshire and Derbyshire it did not decline and in this respect the north Midlands fared better than most areas because there were few parts of Britain where textile employment increased significantly after 1850. Nottinghamshire's advantage was its dominance in the production of 'that most fashionable of all Victorian products'—machine-made lace. Lace employment expanded by the equivalent of some 16,000 jobs between 1851 and 1911, about the same as the number lost in the Nottinghamshire and Derbyshire silk and hosiery industry. The north Midland cotton mills employed almost the same number in 1911 as they employed 60 years earlier.

the Midlands, is also apparent in Region Seven. This region, like the Midlands, combined moderately high wages with moderately favourable employment trends. It was less industrialized than the Midlands and as farm employment fell demand for labour suffered accordingly. On the other hand it supported few textile workers of any description in 1850 and as a consequence, unlike some parts of the Midlands and much of the rural south, had little to lose from free trade in textiles or the development of factory production in other areas. It also enjoyed a modest share in the expansion of mining, less than the Midlands but more than the rural south. However, the greatest contrast with the low-wage areas was to be seen in the vicinities of Middlesbrough and Hull. While most of the region was little affected by the more expansive trends in the economy, Middlesbrough provides perhaps the best example in Britain of sudden and sustained industrialization. This began at the start of our period. In 1850 Middlesbrough supported only 8,000

TABLE 4–7

*Numbers Occupied per 1,000 Population:*
*Region Seven (Lincs., Rutland, E. and N. Ridings)*

| Occupation category | Britain | | | Region 7 | | |
|---|---|---|---|---|---|---|
| | 1851 | 1911 | Change | 1851 | 1911 | Change |
| 1. Metals | 21 | 33 | +12 | 10 | 42 | +32 |
| 2. Domestic Service | 48 | 45 | −3 | 56 | 50 | −6 |
| 3. Wool | 14 | 7 | −7 | 1 | — | −1 |
| 4. Cotton etc. | 34 | 19 | −15 | 5 | 1 | −4 |
| 5. Silk, Straw, Gloves, Hats, Stockings | 15 | 4 | −11 | 2 | — | −2 |
| 6. Mines and Quarries | 16 | 27 | +11 | 2 | 8 | +6 |
| 7. Shoemakers, Millers, Tailors, Saddlers, Carpenters | 32 | 20 | −12 | 36 | 17 | −19 |
| 8. Railways | 3 | 12 | +9 | 6 | 19 | +13 |
| 9. Chemicals, Pottery, Glass, Paper | 4 | 6 | +2 | 1 | 3 | +2 |
| 10. Coachbuilding, Shipbuilding | 2 | 4 | +2 | 2 | 6 | +4 |
| 11. 'New' Industries (Cars, Cycles, Electrical) | — | 5 | +5 | — | 2 | +2 |
| 12. Commerce | 3 | 22 | +19 | 2 | 15 | +13 |
| 13. Agriculture | 85 | 26 | −59 | 140 | 66 | −74 |

*Source:* Census of Occupations. For details of occupations included in these categories, see the appendix to this chapter.

inhabitants; iron ore was discovered in the vicinity in 1851 and
by 1911 the population was 120,000. Besides helping to explain
why wages there were higher than elsewhere in the region[1],
industrial developments on Teeside were largely responsible for
the extraordinarily rapid growth of employment in the region's,
'metal' trades in which Region Seven compared favourably
not only with the Midlands and rural south-east but with each
of the other ten regions.[2] Increased demand for labour in Hull
derived mainly from the city's function as the port linking the
industries of Lancashire and West Riding with Europe. Hull's
contribution to regional prosperity was considerable but more
diverse, and probably less substantial, than developments in the
Middlesbrough area.[3]

# VIII

REGION EIGHT (Lancs., Cheshire, and the W. Riding—see
Map 1)

In Region Eight the general correlation between wage levels
and demand for labour, which has been described in each of the
regions so far examined, was less in evidence. Wages were high
throughout the period; Lancashire, Cheshire, and the West
Riding are the counties of the 'classic' industrial revolution
and there is little doubt that the level of wages in 1850 owed
much to the unusually buoyant labour requirements of the
late eighteenth century and the first half of the nineteenth
century. The tendency for historians and social commentators,
fascinated by the more sordid consequences of industrialization,
to overlook the remarkable prosperity of these counties was
mentioned earlier. Attempts by the poor law authorities to

1. See above, p. 36.
2. Category 1 in Table 4–7. The increase in employment, some 52,000 jobs
   over the period, was equivalent to twice the number of farm jobs lost in the
   region.
3. Hull was Britain's third port by the 1870s. On the expansion of the port,
   and the growth of employment in processing industries and fishing, see
   L. M. Brown in *V. C. H. Yorkshire, East Riding*, i (1969), 219–27, 245–60.

encourage migration from south to north, and the South British Manufacturing Company which was floated in 1836 because its promoters believed that cotton manufacture could only expand in the south of England as there was now insufficient labour in the traditional cotton areas, are somewhat

TABLE 4–8

*Numbers Occupied per 1,000 Population:*
*Region Eight (Lancs., Cheshire, and the W. Riding)*

| | | Britain | | | Region 8 | |
| Occupation Category | 1851 | 1911 | Change | 1851 | 1911 | Change |
| --- | --- | --- | --- | --- | --- | --- |
| 1. Metals | 21 | 33 | +12 | 26 | 43 | +17 |
| 2. Domestic Service | 48 | 45 | −3 | 36 | 31 | −5 |
| 3. Wool | 14 | 7 | −7 | 55 | 24 | −31 |
| 4. Cotton etc. | 34 | 19 | −15 | 101 | 73 | −28 |
| 5. Silk, Straw, Gloves, Hats, Stockings | 15 | 4 | −11 | 18 | 4 | −14 |
| 6. Mines and Quarries | 16 | 27 | +11 | 17 | 29 | +12 |
| 7. Shoemakers, Millers, Tailors, Saddlers, Carpenters | 32 | 20 | −12 | 26 | 18 | −8 |
| 8. Railways | 3 | 12 | +9 | 4 | 12 | +8 |
| 9. Chemicals, Pottery, Glass, Paper | 4 | 6 | +2 | 4 | 6 | +2 |
| 10. Coachbuilding, Ship-building | 2 | 4 | +2 | 2 | 2 | — |
| 11. 'New' Industries (Cars, Cycles, Electrical) | — | 5 | +5 | — | 4 | +4 |
| 12. Commerce | 3 | 22 | +19 | 4 | 22 | +18 |
| 13. Agriculture | 85 | 26 | −59 | 38 | 10 | −28 |

*Source:* Census of Occupations. For details of occupations included in these categories, see the appendix to this chapter.

better guides to the state of the labour market in the first half of the century than accounts of handloom weavers' wages and the living conditions of Irish immigrants.[1] The influence of early industrial development is reflected in the employment structure in 1851 (Table 4–8). Mining, commerce, the railways, and the 'metal' trades, all growth occupations, were each over-represented.[2] Agriculture was less important than in any other

1. On the above points see D. Bythell, *The Handloom Weavers* (Cambridge, 1969), pp. 62–3, 81, 237, 253–5; A. Redford, *Labour Migration in England, 1800–50* (Manchester, 1964 edn.), p. 102; and above, pp. 37–9.
2. In Britain as a whole these four occupational categories employed half as many as were employed in agriculture; in Region 8 they gave employment to one third more than the number in agriculture.

region and only half as important as it was in Britain as a whole. The position with regard to domestic service was scarcely less favourable; mill employment, better paid and less onerous, offered 'a constant temptation for girls and young women to enter the factory rather than engage in domestic service'.[1] In 1851 domestic service and agriculture together gave employment to fewer than the cotton industry and to less than half the number employed in cotton and wool combined.

These same general features—above average employment in the better-paid sectors and a considerably less than average proportion of the labour force in agriculture—are evident in each occupational census between 1851 and 1911. But the rest of the country did not stand still and, other things remaining equal, if the rate of increase in demand for labour in Lanca- shire, Cheshire, and the West Riding was to protect wage differentials against market forces which worked towards a 'one-wage' equilibrium it needed to remain more buoyant than average. However, when the rate of growth of demand for labour in the region is compared either with the national average or with the rate in areas like south Wales and North- umberland and Durham there is little evidence that this con- dition was met. Demand grew scarcely faster than average; of the occupations shown in Table 4–8 only the 'metal' trades expanded substantially faster than average and even in this occupation expansion in Region Eight was less than that in Regions Seven (Lincs., Rutland, E. and N. Riding) and Twelve (central Scotland)[2] and does not compare with the massive increase in demand generated by mining in Regions Four (south Wales) and Ten (Northumberland and Durham).[3]

1. D. Chadwick, 'On the Rate of Wages in Manchester and Salford, and the Manufacturing Districts of Lancashire, 1839–59', p. 7. On the significance of employment in domestic service see above, p. 140 n. 2
2. Tables 4–7, 4–8, 4–12. For regions see Map 1.
3. As mentioned earlier (above p. 131) changes in the proportion of the population in various occupations are by no means a perfect indicator of the level of demand for labour. Rapid expansion on all fronts combined with a rapid increase in population and no change in the proportion employed in different occupations could occur, even though it was unlikely, and if it did it would not be reflected by changes in numbers employed per thousand population. However, this was not the case in Region 8. Lancashire, Cheshire, and the West Riding were a major attraction for

The region did enjoy one advantage over most other areas; as a consequence of industrial development in the first half of the nineteenth century, and earlier, agriculture's contribution to the labour requirements of expanding sectors was relatively small.[1] However, against this must be set a considerable disadvantage not yet mentioned—after 1850 textiles no longer contributed directly to the expansion of demand. Cotton employment continued to rise, but more slowly than the natural increase of the population; the absolute number in the various branches of wool manufacturing in 1911 was almost the same as sixty years earlier; and employment in the silk trade had fallen from 54,000 to 8,000.[2] The importance of these developments may be gauged from Table 4–8; in 1851 textile manufacture was the region's chief employment. At that time the various branches of cotton and wool manufacture employed some 600,000; in 1911 they employed 855,000, or some 350,000 fewer than the number required to keep demand for labour constant as a proportion of the population. Over the same period employment in mining, 'metals', on the railways, and in the manufacture of chemicals, glass, pottery, and paper

---

migrants in the first half of the century but their net migration gain in the second half was slight (below, p. 247). Between 1851 and 1911 Britain's population increased by some 96 per cent, Region 8's by 130 per cent. The increase in Region 8 was above average but considerably less above average than the rate of increase in Regions 4 (south Wales) and 10 (Northumberland and Durham), and less too than its own 208 per cent increase between 1801 and 1861. This process was cumulative; between 1891 and 1911 the population of Region 8 grew no faster than the population of Britain. All population figures from Mitchell and Deane, op. cit., pp. 6, 20–2.

1. The decline in farm employment between 1851 and 1911, relative to population, was less in Region 8 than any other region.
2. The decline of silk employment was sufficient to leave considerable pockets of unemployment and to affect wages in those parts of Cheshire and south Lancashire where the industry had been concentrated. (On Courtaulds' expansion at Leigh in 1898 see above, p. 117 n. 4.) In this local case the relationship between demand and wages seems fairly close and it is worth noting also that in the case of cotton and wool the more buoyant demand for labour from the cotton trade occurred alongside a far faster increase in wages (G. H. Wood, *Wages in the Cotton Trade*, p. 147; H. A. Clegg, A. Fox, and A. F. Thompson, *A History of British Trade Unions since 1889*, i. 186). There is a similar positive relationship between the rate of expansion of the mine labour force in Lancashire and Yorkshire (particularly south Yorkshire) and wages trends in the two coalfields. See above, pp. 41–2, and, for employment figures, Rowe, *Wages in the Coal Industry*, p. 14.

increased by 611,000;[1] this increase was 416,000 more than the number necessary to keep up with the natural growth of the labour force but not much more than sufficient to offset the shortfall in textile expansion. These comparisons are crude and also give an over-pessimistic impression because they fail to distinguish between male and female workers, but they afford some measure of definition to the relative decline in textile employment and, together with the figures given earlier, show clearly that the Lancashire, Cheshire, and West Riding region was no longer a focal point of change. They also suggest that the region's continuing high wage levels cannot be explained to any significant extent by an unusually rapid expansion in demand for labour.

# IX

REGION NINE (Cumberland and Westmorland—see Map 1)

Table 4–9 shows that employment trends in Cumberland and Westmorland were even less favourable to above-average wages than those in Region Eight. Some sectors grew faster than average (mining was the most obvious of these)[2] but by the 1880s employment in the 'metals' sector was no more than keeping pace with population[3] and the proportion employed in the coal and metal trades together remained modest compared with areas like south Wales or Northumberland and Durham.[4] In addition to mining the region seems to have benefited more

1. Occupational groups 1, 6, 8, 9 in Table 4–8.
2. The Cumberland coastal strip developed rapidly after 1860 and the population of Workington quadrupled in 30 years.
3. Cumberland had always been a high-cost iron producer; it was remote, it lacked local coking coal, and with the development of the Thomas process lost the advantage of its non-phosphoric ores. O. Wood, 'The Development of the Coal, Iron and Shipbuilding Industries of West Cumberland, 1750–1914', Ph.D. thesis, University of London (1952), pp. 265–75, 287.
4. Tables 4–4, 4–9, 4–10. In south Wales (Region 4) the increased demand for labour from the mining and metal occupations between 1851 and 1911 was ten times the decline in the agricultural labour force; in Cumberland and Westmorland the mining and metal occupations gained only slightly more than agriculture lost.

TABLE 4–9

*Numbers Occupied per 1,000 Population:*
*Region Nine (Cumberland and Westmorland)*

| | Britain | | | Region 9 | | |
|---|---|---|---|---|---|---|
| Occupation Category | 1851 | 1911 | Change | 1851 | 1911 | Change |
| 1. Metals | 21 | 33 | +12 | 12 | 24 | +12 |
| 2. Domestic Service | 48 | 45 | −3 | 40 | 48 | +8 |
| 3. Wool | 14 | 7 | −7 | 8 | 3 | −5 |
| 4. Cotton etc. | 34 | 19 | −15 | 40 | 6 | −34 |
| 5. Silk, Straw, Gloves, Hats, Stockings | 15 | 4 | −11 | 4 | — | −4 |
| 6. Mines and Quarries | 16 | 27 | +11 | 24 | 48 | +24 |
| 7. Shoemakers, Millers, Tailors, Saddlers, Carpenters | 32 | 20 | −12 | 36 | 18 | −18 |
| 8. Railways | 3 | 12 | +9 | 4 | 18 | +14 |
| 9. Chemicals, Pottery, Glass, Paper | 4 | 6 | +2 | 4 | 3 | −1 |
| 10. Coachbuilding, Ship-building | 2 | 4 | +2 | 4 | — | −4 |
| 11. 'New' Industries (Cars, Cycles, Electrical) | — | 5 | +5 | — | — | — |
| 12. Commerce | 3 | 22 | +19 | 1 | 9 | +8 |
| 13. Agriculture | 85 | 26 | −59 | 119 | 51 | −68 |

*Source:* Census of Occupations. For details of occupations included in these categories, see the appendix to this chapter.

than most from railway development, but there were few other employment trends favourable to high wages.[1] Commercial employment grew very slowly. Shipbuilding reached its peak in the 1880s and employed only a few hundred in 1911, and there was no other significant industrial development outside the coal and iron sector. Moreover, the region had some declining textile trades; there were more engaged in cotton manufacture than mining at the beginning of the period but the 1891 census shows that forty years of competition with Lancashire had left few remaining. Further, and here the contrast with Region Eight (Lancs., Cheshire, and the West Riding) is greatest, the most important occupation in the region at the beginning of the period was agriculture and the contraction of farm employment in the following half-century

1. Two of the main routes to Scotland passed through the area and Carlisle was an important servicing and maintenance depot.

released large numbers to offset the modest demand from the mines, iron mills, and railway companies.

Wages in this region were not as high as those in Lancashire and the West Riding, but nor were they low; for the most part they ranged between average and moderately high. While the demand pattern just described is less compatible with low wages than patterns in the rural south it is far from sufficient to explain above-average wages and in particular it fails to explain the very high level of farm wages in the region.[1] As in Region Eight, above-average wages appear to have existed despite rates of increase in demand for labour which were scarcely, if at all, better than the national average.


# X


Region Ten (Northumberland and Durham—see Map 1)

With Region Ten we return to the earlier pattern in which relative demand for labour and relative wage levels had much in common. The position in this region requires little elaboration—Table 4–10 shows an occupational structure in most respects favourable to high wages, and wages in Northumberland and Durham were always among the highest in Britain.

The greatest impetus to expansion was coal production; between 1851 and 1911 the mine labour force increased more than five times. The development of shipbuilding, which was especially rapid in the last two decades of the century, was an

---

1. Farm wages were far nearer to average at the end of the period than in the 1850s and 1860s (see above, p. 43). This is not surprising given the employment trends shown above; the remarkable thing is that wages were so far above average at the beginning of the period and remained better than average in the early twentieth century. One advantage the region enjoyed with regard to farm wages was the long-term divergence between livestock and grain prices. Caird noted of Cumberland in 1851: 'The humidity of climate has given to those who cultivate the soil with a wise desire to enlist nature on their side a preference for stock over corn farming' (J. Caird, *English Agriculture in 1850–51*, pp. 350–1). This trend, however, gave no advantage over low-wage areas like the south-west or rural Wales.

important secondary influence.[1] There were other, more passive, features no less conducive to high wages. The most obvious of these is the relative insignificance of agriculture; it already employed fewer than mining in 1851 and by 1911

### TABLE 4–10
*Numbers Occupied per 1,000 Population:*
*Region Ten (Northumberland and Durham)*

| Occupation category | Britain | | | Region 10 | | |
|---|---|---|---|---|---|---|
| | 1851 | 1911 | Change | 1851 | 1911 | Change |
| 1. Metals | 21 | 33 | +12 | 29 | 40 | +11 |
| 2. Domestic Service | 48 | 45 | −3 | 37 | 31 | −6 |
| 3. Wool | 14 | 7 | −7 | 4 | — | −4 |
| 4. Cotton etc. | 34 | 19 | −15 | 1 | — | −1 |
| 5. Silk, Straw, Gloves, Hats, Stockings | 15 | 4 | −11 | 3 | — | −3 |
| 6. Mines and Quarries | 16 | 27 | +11 | 65 | 98 | +33 |
| 7. Shoemakers, Millers, Tailors, Saddlers, Carpenters | 32 | 20 | −12 | 32 | 11 | −21 |
| 8. Railways | 3 | 12 | +9 | 6 | 11 | +5 |
| 9. Chemicals, Pottery, Glass, Paper | 4 | 6 | +2 | 10 | 4 | −6 |
| 10. Coachbuilding, Ship-building | 2 | 4 | +2 | 9 | 21 | +12 |
| 11. 'New' Industries (Cars, Cycles, Electrical) | — | 5 | +5 | — | 3 | +3 |
| 12. Commerce | 3 | 22 | +19 | 1 | 15 | +14 |
| 13. Agriculture | 85 | 26 | −59 | 59 | 11 | −48 |

*Source:* Census of Occupations. For details of occupations included in these categories, see the appendix to this chapter.

employed only one person for every fourteen dependent on mining, 'metals', and the shipbuilding trades. Further, competition from the mills of Lancashire, Nottingham, and the West Riding was of no consequence in this region because Northumberland and Durham employed very few textile workers at the beginning of the period.

1. These two sectors far more than compensated for less than average expansion in the non-textile manufacturing industries. However, the low level of employment in these industries (categories 9 and 11 in Table 4–10) at the end of the period was a sign that the north-east, like south Wales, relied too heavily on the basic industries and was under-represented in those sectors which were to be most prosperous in the inter-war years.

# XI

REGION ELEVEN (south Scotland—see Map 1)

The counties of southern Scotland had few of the advantages of Northumberland and Durham (Region Ten) but much in common with Cumberland and Westmorland (Region Nine). Industrial and commercial expansion was extremely limited— it was predominantly a farming area and remained so throughout the period. Only two regions had a larger share of their population employed on the land in 1851, no region exceeded the south of Scotland in this respect in 1911, and at both dates it employed the smallest proportion of any region in the 'metals' group of occupations. The only sector, other than domestic service,[1] where there was a significantly faster than average increase in demand for labour was wool manufacture. The border woollen industry employed 4,000 in 1851, over 14,000 in 1891—although the numbers involved are not large compared with employment in Yorkshire they represent a remarkable achievement at a time when Norfolk, Suffolk, Gloucestershire, Devon, and similar centres were declining in the face of West Riding competition and when there was no long-term increase in employment in Yorkshire itself.[2] However, with the exception of whatever benefit farm wages derived from favourable trends in livestock prices[3] there were

1. On domestic service see above, p. 140 n. 2.
2. The border woollen industry specialized in tweeds, a sector of the market where sales depended less upon price than upon quality, design, and the monopoly advantages conferred on any area which can differentiate its product to the extent that the public rejects similar goods from other areas as different and inferior. Yorkshire and Europe produced cheaper 'tweeds' but the public cheerfully paid more for the Scotch cloth. Bremner accounted for the area's success in terms of the 'genuineness' of the article and the consistent 'anti-shoddy' policy. Expansion ceased in the 1890s due to increased competition and higher tariffs abroad, particularly in the United States. The Hawick hosiery trade fared better than most minor centres but there was no long term increase in numbers employed—D. Bremner, *The Industries of Scotland*, p. 157; W. H. Marwick, *Scotland in Modern Times* (1964), p. 95.
3. See above, pp. 148–9. This advantage was shared with much of the rest of Scotland, Wales, and the west of England. Wheat, the crop most affected by foreign competition, in the 1870s accounted for only 4 per cent of Scotland's arable acreage. R. H. Campbell, *Scotland since 1707*, p. 155.

## TABLE 4–11
### Numbers Occupied per 1,000 Population:
### Region Eleven (South Scotland)

| | Britain | | | Region 11 | | |
| Occupation Category | 1851 | 1911 | Change | 1851 | 1911 | Change |
| --- | --- | --- | --- | --- | --- | --- |
| 1. Metals | 21 | 33 | +12 | 7 | 8 | +1 |
| 2. Domestic Service | 48 | 45 | −3 | 44 | 54 | +10 |
| 3. Wool | 14 | 7 | −7 | 15 | 46 | +31 |
| 4. Cotton etc. | 34 | 19 | −15 | 11 | 4 | −7 |
| 5. Silk, Straw, Gloves, Hats, Stockings | 15 | 4 | −11 | 11 | 15 | +4 |
| 6. Mines and Quarries | 16 | 27 | +11 | 4 | 8 | +4 |
| 7. Shoemakers, Millers, Tailors, Saddlers, Carpenters | 32 | 20 | −12 | 29 | 19 | −10 |
| 8. Railways | 3 | 12 | +9 | 4 | 12 | +8 |
| 9. Chemicals, Pottery, Glass, Paper | 4 | 6 | +2 | — | — | — |
| 10. Coachbuilding, Shipbuilding | 2 | 4 | +2 | — | — | — |
| 11. 'New' Industries (Cars, Cycles, Electrical) | — | 5 | +5 | — | — | — |
| 12. Commerce | 3 | 22 | +19 | 1 | 15 | +14 |
| 13. Agriculture | 85 | 26 | −59 | 147 | 96 | −51 |

*Source:* Census of Occupations. For details of occupations included in these categories, see the appendix to this chapter.

no other favourable influences of note and the over-all impression is that the south of Scotland, even more than Cumberland and Westmorland, was an area with a considerably less than average share of those employment trends favourable to high wages. But wages in the region were not low;[1] the rural south of Scotland, it seems, like Cumberland and Westmorland, was a region where demand for labour was slack but other market forces were sufficiently strong to offset the influence of demand upon wages.[2]

1. See above, pp. 47–50. Farm wages in particular compared well with wages in other areas and farmwork was by far the most important occupation.
2. This conclusion is underlined by consideration of the timing and quantitative significance of expansion of demand in the woollen industry. Over the period as a whole the industry added to its labour force not much more than half the number that left agriculture, and the proportion would be considerably less if males only were considered. Further, farm wages compared as well with other areas in 1906 as in the late 1860s (above, pp. 47–8), whereas the expansion of the woollen industry began in mid century (Campbell, op. cit., pp. 115–16) and ceased in the 1890s—between 1891 and 1911 employment fell.

# XII

REGION TWELVE (central Scotland—see Map 1)

If Region Eleven (south Scotland) was an area characterized by absence of significant pressure on the labour market from the side of demand, Region Twelve was quite the opposite. This position was broadly consistent with one of the main features of wages in the region—steady improvement relative to the rest of Britain.[1] In 1851 central Scotland enjoyed at least an average share in each of the seven occupational categories in Table 4–12 which were to expand faster than population in the following sixty years; and from this promising start it secured a more than proportionate share in subsequent expansion.[2]

Between 1851 and 1911 employment in the 'metal' trades increased more than four times; in terms of numbers employed as a proportion of population this was over twice the average increase and greater than the increase in eleven of the other twelve regions. Before 1830 Scottish iron was easily outsold south of the border and in danger of losing local markets as transport costs fell. Relief, and expansion, came with the 'hot-blast' and successful exploitation of west Scotland's blackband ironstone; by the middle of the century the area accounted for a quarter of Britain's iron output and over 90 per cent of pig-iron exports.[3] In the 1850s competition from the north-east put an end to the extraordinary progress of the previous decade and there was a further slackening of pace in the 1870s, but expansion remained faster than average until after 1890 and it was no slower than average between then and the First World

1. Relative wage rates varied according to occupation, the general position was that wages were below average in the mid-nineteenth century, near or a little above average half-way through the period, and well above average in the early twentieth century, see above, pp. 50–3.
2. Slightly below average expansion in categories 8, 9, 11 (Table 4–12) was heavily offset by expansion in the heavy industries (categories 1, 6, 10).
3. Campbell, op. cit., pp. 118–19, 127, and Clapham, *An Economic History of Modern Britain*, ii. 47.

TABLE 4–12

*Numbers Occupied per 1,000 Population:*
*Region Twelve (Central Scotland)*

| Occupation category | Britain | | | Region 12 | | |
|---|---|---|---|---|---|---|
| | 1851 | 1911 | Change | 1851 | 1911 | Change |
| 1. Metals | 21 | 33 | +12 | 23 | 49 | +26 |
| 2. Domestic Service | 48 | 45 | −3 | 40 | 30 | −10 |
| 3. Wool | 14 | 7 | −7 | 8 | 4 | −4 |
| 4. Cotton etc. | 34 | 19 | −15 | 96 | 17 | −79 |
| 5. Silk, Straw, Gloves, Hats, Stockings | 15 | 4 | −11 | 6 | 2 | −4 |
| 6. Mines and Quarries | 16 | 27 | +11 | 29 | 46 | +17 |
| 7. Shoemakers, Millers, Tailors, Saddlers, Carpenters | 32 | 20 | −12 | 28 | 17 | −11 |
| 8. Railways | 3 | 12 | +9 | 4 | 12 | +8 |
| 9. Chemicals, Pottery, Glass, Paper | 4 | 6 | +2 | 6 | 7 | +1 |
| 10. Coachbuilding, Ship-building | 2 | 4 | +2 | 2 | 15 | +13 |
| 11. 'New' Industries (Cars, Cycles, Electrical) | — | 5 | +5 | — | 3 | +3 |
| 12. Commerce | 3 | 22 | +19 | 5 | 26 | +21 |
| 13. Agriculture | 85 | 26 | −59 | 47 | 13 | −34 |

*Source:* Census of Occupations. For details of occupations included in these categories, see the appendix to this chapter.

War. In 1911 only Region Six (Midlands) employed a greater proportion of its population in the 'metal' trades.

A similar expansion in the shipyards began later and was still in full spate at the end of our period. The 1851 census shows that shipbuilding then employed fewer than 2,500; as a proportion of population this was no greater than that in the south of England and far less than the proportion in the north-east. But the Clyde already dominated steamship production;[1] it became the world's first shipbuilding centre and, by 1870, 'the chief growth point of the Scottish economy'.[2]

Coalmining was another thriving and well-paid occupation whose labour requirements helped improve wages in agriculture

1. It produced over half Britain's steam tonnage as early as 1835. J. B. S. Gilfillan and H. A. Moisley in R. Miller and J. Tivy (eds.), *The Glasgow Region* (Glasgow, 1958), p. 172.
2. A. V. Cairncross in ibid., p. 223; Campbell, op. cit., p. 231.

and similar declining sectors. However, while this had a favourable effect upon the general wage level compared with earnings in non-mining regions, the relative level of colliery wages, considered on their own, requires comparison between coalfields; and in this respect central Scotland was less well placed. Rowe's employment figures for 1889 and 1913 show that Lanark expanded faster than north Wales, Lancashire and Cheshire, Somerset, and the Forest of Dean, but less rapidly than each of eleven other fields.[1] This relationship, in fact, supports the hypothesis that the general level of wages in the region was partly determined by the high rate of increase in demand for labour because mine wages and mine employment were both exceptions to the general pattern.[2] The cotton industry falls in the same category; it employed 87,000 in 1851, only 14,000 in 1911, and at a time when most wages in central Scotland improved relative to wages in other regions Lancashire's advantage in cotton wages was maintained and probably increased.[3]

The cotton trade was probably the single most important exception to the general pattern of long-term expansion. Over the period as a whole employment in this industry fell by twice the number of jobs lost in agriculture and between 1851 and 1871 farm and cotton employment fell by 17,000 and 50,000

1. Rowe, *Wages in the Coal Industry*, p. 14. The comparatively modest rate of growth may be put down to the slackening in the rate of expansion of the local iron industry and, after 1880, problems of exhaustion. East Scotland, with greater reserves and a smaller dependence on local markets, was less affected by these developments but by 1880 foreign and inter-district competition were exercising a similar moderating influence on the rate of expansion. Rowe, ibid., p. 33; Campbell, op. cit., pp. 131–2, 238–42.
2. On mine wages see above, p. 52.
3. The Scots cotton trades showed signs of stagnation long before 1850. Production methods were inferior to those of Lancashire and, like the Norfolk woollen producers earlier, the Scots trade concentrated on supplying the finer cloths, a commitment which precluded full participation in the growing eastern trade and channelled their main efforts into the fiercely competitive European and American markets. Market trends similar to those which had favoured Yorkshire against Norfolk now favoured Lancashire against Scotland. The main collapse occurred soon after the beginning of our period; first as part of the aftermath of the 1857 financial crisis and then during the cotton famine from which the Scots trade never recovered. Campbell, op. cit. pp., 107–11; Miller and Tivy, op. cit., pp. 179–80. On wages in the cotton trades see above, p. 52 n. 3.

respectively; males accounted for rather more than half the latter figure. These were considerable losses and probably help to explain low wages in the region at the beginning of the period[1] but against the background of rapid expansion in the heavy industries they were far from disastrous. Between 1851 and 1871 the 'metal' trades, mining, and shipbuilding together employed sufficient extra labour more than to offset the decline in agriculture and the loss of male work in the cotton trade[2] and over the whole period 1851–1911 they expanded by some 274,000 jobs, nine times the agricultural exodus and about three times the number lost in agriculture and cotton combined.

There appears to be a fairly strong case for regarding the level of demand as a major determinant of wages in central Scotland. The long-term demand for labour was buoyant and wages were characterized by long-term improvement relative to other parts of Britain. In addition, the exceptions to the generalization about demand—coal and cotton—were also exceptions to the general trend in wage rates.[3]

1. See above, pp. 50–3.
2. The 'metal' trades, mining, and shipbuilding employed some 61,000 more in 1871 than they employed 20 years earlier, or some 16,000 more than the total decline in agriculture and the loss of male employment in the cotton trade in the same period. Given this background it is hardly surprising that Purdy found the agricultural labour market comparatively buoyant in the early 1860s (F. Purdy, 'On the Earnings of Agricultural Labourers in Scotland and Ireland', p. 435). See also G. Houston: 'The over-supply of rural labour which developed in some districts of England was not a feature of central Scotland at this time' ('Farm Wages in Central Scotland from 1814 to 1870', p. 228). The agricultural labourer also benefited from the same trends in farm prices which helped labourers in Region 11 (south Scotland—see above, p. 172) and these influences may have been more important in central Scotland because of the proximity of large urban markets.
3. On the evidence of farm wages between 1867 and 1907 wages in Region 12 increased more rapidly than wages in any other region except south Wales (Region 4—see above, pp. 51, 64). The occupational statistics themselves, and the use of changes in numbers employed as a proportion of population to measure demand, leave far too much to be desired in the way of accuracy to permit meaningful correlation tests (see above, pp. 130–1), but it is worth noting that the increase in numbers employed as a proportion of population in the metal trades, mining, coach and shipbuilding, and commerce (i.e. categories 1, 6, 10, 12 in Table 4–12) was greater between 1851 and 1911 in Region 12 than in any other region. Similar comparisons between the employment structure of central Scotland in 1851 and those of Britain as a whole and regions where wages were far higher than in central Scotland (see e.g. Tables 4–1, 4–6, 4–8, 4–10) suggest that, even

# XIII

REGION THIRTEEN (northern Scotland—see Map 1)

The link between wages and demand for labour is equally
clear in the north of Scotland. This region shared in the long-
term improvement of Scottish farm wages but earnings were
always well below average.[1] It requires no more than cursory
examination of Table 4–13 to see that the level of demand for
labour was entirely conducive to low wages. At the beginning
of the period the greater part of the labour force was in occupations where earnings were low and unlikely to rise as a consequence of rapid recruitment. Employment in the 'metal'
trades was less important than in all but two of the other
twelve regions; there was no significant share in the stimulus
from mining expansion; the railways brought less employment
than to other parts of Britain; and while the region was initially
at no great disadvantage with regard to commercial employment
it fell well below average by the 1880s.

This highly unpropitious situation was slightly relieved by
one or two more favourable trends. The major fall in demand
in category 4 of Table 4–13, which occurred mainly in the linen
trade, was offset by the expansion of jute manufacture in the
same area and utilizing much of the labour and capital hitherto
engaged in the manufacture of linen.[2] There was the further
advantage that in the middle of the nineteenth century northern

---

after allowing for the difficulties in the cotton industry, wages in central
Scotland at the beginning of the period were lower than consideration of the
employment structure would lead one to expect—farm wages were below the
level in rural southern Scotland. This situation is similar to that noted in
south Wales (above, pp. 152–3). In the latter case it was suggested that
wages may have been affected by the presence of surplus labour in nearby
central Wales and south-west England; central Scotland may have been
similarly affected by heavy migration from Ireland and the Highlands
(see below, pp. 291–3).

1. Within the region wages were lowest in the crofting counties of the north
and west, see above, pp. 53–6.
2. P. Deane and W. A. Cole, *British Economic Growth 1688–1959*, p. 205.
Jute employment is not included in Table 4–13.

Scotland had no important domestic industries of the kind which were to succumb to factory competition in the following half-century. But these redeeming features amount to very little; agriculture, declining and badly paid, was at all times the most

TABLE 4–13

*Numbers Occupied per 1,000 Population:*
*Region Thirteen (Northern Scotland)*

| Occupation category | Britain | | | Region 13 | | |
|---|---|---|---|---|---|---|
| | 1851 | 1911 | Change | 1851 | 1911 | Change |
| 1. Metals | 21 | 33 | +12 | 8 | 15 | +7 |
| 2. Domestic Service | 48 | 45 | −3 | 41 | 40 | −1 |
| 3. Wool | 14 | 7 | −7 | 7 | 5 | −2 |
| 4. Cotton etc. | 34 | 19 | −15 | 54 | 12 | −42 |
| 5. Silk, Straw, Gloves, Hats, Stockings | 15 | 4 | −11 | 4 | 3 | −1 |
| 6. Mines and Quarries | 16 | 27 | +11 | 3 | 5 | +2 |
| 7. Shoemakers, Millers, Tailors, Saddlers, Carpenters | 32 | 20 | −12 | 27 | 17 | −10 |
| 8. Railways | 3 | 12 | +9 | 1 | 8 | +7 |
| 9. Chemicals, Pottery, Glass, Paper | 4 | 6 | +2 | 1 | 3 | +2 |
| 10. Coachbuilding, Ship-building | 2 | 4 | +2 | 2 | 4 | +2 |
| 11. 'New' Industries (Cars, Cycles, Electrical) | — | 5 | +5 | — | 1 | +1 |
| 12. Commerce | 3 | 22 | +19 | 3 | 15 | +12 |
| 13. Agriculture | 85 | 26 | −59 | 132 | 70 | −62 |

*Source:* Census of Occupations. For details of occupations included in these categories, see the appendix to this chapter.

important occupation.[1] At the beginning of the period the 'metal' trades, the railways, mining, and commerce, together employed hardly one tenth of the number in agriculture; between then and 1914 this group of expanding occupations gave employment to an extra 36,000 but in the same period

1. Large parts of this region, especially those counties north and west of Glen More, failed to share in the benefits of contemporary price trends (see above, pp. 148–9, 172, 177 n. 2). The Highlands were characterized by poor farming and poor soil; agriculture was only partly market-oriented. Cattle raising was affected by competition from more efficient and better-endowed areas, sheep farming by falling prices and deteriorating pasture. Campbell, op. cit., pp. 293–4.

the farm labour force fell by 58,000—these figures summarize most of what we need to know about employment in the north of Scotland.

In the south and east of the region employment trends, and wages, were considerably better than the regional average. The disparity between the economic progress of the Highlands and the area to the south-east has been shown clearly by Malcolm Gray; the Highlands were 'obstinately archaic and peasant-minded' and some of the farming he describes would have distressed the better sort of sixteenth-century English yeoman.[1] The combination of poor farming, poor resources, and high fertility created problems in the Highlands long before 1850.[2] Emigration and the clearances brought unwelcome relief but sundry less serious variations on the malthusian theme continued until the First World War.[3] In the south-east of the region, by contrast, farms were larger, they exhibited more of the 'intelligence, enterprise and skill that mark East Lothian and its neighbours', and men were 'in no great excess over the demand for labour'.[4] While the figures in Table 4–13 throw no light on the long-term improvement in relative wages in the region as a whole—a fact which suggests the presence of differentials in natural increase, in migration rates, or some other variable—they are compatible with below-average wages, and the positive relationship between demand for labour and wages which appears to have existed within the region reinforces the hypothesis that in the region as a whole low wages were in part, and probably in large part, a consequence of low demand for labour.

1. 'The crofters have no notion of following the rotation system in cropping. The only change is from oats to potatoes, and from potatoes to oats . . . It is by no means uncommon to sow oats for three or four years in the same spot, and that without giving it any manure' (M. Gray, *The Highland Economy, 1750–1850* (Edinburgh, 1957), pp. 193, 207).
2. Like Ireland the Highlands exhibited the remarkable propensity of peasant communities occasionally to allow population to grow beyond the level resources could comfortably sustain. If these two areas are any guide, the utopian 'three acres and a cow' schemes of O'Connor and others could have precipitated a British disaster of Irish proportions.
3. Campbell, op. cit., p. 297.
4. Gray, op. cit., pp. 223–7, 232.

## XIV

The relationship between wages and demand for labour in various parts of the country was generally positive. This conclusion, of course, is much what impressions derived from existing national and regional economic histories would have led us to expect. The contribution of this chapter has been the attempt to test and substantiate these impressions by providing quantitative guides on the extent and composition of demand variations in a form which allows comparison of the influence of employment trends within regions, between regions, and between individual regions and the national average. These comparisons show a remarkable diversity of experience and suggest that nineteenth-century Britain is a good example of 'regional dualism'.[1] In terms of the debate among economists on the nature of regional inequalities in unregulated economies,[2] the analysis suggests that, while there was little evidence of increased inequality after 1850 and some evidence of convergence after 1890, the most notable feature was the way in which the play of market forces worked to maintain the advantages of prosperous areas. In addition, to the extent that a study of regional demand for labour is at the same time a rudimentary regional economic history, this chapter has indicated the probable answer to one of the questions raised earlier—viz. the appropriateness of terms like 'the Great Depression', 'the mid-Victorian boom', and other historical generalizations which assume a high degree of homogeneity in the economy.

The relationship between demand and wages was not in all places as close as might have been expected. While demand for labour was generally greatest in areas where wages were high, and substantial changes in demand such as occurred in south

1. On the nature of 'regional dualism' see J. G. Williamson, 'Regional Inequality and the Process of National Development', *Economic Development and Cultural Change*, xiii (1964–5).

2. See above, p. 3.

7

Wales and central Scotland were reflected by changes in relative wages, there were several exceptions to this pattern[1] which suggest the existence of regional variations in the influence of other market forces yet to be examined. These forces would require investigation even if the relationship between demand and wages had been perfect because the establishment of any kind of positive relationship between demand and wages raises important questions about other parts of the labour market—in particular it suggests hypotheses about labour mobility because in one sense an index of the way variations in demand influenced wages is also an index of labour immobility, of the extent by which labour's response to incentives was less than perfect. In a similar fashion the conclusions of this chapter raise questions about investment mobility; employers recruited most labour where wages were highest and least where they were low, a situation consistent with entrepreneurial inertia. However, capital may have enjoyed compensating differentials—low-wage labour is not necessarily cheap. The most likely compensating differential, variations in productivity, is the subject of the following chapter.

1. See above, pp.152–3, 164–70, 173, 177 n. 3. Wages in Lancashire and the West Riding were higher than might have been expected from a consideration of variations in demand alone; the same was true of Cumberland and Westmorland and the rural south of Scotland, while in south Wales and central Scotland, at the beginning of the period, wages were below the level suggested by the nature of demand for labour.

# APPENDIX TO CHAPTER FOUR

## I

### NOTES ON THE OCCUPATIONAL CENSUS

These notes indicate the more important of the problems which arise when using the occupational census to compile indices of the kind shown in Tables 4–1 to 4–13. Most difficulties affect all parts of Britain and for this reason they are unlikely to seriously diminish the utility of Tables 4–1 to 4–13 which emphasize spatial rather than chronological comparisons. However, census errors and ambiguities are such that it would be unwise to rely heavily upon individual figures in the tables; they should be regarded not as exact indicators but as reasonably reliable guides to the numbers and proportions involved. For more detailed regional occupational statistics than those shown in Tables 4–1 to 4–13, including similar decennial figures for 1861, 1871, 1881, 1891, and 1901, see Tables C–1 to C–13 in my dissertation, 'Regional Wage Variations in Britain, 1850–1914', Ph.D. thesis, University of London (1971), pp. 471–96. For additional comment on the occupational census see J. Bellamy, 'A Note on Occupational Statistics in British Censuses', *Pop. Stud.*, vi (1952–3), and *Census Reports of Great Britain, 1801–1931*, Guide to the Official Sources No. 2 (H.M.S.O., 1951).

1. The census normally arranged workers according to the nature of their employment rather than the product of their labour. It is impossible to tell what proportion of men in occupations like 'carpenter and joiner' were part of specific industries—maintenance carpenters in cotton mills for example.
2. The components of the various occupational classes were not always consistent from one census to the next, hence it is impossible to rely on census classes as a guide to the number in any occupation over time.[1] One example will illustrate the problem: in the 'agricultural' classification farmers, shepherds, and agricultural labourers appeared in each census, but several minor occupations moved in

---

1. The degree of comparability is lowest between 1871 and 1881. Mitchell and Deane, op. cit., p. 56. Charles Booth reworked the summary figures of the 1841–81 censuses and presented them in a form which facilitates comparisons over time ('Occupations of the People of the United Kingdom, 1801–81').

and out of the category from one census to the next. Land surveyors and estate agents appeared in 1861 but disappeared in 1881; land-drainage workers appeared in 1871 and 1881 but not thereafter; teamsters and carters were introduced for the first time in 1891.[1] The occupational categories used to compile Tables 4–1 to 4–13 were selected with a view to minimizing error from chronological in-consistency in cenus categories.[2] A search for logic in classification can be seen in the comments of successive Registrar Generals—but their endeavour sometimes led them in the wrong direction. In 1851, for example, the main criterion was the material used by the worker; as a result, workers in wool and silk manufacture appeared alongside tallow chandlers, butchers, and others who worked with animal sub-stances, while cotton operatives appeared alongside greengrocers, bakers, and others who worked with vegetable matter.

3. There is some inconsistency and double-counting in the census arising from the ambiguity of certain occupational descriptions and the fact that certain occupations were known by various names in different parts of Britain. In 1861, for example, the county totals of 'clerks' had to be adjusted because the description had been used by both clergymen and commercial clerks. More serious are the numbers returned under amorphous categories; in particular those returned as 'spinners', 'weavers', or 'labourers'.[3] How many agricultural labourers or coal miners were returned as general labourers, and how much they affect the accuracy of the figures in Tables 4–1 to 4–13, is impossible to say except to note that the accuracy of the census probably improved over time. Other errors occurred at first source, due to ignorance or to what the Registrar General in 1891 termed, 'the foolish but very common desire of persons to magnify the im-portance of their occupational condition'. He was sceptical, for example, about the high proportion of hawkers and costermongers who returned themselves as employers of labour and he drew at-tention also to lads and girls who were actually engaged in the manu-facture of false teeth but who returned themselves as dentists.

1. The treatment of farmers' wives and daughters was particularly erratic. On these see above, pp. 118–19 and J. Bellamy, 'A Note on Occupational Sta-tistics in British Censuses', p. 306.
2. Comparisons between regions at any one date, of course, are not much affected by changes in definition between censuses. In 1871, however, the classifications used for Scotland differed slightly from those used for England and Wales.
3. The 1851 census, for example, in many cases returned unspecified 'weavers' under census class 13, sub-division 12; 'persons working and dealing in flax and cotton'.

4. County figures in the 1851–91 censuses are for 'registration' counties whereas those for 1901 and 1911 are for 'administrative' counties. The difference between the two was seldom great and in view of the number of other minor inaccuracies, and the fact that there were considerable numbers who lived in one county and worked in another, no attempt has been made to standardize boundaries.

5. Many people were engaged in more than one occupation, particularly in the early part of the period. In these cases the usual census practice was to return the person under the occupation in which he spent the greater part of his time.

6. There was some variation in the treatment of unemployed and 'retired' workers. The unemployed were usually assigned to the occupation they followed when last in work. The 'retired' were returned under their former occupations in 1851, 1861, and 1871, but in subsequent censuses they were included with the unemployed.

### *Census Categories used in Tables 4–1 to 4–13*
*Category 1    Working with Metals*

*1851*
Census class XI (10)
Census class XI (11)                    Engine and Machine Maker; Tool-
                                        maker
Census class XIV (9)–XIV (14) inclusive *except* the following:
                                        Copper Miner; Tin Miner; Lead
                                        Miner; Iron Miner; Ironmonger.

*1861 and 1871*
Census class X (9)                      Gunsmith; Gun Manufacturer.
Census class X (10)
Census class XV (9)–XV (14) *except* Ironmonger; Hardwareman;
                                        Dealer.

*1881*
Census class 10 (1), 10 (2).
Census class 10 (5)                     *except* 'Others'
Census class 21 (8)                     *except*    Ironmonger;    Hardware
                                        dealer, Merchant.
Census class 21 (9), 21 (10), 21 (11), 21 (12).

*1891*
Census class 10 (1), 10 (2), 10 (5).
Census class 21 (8)                     *except* Ironmonger; Hardware
                                        dealer; Merchant.
Census class 21 (9), 21 (10), 21 (11), 21 (12).

*1901*

Census class X (1), X (2), X (3), X (4), X (6), X (7).

Census class X (10)          Other dealers in Metals, Machines, etc.

*1911*

Census class X (1), X (2), X (3), X (5), X (7), X (8).

*Category 2   Domestic Service*

*1851*

| Census class VI (2) | Charwoman | Gardener |
| | Coachman | Groom |
| | Cook | Housemaid |
| | Domestic Servant (General) | Inn Servant |

*1861*

Census class V (2)          *except* Hospital Nurse; House-keeper; Nurse; Nurse (not Domestic Service).

*1871*

Census class 5 (2)          *except* Cook (not Domestic Service); Housekeeper; Nurse; Nurse (not Domestic Service).

*1881*

Census class 4 (1)

Census class 4 (2)          Charwoman.

*1891*

Census class 4 (1)

Census class 4 (2)          Charwomen; Office Keeper; Caretaker (not government).

*1901*

Census class IV (1)

Census class IV (2)          Domestic coachmen, grooms.

Census class IV (3)          College, Club, Service; Caretakers; Office, Park, Lodge, Gate, etc. Keepers (not government); Charwomen.

*1911*
Census class IV (1)
Census class IV (2)                    Domestic—Coachmen, Grooms;
                                       Domestic—Motor   Car   Drivers,
                                                 Attendants.
Census class IV (3)                    Caretakers; Office, Park, Lodge,
                                       Gate etc. Keeper (not govern-
                                       ment); Charwomen; Day Girls,
                                       Day Servants.

*Category 3    Workers in Wool*

*1851*
Census class XII (6)

*1861 and 1871*
Census class XI (1)

*1881 and 1891*
Census class 17 (1)
Census class 17 (5)                    Carpet, Rug, Manufacture.

*1901 and 1911*
Census class XVIII (2)
Census class XVIII (5)                 Carpet, Rug, Felt Manufacture.

*Category 4    Workers in Cotton, Flax, Lace.*

*1851*
Census class XIII (12)                 *except* Draper.

*1861 and 1871*
Census class XI (3)

*1881 and 1891*
Census class 17 (3)

*1901*
Census class XVIII (1)
Census class XVIII (5)                 Lace Manufacture.
Census class XVIII (6)                 Textile Bleachers, Dyers,
                                          Printers.

*1911*

| | |
|---|---|
| Census class XVIII (1) | |
| Census class XVIII (4) | Flax, Linen Manufacture. |
| Census class XVIII (5) | Lace Manufacture; Thread Manufacture. |
| Census class XVIII (6) | Textile Bleachers, Dyers, Printers. |

*Category 5     Workers in Silk and Straw and the Manufacture of Gloves, Stockings and Hats*

*1851*

| | |
|---|---|
| Census class VI (3) | Straw Hat and Bonnet Maker; Hose, Stocking-Manufacture, Glover (material not stated), Hatter, Bonnet-Maker, Cap-Maker. |
| Census class XII (7) | |
| Census class XIII (10) | Straw Plait Manufacture. |

*1861*

| | |
|---|---|
| Census class XI (2) | |
| Census class XI (5) | Straw Plait Manufacture; Straw Hat, Bonnet Maker; Hose, Stocking Manufacture; Glover, Leather; Glove Knitter; Hatter, Hat Manufacture; Bonnet Maker, Cap Maker. |

*1871*

| | |
|---|---|
| Census class 11 (2) | |
| Census class 11 (5) | Straw Plait Manufacture; Hosiery Manufacture; Glover (Leather); Glove Maker (all except leather); Hatter, Hat Manufacture. |

*1881 and 1891*

| | |
|---|---|
| Census class 17 (2) | |
| Census class 18 (1) | Straw Hat, Bonnet, Plait Manufacture; Hosiery Manufacture; Glover, Glove Maker; Hatter, Hat Manufacture (not straw). |

*1901*

| | |
|---|---|
| Census class XVIII (3) | |
| Census class XVIII (5) | Hosiery Manufacture. |
| Census class XIX (1) | Straw Plait Manufacture; Straw Hat, Bonnet Manufacture; Glove Makers; Felt Hat Manufacture; Makers of other Hats and Caps etc. |

*1911*

| | |
|---|---|
| Census class XVIII (3) | |
| Census class XVIII (5) | Hosiery Manufacture. |
| Census class XIX (1) | Straw Plait Manufacture; Straw Hat, Bonnet Manufacture; Glove Makers; Felt Hat Manufacture; Makers of Cloth Hats and Caps; Makers of Other Hats and Caps. |

*Category 6    Workers in Mines and Quarries*

*1851*

| | |
|---|---|
| Census class XIV (1) | Coal Miner. |
| Census class XIV (2) | Stone Quarrier. |
| Census class XIV (2) | Slate Quarrier. |
| Census class XIV (2) | Limestone Quarrier, Burner. |
| Census class XIV (9) | Copper Miner. |
| Census class XIV (10) | Tin Miner. |
| Census class XIV (12) | Lead Miner. |
| Census class XIV (14) | Iron Miner. |

*1861*

| | |
|---|---|
| Census class XV (1) | Coal Miner; Copper Miner, Tin, Lead, Iron, Miners. |
| Census class XV (3) | Stone Quarrier; Stone Cutter, Polisher; Slate Quarrier; Limestone Quarrier and Burner. |

*1871*

| | |
|---|---|
| Census class 15 (1) | Coal, Copper, Lead, Iron, Tin Miner. |
| Census class 15 (3) | Stone Quarrier, Stone Merchant, Cutter, Dresser; Slate Quarrier; Limestone Quarrier; Lime-Burner. |

*1881*

| Census class 21 (1) | Coal, Tin, Copper, Ironstone, Lead Miners. |
| Census class 21 (3) . | Stone Quarrier; Stone Cutter, Dresser, Dealer; Slate Quarrier; Slate Worker, Dealer. |

*1891*

| Census class 21 (1) | Coal, Tin, Copper, Ironstone, Lead Miners. |
| Census class 21 (3) | Stone Quarrier, Cutter, Dresser, Slate-Quarrier, Worker. |

*1901*

| Census class IX (1) | Coal and Shale Mine-Hewers. |
| | Coal and Shale Mine—Other workers. below ground. |
| | Coal and Shale Mine—Workers above ground. |
| | Tin, Copper, Ironstone, Lead Miners. |
| Census class IX (2) | Stone-Quarriers, Cutters, Dressers. |
| | Slate-Quarriers, Workers. |

*1911*

| Census class IX (1) | Coal and Shale Mines—Workers at the face. |
| | Coal and Shale Mines—Other workers below ground. |
| | Coal and Shale Mines—Workers above ground. |
| | Iron—Miners and Quarriers |
| | Tin, Copper, Lead Miners |
| | Stone-Miners, Quarriers |
| | Stone-Cutters, Dressers |
| | Slate-Miners, Quarriers. |

*Category 7*    *Workers in Various Craft Occupations—Boot and Shoe Makers, Carpenters, Millers, Saddlers, Harness Makers, Tailors.*

*1851*

| | |
|---|---|
| Census class VI (3) | Shoe Maker; Patten and Clog Maker; Tailor. |
| Census class XI (13) | Saddler, Whip Maker; Other Harness Makers. |
| Census class XI (15) | Carpenter, Joiner. |
| Census class XIII (1) | Miller. |

*1861 and 1871*

| | |
|---|---|
| Census class X (12) | |
| Census class X (14) | Carpenter, Joiner. |
| Census class XI (5) | Shoemaker, Bootmaker; Patten and Clog Maker; Tailor. |
| Census class XII (2) | Miller. |

*1881*

| | |
|---|---|
| Census class 11 (1) | Carpenter, Joiner. |
| Census class 12 (2) | |
| Census class 16 (3) | Corn Miller. |
| Census class 18 (1) | Tailor; Shoe Boot, Maker, Dealer; Patten, Clog Maker. |

*1891*

| | |
|---|---|
| Census class 11 (1) | Carpenter, Joiner. |
| Census class 12 (2) | |
| Census class 16 (3) | Corn Miller. |
| Census class 18 (1) | Tailor; Boot and Shoe Maker; Patten, Clog Maker. |

*1901 and 1911*

| | |
|---|---|
| Census class XII (1) | Carpenters, Joiners. |
| Census class XVI (2) | |
| Census class XIX (1) | Tailors; Boot, Shoe Makers; Slipper Makers; Patten, Clog Makers. |
| Census class XX (1) | Millers, Cereal Food Manufacturers. |

*Category 8    Workers on the Railway*

*1851*

| | |
|---|---|
| Census class VIII (1) | |
| Census class XIV (2) | Railway Labourer, Platelayer. |

*1861*
Census class VII (1)
Census class XV (3)            Railway Labourer, Platelayer.

*1871*
Census class 7 (1)
Census class 15 (3)           Railway Labourer; Platelayer, Navvy.

*1881 and 1891*
Census class 6 (1)
Census class 21 (3)           Platelayer, Railway Labourer, Navvy.

*1901 and 1911*
Census class VI (1)
Census class XII (2)          Navvies, Railway Contractors' Labourers.

*Category 9   Workers in the Chemical, Pottery, Glass and Paper Industries*

*1851*
Census class XI (17)
Census class XIII (13)        Paper Manufacture.
Census class XIV (3)          Earthenware Manufacture.
Census class XIV (4)          Glass Manufacture.

*1861*
Census class X (17)
Census class XIV (5)          Paper Manufacture.
Census class XV (4)           Earthenware Manufacture.
Census class XV (5)           Glass Manufacture.

*1871*
Census class 10 (16)          (England and Wales)
Census class 10 (17)          (Scotland)
Census class 14 (5)           Paper Manufacture.
Census class 15 (4)           Earthenware Manufacture.
Census class 15 (5)           Glass Manufacture.

*1881*
Census class 14 (1)
Census class 14 (2)
Census class 14 (3)           Manufacturing Chemist; Alkali Manufacture.

| Census class 20 (4) | Paper Manufacture. |
| Census class 21 (4) | Earthenware, China, Porcelain Manufacture; Glass Manufacture. |

*1891*

| Census class 14 (1) | |
| Census class 14 (2) | |
| Census class 14 (3) | Manufacturing Chemist; Alkali Manufacture. |
| Census class 20 (4) | Paper Manufacture; Paper Box, Paper Bag Maker. |
| Census class 21 (4) | Earthenware, China, Porcelain, Manufacture; Glass Manufacture. |

*1901*

| Census class XIV (1) | Earthenware, China, Porcelain Manufacture; Sheet, Plate-Glass Manufacture; Glass Bottle Manufacture; Other Workers in Glass Manufacture. |
| Census class XV (1) | |
| Census class XV (2) | |
| Census class XV (3) | Manufacturing Chemists; Alkali Manufacture. |
| Census class XVII (1) | Paper Manufacture; Paper Box, Paper Bag Makers. |

*1911*

| Census class XIV (1) | Earthenware, China, Porcelain Manufacture; Sheet, Plate-Glass Manufacture; Glass Bottle Manufacture; Other Workers in Glass Manufacture. |
| Census class XV (1) | |
| Census class XV (2) | |
| Census class XV (2) | Manufacturing Chemists, Alkali Manufacture. |
| Census class XVII (1) | Paper Manufacture; Paper Bag Makers; Cardboard Box Makers. |

*Category 10    Workers in Coachbuilding, Shipbuilding*

*1851*

Census class XI (12)                 Coachmaker; Others connected
                                     with carriage making.

Census class XI (14).

*1861 and 1871*

Census class X (11)                  Coachmaker.
Census class X (13)

*1881*

Census class 12 (1)                  Coachmaker.
Census class 13 (1)
Census class 13 (2)

*1891*

Census class 12 (1)                  Coach, Carriage Makers.
Census class 13 (1)
Census class 13 (2)

*1901*

Census class X (8)
Census class X (9)                   Coach, Carriage Makers.

*1911*

Census class X (9)
Census class X (10)                  Coach, Carriage Makers.

*Category 11    New Industries*

*1911*

Census class X (4)
Census class X (10)                  Cycle Makers; Motor Car Chassis
                                     Makers; Motor Car Mechanics;
                                     Motor Car Body Makers.

*Category 12    Workers in Commerce*

*1851*

Census class VII (1)                 Merchant; Accountant; Commer-
                                     cial Clerk; Commerical Travel-
                                     ler.

*1861*

Census class VI (1)

*1871*
Census class 6 (1)

*1881 and 1891*
Census class 5 (1)
Census class 5 (2)
Census class 5 (3)

*1901 and 1911*
Census class V (1)
Census class V (2)
Census class V (3)
Census class V (4)

*Category 13    Workers in Agriculture*

*1851*
Census class IX (1)              Farmer; Grazier; Farm Bailiff;
                                 Agricultural Labourer (out-
                                 door); Shepherd; Farm Servant
                                 (indoor).

*1861*
Census class VIII (1)            Farmer, Grazier; Farm Bailiff;
                                 Agricultural Labourer; Shep-
                                 herd; Farm Servant (indoor);
                                 (in Scotland only) Ploughman
                                 and Cattleman.

*1871*
Figures shown in S. B. L. Druce, 'The Alteration in the Distri-
bution of the Agricultural Population of England and Wales',
*J.R.Ag.S.* 2nd Ser., xxi, (1885). Druce's figures cover the following
categories; Farmer, Grazier; Farm Bailiff, Agricultural Labourer,
Shepherd, Farm Servant (indoor); Agricultural Machine Proprietor,
Attendant; Others engaged in Agriculture.

*1881, 1891, 1901*
Figures from *Report on the Decline of the Agricultural Population*,
P.P. 1906, XCVI, pp. 114–17. These figures cover the following categories; Farmers and Graziers; Farm Bailiffs and Foremen; Shepherds; Agricultural Labourers and Farm Servants.

*1911*
Census class VII (1)

Farmers, Graziers; Farm Bailiffs, Foreman; Shepherds; Agricultural Labourers—in charge of cattle, horses, and not distinguished; Crofter (in Scotland only).

# 5

# PRODUCTIVITY

## I

CHAPTER Four showed that throughout the period employers continued to invest capital and to recruit workers in those areas where demand for labour was already substantial—there is no evidence of a general mobilizing of capital to employ low-wage labour after the fashion postulated by neo-classical general equilibrium theory. It does not necessarily follow, however, that because capital was immobile in this sense it was also immobile in the sense that it failed to respond to incentives.[1] If low wages were offset by low productivity two important consequences would follow. First, there would be far less reason to suspect that capital failed to respond to spatial incentives and, second, it would be reasonable to suppose that variations in labour productivity helped to maintain existing wage differentials.

There are fairly good *a priori* reasons for assuming the existence of a positive relationship between wage levels and labour productivity levels. The rapid development of heavy industry in west-central Scotland in the 1830s and the extraordinary growth of towns like Middlesbrough and Barrow-in-Furness, both examples of capital mobility in response to raw material discoveries and technical change, are sufficient reasons to exclude the possibility that investment failed to respond to wage incentives as a consequence of some all-pervasive torpidity. In agriculture there is the example of Scottish capital moving into East Anglia in the 1880s attracted not by cheap labour but by low rents and good leases.[2]

1. Each of these usages is different from the most commonly used concept of 'capital mobility' which refers to the movement of funds between areas, between individuals, and between institutions regardless of the spatial distribution of the investment the funds make possible.
2. J. H. Clapham, *An Economic History of Modern Britain* (Cambridge, 1951 edn.), iii. 84.

The uneven distribution of natural resources and its effect upon output-per-man in mining and similar occupations provides one obvious example where variations in productivity and wages were closely linked. The *Returns of Wages Published between 1830 and 1886*[1] presented Staffordshire colliers' earnings for 1843 in two categories: 'working thick coal' and 'working thin coal'. The first of these were paid 4*s*. a shift, the second 2*s*. 8*d*.—this example illustrates a relationship which influenced wages on every coalfield. Labour accounted for a very high proportion of total cost in mining; as a consequence there was a strong positive relationship between relative labour productivity and relative wages and a major determinant of variations in productivity was geology.[2] The ill-paid miners of Somerset showed their awareness of the link between pay, productivity, and the inability of local owners to pay better wages when they opposed trade union proposals for a national minimum wage in 1912.[3] The Forest of Dean was another field where wages were well below average for reasons very similar to those which affected Somerset:

Q. From the point of view of productivity how has it stood with regard to percentage with the rest?
A. Behind.
Q. From the point of view of wages how has it stood with regard to percentage with the rest?
A. Behind.
Q. From the point of view of profit how has it stood?
A. Behind.[4]

A great many similar examples could be cited: G. C. Allen described how centuries of mining of the 'most elementary character' caused much of the southern part of the south Staffordshire field to resemble a 'water-logged rabbit warren', so that by the 1860s there were already signs of exhaustion, falling employment, and failing output—a situation which

1. P.P. 1887, LXXXIX, p. 25.
2. Rowe, *Wages in the Coal Industry*, pp. 119–20, 123.
3. See above, p. 16.
4. Evidence on the Forest of Dean, *Coal Industry Commission*, P.P. 1919, XI, p. 293; see also 1919, XII, para. 21380 of the same commission and H. S. Jevons, op. cit., p. 80. On wages in this field see above, pp. 16–17.

doubtless helps to account for the relative decline in south
Staffordshire mine wages mentioned in Chapter One.[1]

# II

Occupations in which high wages were compensated by
natural advantages provide one category of cases where wage
differentials were in part a consequence of variations in productivity. However, there were many economic activities where
capital was not tied to raw materials and yet failed to respond
to wage variations. Gunnar Myrdal, a leading critic of neo-
classical general equilibrium theory as applied to regional
inequalities, claims 'all history shows that the cheap and
often docile labour of under-developed regions does not usually
attract industry.' [2] The situation in Britain after 1850 is
certainly consistent with his claim but conditions in 'pre-
industrial' Britain, when most manufacturing was carried on
in small workshops or through some variation of the putting-
out process, cast some doubt on his generalization. At that time
capital was not slow to exploit surplus labour and, as a consequence, low wages were a fairly important factor in industrial

1. Allen, *Birmingham and the Black Country*, pp. 85–6, 142, 194, and see
   above, p. 31. The examples mentioned above are intended merely to
   illustrate a general situation. The existence of mine output and employment
   figures for the period after 1870 affords rather more scope for a detailed
   study of the relationship between productivity and coal wages than would
   be possible for most industries. However, the investigation would not be as
   easy as it might appear. First, because coal is not homogeneous—thus
   productivity would need to be measured in terms of value rather than
   physical output. Second, because price was also a function of market size;
   a low physical productivity pit, for example, might secure high productivity
   per head in value terms by restricting sales to within a few miles of the pit-
   head. Third, because productivity was closely related to output so that
   productivity could be varied by employing more or fewer men; for example,
   a small number of men slowly extracting the choice seams in a poorly
   endowed area could achieve very high productivity levels although the
   absence of the expansion which occurred elsewhere would probably be
   reflected by low earnings. For these various reasons a detailed investigation
   of the relationship between wages and productivity would need to incorporate data on the reserves of each coalfield, the rate of expansion possible
   without rapid falls in productivity, and several other variables besides
   wage rates and output per man-year.
2. G. Myrdal, *Economic Theory and Under-Developed Regions* (1957), p. 31.

location: 'the most important reason for the growth of the
woollen industry in certain parts of the countryside was the
search for cheap labour. Labour was the main factor of production in most industries in pre-industrial England and producers selling in competitive national and international
markets were very conscious of their labour costs.' [1] Ambrose
Crowley established his ironworks in the north because the
north, he noted, was 'verry poore and populous soe workmen
must of necessity increase'; similarly the overpopulated villages
of the east Midlands attracted London hosiery and footwear
manufacturers and, according to Clapham, low wages helped the
West Riding worsted industry in its struggle with Norfolk.
Clapham also quoted the opinion of a contemporary historian
that the ancient baize manufacture of Essex was lost to the
north and west 'where provisions are cheaper, the poor more
easily satisfied, and coals are very plentiful'.[2] One reason for
the diminished attraction of low wages in the nineteenth
century was a widespread and significant change in methods of
production. In very broad terms, economic activity was
relatively labour intensive in the earlier period and became
increasingly less so from the mid-eighteenth century onwards.
Whatever the initial reasons for investing in a particular area,
and these often included low wages, the combination of capital
and up-to-date technology[3] made for reduced costs, better
labour productivity, and higher wages. In the typical case
costs were sufficiently reduced for labour to secure a considerable rise in wages without jeopardizing the employers'

1. L. A. Clarkson, *The Pre-Industrial Economy in England, 1500–1750*
   (1971), p. 94.
2. S. Pollard, *The Genesis of Modern Management* (1968 edn.), p. 197 (subsequently referred to as Pollard, *Modern Management*); Clarkson, op. cit.
   p. 97; J. H. Clapham, 'The Transference of the Worsted Industry from
   Norfolk to the West Riding', *Economic Journal*, xx (1910), 201; *idem, An
   Economic History of Modern Britain* (Cambridge, 1950), i. 44. On this theme
   generally see also D. S. Landes, *Cambridge Economic History of Europe*
   (Cambridge, 1965), vi, Pt. I, 277.
3. In this account more capital-intensive production and the use of advanced
   technology are regarded as near synonymous. Their separate influences
   would in any case be difficult to distinguish although it should be noted
   that most studies of the role of capital in the industrial revolution, particularly those on the cotton industry, stress the very considerable results
   obtainable from modest capital investment in advanced technology.

ability to compete with the less capital-intensive output of low-wage labour. In these circumstances low wages lost their attraction. Well-paid labour was no longer necessarily dear and badly paid labour not necessarily cheap. Moreover, as production in the advanced areas increased external economies developed and tied capital more firmly to high wages.[1]

This pattern is too well known to require much elaboration. D. C. Coleman has described how, during the 1820s and 1830s, large silk-manufacturing units with 'up-to-date throwing machinery and efficient sources of power' prospered in the high-wage north while 'small, remote, old-fashioned mills' in the south went under.[2] The beneficial effect of steam power upon Nottingham lace wages has been described by Roy Church,[3] and some of the consequences of competition between Nottingham and low-wage counties like Buckinghamshire, and between provincial factories and East End sweat-shops were mentioned earlier. Clara Collet described conditions in the cap-making trade: 'The small masters can only compete with the large masters, who have good machinery, by working long hours and paying low wages . . . . The factory system in this trade is beating the small workshops out of the field.'[4]

1. The description above is a very generalized account of the typical order of events. There was a great diversity in the way these events affected different industries; Ch. 4 of this investigation mentions several industries whose mechanization had scarcely begun in 1850. There were also several exceptions to the pattern described. Heathcoats, the lace firm which moved from Nottingham to Tiverton in 1816 partly as a consequence of Luddite activities, is perhaps the best-known of these. According to Church the firm suffered by isolating itself from the inspiration that comes from being at the centre of things; few copied its example. R. A. Church, *Economic and Social Change in a Midland Town: Victorian Nottingham 1815–1900*, pp. 45–6, 66, 78. At certain times, particularly in the 1830s, there was talk of moving to the low-wage south and even to Ireland among some of the textile manufacturers of Lancashire and Glasgow—but no movement of consequence occurred; see above, p. 165, and below, p. 300.
2. D. C. Coleman, *Courtaulds*, i. 60–7.
3. Church, op. cit., pp. 266–8; *idem*, 'Technological Change and the Hosiery Board of Conciliation and Arbitration, 1860–84', *Yks. Bull.*, xv (1963), 53. The introduction of steam power to shipping conferred similar advantages upon merchant seamen; in 1860 wages were said to average 54s. a month on sailing ships and 64s. a month on steamships (Bowley, *Wages in the U.K.*, p. 79).
4. Booth, *Life and Labour*, 1st Ser., iv. 294 and, for other examples, Ibid., pp. 63, 339.

While the combination of advanced production techniques and high labour productivity has a large part in explaining why demand for labour was concentrated in high-wage areas, it should also be noted that if labour productivity rose sufficiently fast in a particular area the increase in employment there might be far less than the increase in output and high wages might then occur in conjunction with quite modest increases in demand for labour. It was noted earlier that the Lancashire, Cheshire, and West Riding region was an exception to the general correlation between the level of wages and the rate of increase in demand for labour,[1] and it is probably significant that in at least one of the region's major industries increasing productivity and high wages were combined with slowly expanding employment. Between 1851 and 1911 cotton output rose at least threefold and earnings rose rapidly while employment increased by less than half.[2] According to Wood, earnings rose 69 per cent between 1860 and 1906; of this increase, 13 percentage points were a consequence of adults replacing children, 7 were due to higher piece-rates, and 49 (i.e. about 70 per cent of the total) were due to higher productivity.[3] Productivity rose sufficiently for employers to meet demand with little extra labour and at the same time made it possible for labour to negotiate wages far higher than might otherwise have been expected in an industry whose share of the total labour force was falling.

The quality of management can be considered separately as a third link between labour productivity and wage differentials. When high labour productivity and heavy capital investment were found together they were normally associated with good management, and management and investment were so closely linked that it may be pedantic to consider them apart. They can be separated in some respects however; there are cases, such as the attempt to establish cotton manufacturing at Hull in the

1. See above, pp. 164–8.
2. See above, p. 167; Mitchell and Deane, op. cit., p. 179; and G. H. Wood, *Wages in the Cotton Trades*, pp. 139, 146–7.
3. G. H. Wood, *Wages in the Cotton Trades*, p. 139.

1830s and 1840s,[1] where heavy investment in up-to-date plant failed to benefit either capital or labour because good management extended no further than building and equipping the mills; further, there are many managerial functions which require little or no capital and for this reason the separate influences of the two variables were possibly more easily distinguished in pre-industrial Britain. As the industrial revolution got under way, however, the two variables became closely linked; at the same time technical change, the increased scale of enterprise, and falling transport costs, were all increasing the potential influence of good management and adequate capital upon productivity, wages, and the prosperity of different regions.[2] These influences, combined with the uneven distribution of natural resources, must have played a major part in the maintenance of those remarkable contrasts in regional prosperity described in Chapters One and Four which made nineteenth-century Britain a good example of 'regional dualism'.[3] There was, of course, nothing entirely novel about the existence of contrasts in the prosperity of different regions—Gilboy has emphasized the distinction between the West Country and the north in the eighteenth century, and the reputation of the advanced north-eastern coalfield was established sometime before this[4]—but changes in the method of production after 1750 so much enhanced the possible influence of capital and management upon productivity that, contrary to what might be expected in a century of falling transport costs and widening horizons, the likelihood of large variations in regional prosperity failed to diminish and probably increased.

---

1. L. M. Brown, *V. C. H. Yorkshire, East Riding*, i (1969), 223–4.
2. On the role of the railways in industrial location see below, pp. 266–72.
3. See above, p. 181.
4. The West Country, according to Gilboy, was characterized by apathy and indifference, 'weighed down by tradition', and lacking in the dynamic elements of the kind likely to provide a 'fertile ground for the introduction or expansion of new industrial methods'. The north, by contrast, was distinguished by evidence of restlessness, ambition, and flexibility (E. W. Gilboy, *Wages in Eighteenth Century England*, pp. 133–4). On the reputation of the north-eastern coalfield see, Pollard, *Modern Management*, pp. 56, 81–2, 152.

# III

A further possible connection between wages and productivity
is variation in the intrinsic quality of labour. Until now it has
been assumed that labour itself was homogeneous and higher
labour productivity, where it occurred, a consequence of
combining labour with more capital, better resources, or
superior management. But these were not the only causes of
high labour productivity—differences in the quality of labour
were among the influences which helped to maintain the advantages of the well-paid regions. One distinguishing feature of
the more dynamic parts of Britain was that they acquired a
labour force that was more flexible, more energetic, and more
skilled in the operation of advanced equipment. These qualities
were an important external economy and among the forces
which kept capital from moving to low-wage areas; they were
in part a consequence of education and training in a pro-
gressive society and in part a consequence of selective migration.[1]

Another cause of spatial variations in labour productivity
was the link between productivity and diet. The vicious circle
of low productivity, low wages, and malnutrition[2] is more
often associated with dualism of the 'colonial' type than with
conditions of the kind that existed in nineteenth-century
Britain. However, although Britain in the nineteenth century
was rich compared with many African and Asian countries in
the mid-twentieth century, the pervasiveness of the subsistence wage concept in economic theory before 1850, and the
findings of Booth, Rowntree, and similar investigators at the
end of the century, suggest that a considerable number of
workers may have earned less than the level where the link
between diet and productivity ceases to be significant. The
opinions of certain railway contractors lend weight to this
hypothesis. In evidence before the *Select Committee on Railway
Labourers* Captain Moorsom, the resident director of the Chester
and Holyhead line, drew attention to the favourable effect of

1. Some examples are given below, pp. 216–17.
2. Poor accommodation and clothing might be added to malnutrition.

railway construction upon Welsh workmen: 'how much better they feed and how they are emulating the English in the amount of work they can do. The position at the beginning was five Welshmen to three Englishmen in filling waggons, and now they are coming to par.' [1] Peto compared ill-fed Irishmen with well-paid, but no dearer, English labour and Brassey was similarly unflattering about the French, citing cases where French labour proved more expensive than Englishmen paid twice as much: 'the meagre diet of the French labourers rendered them physically incapable of vieing with the Englishmen.' [2] Navvying, of course, required exceptional energy but it was also extraordinarily well paid by the standards of the time. There were many occupations which were less arduous but sufficiently badly paid to support the hypothesis of significant links between wages, diet, and labour productivity. Farm-work is an obvious example; there is surely significance in the fact that Brassey recruited mainly in the high-wage north, yet it still required a year of high wages and good feeding before farm labourers became competent navvies.[3] The position in agriculture is particularly important; first, because large numbers were employed in agriculture and, second, because the level of farm wages exercised a considerable influence on wages in other occupations.[4] For these reasons, and because general accounts of nineteenth-century agriculture give labour pro-ductivity less attention than it deserves, the situation merits closer investigation.[5]

1. *S.C. on Railway Labourers*, P.P. 1846, XIII, Evidence, para. 1795.
2. T. Coleman, *The Railway Navvies* (1968 edn.), p. 70; T. Brassey, *Lectures on the Labour Question* (1878, 3rd edn.), pp. 13, 280.
3. T. Brassey, *Work and Wages* (1916), pp. iv–v.
4. See above, pp. 4, 65–6.
5. The following analysis of the relationship between wage levels and labour productivity in agriculture is an abridged and revised version of an article which appeared in the *Economic History Review* in 1967. For subsequent discussion on some of the points raised in this article, and an attempt to quantify regional variations in farm labour productivity using harvest piece-rates, see D. Metcalf, 'Labour Productivity in English Agriculture, 1850–1914: A Theoretical Comment', and my rejoinder in *Ec.H.R.*, 2nd Ser., xxii (1969); P. A. David, 'Labour Productivity in English Agriculture, 1850–1914: Some Quantitative Evidence on Regional Differences', *Ec.H.R.*, 2nd Ser., xxiii (1970); E. H. Hunt, 'Quantitative and Other Evidence on Labour Productivity in Agriculture, 1850–1914', ibid.

The fact that farmers in the low-wage south paid their labour considerably less than rates current in parts of the north and Midlands and yet appear not to have prospered from their advantage is both remarkable in itself and suggests the existence of a positive relationship between wages and productivity. Recent writing on agriculture has placed great emphasis upon trends in arable and livestock prices after 1850 and the consequent contrast in the fortunes of different areas, but spatial variations in wage rates were at least as great. The advantage that farmers in Lancashire derived from buoyant livestock prices is scarcely sufficient to explain the contrast between their fortunes and the 'depressed' farmers in East Anglia when the latter could obtain labour for three-quarters or less of the level of wages in Lancashire and, in addition, had lower rents. Moreover, the ability of Lancashire farmers to pay higher wages than farmers in the south-west clearly owed little to price trends because both areas were largely pastoral.

Assessing productivity levels in agriculture is difficult. The diversity of output, the paucity of production figures, the vagaries of the weather, the great variety of soils, and the numerous tasks involved in farm work are such that it is probably impossible to produce realistic figures of output per man for every area.[1] In the absence of comprehensive statistical evidence it is necessary to fall back upon literary evidence and fragmentary statistics based upon comparisons between individual farms or small areas. Fortunately, evidence of this type is available in sufficient quantity and quality. In broad terms, contemporary opinion agreed that agricultural labour in the south and in East Anglia was inferior in quality to that in much of Scotland, the north of England, and the north Midlands—a pattern which suggests a close correlation between wages and productivity. This opinion was frequently substantiated by farm accounts, which, although not based upon any large-scale or random sample, nevertheless, by their

1. Paul David attempted to provide such an index based upon harvest piece-rates but his figures, and the conclusion he draws from them, are not convincing—see above, p. 205 n. 5.

volume and unanimity of conclusion, leave one with little
doubt as to the truth of the main thesis. During his mid-
century tour James Caird made comparisons between the labour
productivity of different areas. He looked particularly at
agricultural workers on Salisbury Plain whose labour he
considered more costly than labour in areas where higher wage
rates were paid.[1] The 1867 *Commission on the Employment of
Children, Young Persons, and Women in Agriculture* contained
similar evidence. J. T. Blackburn, a farmer from Aldershot,
based his opinion upon experience of using Scottish as well as
Hampshire labourers. He was of the opinion that, 'Two Scotch-
men will at any description of work equal three English
labourers.'[2] In the same inquiry George Culley, one of the
assistant commissioners, remarked that the cost of labour in
low-wage Bedfordshire was up to 7s. p.a. an acre greater than
in Northumberland and another assistant commissioner quoted
the opinion of a steward to the Duke of Bedford that: 'Whereas
in Lancashire a man would get 2s. 6d. a day, and in Devon
1s. 8d. a day, the former would do for 7d. the same as the latter
for 1s. 8d.'[3] The following comparison of labour costs in Norfolk
and Forfarshire, published in *The Times* of 17 October 1874 as
part of a speech made by C. S. Read, M.P., to the Agricultural
Association, is of particular interest in that it goes into some
detail about the nature of the areas in question and thus
removes the possibility that labour costs are being compared
for areas in which arable and pastoral farming were not found
in equal proportions:

Mr. Barclay, the Member for Forfarshire, is, like me, a tenant-
farmer .... He farms 380 acres arable land, which is exactly the
acreage of land I have at Honingham. He has 75 acres of rough
pasture, and I have 40 acres of good permanent grass; he grows 20
acres more corn than I do, but he has less roots and more grass seeds
than I have ... I should say he would require as much manual
labour on his farm as I do on mine. But mark the difference. For

1. Caird, op. cit., pp. 84–5.
2. *Commission on the Employment of Children, Young Persons, and Women in
   Agriculture*, P.P. 1867–8, XVII, First Report, p. 160.
3. Ibid., p. xxviii and Second Report, P.P. 1868–9, XIII, Report H, p. 48.

four years ending 1871 the average annual payment for labour. . . was £400, while mine was £750. . . You must surely admit that . . . the Scotchman is a sharper and keener man of business than I am; and I also come reluctantly to the conclusion that the highly-paid Scottish hind is a cheaper and better man than the Norfolk labourer, and that after all there is no such thing as cheap labour.

The declining prosperity among some sectors of agriculture after 1872 gave rise to a great deal of regional analysis of labour cost and the agricultural journals of the period include many examples of the varying quality of farm labour in different regions.[1] There is similar evidence in the Royal Commission on Agricultural Depression[2] and in a paper by A. Wilson Fox on the wages and conditions of agricultural labourers read before the *Royal Statistical Society* in 1903.[3] In all, we are left in no doubt that contemporaries believed that productivity varied substantially in different parts of the country. The evidence supporting their opinion was empirical and impressionistic but the frequency and consistency of this evidence, together with the fact that substantial wage variations existed and were not reflected by spatial variations in farm prosperity, suggest that they were right.[4] There is further evidence which suggests strongly that a major cause of regional variations in productivity was variation in diet together with certain attitudes towards work of a kind often associated with low wages and under-employment.

A number of other factors could conceivably have accounted for the variations in productivity described above. Soil conditions are one possibility. Recent work on agricultural history has emphasized the difficulties of farmers who worked the heavy clays, and in Oxfordshire and large parts of Essex, Sussex, and some other low-wage counties the clay soil must

1. See e.g. F. Clifford, 'The Labour Bill in Farming'.
2. See e.g. *R.C. on Agricultural Depression*, P.P. 1894, XVIi, Report by R. Hunter Pringle, pp. 46–7, XVIii, p. 544, QQ 31956–7; 1896, XVII, p. 411, QQ 61249–56.
3. Published in *J.R.S.S.*, lxvi (1903).
4. For further evidence on this question and a fuller discussion of the merits of the evidence shown above see the references cited on p. 205 n. 5 above.

have had at least a marginal effect upon labour productivity. But the relationship cannot be pressed far and has probably been over-emphasized. Every county contains a diversity of soils—parts of high wage Northumberland are heavy clay and much of Norfolk consists of light soil.[1] A second possibility is that productivity was lower in some regions because of deficiencies in methods and farm management. But here again no definite and general correlation can be established. Where management was efficient, backed by adequate capital, and equipped with a knowledge of the most advanced techniques, then clearly the productivity of labour and the wage level was likely to benefit. But the relationship was not sufficiently constant to provide a full answer, managerial efficiency varied far more from farm to farm than between major regions. Norfolk provides a good example of this point. Although by then becoming somewhat tarnished, Norfolk's agricultural reputation remained high in the second half of the nineteenth century—but wage-rates and labour productivity there were among the lowest in the land. In Lancashire Caird found that 'good farming . . . is still the exception'[2]—yet Lancashire labourers were well paid and their productivity was as high as that of labourers in almost any other county. Similarly in Durham; Caird noted its neglected drainage and that the old two-crop and fallow system was still the common practice.[3] Durham, of course, was a high wage area, and a county whose labour costs were often favourably contrasted with low-wage counties in the south and east. Clearly high labour productivity and good farming practice were by no means always found together[4] and, although farm methods and soil conditions, together, take us some way towards explaining regional labour

1. On this point see M. K. Ashby, *Joseph Ashby of Tysoe, 1859–1919*, p. 33: 'On drizzling days, walking beside Jasper's team of three horses, on the low clayland under Windmill Hill . . . It was an effort to pull each foot from the clinging sticky earth, and one had a hundred feet! But on the red, light soils of the upper fields work went well, even with a team of only two.'
2. Caird, op. cit., pp. 264–6.
3. Ibid., pp. 331–4.
4. For further discussion on this point, and in particular on capital–labour ratios, see references to the *Economic History Review*, 2nd Ser., xxii and xxiii cited above, p. 205 n. 5.

productivity variations in agriculture, much remains to be explained.

While Britain in the mid nineteenth century can hardly be considered 'under-developed' in the sense that this description is applied to much of Africa, Asia, and Latin America in the mid-twentieth century, conditions within Britain varied enormously and it seems more than possible that the productivity of sectors of England's agricultural labour force was affected by under-nourishment and attitudes to work of a kind usually associated with 'under-developed' economies. When Caird described the low productivity of agricultural labourers on the Salisbury Plain, he also indicated what he considered to be the probable reason for their deficiency. The labourers existed almost entirely upon flour, butter, bread, and potatoes. He observed that they showed 'a want of that vigour and activity which mark the well-fed ploughmen of the northern and midland counties'.[1] This is hardly surprising: their food, even if available in unlimited quantities, contained insufficient protein to ensure continuous health and vigour. Caird's evidence is only a small part of a total which suggests strongly that sectors of the English agricultural labour force were living at a standard which, while adequate to sustain life, fell short of the level needed to ensure maximum labour efficiency. The situation exhibits a well-known feature of under-developed economies: low wage-rates were a cause as well as a consequence of low productivity. Low wages were themselves a barrier to higher wages.

Medical evidence given to the 1843 *Commission on the Employment of Women and Children in Agriculture*[2] described the labourer's diet in the West Country as inadequate to allow recovery when ill health occurred. In Somerset labourers existed largely on bread and potatoes with occasionally a little bacon or cheese, and labourers in East Anglia were fortunate if they tasted meat more than once or twice a week.[3] In south-west

1. Caird, op. cit., pp. 84–5.
2. P.P. 1843, XII, p. 18.
3. Ibid., pp. 19, 217. For other references to diet in the low-wage south see above, pp. 10, 14–15, 17–19.

Wales, it was said, labourers were so ill fed that they were physically incapable of sustained output of the kind common-place in the higher-wage English counties: "a Lincolnshire workman at half-a-crown a day is not dearer than most Welsh labourers at a shilling.'[1] Further evidence of this nature can be found in Appendix Six of the *Sixth Report of the Medical Officer of the Privy Council* by Dr. Edward Smith:

Although the health and strength of the people may be moderately well maintained on the existing dietary, it is more probable that mental vigour and activity, as well as moral courage and enterprise, are less where the diet is low . . . There can be no doubt that the mental and physical condition of the farm labourer and his family is much better in these localities, where remunerative labour other than farm labour can be obtained, than in purely agricultural districts.[2]

He found nutrition levels in some counties to be 50 per cent better than in others[3] and, with one or two exceptions, the least quantity of meat was consumed in the counties with the lowest wage-rates.[4] At this time it was not at all unusual for half a man's wages to be spent on bread and for many, 'fresh meat would come like Christmas, once a year.'[5] Things were somewhat better by the twentieth century but in low-wage areas meat was still seldom seen more than once a week.[6]

Dr. Edward Smith's survey of 1864 was extraordinarily comprehensive for such an early date, and his conclusions are of special value,[7] but, inevitably, much of the other nineteenth-century evidence is of a piecemeal nature, definitely non-random, and possibly even open to the charge of being un-representative. Twentieth-century evidence provides a more

1. C. S. Read, 'On the Farming of South Wales', p. 148.
2. P.P. 1864, XXVIII, pp. 264–5.
3. Ibid., p. 17.
4. Ibid., pp. 246–7.
5. J. Arch, *Joseph Arch. The Story of his Life* (1898), p. 101.
6. A. Wilson Fox, 'Agricultural Wages in England and Wales in the Last Fifty Years', pp. 291–2. For details of expenditure on meat and bread by farm labourers in different parts of Britain in 1902 see above, p. 78. n. 3.
7. Royston Lambert has described the inquiry as 'a model of social-survey technique, unsurpassed for generations to come' (*Sir John Simon, 1816–1904* (1963), p. 341).

scientific and sounder background. Professor A. C. Pigou, writing in 1913, found it 'evident, without any elaborate study of retail prices and food values, that many agricultural labourers must be earning less than is required to maintain the full physical efficiency of themselves and their families'.[1] Other investigators were not content to be satisfied with impressions and conducted large-scale and well-organized inquiries. H. H. Mann, in his survey of the village of Ridgemount in Bedfordshire, found 38·5 per cent of the working-class families living in primary poverty,[2] that is, income was so low as to result in physical inefficiency even when spent to the best effect; it often was not, and wages in Bedfordshire were by no means the lowest in the country. In 1913 another large-scale survey was completed by B. S. Rowntree and M. Kendall.[3] Using the standards considered by Prof. Atwater to be the minimum for persons engaged in moderate work,[4] they allowed 2s. a week for rent, nothing for tobacco, beer, or any other luxuries, and concluded that a family of five could not maintain physical efficiency on less than 20s. 6d. a week. In only five counties did agricultural labourers' wages reach this level. The lowest-paid fell far short of requirements even though wages at this time were far higher than they had been in the third quarter of the nineteenth century. The diet of one Oxfordshire family had a deficiency of 37 per cent in protein and 20 per cent in energy.[5] Not surprisingly the general deficiency in protein food was greater than in energy food—energy foods are both filling and cheap. Both of these surveys made allowances for additional income obtained by way of non-monetary payment, from the labourer's garden, and from family earnings, and they based their minimum diet on a level

---

1. 'A Minimum Wage for Agriculture', *The Nineteenth Century and After*, lxxiv (1913), 1174.
2. H. H. Mann, 'Life in an Agricultural Village in England', pp. 161, 176.
3. B. S. Rowntree and M. Kendall, *How the Labourer Lives*.
4. 125 grammes of protein, 3,500 calories. This assessment compares with current assessments. *The Manual of Nutrition*, Ministry of Agriculture, Fisheries and Food (1961), p. 15, gives the requirements of a carpenter working an eight-hour day as 3,180 calories.
5. Rowntree and Kendall, op. cit., pp. 28, 30–1, 45.

'more austere than that provided in any workhouse in England
or Wales'.[1]

The consequences of malnutrition were reinforced by what
might be called 'non-economic' attitudes towards work. In
backward economies low wages and malnutrition are often
associated with the presence of considerable under-employment.
Under-employment is an indication of population pressure and
gives rise to attitudes towards work characterized by the lack
of emphasis on efficient working. Rather, the main emphasis
is upon providing employment for as many as possible. There
is ample evidence to demonstrate the existence of population
pressure, under-employment, and attitudes of this kind in the
low-wage parts of the English rural economy; some of this
evidence was mentioned in Chapters One and Four above—the
incidence of poor relief, for example (above, p. 148 n. 1), which is
a reasonable indicator of population pressure and the presence
of under-employment.[2] The 1834 *Poor Law Commission* showed
clearly the coincidence between areas of high outdoor relief and
areas of low wages; the same relationship was noted by Dr. J.
Mitchell in 1834, by Caird in 1850, and continued up to the
First World War.[3] Wherever surplus labour was present employees felt little incentive to work efficiently and farmers were
inclined to employ more labour than they really required. This
situation was particularly true of arable areas where the harvest
provided work for a larger number than could usefully be
employed during the rest of the year.[4] In high-wage areas the

1. Ibid., pp. 28, 304.
2. See, in addition, M. Blaug's work on the 1834 poor law which emphasizes
   the relationship between under-employment and areas of high outdoor
   relief. He shows also that farm wages in the south at that time were generally below the level necessary to provide adequate sustenance and describes
   British agriculture in 1834 as a 'classic case of underemployment in backward economies'. M. Blaug, 'The Myth of the Old Poor Law and the Making
   of the New', *J.E.H.*, xxiii (1963), 160–2; *idem*, 'The Poor Law Reexamined',
   *J.E.H.*, xxiv (1964), 243.
3. *Factories Inquiry Commission*, P.P. 1834, XIX, pp. 40–1; Caird op cit.,
   pp. 514–15: 'the counties that stand high in the scale of poor rates, stand
   low in the scale of wages.'
4. L. P. F. Smith has estimated that, in 1939, on a farm which used little
   machinery, approximately half of the total man-hour requirements fell
   within 8 weeks of the year. 'The Productivity of British Agriculture',
   *Manchester School of Economic and Social Studies*, xviii (1950), 3–4.

seasonal employment cycle was less significant partly because
these areas were, for the most part, less concerned with arable
farming, and also because migrant Irishmen and other seasonal
workers filled the need for additional workers at peak periods.
It is significant that few Irish gangs visited the low-wage
areas. Wilson Fox said they went to Scotland and also 'worked
in the harvest in the north, where farmers had hired men for
the ordinary work, and there were no extra men about, as there
were in the open villages in the Eastern counties'; few Irish
were to be found in agriculture below the north of Cambridgeshire.[1] Perhaps the best-known 'make-work' device in the low-
wage areas was the continued use of the flail for threshing long
after more efficient mechanical means were available.[2] Farmers
took on more people than they needed for a variety of reasons.
To some extent, particularly before 1865, it was a question of
either employing extra men or supporting them out of the
parish rates which were largely paid by property owners.
Employers were motivated also by the feeling that it was their
duty to shield local labourers from the more extreme consequences of labour surplus by employing as many men as
possible.[3]

In all, the evidence from agriculture suggests that the more
backward parts of the English rural economy were trapped in

1. Wilson Fox, *J.R.S.S.*, lxvi (1903), 358; E. J. T. Collins, 'Harvest Technology and Labour Supply in Britain, 1790–1870', Ph.D. thesis, University
   of Nottingham (1970), p. 127.
2. See above, p. 137. For other examples see E. J. T. Collins, op. cit.,
   pp. 18–19; G. E. Evans, *Ask the Fellows who Cut the Hay*, pp. 93–7.
3. 'In over-populated countries the code of ethical behaviour so shapes itself
   that it becomes good form for each person to offer as much employment as
   he can.' W. A. Lewis, 'Economic Development with Unlimited Supplies of
   Labour', *Manchester School of Economic and Social Studies*, xxii (1954),
   p. 142. On this theme see also E. J. T. Collins, op. cit., pp. 273–8. However,
   when farmers' generosity was interpreted to imply that agriculture was
   experiencing prosperity they sometimes acted to correct this impression.
   See, for example, Caird's reference to the Cambridgeshire farmers who sent
   some of their men to the workhouse upon hearing it said in Parliament that
   there was no agricultural distress because labourers were fully employed.
   Caird, op. cit., p. 472. Compared with local farmers, the Scots who migrated
   to East Anglia in the 1880s appear to have been moved less by feelings of
   social responsibility and more by the desire to maximize profits: 'The first
   thing was to reduce the number of men and horses.' P. McConnell, 'Experiences of a Scotsman on the Essex Clays', *J.R.Ag.S.*, 3rd Ser., ii (1891), 317.

a circle of circumstances common to under-developed economies. Surplus population was disguised by under-employment and the peak harvest demand. Population pressure kept wages low, and the combination of low wages and surplus population affected productivity in two ways. First, nutrition levels were insufficient to ensure efficient work. Second, the labour surplus was reflected in attitudes to work characterized by attempts to maximize employment rather than to maximize efficiency. Low productivity, in turn, was a barrier to higher wages. The regional disparity in labour productivity in agriculture and its gradual disappearance were important factors affecting agricultural efficiency. Improvements in labour productivity as a result of rising real wages may have been as influential as the contribution to farm efficiency of better drainage; they were probably more influential than developments in agricultural machinery, almost certainly of greater consequence than changes in the size of holdings, and should perhaps be given equal weight with price trends in explanations of spatial variations in farm prosperity.

The exact combination of influences at work in agriculture was unlikely to be found elsewhere—in particular the influence of diet on productivity was less important in better-paid occupations—but there is plentiful evidence that some of the other links between farm labour productivity and wages also operated in towns. An engagingly frank reply by the secretary of the Bristol Society of Ironfounders in 1897, when asked to account for low wages in the south-west, suggests town and country labour in that region at least had much in common— he spoke of the 'poorness of the work done by the men, and their slowness', and went on to mention out-of-date and inefficient machinery.[1] Birmingham, by contrast, combined high wages and high labour productivity; the quality of labour in Birmingham is considered one of the attractions to manufacturers who moved there after 1880.[2] Tawney's inquiry into the working of minimum wage legislation in tailoring compared the high

1. F. W. Lawrence, *Local Variations in Wages*, p. 42.
2. B. M. D. Smith, *V.C.H. Warwickshire*, vii. 189. On wages in Birmingham see above, pp. 32–4.

pay and productivity of women in Leeds and other northern
centres with the less favourable position in the south. One
Leeds employer commented: 'Badly paid labour . . . is the
dearest you can employ . . . . We must have the best labour in
the market, and to get it we must pay the best price.' The
opinion of the manager of a southern factory who had come
from Yorkshire is particularly interesting: 'In this part of the
country . . . the women don't work as hard as they do in the
north, because they have such a low standard of living. They do
not know how to spend their money'.[1] Earnings in parts of the
East End tailoring trade compared badly with earnings in
Leeds but the great majority of London trades were well paid
and there is more evidence here of links between wages and
productivity. The better-paid London trades were great
beneficiaries of selective migration. There was 'a natural
flow . . . of the better workmen towards London' and, no
doubt, to other high-wage towns. At the same time there was a
tendency for inferior workmen to shun these centres and
gravitate towards employment where rates were commensurate
with their ability.[2] There are interesting insights into the
mechanics of this process in the autobiography of Thomas
Wood, an engineer who had served his apprenticeship in the
country. In 1845 he contemplated his chance of employment at
Platts of Oldham which,

employed near 2,000 hands, whose tools were mostly Whitworth's
make—I, who had never worked in a shop with more than eight or
ten men and with country-made tools, the very best of which Platts
would have thrown away as utterly useless. So I had cause for fear
that I should not succeed and be found as efficient as other men in a
place where no favour was shown—no paying a man what he was
worth, but the ostensible rule was a fixed standard of wage, and if the
man was not worth it he must go.[3]

Inferior workmen could often find work in high-wage centres
because there were considerable local variations beneath the

1. R. H. Tawney, *Minimum Rates in the Tailoring Industry*. pp. 118–20, 126.
2. C. Booth, *Life and Labour*, 1st Ser., iii. 74; 2nd Ser., v. 166.
3. T. Wood, *Autobiography* (1956), p. 14.

regional wage pattern,[1] but some of the less profitable industries and the small inefficient firms which gained least from city external economies moved to low-wage areas along with inferior labour. G. C. Allen has described movement of this kind from Birmingham to centres like Stourbridge and from the Black Country to outlying villages, and Roy Church noticed a similar movement of the smaller hosiery and lace manufacturers away from Nottingham.[2] Differences in labour productivity of the kind described here doubtless account for much of the large residual that remained unexplained at the end of F. W. Lawrence's survey of urban wage variations[3] and, together with other external economies whose value was usually proportional to population, go some way to explain the positive correlation between town size and wages which was noted several times in Chapter One.[4]

# IV

The questions raised at the beginning of this chapter can now be answered. There were doubtless instances when entrepreneurs missed opportunities to move with profit but there is no general case for regarding regional wage variations as a consequence of the failure of investment to respond to spatial

1. See above, p. 56. Firms that paid below the going rate made do with the worst workmen. On the relationship between local wage variations and variations in productivity see J. W. F. Rowe, *Wages in Practice and Theory*, p. 66: H. S. Jevons, op. cit., pp. 351–2; and Phelps Brown, *Industrial Relations*, p. 284.
2. Allen, *Birmingham and the Black Country*, pp. 80, 222; Church, op. cit., p. 249.
3. He concluded, by a process of elimination having examined prices, female employment, trade union strength, and other variables, that much was left to be accounted for by 'the difference in character of the people . . . So that where the higher wages are paid they are merely a higher price for a better article', (Lawrence, op. cit., p. 52).
4. Ch. 4 showed that the advantages of the great urban centres were weakening by 1900 but this development had little impact before the First World War. See above, pp. 135–6, 140–1, 146. There were some signs of these changes as early as the 1880s but little of consequence before the turn of the century. Phelps Brown, *Industrial Relations*, pp. 10–11.

incentives. Demand for labour was concentrated in high-wage areas because high wages were compensated by high productivity—not because capital was blind to opportunities elsewhere. Changes in technology after 1750, and associated changes in the nature and importance of capital, management, and labour in the production process, brought about a substantial increase in productivity, reduced the share of labour in total cost, broke down the positive relationship between wages and labour costs, and increased the likelihood of large variations in productivity between firms and different regions.[1] In most respects the industrial revolution was a great leveller; it eroded the idiosyncrasies of regions and localities and gave added impetus to most of the forces edging Britain towards a monolithic economy. Some of these developments were probably conducive to the erosion of regional wage differentials but the influence of industrialization on labour productivity had the opposite effect—it made regional variations in labour productivity more likely and the possibility of persistent and substantial wage variations less remarkable.

This Chapter and Chapter Four have shown that the nature of demand for labour between 1850 and 1914 was such that any erosion of wage differentials was more likely to be a consequence of responses from the supply side of the market. At the same time, because capital did not move to low-wage areas the magnitude of changes in the supply of labour necessary to effect a reduction in wage differentials was greater than it would have been had capital been attracted by low wages. The remaining chapters examine the relationship between wage differentials and the supply of labour beginning with the most fundamental of the possible responses—variations in the rate of natural increase.

1. It is quite probable that capital felt less compulsion to move to low-wage labour between 1850 and 1914 than in any other period before 1700 or after 1930. Substantial regional variations in productivity exist today but the government exerts considerable compensatory influence by subsidizing public or private investment in depressed regions and by placing difficulties in the way of firms anxious to increase demand for labour in the more prosperous areas. The main reason for supposing that capital was more responsive to cheap labour before 1700 was the relatively close relationship between wage rates and the cost of labour at that time.

# 6

## POPULATION AND FERTILITY

### I

BETWEEN 1851 and 1911 the population of Britain doubled
but population growth, like demand for labour, was not experienced equally throughout the nation. This chapter begins
an examination of the degree of harmony between wage levels
and supply. Were there spatial variations in population growth
between regions of a kind likely to modify wage differentials,
and how substantial were variations in population growth
compared with the spatial differences in demand for labour
described in Chapter Four? Different rates of population
growth could be a consequence of migration or variations in
the rate of natural increase; but which of these was more important, and to what extent was variation in rates of natural
increase a response of birth-rate to demand?

Figure 6–1 shows population growth by regions; only one
region lost population between 1851 and 1911 but rates of
growth varied sufficiently to effect substantial changes in the
spatial distribution. While there was a threefold increase in
the population of south Wales and in the population of
Northumberland and Durham, south Scotland declined and the
populations of northern Scotland and rural Wales grew hardly
at all. The contrast between counties was even greater: the
population of Glamorgan grew faster than that of the United
States but there were twenty-four counties which supported
fewer inhabitants in 1911 than 60 years earlier.[1] Economic
theory suggests that the wage differentials described in Chapter

---

1. The counties which lost population were: Cornwall, Hereford, Huntingdon,
   Rutland, Anglesey, Brecknock, Cardigan, Pembroke, Radnor, Argyll,
   Berwick, Caithness, Dumfries, Inverness, Kinross, Kirkcudbright, Nairn,
   Orkney, Perth, Ross and Cromarty, Roxburgh, Shetland, Sutherland,
   Wigtown.

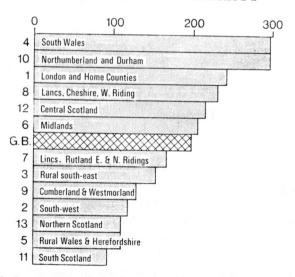

FIG. 6–1. Population of Regions in 1911 when 1851 = 100. *Source*: see appendix to this chapter. For key to regions see Map 1.

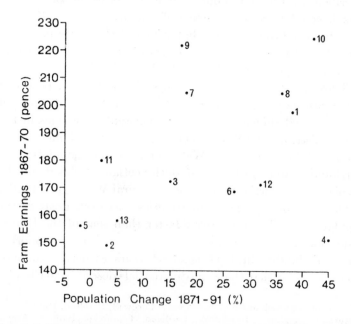

FIG. 6–2. Wages and Population Change 1871–91: Regions. For key to regions see Map 1. Earnings are from Table 1–4. For source of population figures, and notes on their compilation, see the appendix to this chapter.

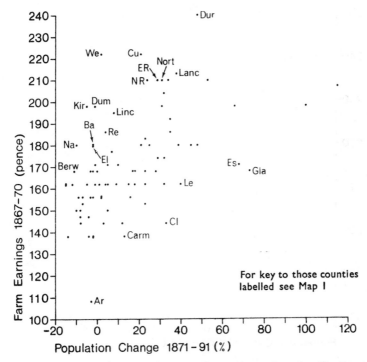

FIG. 6–3. Wages and Population Change 1871–91: Counties. Earnings are from Table 1–3. For source of population figures, and notes on their compilation, see the appendix to this chapter.

One were probably prominent among the influences responsible for these differences, that wage differentials, together with the employment opportunities usually associated with high wages, coaxed labour from low to high wage regions and perhaps also encouraged communities to order their procreative activities with some regard for local labour requirements after the pattern which Chambers may have discovered in the Vale of Trent and Braun in the region of Zurich.[1]

The relationship between population change and wage rates is shown in Figs. 6–2, 6–3, 6–4, and 6–5 which compare earnings in agriculture at two dates (1867–70 and 1898) with the rate

1. J. D. Chambers, *The Vale of Trent 1670–1800,* Economic History Review Supplements No. 3 (1957), pp. 52–3; R. Braun, 'The Impact of Cottage Industry upon an Agricultural Population' in D. S. Landes (ed.), *The Rise of Capitalism* (New York, 1966), pp. 53–64.

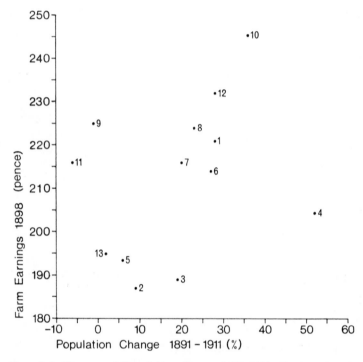

FIG. 6–4. Wages and Population Change 1891–1911: Regions. For key to regions see Map 1. Earnings are from Table 1–4. For source of population figures, and notes on their compilation, see the appendix to this chapter.

of change in population in twenty years after 1871 and 1891 respectively.[1] The coefficients of correlation of the readings shown are 0·39, 0·50, 0·31, 0·45 in Figs. 6–2, 6–3, 6–4, and 6–5 respectively, which indicate a moderately significant relationship where rates of change in population were far from exactly proportional to wage levels but population tended to increase faster in the higher-wage areas.[2] The data on which this conclusion is based are very crude: farm wages were not always a good indicator of general wage levels, least of all in counties like Essex which combined substantial wage variations within

1. On the representativeness of farm wages see above, pp. 4, 65–66.
2. It might be noted in passing that this situation suggests a further shortcoming in existing indices of real wages; several indices take account of the changing occupational structure but none takes account of the changing spatial structure. On this point see above, pp. 2–3.

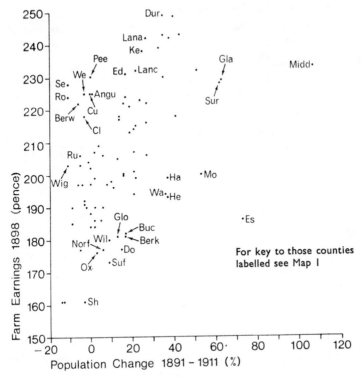

Fᴵɢ. 6–5. Wages and Population Change 1891–1911: Counties. Earnings are from Table 1–3. For source of population figures, and notes on their compilation, see the appendix to this chapter.

its boundary and rapid population growth in those parts where agriculture was unimportant. Further, when population is measured over two decades the wage levels at any one date will not be long representative of an area whose relative wage position was changing. For these reasons the relationship between wages and population growth was almost certainly closer than the scatter diagrams and correlation coefficients suggest and particular caution is necessary in assessing the significance of deviations from trend.[1] In south Wales (Region 4), for example, wages were rising faster than average[2] and

1. For broadly similar reasons no regression lines are shown in Figs. 6–2 to 6–5 or in Figs. 6–5 to 6–11 below which use similar data.
2. See above, p. 21–4.

this partly accounts for its deviant position in Figs. 6–2 and
6–4. There are two areas which deviate from trend sufficiently
to be of possible significance: Fig. 6–5 shows a number of low-
wage counties in the south of England whose population increases was as rapid as the increase in a great many high-wage
counties, and, more significant, Figs. 6–2, 6–3, 6–4, and 6–5 all
show parts of the north of England and southern Scotland
which deviated in the opposite direction by combining modest
increases in population with high wages.[1] In Cumberland,
Westmorland, Berwick, Peebles, and Selkirk farm earnings in
1898 ranged from 18s. 6d. to 19s. 2d. yet in the following two
decades none of these counties did more than maintain their
1891 level of population while a group of eight southern
counties[2] whose earnings ranged between only 14s. 5d. and
15s. 2d. registered population increases of between 3 per cent
and 17 per cent.

# II

How much did the pattern of redistribution shown in Fig.
6–1 owe to migration and how much to spatial variations in
the rate of natural increase? To the extent that migration was
age-selective, and therefore could affect the number of births
and deaths, the distinction between the two is of limited value.
At this stage, however, migration and natural increase, from
whatever cause, are considered separately. The effects of
migration upon fertility will be examined later.

It is possible that natural increase followed a pattern of its
own unconnected, or only tenuously connected, with the labour

1. It is worth noting that many of the counties concerned (see Figs. 6–3, 6–5)
were rural counties noted in Chapter Four for their combination of high
wages and mediocre demand for labour (see sections IX and XI of Chapter
Four). In other words, population growth in these counties was less than
the level of wages might lead us to expect but much as might be suggested
by the level of demand for labour. This relationship implies that high wages
were in part a consequence of low rates of population increase or high rates
of out-migration.
2. Berkshire, Buckinghamshire, Dorset, Gloucestershire, Norfolk, Oxfordshire,
Suffolk, Wiltshire.

market. There is, after all, more to man than the economic man, particularly with regard to his procreative activities, and it is possible that men multiplied fastest where they were least needed. Evidence can be found to support a variety of hypotheses. On the one hand there are influences like the old Poor Law which encouraged the proliferation of population in rural areas despite the absence of reciprocal increase in demand, and encouraged it most where wages were low.[1] On the other there is Chambers's work on the Vale of Trent and Braun's on Zurich both of which suggested the possibility of a positive relationship between fertility and demand for labour.[2] A similar link is assumed in the various forms of subsistence wage theory. There is too, of course, the well-known example of the mining population which was both well paid and 'notoriously prolific',[3] although whether its fecundity was a response to pressures from the labour market, to the shortage of female employment in most mining districts, or to some more fundamental social and biological motivation associated with mining life is difficult to determine.

Table 6–1 shows the relative importance of natural increase and migration. The excess of births over deaths accounted for by far the greater part of population change in almost every region. In areas where migration was high, and natural increase low, migration sometimes played the major role in shaping population trends[4] but the more general pattern was that illustrated by south Wales (Region Four) where the change wrought by migration between 1851 and 1861 was barely a quarter of that due to natural increase and never exceeded half of the natural increase in the following five decades.[5] However, if we turn from comparisons of the relative contribution of migration and natural increase to chronological change and look instead at the range of regional variation

1. For examples of incentives to marriage in the rural south, some of which persisted long after 1850, see below, p. 237 n. 1.
2. See above, p. 221. See also Deane and Cole, op. cit., p. 117.
3. Redford, op. cit., p. 56.
4. In south Scotland after 1881, in northern Scotland and Cumberland and Westmorland in the first decade of the twentieth century, and in rural Wales in the 1870s. Table 6–1.
5. Table 6–1.

TABLE 6–1   *Natural Increase and Migration, 1851–1911: Regions*

| | 1851–61 (a) | (b) | (c) | 1861–71 (a) | (b) | (c) | 1871–81 (a) | (b) | (c) | 1881–91 (a) | (b) | (c) | 1891–1901 (a) | (b) | (c) | 1901–11 (a) | (b) | (c) |
|---|---|---|---|---|---|---|---|---|---|---|---|---|---|---|---|---|---|---|
| Region 1 (London and Home Counties) | 18 | 11 | 7 | 19 | 13 | 6 | 19 | 15 | 5 | 17 | 15 | 2 | 16 | 13 | 4 | 11 | 13 | −2 |
| Region 2 (South-west) | 3 | 11 | −8 | 4 | 12 | −8 | 1 | 11 | −11 | 3 | 11 | −8 | 4 | 10 | −5 | 5 | 9 | −4 |
| Region 3 (Rural south-east) | 4 | 12 | −8 | 7 | 13 | −6 | 6 | 14 | −7 | 8 | 13 | −5 | 8 | 11 | −3 | 10 | 10 | — |
| Region 4 (South Wales) | 19 | 15 | 4 | 15 | 16 | −1 | 17 | 18 | −1 | 23 | 17 | 7 | 19 | 17 | 2 | 28 | 19 | 9 |
| Region 5 (Rural Wales and Herefordshire) | 3 | 10 | −6 | 3 | 11 | −7 | 2 | 11 | −9 | −4 | 9 | −13 | 2 | 8 | −6 | 2 | 8 | −6 |
| Region 6 (Midlands) | 14 | 15 | −1 | 12 | 16 | −4 | 15 | 18 | −2 | 10 | 16 | −6 | 14 | 15 | −1 | 11 | 14 | −3 |
| Region 7 (Lincs., Rutland, E. and N. Ridings) | 5 | 13 | −8 | 9 | 14 | −5 | 14 | 15 | −2 | 5 | 14 | −9 | 8 | 12 | −4 | 12 | 12 | −1 |
| Region 8 (Lancs., Cheshire, and the W. Riding) | 15 | 13 | 3 | 17 | 13 | 4 | 20 | 15 | 5 | 13 | 13 | NIL | 12 | 11 | 1 | 10 | 11 | −1 |
| Region 9 (Cumberland and Westmorland) | 5 | 12 | −7 | 7 | 12 | −5 | 10 | 14 | −4 | 6 | 15 | −9 | NIL | 12 | −12 | −1 | 10 | −11 |
| Region 10 (Northumberland and Durham) | 24 | 17 | 7 | 28 | 19 | 9 | 21 | 21 | 1 | 17 | 18 | −1 | 17 | 17 | 1 | 15 | 17 | −2 |
| Region 11 (South Scotland) | | | | NIL | 13 | −13 | 5 | 12 | −8 | −2 | 11 | −13 | −6 | 8 | −13 | −1 | 7 | −8 |
| Region 12 (Central Scotland) | | | | 15 | 14 | 1 | 16 | 15 | 1 | 13 | 15 | −3 | 17 | 14 | 3 | 10 | 14 | −4 |
| Region 13 (Northern Scotland) | | | | 4 | 12 | −8 | 5 | 12 | −7 | 1 | 12 | −10 | 2 | 10 | −8 | NIL | 8 | −9 |

Column (a) Population Change     (b) Natural Increase     (c) Migration

Notes: All figures are percentages of the population at the beginning of the decade. For sources and other notes see the appendix to this chapter. Regions are shown on Map 1. As a consequence of showing percentages to the nearest whole number the sum of figures in columns (b) and (c) for any one region is sometimes one greater or less than the figure in column (a).

between the two influences, which is the more pertinent consideration for our purpose, the impression changes. For while in most regions population change was primarily a consequence of the excess of births over deaths the rate of natural increase was less varied than the rate of migration. Between 1891 and 1901, for example, the rate of natural increase was lowest in Regions Eleven and Five (8 per cent), highest in Regions Four and Ten (17 per cent)—a difference of 9 per cent. But the changes due to migration ranged from a gain of 4 per cent in Region One to a loss of 13 per cent in Region Eleven—a difference of 17 per cent.[1] And this pattern was general. Decennial variation in the regional rate of natural increase ranged from 8 to 12 per cent while variation in the extent that regions were affected by migration was never less than 15 per cent and was 22 per cent in the decade after 1861.[2]

Although migration was the more powerful determinant of differentials in the rate of population growth, variations in natural increase were not insignificant. In the decade after 1901 the people of south Wales (Region 4) added nearly one fifth to their number by natural increase while west-countrymen on the other side of the Bristol Channel (Region Two) multiplied at less than half this rate.[3] In Scotland the rate of natural increase in the central counties (Region 12) was twice that in the south (Region 11).[4] It is interesting also to note that even where natural increase was lowest it was not unduly low in historical terms. Decennial increases of 8 or 9 per cent are sufficient to double population in less than a century; such rates were rarely experienced in Britain before 1700. In the nineteenth century increases of this order were commonplace in areas where demand for labour was extraordinarily low.[5]

1. Table 6–1.
2. Ibid.
3. Table 6–1. This part of the analysis is concerned only with the excess of births over deaths; this is the crudest of all measures of natural increase and takes no account of age structure and sex ratio. The comment above by no means implies that fertility in south Wales was twice that in the West Country; the former gained by migration, the latter lost, and it is probable that not a few of the babies born in south Wales were conceived in the West Country. There is also, of course, the possibility of significant differences in mortality between the two regions.
4. Table 6–1.
5. Ibid. and Ch. 4 above.

Natural increase followed a similar pattern in most regions; a rising trend at first followed by decline after the 1870s and with a tendency for the decline to slow or cease at the end of the period.[1] Within this pattern each region maintained an approximately constant station relative to other regions. We can see here again a feature noted earlier with regard to relative wage rates and demand for labour—the tendency for distinctive regional characteristics to prevail throughout the period. Two mining regions, south Wales (Region 4) and Northumberland and Durham (Region 10), occupied first and second place in each decade with the Midlands (Region 6) and central Scotland (Region 12) not far behind. Rural Wales (Region 5), south Scotland and nothern Scotland (Regions 11 and 13), and the south-west (Region 2) were no less clearly the regions where natural increase was always least.[2]

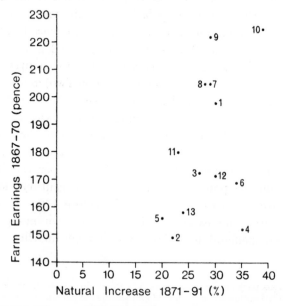

Fig. 6–6. Wages and Natural Increase 1871–91: Regions. For key to regions see Map 1. Earnings are from Table 1–4. For source of natural increase figures, and notes on their compilation, see the appendix to this chapter.

1. Table 6–1.
2. Table 6–1.

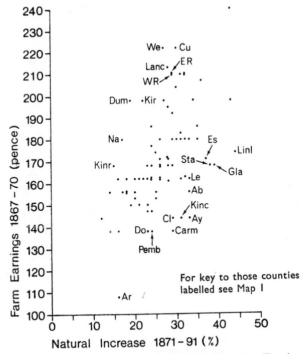

F IG. 6–7. Wages and Natural Increase 1871–91: Counties. Earnings are from Table 1–3. For sources of natural increase figures, and notes on their compilation, see the appendix to this chapter.

How does this pattern of natural increase compare with wage levels? The coalfields, where wage levels and rates of natural increase were both high, suggest at least one complementary relationship but elsewhere the position may have been less harmonious. Figures 6–6 to 6–9 show the relationship in a similar fashion to the comparison between total population change and earnings in Figs. 6–2 to 6–3, using identical wage material, and with similar reservations about method and the degree of significance that may reasonably be attached to what is shown.

The scatter diagrams suggest a relationship between wages and natural increase remarkably similar to that between wages and change in population (Figs. 6–2 to 6–5). The readings, which form a broad pattern sloping upwards from left to right, and the coefficients of correlation, 0·45, 0·47, 0·51, 0·51 in Figs.

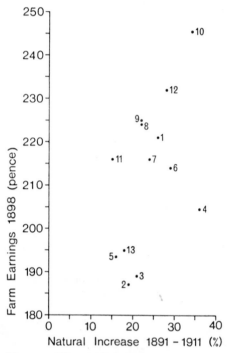

FIG. 6–8. Wages and Natural Increase 1891–1911: Regions. For key to regions see Map 1. Earnings are from Table 1–4. For source of natural increase figures, and notes on their compilation, see the appendix to this chapter.

6–6, 6–7, 6–8, and 6–9 respectively, lend moderate support to the hypothesis that men multiplied at a rate which had some relation to local wage rates and demand for labour[1] although it does not necessarily follow that natural increase was therefore a force which worked towards the erosion of wage differentials.[2] The areas which diverge from trend, by combining high wages with modest rates of natural increase or high rates of

1. Figs. 6–6, 6–7, 6–8, and 6–9 show wages not demand. Demand is discussed in Ch. 4; it correlated closely with wages although there were parts of the country where the correlation was not close and the relationship between natural increase and demand was rather closer than that between natural increase and wages. In this case again the position resembles that shown in Figs. 6–2 to 6–5 (see above, p. 224 n. 1.)
2. It would be possible for natural increase to have almost the opposite effect even if the relationship between natural increase and wages was perfect (i.e. a coefficient of correlation of 1) if, for example, very large variations in wages were combined with very small variations in rates of natural increase. See also below, p. 238 n. 2.

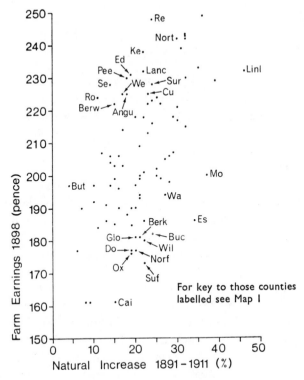

Fig. 6–9. Wages and Natural Increase 1891–1911: Counties. Earnings are from Table 1–3. For sources of natural increase figures, and notes on their compilation, see the appendix to this chapter.

natural increase with modest wages, are also remarkably similar to the deviant areas in Figs. 6–2, 6–3, 6–4, 6–5. Some of these, Essex and south Wales in particular, can again be partly explained by shortcomings in the methods and statistics.[1] But, again, we are left with a group of low-wage counties in the south and a group of high-wage counties on both sides of the Scottish border which deviated from trend in a manner conducive to the maintenance of spatial wage differentials. In Fig. 6–8, for example, the rates of natural increase in the two lowest wage regions, both in the south of England (Regions 2 and 3), were not less than those in the high-wage rural north of England and southern Scotland (Regions 9 and 11).

1. See above, pp. 222–4.

# III

It would be very rash to imagine that the moderate correlation between wages and rates of natural increase shown above implies that the birth-rate responded to market conditions. To assess the response of birth-rates to wages requires a measure far less crude than the simple excess of births over deaths; ideally age-specific fertility rates for all women should be compared with wage levels over the periods covered in Figs. 6–2 to 6–9. Unfortunately these figures are not available. The first census of fertility was taken in 1911 and was confined to married women.[1] A great deal more can be deduced from this census, however, than its timing might imply, because what it measured was not just fertility in that one year but the history of all mothers alive in 1911; while it can tell us little about the 1850s and 1860s it is a reasonable guide to fertility over several decades in the second half of our period. Part II of the census[2] included a geographical analysis with sufficient data to test whether the correlation which existed between wages and natural increase remains when the figures are purged of the distorting influence of migration.

Some of it remained—but very little. In broad terms fertility tended to be higher north of a line from the Wash to the Severn and lower to the south of it.[3] This pattern might suggest some correlation with wage levels—but closer examination undermines the first impression. In Chapter One it was shown that

---

1. *Census Reports of Great Britain, 1801–1931*, Guide to Official Sources No. 2. (H.M.S.O., 1951), p. 89. Gross reproduction rates for English and Welsh counties have been calculated for much of the period but these take us little further because females were as mobile as males (see below p. 283) and gross reproduction rates reflect the influence of migration upon age structure. Additional distortion would arise from the natural tendency of would-be migrants to remain single and to contemplate matrimony after settling in their new surroundings. For gross reproduction rates see D. V. Glass, *Population Policies and Movements in Europe* (Oxford, 1940), pp. 62–3; E. Charles and P. Moshinsky in L. Hogben (ed.), *Political Arithmetic*, pp. 108–21.

2. *Census of England and Wales 1911. Vol. XIII Fertility of Marriage Pt. II* (subsequently, *Fertility of Marriage*).

3. Ibid., pp. cxli–ii.

there were several low-wage areas to the north of this line; rural Wales was one of them and age-standardized fertility rates in rural Wales were among the highest in Britain; the same was true of the Highlands of Scotland.[1] There were, too, some high-wage areas, like the Lancashire textile districts, where fertility was distinctly below average.[2]

TABLE 6–2

*Age-Standardized and Actual Fertility of Wives aged under 45 in 1911*[3]

| | Total Fertility | | Effective Fertility (children surviving) | |
|---|---|---|---|---|
| | Age-standardized | Actual | Age-standardized | Actual |
| England and Wales | 100 | 100 | 100 | 100 |
| Wales | 110 | 110 | 109 | 109 |
| Midlands | 100 | 100 | 102 | 102 |
| North | 101 | 101 | 98 | 98 |
| South | 95 | 95 | 98 | 97 |

Table 6–2 shows variations in age-standardized fertility between the four large census divisions; they bear little relationship to what we know of the regional wage pattern.[4] Actual average fertility rates are included in Table 6–2 because the age-standardized fertility of married women will not reveal fertility variations arising from delayed marriage: in fact the two series are almost identical.[5] To establish the degree of

1. Ibid, pp. cxxvi, cxlii–iii.
2. Ibid., pp. cxxix, cxxxv, cxli, cxlii.
3. Ibid., pp. cxxii.
4. See e.g. the figures of regional farm earnings, Table 1–4.
5. While non-age-standardized fertility rates are not affected by variations in age at marriage they are, of course, affected by migration—however, there was also no significant relationship between earnings and non-age-standardized fertility rates in rural districts which were more uniformly affected by migration than regions or counties (see below, p. 235 n. 1). The census failed to provide details of fertility by local areas for marriages of completed fertility—*Fertility of Marriage*, Part II, p. cxxi. The relationship between farm labourers' wage rates and standardized fertility of wives in the rural parts of administrative counties who had been married 25–30 years was not significant—see below, p. 235 n. 1.

relationship, or lack of relationship, more precisely, and in a form comparable with the earlier findings, farm earnings in 1898 and age-standardized fertility in rural districts are shown in Figs. 6–10 and 6–11. Rural districts are used to minimize the effect of occupational differentials and because they are the areas where any relationship between fertility and farm wages will be most apparent.[1] The absence of any significant

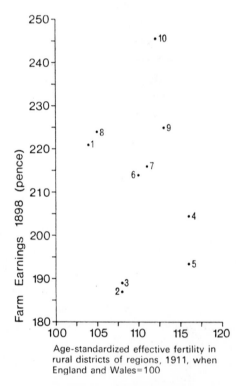

FIG. 6–10. Wages and Age-Standardized Fertility 1911: Regions. For key to regions see Map 1. Earnings are from Table 1–4. For sources and other notes see text.

1. On this point see *Fertility of Marriage* Part II, p. cxlii. Fertility figures are taken from *Fertility of Marriage* Part II, pp. cxxv–vi. Regional figures are the unweighted average of administrative areas within each region. The figures for counties composed of two or more parts (e.g. East and West Sussex) have been averaged and represented on Fig. 6–11 as a single county. The fertility readings relate to births over a considerable time-span and relative wage rates were fairly constant (see above, p. 57) so 1898 is as good a date to use as any in the late-nineteenth or early-twentieth centuries.

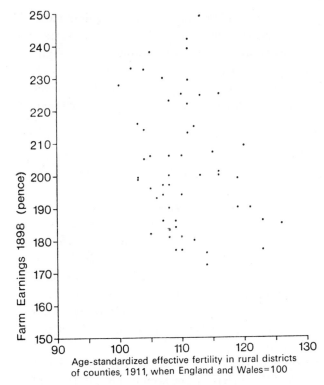

FIG. 6–11. Wages and Age-Standardized Fertility 1911: Counties. Earnings are from Table 1–3. For sources and other notes see text.

relationship between the two variables is readily apparent particularly when Figs. 6–10 and 6–11 are compared with Figs. 6–8 and 6–9 which show wages and natural increase at the same date. The coefficients of correlation for Figs. 6–10 and 6–11 were −0·09 and −0·26; for Figs. 6–8 and 6–9 it was 0·51 in each case.[1] These findings suggest strongly that the

1. The precise position of each county varies slightly according to whether the measure used is total fertility or effective fertility, and according to age groups. Figs. 6–10 and 6–11 show age-standardized effective fertility ratios of all wives under 45 at the time of the census. The rank order of counties was compared with that for age-standardized effective fertility of wives who had been married 25–30 years (*Fertility of Marriage*, Part II, pp. cxxxix–cxli); the comparison suggested that the relationship between earnings and effective fertility in this group was probably no more significant than that between earnings and the effective fertility of all wives under 45— the coefficient of correlation was 0·13 for wives married 25–30 years and −0·26 for all wives under 45. Infantile mortality was lower in the south and

birth-rate was not adjusted to market requirements. The approximate correlation between natural increase and wage rates shown earlier was mainly a consequence of the effect of migration upon age structure and the greater part of that substantial redistribution of population which occurred between 1850 and 1914, either directly or indirectly, was a consequence of migration.[1]

The exact relationship between earnings and age-standardized fertility varied from one part of the country to another; there was a clear and positive correlation on the coalfields which were deservedly renowned both for high wages and prodigious rates of natural increase although, as suggested earlier, it would be unwise to suppose that high fertility was necessarily a response to demand. Lancashire is the best example of a very different type of relationship: high wages combined with low fertility. Low fertility in Lancashire was probably a consequence of unusual opportunities for female employment and may be considered among the influences which helped the county to remain a high-wage area despite a moderate rate of increase in demand for labour.[2]

Another aspect of the fertility pattern not conducive to the erosion of wage differentials can be seen in Figs. 6–10 and 6–11. In rural areas wages were low and demand for labour was slack,

---

Footnote 1 (continued)

for this reason a comparison of earnings and total fertility might produce a marginally less random relationship but the absence of relationship in Figs. 6–10 and 6–11 is so striking that it is very unlikely that the difference would be sufficient to affect the conclusion, and from the point of view of assessing the influence of birth-rate on the labour market effective fertility is the pertinent variable. A cursory comparison of earnings and actual average family size was made to test whether age-standardized comparisons were hiding significant earnings-related variations in age at marriage, but the relationship appeared no more significant than that shown in Figs. 6–10 and 6–11.

1. This conclusion follows from the evidence in Table 6–1 as well as the discussion above. It may be of some significance to the debate on the cause of population growth in the eighteenth century. It is, of course, possible that birth-rates in the eighteenth century responded quite differently to changes in demand for labour, but it is also possible that studies like that of Professor Chambers (see above, p. 221) which found high rates of natural increase in prosperous areas were measuring only the effect of migration upon age structure.

2. Charles and Moshinsky in Hogben (ed.), op. cit., pp. 143, 159, 205–6. On demand for labour in Lancashire see above, pp. 164–8.

yet age-standardized effective fertility in the rural districts of every English and Welsh county was above the average for England and Wales as a whole. This uncalled-for increase in the supply of labour imposed strain on all rural economies, most of all in the rural south where wages were lowest.[1] The south was losing employment in agriculture and domestic industry and failed to obtain more than a very small share of industrial and commercial expansion, yet it shared whole-heartedly in the demographic revolution. In Region Three (rural south-east) between 1851 and 1911 the decennial rate of natural increase was never less than 10 per cent (Table 6–1). This was sufficient to double population every seventy years and was achieved despite the disproportionate loss of the more fertile members of the community. In these circumstances each extra mouth dependent upon the labourer's meagre earnings constituted a minor malthusian crisis—each child that grew up to compete for the limited amount of ill-paid work available exercised a similar influence upon the village economy. Situations of this kind and their quasi-malthusian consequences are commonplace

---

1. Fertility in the rural south was below the average of all rural districts but by a much smaller margin than the differential in wages might lead us to expect, and there were some low-wage counties in the south, Suffolk for example, where fertility was higher than in most northern counties (*Fertility of Marriage*, Part II, pp. cxxv–cxxvi). The rural south had been most affected by the old poor law and its encouragement of early marriage—see e.g. J. L. and B. Hammond, *The Village Labourer* (1966 edn.), p. 180; *V.C.H. Wiltshire*, iv. 83; Chambers and Mingay, *The Agricultural Revolution*, p. 146. Custom and charity extended the practice of giving married men more pay, and preference when work was scarce, long after 1834. In Suffolk the farmers of Clare and Cavendish were paying unmarried men 2s. or 3s. (i.e., some 25–40 per cent below the rate for married men in 1849, a practice the *Morning Chronicle* investigator considered almost compulsive to early marriage (*M.C.* 5 Dec. 1849); see also F. Clifford, *The Agricultural Lock-out of 1874*, pp. 209–10. The *Morning Chronicle* survey recorded similar conditions in several other southern counties and the report on Durham included the observation that the practice of paying ordinary labourers more if they were married was 'utterly unknown in any parts of the north' with which the correspondent was acquainted. Ibid. 24 Oct., 29 Dec. 1849, 9, 26 Jan. 1850; see also Wilson Fox, *J.R.S.S.* (1903), 278. Higher pay for married men was certainly not unknown in the north at this time although the evidence suggests strongly that it was far more usual in the south. How long this practice continued in the low-wage south and its influence on birth-rate, and hence wages, are questions which might repay investigation. There is a further point, 'living in', a practice which favoured late marriage, was most widespread in Scotland and the north of England.

in the under-developed world. The rural south of England had less serious problems than rural India today and it was certainly in better shape than pre-famine Ireland,[1] but it is not difficult to understand why, in the late eighteenth and early nineteenth century, the situation appeared alarming to a southern clergyman and teacher whose main source of information was contacts in other parts of the rural south. While few experienced the ultimate consequence of a malthusian situation, a great many, as we have seen, were under-nourished and population growth exerted powerful and sustained pressure upon incomes and against the erosion of wage differentials between the south and more fortunate regions. The tendency to focus attention on town conditions can easily result in serious underestimation of the role of population pressure in accounting for social distress in the nineteenth century. Rural areas deserve at least as much attention as the cities, Malthus as much as Marx and Engels; and the farm labourers are probably more deserving of compassion than any other major occupational group.

# IV

The rate of natural increase in the low-wage south illustrates what is perhaps the most outstanding characteristic of the relationship between wages and natural increase: that is, while total natural increase varied in a manner which might be considered broadly conducive to the erosion of wage differentials there were several significant exceptions to this pattern and the variations in natural increase were small compared with variations in wages and demand for labour.[2] There were large

---

1. Although the margin which separated it from Ireland was probably no greater than that which separated southern England from the more prosperous parts of the north.

2. The relationship between population increase and incomes is usually more complex than this sentence suggests. It might be argued that while a high rate of population increase has a depressive influence on wage levels in areas of labour surplus it may have an opposite effect on prosperous areas and that the variations in natural increase described above were, therefore, perhaps even less conducive to the erosion of wage differentials than has been suggested—however, it is unlikely that this argument is applicable to conditions in Britain between 1850 and 1914, see below, p. 248 n. 2.

parts of Britain which would have been best served by negative rates of natural increase and others where labour was far less abundant. But population rose rapidly everywhere. It rose rather faster in some areas than others, but only slightly less fast in areas where labour was abundant and wages were lowest, so that its net effect was almost certainly on the side of those forces which were helping to maintain wage differentials.[1] The obvious remedy for a combination of pronounced spatial variations in demand and rapid and indiscriminate increases in supply was migration. The nature of migration and to what extent it alleviated this situation is the subject of Chapter Seven.

1. A specific example may help to give some precision to this point. In the decade after 1861 the highest rate of natural increase (19 per cent) occurred in Region 10 (Northumberland and Durham) and one of the lowest (12 per cent) in Region 2 (south-west) (Table 6–1). Employment in the wide range of occupations analysed in Ch. 4 (see Tables 4.2 and 4.10) rose by 21 per cent in Region 10 and fell by 8 per cent in Region 2, but natural increases occurred in both areas and while there was a difference of 29 per cent in the rate of increase in demand there was a difference of only 7 per cent in rates of natural increase.

# APPENDIX TO CHAPTER SIX

*Notes to Table 6–1 and Figs. 6–1 to 6–9 (Chapter Six) and Figs. 7–1 to 7–4 (Chapter Seven)*

1. Figures of population, natural increase, and migration shown in Table 6–1 and Figs. 6–2 to 6–9 are calculated from a variety of sources. Those for Scotland are taken from the *Hundredth Annual Report of the Registrar General for Scotland* (Edinburgh, 1955), Appendix IX. Those for England and Wales are calculated from decennial censuses: P.P. 1862, L, pt. II, Table E; 1872, LXVIii, pt. II, Table 9; 1883, LXXX, General Report, Tables 7 and 30; 1893–4, CV, Table X; 1903, LXXXIV, Table XVII; 1914–16, LXXXI, Summary Tables, Table 25; 1917–18, XXXV, pp. 47–8. In Figs. 6–1 to 6–5 population figures are taken from Mitchell and Deane, op. cit., pp. 20–3. Those for 1851–91 relate to the areas of ancient counties in 1891; subsequent figures show the area of administrative counties in 1951.

2. London has been excluded from those figs. which show the relationship between county earnings in agriculture and various demographic variables. A small number of other counties for which no figures of earnings in 1867–70 are available have been excluded from those figs. which relate demographic variables to county earnings in 1867–70.

3. Two minor irritants attend any analysis of nineteenth-century census data, boundary changes and the medley of 'official' counties: the registration county, the administrative county, the ecclesiastical county, the ancient county, and others. County boundaries are discussed in detail in the official guide to the census reports (*Census Reports of Great Britain 1801–1931*. Guide to the Official Sources No. 2. (H.M.S.O., 1951), pp. 95–104). The area and population of towns and parishes were considerably affected by boundary changes but in this study, where the smallest unit analysed is the county, the degree of error arising is not large and, wherever possible, has been minimized by using units of uniform acreage. Where the unit of analysis is the region most of the consequences of boundary variations cancel out within the region. In those cases where changes occurred between censuses, natural increase and migration have been calculated for the registration area at the end of the

decade. Boundary changes also resulted in some anomalies and approximations in the census reports—see e.g. P.P. 1903, LXXXIV, p. 108, or the figures for Bute, *100th Report of the Reg. Gen. for Scotland*, p. 92. Another source of fractional error arises from the fact that the registration year commenced on 1 January while the census was usually taken in April. None of these problems is likely to affect the calculations by much more than the error introduced by rounding figures of migration and natural increase to the nearest whole per cent.

4. In England and Wales compulsory registration of births and deaths commenced in 1837, in Scotland in 1855. There was considerable under-registration at first, but registration was reasonably complete during the period for which statistics have been calculated in Chapters Six and Seven, i.e. 1851–1911 for England and Wales, 1861–1911 for Scotland; most of the calculations in Chapters Six and Seven rely upon the census of 1861 and subsequent censuses. On this point see D. V. Glass, 'A Note on the Under-Registration of Births in Britain in the Nineteenth Century', *Pop. Stud.*, v(1951–2), 75–6, 86–7.

5. In Figs. 6–2 to 6–5 the readings along the horizontal axis, which in each case cover two decades, represent the change over the two decades as a whole. In Figs. 6–6 to 6–9 and 7–1 to 7–4 the reading along the horizontal axis represents the sum of the change in the first and second decade calculated separately. In each case the percentage figures used represent the proportion of the total population at the beginning of the period.

# 7

## MIGRATION

IN ECONOMIC theory migration plays a prominent part in the process of redressing regional variations in the relationship between labour demand and supply. However, Chapters Four, Five, and Six showed that in Britain between 1850 and 1914 there were strong forces working to reinforce the existing wage differentials, forces so strong that it would be rash to assume that the slow erosion of regional differentials necessarily implies a high degree of immobility. This chapter considers how effectively migration reconciled the supply of labour with demand between 1850 and 1914; and whether labour at this time was closer to the economic man of classical theory as envisaged by, for example, Marshall, or to the less economic man that Adam Smith had in mind when he wrote that: 'a man is of all forms of baggage the most difficult to be transported.' [1] Section I examines the degree of correlation between wages and migration; section II attempts to establish some generalizations about labour mobility between 1850 and 1914 by comparing it with mobility in other periods; section III looks at the effect of railways upon wage differentials; and section IV considers occupational and spatial migration differentials. Irish and alien immigrants are considered separately in Chapter Eight.

---

1. Marshall drew an analogy between local labour markets and a number of interconnected water-tanks. Wage variations set up by changes in demand or supply of labour, he said, would be obliterated by labour mobility just as a uniform level would ensue if water was taken from, or added to, any of the connected tanks (J. Heads, 'The Internal Migration of Population in England and Wales, 1851–1911', p. 33). The classical theorists were not quite so dogmatic as this comment might suggest but, as B. Thomas pointed out in what remains probably the best survey of nineteenth-century opinion on mobility, their qualifications were 'mainly in the nature of footnotes to the main body of doctrine which has free movement as its fundamental assumption' (B. Thomas, 'Studies in Labour Supply and Labour Costs', p. 18).

# I

Figures 7–1 to 7–4 and Tables 7–1 and 7–2 show migration rates and earnings for regions and counties; they are based upon the same method and much the same material as was used in compiling Figs. 6–2 to 6–9 in Chapter Six.[1] Migration is defined as the net balance of migration across county or region boundaries that occurred between census years and is expressed as a percentage of the population at the beginning of the decade. Like any index of migration this measure falls short of perfection; it tells us very little about the direction of migration flows,[2] and nothing about gross migration or

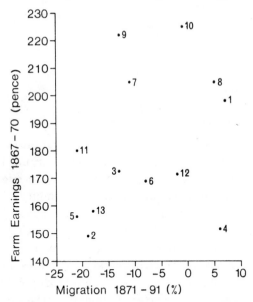

FIG. 7–1. Wages and Migration 1871–91: Regions. For key to regions see Map 1. Earnings are from Table 1–4. For sources of migration figures, and notes on their compilation, see text.

1. For notes on the methods and on the sources and limitations of the wages, population, and migration figures see the appendix to Ch. 6 and above, pp. 222–4. No trend lines are shown in Figs. 7–1 to 7–4, for the reasons outlined above, p. 223.
2. This is discussed in a little more detail below, section IV.

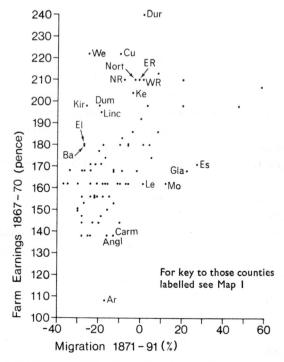

FIG. 7–2. Wages and Migration 1871–91: Counties. Earnings are from Table 1–3. For sources of migration figures, and notes on their compilation, see text.

migration within county boundaries. Gross migration probably exceeded net migration by a considerable margin, but in measuring the influence of migration upon wages net migration is the important variable.[1] The absence of intra-county figures is more regrettable because counties vary so much in size but, as with wage material, we must take the statistics as they come, which is in county bundles.[2] Immigrants to Britain and emigrants from Britain are included in the figures but not distinguished; the only practical importance of this point is that because Britain was a net exporter of population the sum of all county gains and losses is not nil but a negative quantity.

In the six decades before 1911 regional migration rates ranged between a loss of 13·2 per cent and a gain of 9·4 per cent

1. This point is discussed below, pp. 254–5.
2. It is possible, of course, to calculate migration rates for much smaller areas but the time necessary to produce statistics for the whole of Britain substantially more useful than the county figures would be far greater than their importance to the present study warrants.

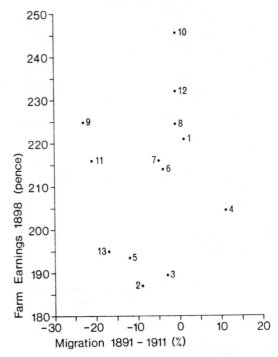

Fig. 7–3. Wages and Migration 1891–1911: Regions. For key to regions see
Map 1. Earnings are from Table 1–4. For sources of migration figures, and
notes on their compilation, see text.

(Table 7–1). There were more substantial changes at county
level; migration added almost a third to the population of
Middlesex in the 1880s; while in the 'seventies Selkirk had a
migration gain of 54 per cent.[1] These examples represent the
exceptional; the over-all role of migration was less dramatic
but it was far from insubstantial. Between 1871 and 1891, for
example, just over three-quarters of all counties experienced
average decennial net migration of at least ±5 per cent and
more than two-fifths averaged at least ±10 per cent.[2] Table 7–1
shows which parts of Britain were most affected by these
trends. South Scotland, northern Scotland, rural Wales, the
south-west, and Cumberland and Westmorland[3] experienced

1. This and all other county migration figures are calculated from the sources
   detailed in the appendix to Ch. 6.
2. Fig. 7–2. The rates shown on Fig. 7–2 are for twenty-year periods.
3. Regions 11, 13, 5, 2, and 9 respectively; for key to regions see Map 1.

9

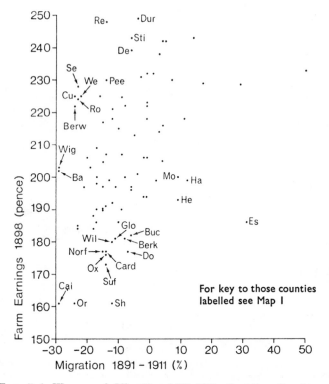

Fig. 7–4. Wages and Migration 1891–1911: Counties. Earnings are from Table 1–3. For sources of migration figures, and notes on their compilation, see text.

the heaviest and most consistent losses. The rural south-east lost population fairly rapidly in the 1850s and 1860s, but less rapidly thereafter and there was a modest gain in the decade before 1911. South Wales after 1871, and the London area until 1901, were the chief areas of absorption. Other industrial areas—the Midlands, the northern textile region, central Scotland, and Northumberland and Durham after 1871—gained surprisingly little by net migration. In very broad terms, the figures show a movement out of agricultural areas and into the London region and two coalfields, the north-east before 1871, and then south Wales. London's attraction was greatest between 1851 and 1881 and there appears to have been a slackening of migration from the rural south by the end of the

TABLE 7–1  *Decennial Net Migration 1851–1911: Regions*

| Region | 1851–61 Gain or loss (%) | Region | 1861–71 Gain or loss (%) | Region | 1871–81 Gain or loss (%) | Region | 1881–91 Gain or loss (%) | Region | 1891–1901 Gain or loss (%) | Region | 1901–11 Gain or loss (%) |
|---|---|---|---|---|---|---|---|---|---|---|---|
| 1 | +6·9 | 10 | +8·7 | 8 | +4·9 | 4 | +6·5 | 1 | +3·7 | 4 | +9·4 |
| 10 | +6·7 | 1 | +5·7 | 1 | +4·8 | 1 | +2·3 | 12 | +3·1 | 3 | +0·3 |
| 4 | +3·8 | 8 | +4·4 | 12 | +0·7 | 8 | +0·1 | 4 | +1·7 | 7 | −0·6 |
| 8 | +3·3 | 12 | +0·6 | 10 | +0·6 | 10 | −1·1 | 8 | +0·8 | 8 | −1·3 |
| 6 | −0·6 | 4 | −1·5 | 4 | −0·8 | 12 | −2·5 | 10 | +0·7 | 10 | −2·0 |
| 5 | −6·3 | 6 | −3·9 | 7 | −1·7 | 3 | −5·4 | 6 | −0·8 | 1 | −2·3 |
| 9 | −7·1 | 7 | −4·9 | 6 | −2·2 | 6 | −5·7 | 3 | −3·2 | 6 | −3·0 |
| 7 | −8·0 | 9 | −5·1 | 9 | −3·9 | 2 | −8·3 | 7 | −4·3 | 2 | −3·8 |
| 3 | −8·2 | 3 | −5·6 | 3 | −7·3 | 7 | −8·8 | 2 | −5·4 | 12 | −4·2 |
| 2 | −8·4 | 5 | −7·5 | 13 | −7·4 | 9 | −9·3 | 5 | −5·8 | 5 | −6·0 |
| 13 | −8·2 | 2 | −7·9 | 11 | −7·8 | 13 | −10·3 | 13 | −7·6 | 11 | −7·7 |
| 11 | −13·2 | 13 | −8·2 | 5 | −8·5 | 5 | −12·8 | 9 | −12·3 | 13 | −8·9 |
| | | 11 | −13·2 | 2 | −10·9 | 11 | −13·2 | 11 | −13·2 | 9 | −10·8 |

For sources and comment on these figures see text and the appendix to Ch. 6.
Compulsory registration of births and deaths in Scotland began only in 1855; for this reason the first column in Table 7–1 is incomplete.

| | |
|---|---|
| Region 1. London and Home Counties | Region 8. Lancs., Cheshire, and the W. Riding |
| Region 2. South-west | Region 9. Cumberland and Westmorland |
| Region 3. Rural south-east | Region 10. Northumberland and Durham |
| Region 4. South Wales | Region 11. South Scotland |
| Region 5. Rural Wales and Hereford-shire | Region 12. Central Scotland |
| Region 6. Midlands | Region 13. Northern Scotland |
| Region 7. Lincs., Rutland, E. and N. Ridings | For Regional boundaries see Map 1. |

century. The latter feature formed a substantial part of a
general trend which is apparent in the horizontal dispersion of
readings in Figs. 7–1 to 7–4 and which is shown clearly
in Table 7–4; the spread was greater in the earlier period
and there seems to have been a reduction in net migration
across county boundaries after 1891. This raises the possibility
that labour was less mobile after 1891 than before.[1]

To what extent was migration in harmony with the pattern
of wage differentials? The coefficients of correlation of the
readings in Figs. 7–1 to 7–4 are 0·33, 0·47, 0·15, 0·33 respectively.
These figures suggest a moderately significant relationship in
which migration was probably conducive to the erosion of
wage differentials;[2] given the magnitude of migration and the

1. It is, however, at this stage no more than a possibility: county net migra ion
   is one of several ways of measuring mobility and its limitations have already
   been mentioned. In terms of another, although much cruder, measure—
   gross emigration—the first decade of the twentieth century compares favourably with any other. Mitchell and Deane, op. cit., pp. 47–8.
2. The relationship was probably closer than these figures and the scatter
   diagrams suggest, see above, pp. 221–3. Erosion of wage differentials is
   by no means a certain consequence of migration from low- to high-wage
   areas. Out-migration may retard the recovery prospects of an area by
   removing local purchasing power and the most productive workers. Similarly, further progress in a developing area might be consequent upon securing by migration a supply of labour, particularly young and skilled labour,
   and a larger local market. However, the net effect of migration upon spatial
   wage differentials in Britain between 1850 and 1914 was almost certainly
   that postulated by neo-classical equilibrium theory. A few of the problems
   which beset counties like Wiltshire and Dorset might have been eased by
   lower rates of migration but other, more serious, problems would have been
   aggravated and it is very difficult to envisage likely circumstances in which
   the net effect of lower rates of out-migration upon local incomes could have
   been other than detrimental. That the net influence of migration upon wage
   levels in the more prosperous urban areas might have been beneficial is
   rather more of a possibility although it seems unlikely. Young people and
   workman of more than average ability were probably over-represented
   among migrants (see above, pp. 108, 216 and below, p. 276 n. 1) and the
   high-wage areas benefited from this selective migration. On the other hand,
   while labour was less abundant in high-wage areas than elsewhere in Britain,
   rates of natural increase were high and labour was seldom scarce. Unskilled
   labour of the kind likely to dominate migration from low-wage areas was
   least scarce of all—on this point see below, pp. 299–304. Moreover, high-
   wage urban areas probably contributed disproportionately to overseas
   migration (see below, pp. 277–8) and one of the more likely consequences of
   a lower rate of migration from low-wage areas was a reduction in the flow
   of labour from high-wage centres to destinations abroad. For a fuller
   discussion of the relationship between migration and incomes see, B. Okun
   and R. W. Richardson, 'Regional Income Inequality and Internal Population Migration', *Economic Development and Cultural Change*, ix (1961).

íact that some areas had population losses and others gains (in marked contrast to the relationship between wages and natural increase),[1] it seems likely that migration contributed fairly substantially to the erosion of differentials.[2] The degree of correlation, and the identity of the areas which deviated from trend, are both very similar to those in the relationship between earnings and population increase and between earnings and natural increase which were examined in Chapter Six.[3] This, of course, was to be expected because in Chapter Six it was shown that migration was both the major cause of variations in the rate of total population increase and, via its influence upon age structure, also the main determinant of variations in natural increase. In these circumstances there is little need to repeat here what has already been said of Figs. 6–2 to 6–9.[4] After allowance is made for those deviations from trend which are clearly a consequence of shortcomings in the method, or the statistics,[5] two significant deviant areas remain: a group of high-wage counties in the north, mainly in Regions Nine, Ten, and Eleven, and, in the second part of the period, a number of low-wage counties in the south of England. The extent of deviation is clearest in the case of Regions Nine, Eleven, Two, and Three between 1891 and 1911 (Fig. 7–3). The two northern regions (Nine and Eleven), where average earnings in 1898 were 18s. 9d. and 18s. respectively, had migration losses of over 20 per cent, whereas the two southern regions whose average earnings were 15s. 9d. (Region Three) and 15s. 7d. (Region Two) lost only 3 per cent and 9 per cent of their populations respectively. The same point may be put in another form; in the two low-wage southern regions, taken together, migration disposed of only a little over a quarter of the natural increase in population, in the northern regions it was more than sufficient to offset all natural increase.

1. See above pp. 238–9.
2. The question of the magnitude of migration is considered in detail in the next section of this chapter.
3. See above, pp. 221–4, 229–31.
4. See above, Ch. 6.
5. See above, pp. 222–4.

That the over-all influence of migration was to transfer population from low- to high-wage areas is, of course, what we would expect; the more interesting feature of the pattern shown in Figs. 7–1 to 7–4 is perhaps the number and extent of exceptions to the prevailing trend which cannot be dismissed as due to shortcomings in the method or statistics. These exceptions, whose influence was to modify the over-all erosive effects of migration upon wage differentials, deserve further attention. Some may be partly explained by regional variations described in earlier chapters; for example the combination of high earnings with a long-term migration loss in Northumberland and Durham after 1871 probably owed something to the extraordinarily high rate of natural increase in the area, although this observation provides only part of the answer because, while a high rate of natural increase reduced the opportunities which might otherwise have attracted migrants, it was not sufficient to reduce wages to the national average—a wage premium remained yet it was not accompanied by net in-migration. South Wales might also be added to the two deviant areas which were mentioned above because its position on the scatter diagrams, although in part a consequence of combining two decades of demographic change with earnings at one date,[1] was also a consequence of geography. South Wales was favourably placed to attract a substantial flow of migrants by the inducement of only moderately high wages.[2] Some other deviation might be similarly explained in terms of distance from high-wage areas but much would still remain; several of the southern counties where migration responded tardily to wage differentials were not further from London, south Wales, or the industrial Midlands, than were northern rural counties from areas of similar opportunity. The occupational statistics in Chapter Four add a little more towards an explanation because, while the correlation between wages and demand for labour was close, it was not perfect. Migration rates in Regions Nine (Cumberland and Westmorland) and Eleven (south Scotland) were more consistent with the levels of demand for

1. See above, pp. 223–4.
2. See above, pp. 152–3.

labour than the level of wages[1] and in these cases the high rate of out-migration may be regarded as a response to lack of local employment, although the suggestion that labour in these regions was more mobile than average remains because its response to the situation was sufficiently vigorous to restrict supply to a level where wages remained high despite the scarcity of local employment. In the rural south-east the slackening in the rate of out-migration towards the end of the century was concurrent with signs of revival in the area's fortunes[2] but migration fell by an amount quite dispropor-tionate to the improvement in demand which was by no means sufficient to explain migration gains after 1901 in counties like Buckinghamshire, Bedfordshire, and Dorset when Lancashire, Derbyshire, and Lanarkshire each lost population. Farm earnings in the south-east were lower than in any other region in 1907[3]—yet in the decade after 1901 more entered the region than left. In short, when all allowances have been made for deficiencies in the methods and raw materials and for the influences of distance and variations in natural increase and demand for labour, there remains a substantial residue of spatial variation in response to wage differentials still to be explained. This feature will be considered again in section IV.

## II

We turn now to another of the issues raised at the beginning of this chapter—should labour in this period be regarded as mobile or immobile, on what criteria might an assessment be based, and how useful are generalizations of this kind? The extent and persistence of regional wage variations might suggest that mobility was not only a long way short of the perfect fluidity assumed in classical theory[4] but perhaps also

1. See above, pp. 168–70, 172–3.
2. See above, p. 146.
3. Table 1–4.
4. On this point see above, p. 242.

low in historical terms, particularly when measured against twentieth-century rates. But there were other forces at work in the labour market and these may have been sufficiently powerful to maintain regional wage variations despite relatively high rates of mobility.

Unfortunately economic theory provides little help in resolving these problems. In the whole field of economic theory those parts dealing with the role of wage differentials in allocating labour are perhaps the least satisfactory. Few principles have been soundly established and most generalizations are highly vulnerable to empirical investigation. In 1931 Brinley Thomas considered, 'nothing is easier than to throw inductive missiles at the vulnerable structure of the main theory of wages . . .' [1] The gap between theory and reality has been reduced a little in the last forty years but almost entirely by recognizing the limitations of classical theory and very little by the development of better theory: 'No accepted theory of labour mobility in an advanced industrial society exists . . . the textbook model of the labour market is a highly abstract concept.' [2] Economic historians, in a position to exercise discrimination in the use of theory and less often tempted to theorize without a reasonable regard for the facts, have not accepted the mobility assumptions of classical theory as readily as economists. Historians are necessarily more aware of the formidable barriers to mobility, social and psychological as well as economic, and the persistent tendency among men, even in the mass, to act in a manner which economists might regard as irrational. Professor Youngson Brown lent more support than most historians to classical theory when he suggested that it was a high degree of labour mobility, 'as much as any other element in the situation which made the British nineteenth century economy so prodigious in its achievements'.[3]

1. B. Thomas, 'Studies in Labour Supply', p. 285.
2. J. H. Smith in D. C. Roberts and J. H. Smith (eds.), *Manpower Policy and Employment Trends* (1966), p. 89.
3. A. J. Youngson Brown, 'The Scots Coal Industry, 1854–1886', p. 195. For another, but contradictory, generalization on mobility see H. A. Turner, *Trade Union Growth, Structure and Policy*, p. 172, where there is the curious observation that 'the great labour migrations' were over by the 1850s.

But he was generalizing from his findings on mobility among
the Scots miners, who were probably not a very representative
group, and the mainstream of comment by economic historians
emphasizes the profound influence of friction in the labour
market. The prevalence of migration in stages illustrates one
kind of friction;[1] the handloom weavers and their reluctance to
accept substantial economic inducements to abandon a dying
trade illustrate a second; and the peasant miners of Pembroke
who preferred a low income in their native county to 'the high
wages of "sin and savagery" ' in the valleys of Glamorgan and
Monmouth, a third.[2] Imperfect knowledge was one of the
greatest restraints on the mobility of labour, particularly in
rural areas:

They could give me no distinct notion of Canada ... their only idea
seemed to be that it was ... very far off; whilst some of them enter-
tained the most exaggerated notions of its climate. Told of its opportunities they pricked up their ears and looked in mute astonishment.
Some had heard of New Zealand, others had not. With the name
of Australia they almost exclusively associated the idea of trans-
portation.[3]

Yet, while most comment emphasizes the immobility of labour,
it is usually confined to specific instances and, confronted with
evidence that the response of labour to stimuli was highly
unpredictable, economic historians have usually resisted the
temptation to generalize from individual cases. The census
reports contain a salutary warning of the danger of drawing
broad conclusions from scanty evidence and with undefined

1. See the conclusions of Redford's *Labour Migration in England*, and E. G.
   Ravenstein, 'The Laws of Migration', *J.R.S.S.*, xlviii (1885) and lii (1889).
2. A. H. John, *The Industrial Development of South Wales, 1750–1850*, pp. 61–2.
   Their outlook appears to have been shared by Bristolians who summed up
   their dislike of Cardiff with uncomplimentary remarks on the moral condition of returned migrants and the relative attractions of Cardiff and the
   colonies. F. W. Lawrence, *Local Variations in Wages*, p. 45.
3. From the report on conditions among the rural population of Berkshire,
   Buckinghamshire, Oxfordshire, Wiltshire, *M.C.* 31 Oct. 1849. See also
   accounts of the immense difficulties faced, and partly overcome, by Canon
   Girdlestone during his struggle to persuade labour to forsake Devon for
   the high wages and opportunities of the north, in e.g. F. G. Heath, *The
   English Peasantry*, (1874), Ch. V. For another contemporary comment see
   *R.C. on Labour. The Agricultural Labourer: Wales*, P.P. 1893–4, XXXVI,
   p. 17.

criteria. The Registrar General in 1871, in his introduction to the census, noted 'the improved roads, the railway, the habit of travelling about and the increasing knowledge of workmen', and suggested that 'the English are probably the most migratory people in the world.'[1] The report of the next census, however, weighed up similar evidence and concluded: '. . . the native population shows, after all, stationary habits of a most decided character.'[2] That neither quotation was entirely accurate is almost certain, but which came nearer to the truth is a matter of some interest. The discussion that follows argues that in the second half of the nineteenth century the British population was characterized by a high degree of spatial mobility.

Establishing generalizations about mobility between 1850 and 1914 is a task which lends itself to quantification and the discussion that follows makes extensive use of statistical evidence. The exactitude conveyed by this approach is unintended because while we can have reasonable confidence in the population census, and in the registration of births and deaths, county net migration rates are not perfect measures of mobility.[3] For this reason, and for others that will become apparent, the statistical comparisons should be regarded simply as aids to forming a general impression of mobility levels in the period. The figures are intended to measure 'economic mobility': that is, mobility in response to economic incentives. Figures of net migration across county boundaries are not a very good index of total migration but they are a reasonable measure of 'economic mobility'; it is probable that many individual moves were made for non-economic reasons[4] but mobility of this kind would be unlikely to result in significant net flows and it seems probable that by far the greater part of

---

1. *Census of England and Wales: General Report*, P.P. 1873, LXXIii, p. xxi.
2. *Census of England and Wales: General Report*, P.P. 1883, LXXX, p. 51.
3. See above, pp. 243–4.
4. Very little is known of gross migration rates before 1914. There is some evidence on the relative importance of gross and net migration in more recent times in the *Ministry of Labour Gazette* (July 1965), pp. 299–303, although its reliability has subsequently been questioned, ibid. (Feb. 1968), p. 120.

net migration balances were a consequence of mobility whose direction was determined by economic considerations.[1] Mobility will be judged high, middling, or low in the light of several criteria, the most important being comparisons of mobility rates in the 1850–1914 period with rates before 1840 and after the First World War.[2]

In addition to comparisons of county migration rates at different times, some less rigorous but broader comparisons are possible and perhaps of some significance. Consider first the much debated 'south-east drift'. Between 1951 and 1961 the 'south-east' gained some 163,000 migrants,[3] but this figure was exceeded in four of the six decades between 1851 and 1911

---

1. Similar measures were used by H. Makower, J. Marschak, and H. W. Robinson in their analysis of inter-war labour mobility. *Oxford Economic Papers*, ii (1939), 73–4. See also Ravenstein op. cit. (1885), pp. 181, 198. Ravenstein, well aware of the complexities of total migration, concluded: 'It does not admit of doubt that the call for labour in our centres of industry and commerce is the prime cause of . . currents of migration . . .' A recent government survey concluded similarly after noting the large two-way movement between regions with very different levels of employment: 'It appears that many of the influences which induced employees to move, although presumably powerful and systematic as far as the individual employee was concerned, did not appear to operate systematically on gross movements between Regions' ('Notes on Regional Labour Statistics', *Ministry of Labour Gazette* (July 1965), p. 300).

2. Unfortunately neither of the two most direct measurements of response to economic incentives can be used to compare mobility in the nineteenth and twentieth centuries. The relationship between migration and wage rates after 1850 has been examined but there is little point in repeating the exercise for the 1920s and 1950s because regional wage variations were so much less in these decades that the results would be of little value. Regional unemployment was a feature of both the inter-war years and the 1950s and several studies have measured the relationship between unemployment and migration in these decades, but they cannot be used as a basis for comparison with the nineteenth century because comparable figures of unemployment before 1914 are not available. On the relationship between migration and unemployment between the wars see, in particular, the three articles by H. Makower, J. Marschak, and H. W. Robinson, in Vols. i, ii, and iii of the *Oxford Economic Papers* (1938, 1939, 1940), and F. R. Oliver, 'Inter-Regional Migration and Unemployment, 1951–61', *J.R.S.S.*, Ser. A, cxxvii (1964), Part 1.

3. The south-east is defined here as London, Kent, Middlesex, Surrey, Sussex, Essex, and Hertfordshire. The 'standard London and south-eastern region' is identical save that parts of Essex and Hertfordshire are omitted. *Census of England and Wales*, 1961. Migration Tables, pp. xvi–xvii.

when the total population of the area was considerably less.[1] Rural depopulation is another contemporary problem and one which the recent flowering of Celtic nationalism has made as much a subject of popular debate as the drift to the south-east. The Welsh counties most affected by depopulation in the decade after 1951 were Merioneth, Montgomery, and Radnor which suffered net losses of 7·6, 7·5, and 9·4 per cent respectively,[2] equivalent to an absolute loss of about 8,500 people. Such losses have been the subject of official inquiry[3] and much pleading for special action to reverse the tide: 'the derelict farmsteads . . . abandoned mining projects, the inevitable brake upon the full flowering of Welsh culture . . . the melancholy atmosphere of rural decay . . . action on a grand scale must be taken within the near future for the disease of depopulation shows no signs of abating.' [4] The census returns for the second half of the nineteenth century show that, although less may then have been heard of Welsh rural depopulation, it was no less serious; in fact compared with some decades before 1914 the exodus in the 1950s was of moderate proportions. In only one decade between 1851 and 1911 did Merioneth, Montgomery, and Radnor lose fewer than 8,500 inhabitants[5] and in each of the other five decades migration losses were both absolutely and proportionately greater than the loss sustained in the 1950s.[6] The picture is similar in rural southern Scotland. The seven counties in the southern division of the 1961 census are

1. Net migration into the 'south-east' calculated from census reports 1851–1911, 1951, 1961. For details see notes to Table 7–2.

| | | | |
|---|---|---|---|
| 1851–61 | 212,000 | 1891–1901 | 264,000 |
| 1861–71 | 239,000 | 1901–11 | −160,000 |
| 1871–81 | 230,000 | 1951–61 | 163,000 |
| 1881–91 | 122,000 | | |

2. For sources of this and subsequent references to population and migration see notes to Table 7–2.
3. See e.g. *Depopulation in Rural Wales* (H.M.S.O., 1964).
4. V. C. Davies, 'Some Geographical aspects of the Decline in the Rural Population of Wales', *Journal of the Merioneth Historical and Record Society*, ii (1953–6), 58.
5. In the 1860s when Merioneth registered a modest gain.
6. Between 1881 and 1891 net migration from these three counties amounted to almost 30,000 or 18 per cent of their population at the beginning of the decade.

identical with those in Region Eleven;[1] each of these counties
lost population by migration in the 1950s and the region as a
whole lost the equivalent of nearly 7 per cent of its 1951
population. But here too it would be wrong to allow the attention figures of this order attract today to convey the impression
that depopulation is high in historical terms, because the rate
of depopulation in the 1950s was exceeded in every decade
between 1861 and 1911; in the 'sixties, 'eighties, and 'nineties
the net loss was approximately twice that in the 1950s.[2]
Another insight into labour mobility may be obtained by
considering rates of structural change in the economy. There
have been some very impressive changes in recent decades but
most can be matched by changes of similar proportions in the
period before 1914. The numbers in agriculture fell by rather
more than a quarter of a million between 1921 and 1951,
equivalent to about 16 per cent of the 1921 total; between
1861 and 1891 the decline was 440,000 or 22 per cent of the
labour force of 1861.[3] In the coal industry no fewer than 316,000
jobs were lost in twelve years after 1955, but 309,000 were
created in the twelve years before 1914.[4] Similarly, the contraction of the labour force on the railways by nearly a quarter,
or some 115,000, between 1960 and 1964 was impressive but not
more impressive than the 200,000 men gathered together with
'considerable ease' in the course of a year or so before 1846.[5]

The point was made earlier that there is no single perfect
indicator of relative mobility, nor is there any ideal combination of measures. Those employed so far suggest that mobility
in the years 1850–1914 compared favourably with rates
achieved after 1945 and in the inter-war years. The value of
this impression is that it is derived from several different
aspects of mobility; its main shortcoming, of course, is that
it rests upon rule-of-thumb comparisons of non-comprehensive,

1. Berwick, Dumfries, Kirkcudbright, Peebles, Roxburgh, Selkirk, Wigtown.
   *1961 Census of Scotland*, Vol. viii. Internal Migration, p. xxvi.
2. See Table 7–2.
3. Mitchell and Deane, op. cit., pp. 60–1.
4. *The Times*, 15 Nov. 1967, p. 25. Mitchell and Deane, op. cit., pp. 118–19.
5. *The Economist*, 10 July 1965, p. 140; B. R. Mitchell, 'The Coming of the
   Railway and United Kingdom Economic Growth', *J.E.H.*, xxiv (1964), 323.

and sometimes only approximate, statistics. However, crude as they are, these comparisons are useful; first, because they each point in one direction and, second, as a check upon the more precise and comprehensive results of the analysis of county migration rates which forms the next stage of the investigation.

Certain aspects of county migration have been studied, particularly by geographers. R. H. Osborne has investigated the relationship between residence and place of birth in England and Wales in 1951 and in Scotland in 1851, 1901, and 1911. Among other things he has found that in Scotland the proportion of people living outside their county of birth was greater in 1901 than in either 1851 or 1951.[1] J. W. Webb has drawn attention to what he considers high rates of mobility in England and Wales in the decade after 1921 and suggested that labour was more mobile in the 1920s than in previous decades.[2] This conclusion conflicts with the pattern suggested by the rough comparisons we have made so far but the difference may arise because Webb's investigations extended back only to 1900. The investigations of Saville, and Friedlander and Roshier, also restricted to England and Wales, cast doubt on Webb's interpretation. Saville found that in several mainly rural counties migration rates, measured as a proportion of the natural increase, were lower between 1901 and 1931 than in the previous fifty years.[3] Friedlander and Roshier also suggest that mobility was lower in the twentieth century although their findings rest on a basis of comparisons between decennial rates before 1911 and rates over twenty-year periods after 1921 which, as they point out, introduces a downward bias into the post-1911 figures.[4] Useful as they are, these studies leave us

1. R. H. Osborne, 'Internal Migration in England and Wales, 1951', *The Advancement of Science*, xii (1955–6); *idem*, 'The Movements of People in Scotland, 1851–1951', *Scottish Studies*, ii (1958), 33–4.
2. J. W. Webb, 'The Natural and Migrational Components of Population Change in England and Wales, 1921–31', *Economic Geography*, xxxix (1963), 131.
3. Saville, op. cit., pp. 48–53.
4. They consider, however, that the probable downward bias is less than sufficient to explain away the likelihood of lower mobility after 1881. D. Friedlander and R. J. Roshier, 'Internal Migration in England and Wales: Part I'. *Population Studies*, xix (1965–6), 266–8.

TABLE 7-2  *Decennial Net Migration 1861–1961: Regions*

| 1861–71 | | 1871–81 | | 1881–91 | | 1891–1901 | | 1901–11 | | 1921–31 | | 1951–61 | |
|---|---|---|---|---|---|---|---|---|---|---|---|---|---|
| Region | Gain or loss (%) | Region | Gain or loss (%) | Region | Gain or loss (%) | Region | Gain or loss (%) | Region | Gain or loss (%) | Region | Gain or loss (%) | Region | Gain or loss (%) |
| 10 | +8·7 | 8 | +4·9 | 4 | +6·5 | 1 | +3·7 | 4 | +9·4 | 3 | +4·6 | 3 | +10·5 |
| 1 | +5·7 | 1 | +4·8 | 1 | +2·3 | 12 | +3·1 | 3 | +0·3 | 1 | +4·5 | 2 | +2·6 |
| 8 | +4·4 | 12 | +0·7 | 8 | +0·1 | 4 | +1·7 | 7 | −0·6 | 2 | +0·6 | 6 | +1·5 |
| 12 | +0·6 | 10 | +0·6 | 10 | −1·1 | 8 | +0·8 | 8 | −1·3 | 6 | −1·0 | 7 | −1·1 |
| 4 | −1·5 | 4 | −0·8 | 12 | −2·5 | 10 | +0·7 | 10 | −2·0 | 7 | −1·7 | 1 | −1·2 |
| 6 | −3·9 | 7 | −1·7 | 3 | −5·4 | 6 | −0·8 | 1 | −2·3 | 8 | −2·1 | 5 | −1·6 |
| 7 | −4·9 | 6 | −2·2 | 6 | −5·7 | 3 | −3·2 | 6 | −3·0 | 5 | −3·2 | 4 | −1·8 |
| 9 | −5·1 | 9 | −3·9 | 2 | −8·3 | 7 | −4·3 | 2 | −3·8 | 11 | −5·7 | 9 | −2·0 |
| 3 | −5·6 | 3 | −7·3 | 7 | −8·8 | 2 | −5·4 | 12 | −4·2 | 9 | −6·7 | 8 | −2·1 |
| 5 | −7·5 | 13 | −7·4 | 9 | −9·3 | 5 | −5·8 | 5 | −6·0 | 12 | −8·3 | 10 | −3·1 |
| 2 | −7·9 | 11 | −7·8 | 13 | −10·3 | 13 | −7·6 | 11 | −7·7 | 10 | −9·2 | 12 | −4·5 |
| 13 | −8·2 | 5 | −8·5 | 5 | −12·8 | 9 | −12·3 | 13 | −8·9 | 13 | −9·7 | 13 | −6·3 |
| 11 | −13·2 | 2 | −10·9 | 11 | −13·2 | 11 | −13·2 | 9 | −10·8 | 4 | −11·9 | 11 | −6·7 |

*Source:* For 1861–1911 see Table 7-1; *Census of England and Wales, 1931,* Preliminary Report, Table III; General Report, Tables XI, XII. *Annual Report of the Registrar General for Scotland,* 1954, pp. 82–137; *Census of England and Wales 1961,* County Reports, Tables 1 and 2; *Census of Scotland 1961,* Vol. iii. Age, Marital Condition, and General Tables, Table B, Table 7a.

Region 1. London and Home Counties
Region 2. South-west
Region 3. Rural south-east
Region 4. South Wales
Region 5. Rural Wales and Herefordshire
Region 6. Midlands
Region 7. Lincs., Rutland, E. and N. Ridings
Region 8. Lancs., Cheshire, and the W. Ridings
Region 9. Cumberland and Westmorland
Region 10. Northumberland and Durham
Region 11. South Scotland
Region 12. Central Scotland
Region 13. Northern Scotland
For regional boundaries see Map 1.

## TABLE 7–3
### *Sum of Migration Gains and Losses: Regions*

| 1861–71 | 1871–81 | 1881–91 | 1891–1901 | 1901–11 | 1921–31 | 1951–61 |
|---------|---------|---------|-----------|---------|---------|---------|
| 77·2    | 61·5    | 86·3    | 62·6      | 60·3    | 69·2    | 45      |

*Source:* Table 7–2

No figures for migration in the 1930s are given here, but the work of
Makower, Marschak, and Robinson suggests that migration in that decade
was less than in the twenties. H. Makower, J. Marschak, and H. W. Robinson, 'Studies in the Mobility of Labour: A Tentative Statistical Measure',
*Oxford Economic Papers*, i (1938), 83; *idem*, 'Studies in the Mobility of
Labour: Analysis for Great Britain. Pt. I', *Oxford Economic Papers*, ii
(1939), 75–6. To check whether the figures in Table 7–3 contain significant
bias consequent upon migration having been measured as a proportion of
population at the beginning of each decade, migration rates for each region
were calculated as a proportion of the figure mid-way between the population at the beginning of the decade and that at its end. This exercise
produced results not significantly different from those shown in Table 7–3,
viz.:

| 1861–71 | 1871–81 | 1881–91 | 1891–1901 | 1901–11 | 1921–31 | 1951–61 |
|---------|---------|---------|-----------|---------|---------|---------|
| 73·9    | 59·1    | 84·4    | 61·9      | 58.6    | 69·6    | 44·1    |

## TABLE 7–4
### *Decennial Net Migration 1861–1961: Counties*

A. Greatest Gain and Loss in each Decade (per cent)

| 1861–71 | 1871–81 | 1881–91 | 1891–1901 | 1901–11 | 1921–31 | 1951–61 |
|---------|---------|---------|-----------|---------|---------|---------|
| +28     | +55     | +31     | +27       | +23     | +24     | +25     |
| −20     | −21     | −21     | −23       | −23     | −43     | −20     |

B. Number of Counties where Migration Gain or Loss
was 8 per cent or over

| 1861–71 | 1871–81 | 1881–91 | 1891–1901 | 1901–11 | 1921–31 | 1951–61 |
|---------|---------|---------|-----------|---------|---------|---------|
| 49      | 45      | 51      | 34        | 26      | 35      | 19      |

C. Sum of Migration Gains and Losses (percentage gains and
losses added without regard to sign)

| 1861–71 | 1871–81 | 1881–91 | 1891–1901 | 1901–11 | 1921–31 | 1951–61 |
|---------|---------|---------|-----------|---------|---------|---------|
| 772     | 803     | 812     | 639       | 570     | 652     | 508     |

*Sources:* as for Table 7–2.

with no more than a tentative, and sometimes contradictory, impression of relative mobility in different periods.[1] Tables 7–2 and 7–3 provide the basis for more certain conclusions; they are based upon decennial data for each English, Welsh, and Scottish county between 1861 and 1911, for one inter-war and one post-war decade.[2]

No region was more affected by in-migration than Region Three (rural south-east) in the 1950s, although Region Four (south Wales) after 1901 and Region Ten (Northumberland and Durham) in the 1860s were scarcely less affected. This case apart Table 7–2 contains little which suggests that mobility increased after the First World War. The highest migration rates occurred in areas which lost population and in this respect no region was more affected than was Region Eleven (south Scotland) in the 1860s, 1880s, and 1890s. Migration losses substantially higher than the highest. experienced in the 1950s were commonplace before 1911, particularly in the 1880s. A crude but more comprehensive comparison of migration in different periods may be obtained by adding the decennial migration rates regardless of sign. This is shown in Table 7–3 and produces a result consistent both with Webb's conclusion[3] and with the hypothesis that migration rates between 1851 and 1911 were not less, and were perhaps greater, than rates in more recent decades.

The hypothesis that labour was relatively mobile in the second half of the nineteenth century is powerfully reinforced by Tables 7–2 and 7–3. We can impose a check on these figures and obtain rather more detail by examining similar data for counties shown in Table 7–4. The county most affected by migration in any one decade was Selkirk where migration added 55 per cent to the population in the decade after 1871; the greatest loss of population occurred in Bute between 1921 and 1931.

1. This is not a criticism of the methods used by their authors who were, for the most part, not directly concerned with the problem investigated here.
2. No figures are shown for the decade before 1861 because registration in Scotland did not commence until 1855. There was, of course, no census in 1941.
3. See above, p. 258.

The highest gain achieved by any county in the 1950s was 25 per cent. This figure had been exceeded in every decade between 1861 and 1901 and the greatest loss in the 1950s, 20 per cent in Bute, was equalled in the 1860s and exceeded in each of the following four decades. With more than 80 counties in all, including some very diminutive counties such as Bute and Selkirk, the figures in section A of Table 7–4 are of limited value,[1] although they suggest, once again, that mobility before the First World War was at least as high as it was in the 1920s and 1950s. Section B of the same table shows the number of counties in each decade in which migration exceeded 8 per cent. A study of migration between 1951 and 1961 suggested 8 per cent as a level beyond which migration creates social problems in towns and rural districts;[2] few of those counties most affected by rural de-population in the 1950s had losses exceeding 8 per cent and these were the subject of government inquiries and much pleading for special action to reverse the flow; for these reasons it seems reasonable to regard 8 per cent as a 'high' rate of county migration. More counties had migration rates of 8 per cent or over between 1861 and 1901 than in the 1920s, and far more reached this level between 1861 and 1901 than in the 1950s. Further, between 1861 and 1891 well over half of all counties experienced 'high' rates of migration. Section C of Table 7–4 shows county migration rates summed regardless of sign. The figures endorse what is by now more than an impression: mobility in the half-century after 1861 was as great or greater than it was in the 1920s and greater than it was in the 1950s.

It is easier to compare migration between 1850 and 1914 with rates after the First World War than with the position before 1850. County figures for the whole of Britain can be compiled only from the decade which began in 1861. England and Wales can be studied from 1841 but this is too late to make possible

1. It should be noted, however, that differences in the size of counties are less important in chronological comparisons of the kind shown in Table 7–4 than in spatial comparisons of the kind described on pp. 243–4, above, because in Table 7–4 migration figures for different decades refer to the same assortment of different-sized counties.
2. J. W. House, *Rural North East England 1951–61*. (Newcastle, 1965), p. 44.

worthwhile comparisons with the second half of the century and too late also to permit meaningful quantitative generalization about mobility before and after the introduction of railways whose impact upon mobility is considered by some writers to have been very considerable.[1]

The migratory habits of pre-industrial Englishmen have several times received attention and investigators have usually discovered greater mobility than they expected, but only in the sense that population was more mobile than implied in earlier works which assumed a very high degree of immobility: 'Although it is an article of popular belief that the rural population in pre-industrial Britain was geographically static, social historians have come to realize that there was in fact a great deal of movement . . .'[2] Given that the 'high' mobility they have discovered was overwhelmingly short-distance mobility,[3] and that net migration rates were a small part of total migration even between county units,[4] little has been found that can usefully be employed in this investigation. There are, however, two other local studies whose findings are of some significance. In the first of these, an examination of the influence of migration upon death-rate in Essex, the author drew attention to the contrast between sporadic out-migration before 1841 and the steady stream thereafter.[5] In the second, A. Constant measured mobility in five east-Midland parishes in terms of the distance that brides and grooms travelled to marry.[6] From the middle of the eighteenth century until the

1. On this point see section III of this chapter.
2. J. Cornwall, 'Evidence of Population Mobility in the Seventeenth Century', *Bulletin of the Institute of Historical Research*, xl (1967), 143. Among other works containing references to pre-industrial mobility see, E. J. Buckatzsch, 'The Constancy of Local Populations and Migration in England before 1800', *Population Studies*, v (1951–2); W. G. Hoskins, *Devon*, p. 173; T. P. R. Laslett, *The World We have Lost* (1965); N. L. Tranter, 'Population and Social Structure in a Bedfordshire Parish', *Population Studies*, xxi (1967).
3. Cornwall, op. cit., pp. 150–1; Buckatzsch, op. cit., p. 64; Hoskins, op. cit., p. 173; Laslett, op. cit., p. 147; Tranter, op. cit., p. 278.
4 See above, pp. 243–4, 254–5.
5. A. B. Hill, 'Internal Migration and its Effects on the Death Rate', *Medical Research Council Reports*, No. 95 (1925), pp. 22–3.
6. A. Constant, 'The Geographical Background of Inter-Village Population Movements in Northamptonshire and Huntingdonshire, 1754–1943', *Geography*, xxxiii (1948).

1840s, when railways were introduced to the area, mobility in this sense hardly changed; it then increased sharply.[1] It is interesting, and perhaps significant, that both these studies emphasize a quickening of mobility shortly before the mid-nineteenth century, although how representative these two areas are is impossible to determine. For the purposes of the broad comparisons that concern us here the most useful work by far is that of P. Deane and W. A. Cole who have collected together much pertinent information on the eighteenth century and from this calculated some tentative county migration rates.[2] Their calculations suggest that net migration across county boundaries was increasing throughout the eighteenth century and in 1800 was approximately twice as great as a century earlier.[3] A comparison between migration in the 1860s and the average of the Deane and Cole estimates for the period 1801–31[4] shows that 27 out of 42 counties had higher rates of migration in the later period and that the total volume of net migration across county boundaries was some 40 per cent greater.[5]

Due allowance must be made for the declared shortcomings of Deane and Cole's estimates but the proportions involved suggest strongly that there was a long-term increase in mobility from 1700 to the mid-nineteenth century. The case for believing that there was an acceleration in the rate of increase in mobility in the second quarter of the nineteenth century is supported by the more detailed studies of Hill and Constant and there is, in addition, a great deal of less quantitative evidence highly consistent with increasing mobility at this time. There were far-reaching changes in transport; Redford, whose opinion on this matter is especially valuable, emphasized the number, magnitude, and speed of economic

1. The author emphasized the close coincidence between the increase in mobility and the opening of railways, an event which quickly stimulated mobility and encouraged long-distance movement (Constant, op. cit., p. 82).
2. Deane and Cole, op. cit., pp. 106–22. Redford's work tells us far more of the character of migration in the first half of the nineteenth century than of its magnitude.
3. Dean and Cole, op. cit., p. 111.
4. Ibid., p. 115 and Tables 7–3 and 7–4 (above).
5. Measured by the methods used in section C of Table 7–4 and compared with the figures shown there. Comparison with the 1870s or 1880s would suggest an even greater increase in mobility from the beginning of the century.

changes consequent upon railway development;[1] the new poor law removed an institutional barrier to mobility;[2] and the geographical distribution of employment was changing rapidly, probably faster than in any earlier period and perhaps fastest of all in the difficult years of the 1840s.[3] The number of hand-loom weavers fell after 1830, rural depopulation became a general feature between 1820 and 1850, and in the same decades the growth of the farm labour force slackened and ceased.[4] Saville found that in south Devon general industrial buoyancy continued long after 1815 but had gone by 1850[5] and at least one other study places the most rapid decline of domestic industry and rural craftsmen in the 1840s.[6]

While we cannot be sure of the precise amount of migration before 1840 the over-all picture is sufficiently clear to allow worthwhile generalizations. There is very little reason to consider that labour was generally immobile in the second half of the nineteenth century. Migration rates then were greater than those of the eighteenth or early-nineteenth century, they were at least as great as those of the inter-war years, and exceeded rates in the 1950s. Mobility was clearly far from perfect but the over-all extent and persistence of regional wage variations cannot be considered as a consequence of labour immobility in any meaningful sense of the word; nor was the decline in regional wage variations after 1914 a consequence of increased mobility.

1. Redford, op. cit., pp. 187–90. The relationship between railways and migration is examined in section III of this chapter.
2. There were further easings of restraints connected with the poor law in 1861 and 1865. How significant those restraints were is not clear. After 1795 a man could be removed only after becoming a burden on the rates and it is possible that the customary and psychological immobility consequent upon attitudes connected with the old poor law—the easy acceptance of low incomes, unemployment, and underemployment, and the stigma attached to schemes of assisted migration and emigration—was a more important constraint than the statutory provisions. Many of these attitudes lasted long after 1834 (see above p. 237 n. 1 and below, pp. 279–80). For a general account of migration under the old poor law see Redford, op. cit., Ch. V.
3. Ibid., p. 129.
4. D. S. Landes in H. J. Habakkuk and M. Postan (eds.) *Cambridge Economic History of Europe* (Cambridge, 1965), vi, Pt. I. 316; Saville, op. cit., pp. 5, 11.
5. Saville, op. cit., pp. 206–10.
6. V. C. Davies, 'Some Geographical Aspects of the Depopulation of Rural Wales since 1841', p. 53.

## III

It has been suggested that in the decades during which Britain acquired a railway system mobility reached an unprecedented level. The forces which increased mobility were closely connected; a typical area of dispersion lost population because farm employment expanded far less rapidly than the supply of labour, other occupations were affected by factory competition, and better transport facilitated migration to areas where wages were high and demand for labour buoyant. There is no doubt of the combined impact of these forces but it is difficult to assess the contribution of any one. These problems merit attention, however, particularly the influence of railways whose total impact on economic life, at one time regarded as near cataclysmic, has become one of the central issues in economic history.

Mobility and the railway system grew together—to what extent was the first development a consequence of the second? This question might appear easily answered because most of the variables are known and measurable. We know which areas lost and which gained population, we know too how much track existed at different dates, where it was, the charges for using it, and the number of passengers it carried. All this sounds conducive to testing the effect of railways upon migration by comparing migration rates before and after railway construction and between those counties with railways and those without. Unfortunately these comparisons would not be helpful because the railway influence extended far beyond its immediate vicinity. A line might modify or reverse a migration loss in rural areas along its route[1] and at the same time stimulate migration from areas at some distance but near enough to be affected by falling freight rates and the erosive influence

1. For examples of this process see *Census of England and Wales 1871*, Vol. II, P.P. 1872, LXVIii, pp. 545–6; K. Walton, 'Population Changes in North East Scotland, 1696–1951', *Scottish Studies*, v (1961), 168–9; Saville, op. cit., p. 211.

of railways upon barriers to mobility. Its power to depopulate
could extend over a considerable distance, much too far to
allow worthwhile tests based upon county data. The Norfolk
textile trades, for example, suffered a competitive disadvantage
because railways were built to serve the West Riding before
Norfolk benefited similarly[1] and railways on the American
prairie affected employment, wages, and migration rates in
every arable parish in Britain almost regardless of their
proximity to local lines.

An aspect of the influence of railways which assumes particular importance in a study of regional wage variations is
whether railways encouraged mobility most in the positive
and direct sense of inducing movement by reducing the cost,
time, and discomfort involved, or indirectly by the con-
solidation they gave to forces which favoured the expansion of
manufacturing and commerce in large towns and the contraction
of employment elsewhere. The two influences obviously over-
lapped but the distinction is useful and important. Two
comments will illustrate the point; the first stresses the railways' direct impact: 'How did the country population attain
their present prosperity? Simply by the emigration to the
towns or colonies of the redundant labourers. This emigration
was scarcely possible until the construction of railways. Up to
that date the farm labourer was unable to migrate; from that
time he became a migratory animal.' [2] The second emphasizes

1. J. K. Edwards, 'Communications and the Economic Development of
Norwich, 1750–1850', *Journal of Transport History*, vii (1965), 102. The
Long Crendon needle trade was similarly affected in its competition with
Redditch. W. Shrimpton, *Notes on a Decayed Needleland*, (Redditch, 1897),
p. 7.
2. R. D. Baxter, 'Railway Extension and its Results', *J.R.S.S.*, xxix (1866),
567. For other comments of this kind see e.g. Thomas Brassey. He claimed
that the railways 'had a marked effect in equalizing the cost of labour
throughout the country' (*Lectures on the Labour Question*, p. 18). Alexander
MacDonald, the Scottish labour leader, talked of 'a great new power . . .
locomotion' improving the miners' bargaining position, . . . 'When they
were dissatisfied with their work or their employer they now had only to
take the railway . . .' (Youngson Brown, 'The Scots Coal Industry', p. 189).
Redford suggested that the railways, 'tapped a vast stagnant reservoir of
labour in the English countryside and transformed the character of English
migration'. (Redford, op. cit., p. 187). See also D. Williams, *The Rebecca
Riots* (Cardiff, 1955), p. 158: 'In time, the railway lessened the pressure
caused by a growing population in a backward area by facilitating migration

the indirect influence: '. . . their effect upon internal migration was probably less in physically moving people from one place to another than in the achievement of a national market.'[1] There is evidence from Belgium and America which might lend support to the first view; Belgian workers were granted extensive travel concessions with considerable effect on the mobility of labour,[2] and, in a different way and for different reasons, the railways exerted a considerable direct influence on migration in the United States.[3] However, unless we give undue weight to unsubstantiated opinions such as those already quoted, there is not much evidence of a substantial direct effect in Britain; perhaps the strongest evidence is the large proportion of revenue which was accounted for by passenger receipts until the late 1840s.[4]

In fact, there is good reason to suggest that the direct influence of railways on migration was not great, and it was certainly considerably less than Baxter and others supposed. The importance of passenger receipts is not necessarily evidence that the indirect effect of railways was initially of small consequence because much freight that continued to travel by water or road travelled more cheaply as a consequence of railway competition.[5] The evidence from Belgium relates to special conditions of exceptionally low-cost travel of a kind that never existed in Britain; before the Act of 1844 and the introduction of 'parliamentary trains' railways may have increased the cost of working-class mobility by putting out of business waggon and coach services which the poor had previously

---

Footnote 2 (continued)

to the industries of Glamorgan and Monmouthshire and it is arguable that if the railway had reached West Wales a decade earlier the riots would not have taken place.'

1. Saville, op. cit., p. 9.
2. B. Thomas, 'Studies in Labour Supply and Labour Costs', pp. 80–1.
3. T. C. Cochran in B. Mazlish (ed.) *The Railroad and the Space Program* (Cambridge, Mass., 1965), pp. 164–5.
4. B. R. Mitchell, 'The coming of the Railway and United Kingdom Economic Growth', *J.E.H.*, xxiv (1964), 317–19; Saville, op. cit., p. 9.
5. See e.g. Mitchell, op. cit., p. 318 and, among others, J. K. Edwards, op. cit., p. 102. Edwards mentions freight reductions of over two-thirds on the Aire and Calder navigation following railway construction.

patronized.[1] The American case too was a special one which involved great distances and, often, the absence of alternative transport, whereas England was small and well served by coach and waggon before railway building commenced. Rapid and comfortable road transport was expensive, and cheap road transport was far slower and less comfortable than the service eventually provided by the railway, but probably not so much slower, nor so much less comfortable, as seriously to deter migration in a small country where most moves were over very short distances. Further, and again contrary to what statements like Baxter's might lead us to expect, there is evidence of considerable mobility before the railway age and of mobility after 1830 which owed nothing to the railways. The parish studies of pre-industrial migration mentioned earlier are not important in this respect because they refer mainly to very local movement;[2] but the Nottingham framework knitters, who travelled on foot each year to Scotland when the Nottingham trade was slack,[3] come into a quite different category. So do the glassmakers, constantly on the move between Scotland, the north-east, Lancashire, the Midlands, Bristol, and London, the 'tramping artisans', and the railway navvies who were reputedly willing to tramp from Kent to Westmorland for an extra fourpence a day.[4] Welshmen travelled to the English Midlands to help in haymaking and harvest in the eighteenth century; the Irish travelled even further to perform similar tasks, and there was a considerable volume of seasonal migration between highland and lowland Scotland.[5] Even when the railways penetrated northern Scotland in the second half of the century they were not much patronized by

---

1. T. R. Gourvish, 'British Railway Management in the Nineteenth Century', University of London Ph.D. thesis, 1967, pp. 30–4; see also H. J. Dyos and D. H. Aldcroft, *British Transport* (Leicester, 1969), p. 171.
2. See above, p. 263.
3. E. G. Nelson, 'The Putting-out System in the English Framework Knitting Industry', *Journal of Economic and Business History*, ii (1929–30), 483–4.
4. T. C. Barker and J. R. Harris, *A Merseyside Town in the Industrial Revolution, St Helens 1750–1900*, p. 284; E. J. Hobsbawm, *Labouring Men* (1964), Ch. 4; T. Coleman, *The Railway Navvies*, p. 234.
5. Redford, op. cit., pp. 132–7; E. W. Gilboy, *Wages in Eighteenth Century England*, pp. 52–3.

seasonal migrants who were either unable to buy tickets or preferred to walk and keep the fare.[1]

Given Britain's size, the existence of other forms of transport, and specific evidence of a great deal of mobility which was not dependent on the railways, it seems unlikely that the direct effect of railways on migration was substantial. The advantages the railway offered in speed, comfort, and cost amounted to no more than one factor among many to be taken into account when contemplating whether or not to abandon home, friends, and existing employment in search of better opportunities elsewhere. The greatest positive effect of railways upon migration perhaps derived from their influence on men's imaginations; they symbolized an acceleration in the rate of progress and the rewards and excitement this offered and thus made men less reluctant to accept change. In addition, travel of any sort widened men's horizons and excursions, shopping expeditions, and similar diurnal mobility of a kind which was probably affected very substantially by railways may have made the prospect of living and working elsewhere less painful to contemplate. The importance of these influences is impossible to measure; while they may have been greater than the improvements railways bought in time, cost, and comfort they were probably still not sufficient to make serious inroads upon the immense barriers which prevent most men changing their home and job when they have work, a reasonable income, and a measure of security. Towards the middle of the century there began those major structural changes in the economy described earlier; these were greatly facilitated by the railways, and gave rise to declining employment opportunities in many parts of the country. Stagnant or diminishing employment opportunities combined with rising population made migration less a matter of choice, and it was probably in this way that the

1. D. F. MacDonald, *Scotland's Shifting Population 1770–1850* (Glasgow 1937), p. 133. The extraordinarily rapid town growth of the 1820s might be added to this evidence of pre-railway mobility. Redford, op. cit., p. 62; Clapham, op. cit. i. 536. See also T. Wood, *Autobiography* (1956) pp. 12–13, 15; in the course of a month spent travelling in search of work in the mid-1840s Wood never once used the railway. When he lost his job at Platts of Oldham in 1847 he walked to Huddersfield and subsequently to Leeds and York.

railways exerted their greatest influence. They allowed factory
manufactured goods to compete effectively with the products
of domestic crafts and industries, they curtailed employment
in canal, river, coasting, and coaching trades, and they brought
the harvests of the American west to compete with the produce
of Britain's farms.[1] As a consequence migration more often
became a matter of necessity—that the actual move might be
made faster and in greater comfort than was possible before
1830 was hardly more than incidental.[2]

The role of the railway appears to have been threefold.
First, by reducing freight rates it increased prosperity in the
more efficient manufacturing centres and made more effective
the spatial variations in productivity described in Chapter
Five.[3] At the same time, and as part of the same process,
employment prospects in rural areas and the less efficient
manufacturing centres were reduced to a level where migration
became unavoidable. Third, and probably least important, it
made migration quicker, more comfortable, and possibly
cheaper. An important corollary of this order of importance is
that while railways were among the forces which helped to
achieve the extraordinarily high rates of mobility in the second
half of the century their contribution to the erosion of wages
differentials was, nevertheless, small or possibly negative. By
reducing transport costs they increased international competition in the supply of foodstuffs and put pressure on the
British arable farmer and his badly paid labourers, they consolidated the advantages of high-wage and efficient manufacturing centres and intensified the difficulties of the low
productivity districts. Each of these influences would tend to

1. For examples and descriptions of this process see Ch. 4 above and, among
   many others, Saville, op. cit., particularly Chs. 1 and 5; A. H. Shorter,
   'The Historical Geography of Manufacturing Industry in the South-west
   of England in the Nineteenth Century', pp. 23–30; V. C. Davies, 'Some
   Geographical Aspects of the Depopulation of Rural Wales since 1841',
   pp. 53–4; P. R. Mounfield, 'The Location of Footwear Manufacture in
   England and Wales', pp. 209, 278–83.
2. Indeed, as was noted earlier, many of the areas most affected by the building
   of railways and by migration were some distance from a railway.
3. The railways also helped the growth of large cities by facilitating the supply
   of food and raw materials.

widen existing wage differentials: at the same time railway-induced mobility worked in the opposite direction, but there is no reason to suppose that the latter influence was the stronger for several decades after 1850.[1] Railways facilitated mobility but probably by no more than they increased its necessity.

Although we have reached a tentative conclusion on the likely effect of railways upon regional wage variations, their contribution to high mobility has proved impossible to measure with any degree of precision; its direct effect was perhaps less than the contribution of technical change in manufacturing—but this is an impression which cannot be proven. Population change may have been more influential than either; population grew rapidly both where it was wanted and where it was not[2] and one consequence of this was high rates of migration. The influence of population growth can be seen in the nature of rural 'depopulation' which began before food imports were important and was a feature of both pastoral and arable areas. It is reflected also in the fact that despite substantial migration from rural areas the rural population was no less in 1911 then seventy years earlier.[3] A single case cited in the Booth survey sums up the position in most of rural Britain. In an East Anglian village where labourers were among the worst-paid in Britain the investigator noted, '. . . a labourer, with a family of twelve. Six are in London already, and the rest will follow when old enough . . .' [4] There are two things remarkable about this family: its mobility and its fecundity—the first was a consequence of the second but the second was so

1. By the late nineteenth century the spatial redistribution of economic activity was slowing down (see Ch. 4 above) and by that time the railway influence was probably in the direction of equalizing wages. Developments in local transport which encouraged working-class commuting at about the same time probably had a similar effect although they may have reduced migration by permitting a greater choice of employment without change of residence. On these developments see R. H. Osborne in K. C. Edwards (ed.), *Nottingham and its Region*, p. 343, E. J. Hobsbawm in R. Glass (ed.), *London; Aspects of Change*, pp. 7–8; M. K. Ashby, *Joseph Ashby of Tysoe, 1859–1919*, pp. 160–1 and above, p. 18.
2. See Ch. 6 above.
3. Deane and Cole, op. cit., p. 10; Caircross, op. cit., p. 77.
4. Booth, *Life and Labour*, 1st Ser. iii. 131.

strong that despite high rates of mobility wages in the village, and in the whole of East Anglia, remained abysmally low.[1]

# IV

While we may generalize about the extraordinary mobility of the labour force as a whole it is likely that there was considerable diversity within the over-all pattern. Clapham noted the extent of regional wage variations and suggested that their existence probably owed something to variations in mobility: 'the men of Surrey may be pictured moving easily over their suburban sands; those of Essex, stuck beyond East London in deep clays or hidden in the folds of their north-western chalk; Buckingham men immobile in vale and beechwood, and Oxfordshire men tied, by affection surely not by inertia, to the valleys of the Windrush and the Evenlode.' [2] The correlation analysis in section I of this chapter suggested certain spatial differentials in mobility, and one of the interesting features which has emerged from the study of labour mobility between the wars is the existence of varying degrees of mobility among different occupational groups and different regions; at that time there was a particular contrast between the highly mobile Welsh and the relatively immobile Lancastrians.[3] We are concerned

1. The implications of a situation where rapid population increase made migration almost imperative, and the earlier conclusion that 'railways facilitated mobility but by no more than they increased its necessity' (above, p. 272). suggest the need to emphasize again the qualification which attached to the conclusions about mobility in section II of this chapter. Labour was highly mobile in the sense that net migration across county boundaries occurred on a scale not exceeded before or since, and in the light of certain other less exacting measures described above (pp. 255–7). This conclusion implies nothing about the innate mobility or immobility of the population. The hypothesis that net migration across county boundaries increased in this period by no more than the necessity to move increased may well be sound, but the definition of mobility used here stops short of considering the imponderables involved in comparisons of this type.
2. Clapham, op. cit. iii. 97–8.
3. B. Thomas several times drew attention to this feature; see his 'Labour Supply and Labour Costs', p. 128 and his articles in *Economica*, N.S., i (1934), 225; iv (1937), 328–9; v (1938), 416–17, 427. See also J. Jewkes and H. Campion, 'The Mobility of Labour in the Cotton Industry', pp. 135–7. Makower, Marschak, and Robinson, op. cit. (1938), p. 111.

here mainly with those parts of the pattern which significantly affected regional wage variations,[1] and in particular with migration differentials between urban and rural areas and among rural areas. Their effect was to modify the erosive influence of migration upon regional wage variations.

The first case, relatively low mobility in rural areas, is scarcely surprising and not difficult to explain.[2] It was there that the obstacles to mobility were most formidable and, although migration from low-wage rural areas could pay unusually high dividends, knowledge of distant opportunities was notoriously deficient. Remoteness, the solitary nature of employment, and the strong hold of tradition and custom all hindered the acquisition of market information. Income comparisons were made more difficult by the necessity to assess the value of payments in kind, by ignorance of the extent to which wage advantages might be offset by higher prices,[3] and by a not entirely unjustified suspicion that high wages might be little more than a premium for skill and extraordinary effort.[4] In Flora Thompson's account of her childhood in a village nineteen miles from Oxford she recalls children asking where was Oxford and what was it like. They were told, incorrectly, that Oxford 'was "a gert big town" where a man might earn as much as five and twenty shillings a week; but as he would have to pay "pretty near" half of it in house rent . . . he'd be a fool to go there.'[5] Much of the market information obtained by rural workers came from their social superiors and they were often ill advised. In the first instance this was because sound

1. The age differential will not be discussed here because there is no evidence which suggests that it directly affected the regional wage pattern. For a brief comment on the relationship between adolescent wage differentials and migration rates see above, p. 111.
2. On this see, e.g. Redford, op. cit., pp. 93–6; F. Clifford, 'The Labour Bill in Farming', pp. 125–6.
3. On this point see also above, p. 105.
4. The connection between diet and productivity is discussed in Ch. 5. Some Norfolk farm labourers returned from Durham giving the reason that they had to work harder and that much of their enhanced income was spent on additional food. R. Hamilton in discussion on Ravenstein op. cit. (1885), p. 233.
5. F. Thompson, *Lark Rise to Candleford* (1945), p. 20.

and comprehensive information was not available from any
source; second, many who considered themselves possessed of
a right and duty to advise the rural labourers were inclined to
idealize rural life. Their advice was characterized by a failure
to appreciate that a diminishing farm labour force is a normal
development in an industrializing economy. It was, moreover,
the opinion of the well-to-do who were well placed to enjoy the
benefits of country life and likely, therefore, to take an unduly
optimistic view of the compensation they offered for long hours
and low wages. 'Can any difference in the rate of wages fully
compensate him [the town worker] for the privations that he
suffers ?', asked Thomas Brassey, a man much given to offering
advice to the lower orders.[1] Farmers and landlords, perhaps
uneasy about the evidence of rural distress but no doubt mainly
because they believed them to be true, eagerly endorsed these
opinions.[2] They may also have been aware that interpretations
of this kind were conducive to a contented and plentiful labour
force for depopulation, no matter how necessary it may appear
to the historian, usually gave rise to concern about labour
shortages, particularly when it was accompanied by rising
wages.[3] In these various ways market knowledge was obscured,
mobility impeded, and the erosion of wage differentials
retarded.

In so far as the poor law was an obstacle to mobility rural
areas were most affected.[4] Tied cottages were a further impediment;[5] and so were low incomes because migration

1. Brassey, op. cit., p. 120. Cobbett's work contains much in similar vein;
   see e.g. his comments on the 'horrible misery' of factory workers and the
   'hell hole' northern manufacturing towns. W. Cobbett, *Rural Rides*, ed.
   G. Woodcock (1967), pp. 273, 341, 394–5.
2. See e.g. John Walker's comments on a paper by G. B. Longstaff, 'Rural
   Depopulation', *J.R.S.S.*, lvi (1893), 436.
3. Canon Girdlestone was strongly opposed by local employers when he tried
   to transfer Devon labourers to the north (Chambers and Mingay, op. cit.,
   pp. 146, 188). See also W. S. Shepperson, *British Emigration to North
   America* (Oxford, 1957), p. 64. When distress was particularly severe
   depopulation might be encouraged as it was in Ireland, but there were few
   cases of this kind in Britain after 1850.
4. Attitudes encouraged by the old poor law influenced mobility well into the
   second part of the century. See above, p. 265.
5. Tied cottages were an especially formidable obstacle to mobility when
   migration jeopardized parents' tenancy. B. Kerr, 'The Dorset Agricultural
   Labourer, 1750–1850', p. 176.

required savings to finance the move itself and as provision
against the risk that employment might not be immediately
available. But the agricultural labourer was perhaps most at a
disadvantage with respect to what might be called the 'psychological' cost of moving. Mobility can be considered in two
broad categories: geographical and occupational. We are concerned mainly with the former but the two were linked and
unless he was prepared to go abroad the agricultural worker,
unlike most others, could seldom contemplate the first alone.[1]
The Scots miners whose market included both sides of the
Atlantic operated within only one of the two migration dimen-
sions and so did the framework knitters and glassworkers who
were mentioned earlier.[2] The importance of 'psychological'
restraints on the mobility of rural workers is reflected by their
prominent place in that part of total migration which took
place in stages.[3] Moving in this way allowed gradual acclimatiza-
tion to new work and surroundings. After the first move subsequent migration was less difficult and in most cases the further
the rural migrant ventured from his starting-point the more

1. There were exceptions of course, see above p. 23. The situation described
   helps to explain why young men, not long used to farm work, figured so
   prominently among rural migrants. However, the possibility of structural
   change being effected by 'wastage' was much impeded by the fact that
   education finished before a boy reached an age where he could earn sufficient
   to keep himself. This left him with little alternative but to live at home and
   take what work was available. Many of these lads migrated before they were
   much older, but not all, and in this way the supply of labour for agriculture
   and other village and small-town occupations remained high relative to
   demand. Their sisters were more fortunate, for domestic service offered a
   roof, food, and some substitute for parental guidance: few jobs offered
   equivalent advantages to young men and this situation underlies higher
   mobility among young females. Saville, op. cit., p. 98, and see below, p.
   283,
2. See above, p. 269, In one sense these examples might be regarded as an
   indication of the obstacles to occupational mobility. There is much similar
   evidence among the lowest-paid city workers like the handknitters of
   Leicester and their counterparts in other textile towns who clung to their
   customary occupation, their independence, and their poverty, when well-
   paid work was available in the same town—see above, p. 34 n. 2. The out-
   door weavers of Coventry were in the same category; they converted
   their homes to miniature steam factories rather than surrender their
   independence and 'respectable, propertied virtues', J. M. Prest, *The
   Industrial Revolution in Coventry*, pp. 94–5.
3. On this point see, Heads, op. cit., pp. 228, 269, 280; B. Thomas, 'Labour
   Supply and Labour Costs', pp. 70–1.

conducive was the environment to mobility. A rising income was part of this process, another part was the company of other migrants, increasingly from areas other than his own, and a third part was better knowledge of market conditions.

The urban worker drew his superior market information from a variety of sources. Trade unions might be one of these; some published regular information on the state of trade in other parts of Britain and north America and many took more positive action to encourage overseas migration. Their advice was doubtless valuable, not least so when it drew attention to bad conditions elsewhere; there were few more powerful reinforcements to inertia than disappointed ex-migrants and there were many of those in agricultural villages.[1] The union role in the encouragement of migration is still debated; it was strongest in the third quarter of the century, more significant than might be suggested by the amount spent on assistance, and felt mainly in urban areas, particularly the high-wage industrial towns of the north and Midlands.[2] Emigration statistics are not sufficiently clear to remove uncertainty about the source of overseas migrants[3] but it is highly probable that the influence of trade unions was partly responsible for a disproportionately high level of emigration from large towns— a feature likely to help maintain existing wage differentials.

1. Migrants were always likely to find themselves at a disadvantage to native labour, victims of discrimination and lack of local knowledge. When the destination had been well chosen this might not be a great handicap, but undirected migration could be a severe barrier to further migration. On these various points see Youngson Brown, 'The Scots Coal Industry', p. 202; R. V. Clements, 'Trade Unions and Emigration, 1840–80', *Pop. Stud.*, ix (1955–6), 170; Heads, op. cit., p. 120.

2. Union restriction on labour supply is discussed further in Ch. 9 below, p. 340. Joseph Arch's union encouraged emigration for a short period in the 1870s and on a more modest scale thereafter but its main impact was short-lived and confined to the south and Midlands. Arch at one time claimed to have assisted 700,000 emigrants but this, as he subsequently admitted, was a gross exaggeration (R. V. Clements, op. cit., p. 173). It is interesting to note how well Arch's own circumstances endorse what has been said of the relative immobility of most rural workers—he was a champion hedge-cutter, well paid, and highly mobile, and thus he differed from most rural workers in a manner highly conducive to his enthusiastic acceptance of migration as a cure for poverty.

3. For a discussion of the evidence see N. H. Carrier and J. R. Jeffery, *External Migration: A Study of the Available Statistics 1815–1950*, Studies on Medical and Population Subjects, No. 6 (H.M.S.O., 1953).

Agriculture was certainly the main reservoir of labour and, because they were so badly paid and could seldom move within Britain without changing their occupations, farm workers had more than most to gain from emigration. These considerations have led several writers to suppose that rural workers contributed disproportionately to emigration in the nineteenth century.[1] But the suggestion that agricultural labourers were more likely to emigrate because they had most to gain overlooks the greater mobility of urban workers and is contradicted by the findings of two detailed investigations of the source and occupations of emigrants.[2]

None of what has been said here should be interpreted as implying that rural labour was immobile in any general sense; the opposite was nearer the truth. The position was, simply, that the urban workers, and particularly the better-paid among them, were more mobile. It was partly because labour's response to migration incentives was not homogeneous that the relationship between migration and wages shown in section I of this chapter was not entirely consistent with what economic theory would lead us to expect.[3] The major industrial areas of the north and Midlands all managed to combine high wages with low migration gains;[4] part of the explanation for this is that the labour they attracted from low-wage areas was in some measure offset by the departure of others abroad and elsewhere in Britain.[5]

The other migration differential which affected the regional wage pattern was suggested by the correlation analysis in section I of this chapter. Mobility in parts of the low-wage rural

---

1. See e.g. W. Hasbach, *A History of the English Agricultural Labourer*, pp. 252–3; Redford, op. cit., pp. 123–4.
2. C. J. Erickson, 'Who were the English and Scots Emigrants to the United States in the late-Nineteenth Century?', in D. V. Glass and R. Revelle (eds.), *Population and Social Change* (1972); R. Duncan, 'Case Studies in Emigration: Cornwall, Gloucestershire and New South Wales, 1877–86', *Ec.H.R.*, 2nd Ser., xvi (1963-4).
3. See above, pp. 248–51.
4. See above, pp. 249–51.
5. Many went to London. Industrial counties sent a disproportionate number of migrants to the capital compared with rural counties at a similar distance (A. E. C. Hare, 'Labour Migration: A study of the Mobility of Labour', pp. 81–2). On emigration from northern towns see Cairncross (1953), op. cit., pp. 69–71.

south appeared to compare unfavourably with rates in much
of the north of England and southern Scotland including
several rural counties which could not have been much affected
by the influences operative in northern cities. If this pattern
existed its influence would have been to modify the erosive
influence of migration on regional wage variations; it would
also help to explain the combination of high, or moderately
high, wages with a very low rate of increase in demand for
labour in Cumberland, Westmorland, and the counties of rural
southern Scotland.[1] The statistics used in section I leave much
to be desired but the suggestion of spatial differentials in
response to wage incentives is sufficiently strong to warrant
further investigation. There is, in fact, considerable literary
evidence consistent with the pattern suggested.

The poor law retarded mobility more before 1834 than after,
and even less after the Union Chargeability Act of 1865; but
where dependence on the old poor law had been greatest the
habits of immobility, the identification of the parish with
security, and the stigma which organized migration and
emigration laid upon subsequent schemes, lasted long after
1865.[2] The north of England never depended on the old poor
law as much as the south and its labour force had fewer in-
hibitions about migration.[3] The contrast between the south
and Scotland was even greater, for Scotland's way of dealing
with poverty was at one time entirely distinct and far more
conducive to mobility. A report of the 1830s contrasted
England where the unemployed poor were 'chained to the
soil' and Scotland where 'the circulation of labour has not been
impeded by an ill-administered system of poor-laws.' [4] The
essence of the Scottish system was that the unemployed were
encouraged and assisted to travel to wherever work was

1. See above, p. 182 n. 1.
2. Many private charities, particularly local charities, continued to exercise
   some residential test; see e.g. H. J. Dyos, 'The Suburban Development of
   Greater London south of the Thames', p. 144.
3. On these points see above, p. 265; Redford, op. cit., pp. 93–6, 99, 104,
   110–11; Shepperson, op. cit., p. 48.
4. *Poor Inquiry (Ireland)*, P.P. 1836, XXXIV, Appendix G to Report, pp.
   xxvi, xxviii.

available and those unwilling to move were refused relief. Provision was most generous in the towns so that migration from the countryside to urban regions was particularly encouraged.[1] After 1845 the distinction between the Scottish and English poor laws diminished but the attitudes encouraged by the Scottish system, like those encouraged by the old poor law in the south of England, must have retained some influence well into the second half of the century.

Another influence which lends substance to the pattern suggested by the correlation analysis was the nature of the farm employment contract. This varied greatly from one locality to the next and between different occupations but the main distinction was between Scotland and the north of England on the one hand, where men were engaged for six months or a year at a time and often accommodated on the farm, and the south and Midlands on the other, where 'living in' was exceptional and men were usually engaged on a daily or weekly basis.[2] These provisions might suggest that the less fettered labourers of the south and Midlands were more mobile than those of the north; in fact the opposite was the case. Despite short tenures southern labourers enjoyed customary security while the much longer, and apparently immobilizing, contracts of the north encouraged mobility—not because men were discharged at the end of their contract but because many, perhaps the majority, customarily discharged themselves and went to the hiring fair to seek a new master, better conditions, and a change of scenery: 'the periodical recurrence of the hiring season suggests to the peasant mind the necessity of being hired.'[3] The origins of this practice are obscure although

1. For accounts of the system in Scotland see MacDonald, op. cit., pp. 106–21; Campbell, op. cit., pp. 204–11, 310–12.
2. This distinction applied still in 1914 and had far from disappeared in 1939. G. Houston, 'Labour Relations in Scottish Agriculture before 1870'. *Ag. Hist. Rev.*, vi (1958), 27; J. D. Wood, 'Scottish Migration Overseas', *Scottish Geographical Magazine*, lxxx (1964), 165; *Second Report on Wages ... Agricultural Labourers*, P.P. 1905, XCVII, p. 2.
3. T. E. Kebbel, *The Agricultural Labourer*, p. 165; see also, J. D. Wood, op. cit., p. 165; *Second Report Wages ... Agricultural Labourers*, P.P. 1905, XCVII, pp. 13, 88; J. A. Symon, *Scottish Farming Past and Present* (Edinburgh and London, 1959), p. 162.

in Scotland it probably owed something to an understandable desire to exploit in full the easing of legal restraints on mobility in the eighteenth century. In the second half of the nineteenth century it was sustained by custom and the existence of the hiring fair; it affected married men almost as much as single[1] and helped to make rural labour in parts of Scotland and northern England an important exception to generalizations about the contrast between urban and rural mobility. Other forces worked in the same direction. Long familiarity with seasonal migration probably contributed to mobility in the north[2] and so did a superior education system; labourers profoundly ignorant of Canada and Australia and able to regard Lancashire as a foreign country were probably less common north of the Trent.[3] In the rural south a further impediment to mobility was the small independent village friendly societies with their non-transferable benefits.[4]

There is evidence which suggests a further distinction between mobility in different parts of the country. A large part of the southern labour force appears to have operated in a particularly

1. A. Symon, op. cit., p. 162; *Second Report on Wages . . . Agricultural Labourers*, p. 88.
2. There were seasonal demands for labour in southern England too but there supply pressed upon demand to an extent that, far from stimulating mobility, harvest requirements encouraged underemployment during the rest of the year. Seasonal migration in Scotland is discussed extensively in MacDonald, op. cit., pp. 125–40; see also R. Molland and G. Evans, 'Scottish Farm Wages from 1870 to 1900', p. 225, and Campbell, op. cit., p. 180. On southern England see *V.C.H. Wiltshire*, iv. 81–3, and above, pp. 213–4.
3. See above, p. 253, and below, p. 283. For comments on education in these areas and its effect on mobility see *M.C.* 12, 19 Jan. 1850; P. de Rousiers, *The Labour Question in Britain*, pp. 304–5. It is interesting to note that the rural south of Scotland emerges rather well from Professor Smout's recent criticism of the long-established belief in the superior quality of Scottish education. T. C. Smout, *A History of the Scottish People, 1560–1830* (1969), Ch. 18.
4. On the village friendly societies, see P. H. J. H. Gosden, *The Friendly Societies in England, 1815–1875* (Manchester, 1961), pp. 25, 52–4, 78. High rates of mobility in the north and the relationship between mobility and high wages have been noted by several writers. See e.g. R. Molland and G. Evans, 'Scottish Farm Wages from 1870 to 1900', pp. 225–6; G. Houston in *J.R.S.S.*, Series A. (1955), 228; D. J. Davies, op. cit., p. 60; F. Clifford, 'The Labour Bill in Farming', pp. 91, 124–5; de Rousiers, op. cit., p. 304; Youngson Brown, 'The Scots Coal Industry', pp. 195, 200–3.

restricted market. They moved overwhelmingly in one direction—towards London. This feature is well documented;[1] Norfolk and Wiltshire, sufficiently far from the capital to rule out the possibility that its attraction was due to proximity, illustrate the general position:[2]

TABLE 7–5

*Enumeration of Norfolk-born and Wiltshire-born:*
*1871, 1901*

| 1871 | Norfolk-born | Wiltshire-born |
|---|---|---|
| Enumerated in: | | |
| London and Middlesex | 87,575 | 49,637 |
| Lancashire | 4,229 | 1,524 |
| Staffordshire | 814 | 950 |
| Glamorganshire | 174 | 1,859 |
| 1901 | Norfolk-born | Wiltshire-born |
| London and Middlesex | 58,867 | 35,186 |
| Lancashire | 8,308 | 2,788 |
| Staffordshire | 1,413 | 1,351 |
| Glamorganshire | 633 | 6,089 |

*Source:* Census of England and Wales, 1871, 1901, Birthplace Tables.

There are a number of possible explanations for the failure of the mining and manufacturing areas to attract southern migrants. Even when London was not closer better communications often made it more accessible. London's influence probably also owed something to its great importance in pre-industrial migration. In the seventeenth and eighteenth centuries,

1. See V. C. Davies, 'Some Geographical Aspects of the Decline in the Rural Population of Wales', p. 60; H. C. Darby, 'The Movement of Population to and from Cambridgeshire between 1851 and 1861', *Geographical Journal*, ci (1943), 124–5; A. B. Hill, op. cit., pp. 40–2; W. G. Hoskins, op. cit., p. 173; R. Lawton, 'Population Migration into and from Warwickshire and Staffordshire, 1841–1901', M.A. thesis University of Liverpool (1950), pp. 188–96; W. Ogle, 'The Alleged Depopulation of the Rural Districts of England', *J.R.S.S.*, lii (1889), 214; Ravenstein, op. cit. (1885), p. 210; C. T. Smith, 'The Movement of Population in England and Wales in 1851 and 1861', *Geographical Journal*, cxvii (1951), 205–10.
2. Wiltshire, for example, is as near to the Birmingham area as to London and nearer to south Wales. Most of Norfolk is as near to the Birmingham area as to London and not much further from Manchester.

before the development of northern and Midland manufacturing
and mining centres, it was far more the obvious destination for
southern migrants then in the nineteenth century and migration streams tend to perpetuate themselves.[1] But there was
more than inertia to sustain the flow to London. Girls commonly
left home before their brothers, many of them to enter domestic
service;[2] the demand for servants was greatest in London and
other southern towns and it was likely that kinship ties and
information received from mothers and sisters propelled men
and boys in the same direction.[3] It seems probable also that
southerners regarded the mining and manufacturing areas with
some repugnance, particularly the coalfields where demand for
labour was greatest but patterns of work and leisure least
familiar. Dorset labourers were said to have considered
migration to the industrial north no less terrible than
migration overseas and some Devon labourers were not sure
that the northern counties were not overseas.[4] How strong
this influence was is difficult to determine but the London
service trades offered ample non-industrial employment and
there was much about the mining and manufacturing areas
that was unpleasant; their least favourable features were well

1. Once set in a particular direction ties of family and friendship and especial
   knowledge of conditions in the receiving area make it likely that migration
   streams will continue. One of the more curious among the many examples
   of this tendency is the reported fact that over 90 per cent of natives of
   Anguilla resident in Britain in the late 1960s lived in and around Slough.
   For more prosaic examples see Booth, *Life and Labour*, 1st Ser. iii. 131–3;
   T. Wilson and P. W. S. Andrews, *Oxford Studies in the Price Mechanism*
   (Oxford, 1951), p. 224; B. Kerr, 'The Dorset Agricultural Labourer
   1750–1850', p. 176; *General Report of the 1871 Census of Scotland*, P.P. 1873,
   LXXIII, p. xxxvi.
2. 'It is this opening for early employment that strips the rural districts of
   their young girls, and causes . . . the lads to exceptionally outnumber the
   girls in country places between the ages of 10 and 20' (*General Report of the
   1891 Census of England and Wales*, P.P. 1893–4, CVI, p. 40). On this point
   see also above, 276 n. 1.
3. 'The letters written home by these country girls settled in domestic service
   in towns have been "probably one of the most powerful and efficient
   migration agencies," ' (D. J. Davies, op. cit., p. 67).
4. Kerr, 'The Dorset Agricultural Labourer', pp. 175–6. Chambers and
   Mingay, op. cit., p. 188.

publicized,[1] and the non-monetary advantages of city life were greatest in the capital. Conditions in the northern towns improved in the second half of the century but these changes were not likely to be appreciated at once; lurid accounts of conditions in the 1820s and 1830s doubtless influenced opinion about the north long after 1850 just as general impressions of the north in the 1950s and 1960s were coloured by what was known of conditions in the inter-war years. Southern attitudes to railway construction may be indicative of opinion and prejudices. The navvies themselves were mainly northerners;[2] they were remarkably well paid but, as a consequence of their fondness for hard drinking, brawling, petty crime, and other debaucheries, they were not highly regarded by respectable members of the working classes.[3] In many rural areas the arrival of the navvies was the first close contact with the industrial world and this event must have reinforced many suspicions about the quality of northern life. Some rural labourers joined the gangs but most wanted no part of it even though by joining they might double their earnings: 'nothing will induce them to submit to what they conceived a degradation, of working upon the works.' [4]

1. The attitudes discussed on pp. 274–5 above are relevant here, particularly Cobbett's remarks on the 'horrible misery' of factory workers and the 'hell hole' manufacturing towns. The contrast between northern towns and the rural south is still sometimes exaggerated: Prest, after describing the wretched conditions of the country silk weavers outside Coventry who lived on 'bread, potatoes, and a little tea, and . . . bacon' suggests that: 'rough as life was . . . it was nothing like so bad as the pitiful life of the Manchester cellars' (Prest, op. cit., pp. 64, 70). While this may be a reasonable description of life in the Manchester cellars it is no guide to the average condition of migrants in that city.
2. T. Coleman, op. cit., pp. 25, 94, 200, 223. The fact that most navvies were northerners is consistent with the regional migration differentials described above.
3. For a general account of their life and impact on country districts see ibid., Chs. 1, 6, 10, and 11.
4. Comment on the attitude of Northamptonshire labourers to construction work on the London and Birmingham line. *S.C. on Railway Labourers*, P.P. 1846, XIII, Evidence, para. 895. Similar attitudes were recorded in Surrey: Q. 'Notwithstanding the very great disparity in wages, they consider themselves a superior class to the railway labourers, and look down upon them though employed at nearly double as much?' A. 'Yes, most decidedly.' Ibid., paras. 2280–4.

# V

The most important point about the relationship between migration and wage differentials, and one which must not be lost to sight in the complexities discussed above, is that migration exercised a powerful influence in the direction of reducing wage differentials. Differentials persisted not because labour was immobile but, for the most part, because the market forces which sustained differentials were so strong that a considerable degree of mobility was necessary merely to prevent them widening. However, not all migration helped to reduce wage differentials—this was in part a consequence of selective migration[1] and also because labour was not equally mobile. Sections I and IV of this chapter showed that some of the higher-wage areas were characterized by above-average mobility; thus there was a certain amount of migration within Britain and to destinations abroad which was 'differential induced' but unlikely to reduce spatial differences in Britain. Moreover, it was shown in section III that the railways, one of the causes of high mobility, for long did little to erode differentials and may have increased them. The following chapter examines the role of two migrant groups who were sufficiently distinguished to merit separate attention—the Irish and the alien immigrants.

1. On this point see above, 248 n. 2.

# 8

# IRISH AND ALIEN IMMIGRATION

Two groups of immigrants were important in the period
1850–1914: the Irish, whose relative influence was greatest at
the beginning of the period, and the Jews from eastern Europe
who came mainly after 1880.

## I

### IRISH IMMIGRATION

Higher wages and plentiful employment in Britain had
attracted the Irish long before the great famine—Adam Smith
noted that they accounted for the greater part of the porters,
coalheavers, and prostitutes of eighteenth-century London.[1] The
pace of migration increased towards the end of the eighteenth
century, and in the 1820s it increased again when famine, in
1821–2, coincided with the introduction of steam ships on the
Irish Sea; but the greatest influx began with the 1845–7
famine.[2] In five years Ireland's population fell by some 1·8
million. Of these, nearly three-quarters of a million died, an
equal number left Europe, and a third of a million or more
entered Britain, raising the total Irish-born to approaching
750,000 or some 3·5 per cent of the population.[3] For the next
thirty years the Irish-born remained at around three-quarters
of a million but their share of the population declined; it was
about 2·6 per cent in 1881. By 1911 the total of Irish-born in

---

1. A. Smith, *The Wealth of Nations*, ed. E. Cannan, i. 161–2.
2. On Irish immigration before the famine see J. E. Handley, *The Irish in
   Scotland, 1798–1845* (Cork, 1943), and Redford, op. cit., Chs. 8 and 9.
3. Ibid., p. 158; P. Deane and W. A. Cole, *British Economic Growth 1688–1959*,
   pp. 8–9; R. Lawton, 'Irish Immigration to England and Wales in the
   Mid-Nineteenth Century', *Irish Geography*, iv (1959), 35–8.

Britain had fallen to 550,000, or 1·3 per cent of the population.[1] Their influence in the labour market was much greater than these figures suggest because, like most immigrant groups, the Irish included a disproportionately large number of young adults. During the famine, and for perhaps a decade after, migration was far less selective and the activity rate among immigrants was probably then less above average than it was before 1845 or after 1860. Even so, in 1851 75 per cent of the Irish-born in England and Wales were aged 20 and upwards when the proportion in this age group in England and Wales as a whole was 55 per cent, and in Liverpool one third of the Irish-born males, but only a quarter of the total male population, were in the 15–45 age group.[2] These figures, at a time of mass exodus when migration was probably less age-selective than usual, suggest that the activity rate among new arrivals was normally well above the native average, although by exactly how much is difficult to assess because the occupational censuses neither gave details of workers' birthplaces nor distinguished new immigrants from those long resident in Britain.[3]

Even if it were possible to inflate the percentage of Irish-born in Britain by a factor to allow for their high activity rate the result would still fall short of their total influence in the labour market because any reasonable definition of the immigrant group would include at least the British-born children of immigrants, and many grandchildren might reasonably be included because marriage took place mainly within the community and the community itself was well defined; the Irish lived in certain areas and worked in a limited range of

1. Ibid. For purposes of comparison it is worth noting that in 1966 immigrants from India, Pakistan, and the Caribbean area accounted for about 1·1 per cent of the population of Britain. K. Jones and A. D. Smith, *The Economic Impact of Commonwealth Immigration* (Cambridge, 1970), p. 166.
2. J. H. Clapham, 'Irish Immigration into Great Britain in the Nineteenth Century', *Bulletin of the International Committee of Historical Sciences*, v (1933), 603; Lawton, op. cit., table facing p. 52; the proportion of Irish-born males refers to Lawton's eight sample areas. The census, of course, recorded all Irish-born; many subsequently left for America and their departure probably modified the immigrant activity rate.
3. On Irish activity rates see J. E. Handley, *The Irish in Modern Scotland* (Cork, 1947), p. 248; J. A. Jackson, *The Irish in Britain* (1963), p. 19; Lawton, op. cit. p. 52.

occupations, they maintained their culture, their faith, and their nationalist sentiments.[1] Denvir's partisan history of the immigrant community talks of, '. . . Irishmen, either native or London born—for one is often quite as good as the other', and of the Liverpool Irish, wherever born, who were 'not out of Ireland at all, but on a piece out of the old sod itself'.[2] Although the relative strength of the Irish-born fell after 1861, that of the Irish community, broadly defined, probably increased as a consequence of its high birth-rate.[3] According to Clapham the 'effectively Irish' proportion of the population in England in 1865 was between 5 and 7 per cent, about twice the proportion of Irish-born, and in 1890 when there were fewer than half a million Irish-born in England and Wales, Cardinal Manning numbered a million 'Irish' in his English flock.[4] These proportions suggest that in the second half of the nineteenth century the 'Irish', broadly defined and allowing for their higher-than-average activity rate, accounted for between 4 and 6 per cent of the labour force.

## II

The Irish were concentrated in the worst-paid urban occupations; a report of 1836 described them taking work of 'the

1. On these points, which apply particularly in the years before 1890, see J. Handley, *The Irish in Scotland, 1798–1845*, p. 84; D. Gwynn, 'The Irish Immigration' in G. A. Beck (ed.), *The English Catholics 1850–1950* (1950), p. 281; J. Tivy in Miller and Tivy, op. cit., p. 261; Jackson, op. cit., Ch. 6 and below, pp. 296–7.

2. J. Denvir, *The Irish in Britain* (1892), pp. 390, 433–4. Bound in green, its cover embellished with a shamrock motif, Denvir's book is typical of much that has been written on the immigrant Irish whose history has been comparatively neglected by serious historians—see below, p. 325 n. 4.

3. Even if the immigrant and native net reproduction rates were identical in similar occupational categories it is likely that the immigrant birth-rate was higher than average because immigrants were associated with high-fertility occupational groups and because young adults were over-represented among new immigrants.

4. Clapham, 'Irish Immigration into Great Britain', p. 603; Lawton, op. cit., p. 38; Gwynn, op. cit., pp. 266–7. Denvir gives similar ratios for Manchester and Liverpool in 1881: according to his calculations Manchester contained 38,500 Irish-born but 80,000 Irish, Liverpool contained 71,000 Irish-born but at least 150,000 Irish (Denvir, op. cit., pp. 431, 434).

roughest, coarsest, and most repulsive description . . . re-
quiring the least skill and practice'.[1] This description was no
less fitting seventy years later. They provided a large part of the
army of unskilled labourers required by the construction
industry and did much of the heavy and unpleasant work on
the Thames and Mersey and in other ports; the greater part of
Manchester's building labourers were Irish even before the
famine and after the famine they provided a majority of unskilled building workers in most of the rapidly expanding
towns. They readily accepted the more arduous and dangerous
tasks in the St. Helens and Clydeside chemical industry which
were shunned by native workmen; they also joined the armed
forces, and were prominent in several of the 'depressed' trades
including handloom weaving.[2] Few became rural workers save
in a small area of south-west Scotland.[3] A recent investigation
of the Irish in mid-nineteenth-century Bradford showed that
they accounted for no more than a handful of the better-paid
white-collar jobs and only 3 per cent of building craftsmen, but
81 per cent of hawkers and peddlers were Irish and over half
the building labourers.[4] In Merthyr Tydfil, the *Morning
Chronicle* survey noted, they provided much of the unskilled
labour but seldom raised themselves to the dignity of skilled
workers: 'Such a wonder as an Irish puddler was never heard
of.' [5]

1. *Poor Inquiry (Ireland) Appendix G*, P.P. 1836, XXXIV, p. iii.
2. On these points see J. Strang, op. cit., p. 311; Jackson, op. cit., pp. 10,
   79–93; Handley, *The Irish in Scotland, 1798–1845*, p. 129; *idem, The Irish in
   Modern Scotland*, p. 135; Lawton, op. cit., pp. 43, 50; Redford, op. cit.,
   pp. 150–2; T. C. Barker and J. R. Harris, *A Merseyside Town in the Industrial Revolution, St Helens, 1750–1900*, p. 283; D. S. Landes, *The Cambridge
   Economic History of Europe*, vi. 316; W. G. Rimmer, 'Leeds and its Industrial Growth. 4. The Working Force', *Leeds Journal*, xxv (1954), 88; *M.C.*
   12 Nov., 3, 14, 18 Dec. 1849. D. Bythell has recently suggested that the
   Irish increment to the Lancashire handloom weavers was not as great as
   once believed (*The Handloom Weavers*, pp. 63–5).
3. D. F. MacDonald, *Scotland's Shifting Population, 1770–1850* p. 79.
4. C. Richardson, 'Irish Settlement in mid-Nineteenth Century Bradford',
   *Yks. Bull.*, xx (1968), 51–2. For similar accounts of their role in other cities
   at this time see, among others, W. Pollard-Urquhart, 'Condition of the
   Irish Labourers in the East of London', *Trans. Nat. Assoc. for the Promotion
   of the Social Sciences* (1862); Lawton, loc. cit.
5. *M.C.* 21 Mar. 1850.

There were a few exceptions to this pattern but none of consequence. The seasonal harvesters, who returned to Ireland in the autumn, are clearly a case on their own. Some 50,000 or more came each year in the early 1840s but harvest machinery and other influences reduced their number to 20,000 by the early 1880s and to only 8,000 in 1913.[1] A number of Irish tailors seem to provide an exception to the generalization that the Irish did only unskilled work and some categories of textile workers brought their skills with them, but the latter were heavily outnumbered by the Irish handloom weavers and unskilled mill workers.[2] The most significant exceptions to the pattern described occurred in the industrial west of Scotland where the Irish made considerable inroads into occupations elsewhere monopolized by natives. They accounted for a substantial proportion of the coalminers in this area and most of the cotton workers including spinners, a contrast to the position in the Lancashire cotton industry where the Irish were largely confined to low-paid work.[3] But even in west Scotland the main contribution of the Irish was the provision of unskilled labour in which role they supplemented, and often displaced, the Highlanders: 'The Irish labourers do all the drudgery of the place.'[4] In so far as the Irish in western Scotland were rather less confined to the lowest rungs of the occupational ladder than their countrymen elsewhere in Britain,

---

1. See Clapham, 'Irish Immigration into Great Britain', p. 604, and the *Report on the Diminution in the Number of Migratory Labourers from Ireland*, P.P. 1884, LXII; Handley, *The Irish in Modern Scotland*, pp. 168–70.
2. See Denvir, op. cit., p. 426; *Poor Inquiry (Ireland) Appendix G*, p. viii; *M.C.* 13 Dec. 1849; Redford, op. cit., pp. 152, 159; Lawton, op. cit., p. 43.
3. In many cases the Irish were introduced to the coal industry as strike-breakers. They were helped too by the stigma which still attached to mining from the days of 'bonded' labour. On these points generally see Redford, op. cit., pp. 151–3; D. Bremner, *The Industries of Scotland*, p. 20; R. H. Campbell, *Scotland since 1707*, pp. 119–20, 129; J. Tivy in R. Miller and J. Tivy, *The Glasgow Region*, p. 260; *Poor Inquiry (Ireland)*, *Appendix G*, p. vii.
4. There is some evidence that in the coal industry Irishmen were more frequently employed as drawers and redesmen than as hewers and according to Redford the main Irish influx to the Scottish textile trades was composed of handloom weavers. Handley, *The Irish in Scotland, 1798–1845*, pp. 89–93, 110–11; Redford, op. cit., 152.

they could be grateful for the area's extraordinary rapid industrial development after 1830 and for the more-than-average reluctance of Scots to enter the mills and coalmines.[1] But they failed to consolidate these early advantages and, as in England and Wales, remained 'largely confined to the lowest ranks of the industrial army'.[2]

Their geographical distribution was similarly persistent. In 1914 the Irish were most numerous in almost exactly those areas where they had been most numerous seventy years earlier. The pattern owed something to proximity; of the large towns, Liverpool and Glasgow always had the greatest proportion of Irish-born. But the migrants were foot-loose, and their distribution was chiefly determined by regional variations in demand for labour. The three main centres of Irish settlement in 1841 were the Glasgow area and Lancashire, which combined ease of access from Ireland with a vigorous appetite for labour, and London.[3] At that time the Irish-born accounted for 2·2 per cent of the population of Britain, but 6 per cent and 13 per cent respectively of the populations of Lancashire and Lanarkshire.[4] On the other hand there were

1. *Poor Inquiry (Ireland), Appendix G*, p.v; Redford, op. cit., p. 151; Handley, *The Irish in Scotland, 1798–1845*, pp. 92–3, 107; Campbell, op. cit., p. 129. If there is any truth in the frequently mentioned reluctance of Scots to work in mills and mines they were remarkable for combining geographical mobility with occupational immobility (see Ch. 7 section IV). However, there are a number of other features which may explain the ease of Irish entry to occupations elsewhere monopolized by natives including the very rapid development of mining in West Scotland, their use as strike breakers, and the fact that Scotland received many experienced textile workers from Ulster.

2. Handley, *The Irish in Modern Scotland*, p. 319; see also Denvir, op. cit., pp. 422, 426; and *Census of England and Wales 1891*, P.P. 1893–4, CVI, pp. 62–3.

3. Over half of the Irish-born in Britain were recorded in Lancashire and Cheshire, Lanark, and Middlesex. *Census of Great Britain (1841)* P.P. 1843, XXII, pp. 399, 458 and p. 78 of Scotland section. London was not enumerated separately in this census; most of the London Irish-born were enumerated in Middlesex.

4. Ibid. 1843, XXII. In England and Wales the proportion was 1·8 per cent, in Scotland 4·8 per cent. Scotland had a considerably greater proportion of Irish-born into the twentieth century. Lawton, op. cit., p. 38. Twelve per cent of the population of Manchester were Irish-born, 17 per cent of the population of Liverpool, and an even higher proportion of the population of Glasgow. Lawton, op. cit., p. 43; Handley, *The Irish in Scotland, 1798–1845*, pp. 101–3.

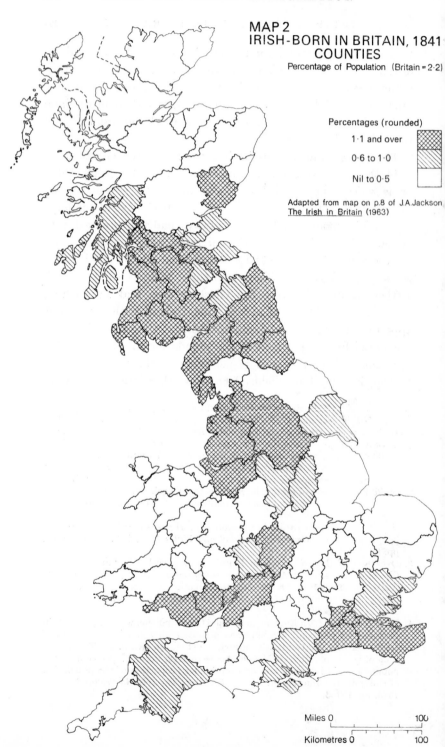

MAP 2
IRISH-BORN IN BRITAIN, 1841
COUNTIES
Percentage of Population (Britain = 2·2)

Percentages (rounded)

1·1 and over

0·6 to 1·0

Nil to 0·5

Adapted from map on p.8 of J.A.Jackson
The Irish in Britain (1963)

Miles 0                    100

Kilometres 0                    100

considerable areas in the south of England, in Wales,[1] and in the
north of Scotland where Irish settlement was of little consequence. Map 2 shows that for the most part these were the
areas where labour was most abundant and which suffered,
in a milder form, the same crisis that afflicted Ireland—
accordingly they were shunned by Irish exiles.[2] For a short
time after the famine the Irish were less clearly confined to the
expanding ports and industrial centres,[3] but by 1851 the
pattern was much the same as a decade earlier with London,
Lanarkshire, Lancashire, and Cheshire accounting for over
half the total; the proportion of Irish-born had by then reached
3·5 per cent in Britain as a whole, 22 per cent in Liverpool,
13 per cent in Manchester and Salford, and 18 per cent in
Glasgow.[4] Towards the end of the century (Map 3) the proportion of Irish-born fell but their distribution remained much
as it was in the 1840s and 1850s, and in 1911 London, Lanarkshire, Lancashire, and Cheshire still accounted for more than
half the total.[5] All this is much as might be expected: Irish
immigrants, for the most part, continued to settle where their
labour was most welcome and, as was shown in Chapter Four,
the long-term pattern of demand for labour in different parts of
Britain changed very little; Irish settlement reflected its consistency.[6]

1. There were fewer than 6,000 Irish-born registered in Wales in 1841; over
   half of these were in Glamorgan. Census, P.P. 1843, XXII, p. 458.
2. Some of these low-wage areas were visited by Irish harvesters (Redford,
   op. cit., Ch. 8) but the seasonal workers probably went most to areas
   proximate to the centres of permanent settlement. In Dorset it was reported
   that the local labourers experienced little competition from migratory
   Irish labour because there were sufficient hands in the country to perform
   even the extra work of harvest time. M.C. 28 Nov. 1849. A pattern of this
   kind was certainly evident by the early twentieth century—see above,
   p. 214; see also the map and comments on distribution in *Reports and
   Tables Relating to Migratory Agricultural Labourers*, P.P. 1900, CI, p. 20.
3. Redford, op. cit., pp. 156–8.
4. *Census of Great Britain 1851*, P.P. 1852–3, LXXXVIIIi, pp. ci–cvi;
   cclxxxvii-ccxcviii; LXXXVIIIii, pp. 664, 1041.
5. Birthplace Tables, *Census of England and Wales*, 1911; *Census of Scotland*
   1911.
6. The continuation of the mid-nineteenth-century settlement pattern has
   been noted by several investigators. See Lawton, op. cit., p. 40; Clapham,
   'Irish Immigration into Great Britain', p. 604; Denvir. op. cit., pp. 402–31.

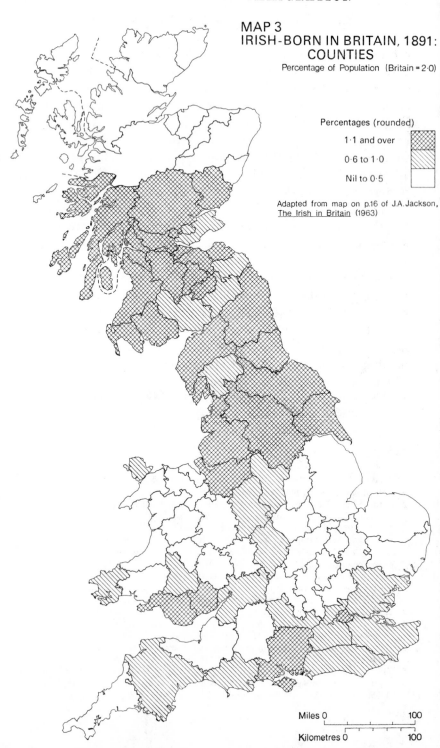

MAP 3
IRISH-BORN IN BRITAIN, 1891:
COUNTIES
Percentage of Population (Britain = 2·0)

Percentages (rounded)

1·1 and over

0·6 to 1·0

Nil to 0·5

Adapted from map on p.16 of J.A.Jackson,
The Irish in Britain (1963)

Miles 0                    100

Kilometres 0              100

# III

The affinity between the pattern of Irish settlement and the regional wage pattern described in Chapter One is very marked. Most immigrants made for centres where work was available and wages high and it seems probable, on first appraisal, that the Irish helped to reduce regional wage differentials.[1] There is a great deal of evidence which suggests this process in operation. Jackson and Gilboy cite cases of Irishmen lowering wages in eighteenth-century London and knowledgeable contemporaries had no doubt of the effect of Irish competition upon wages in Lancashire, the industrial west of Scotland, and parts of rural Scotland: 'From the influx of Irish labourers . . . the rate of wages in the labour market has been greatly reduced.'[2] Redford considered that the most significant social consequence of the Irish influx was their unfavourable effect on native living standards,[3] and native workmen would have enthusiastically endorsed this opinion; their views were made explicit, particularly before 1860, by periodic violence towards the immigrants themselves and those who employed them.[4]

1. Most Irish immigrants were engaged in unskilled manual work but in so far as they were also associated with handloom weaving, the London sweated trades, and other 'depressed' sectors (see above, p. 289) they probably help to account for the existence of pockets of less-well-paid labour in otherwise prosperous areas.
2. Jackson, op. cit., p. 82; E. W. Gilboy, *Wages in Eighteenth Century England* p. 18; *Poor Inquiry (Ireland)*, *Appendix G*, p. xxxiii; MacDonald, op. cit., p. 78; F. Purdy, 'On the Earnings of Agricultural Labourers in Scotland and Ireland', p. 436.
3. Redford, op. cit., p. 159.
4. The violence was frequently on an awesome scale particularly when it involved railway navvies. Natives commonly refused to work alongside immigrants and the contractors took care to segregate them wherever possible. The immigrants were resented for their religion, their nationalism, and their squalor as well as for the competition they brought, but there is no doubt that their economic threat was a major source of resentment. See, among many examples, *S.C. on Railway Labourers*, P.P. 1846, XIII, para. 866–8, 1043, 1419; T. Coleman, *The Railway Navvies* (1968), pp. 93–4; Handley, *The Irish in Scotland, 1798–1845*, pp. 67–8, 166; Jackson, op. cit., pp. 77, 82, 87; Barker and Harris, op. cit., pp. 279–83; B. Kerr, 'Irish Seasonal Migration to Great Britain, 1800–1838', *Irish Historical Studies*, iii (1942–3), 376; A. J. Youngson Brown, 'Trade Union Policy in the Scots Coalfields, 1855–85', *Ec.H.R.*, 2nd Ser., vi (1953–4), 38–9.

When immigrants were used as strike breakers they afforded employers a strategic advantage out of proportion to the numbers involved.[1] On these occasions they clearly weakened unionism and helped to lower wages; at the same time, as a consequence of their spatial distribution, they would tend to reduce regional wage differentials. There is some evidence that the Irish also retarded the long-term development of trade unionism but this influence is more debatable. It is true that they seldom worked easily alongside natives in the same occupation until well into the second half of the nineteenth century. Moreover, their nationalism and loyalty to the Roman Catholic Church[2] held back the development of class solidarity, and while they were sometimes prominent in industrial disputes their efforts were seldom crowned with lasting success. They were impulsive and daring, impatient and resentful of discipline, quick to resort to violence and too willing to embark on ill-considered strikes. Action of this kind, the antithesis of 'scientific unionism', was hardly more conducive than strike-breaking to the development of stable unionism.[3] For these reasons it is almost certain that the Irish offered no net advantage to unionism. But when all these points have been made the significance of the handicap they imposed remains in doubt because until the end of the century unionism was the prerogative of the skilled and highly paid and the occupations where the Irish found work were almost entirely unorganized.[4]

1. The Irish provided a remarkably flexible supply of labour; a letter or an advertisement in an Irish paper produced a speedy response, and there is considerable evidence which shows that in the middle decades of the century they were often recruited specifically to break a strike. See above, p. 290 n. 3 and *Poor Inquiry (Ireland) Appendix G*, pp. xxvii–xxviii; Handley, *The Irish in Scotland 1798–1845*, pp. 110–11; H. M. Pelling, *A History of British Trade Unionism* (1963), p. 48; Redford, op. cit., p. 114.
2. On these points generally see Jackson, op. cit., pp. 115–17. There was an interesting episode in the 1830s when for some years the Roman Catholic Church actively opposed trade unions. Rival friendly societies were established and Roman Catholics were forbidden to join unions under threat of denial of the sacraments. J. Treble, 'The Attitude of the Roman Catholic Church towards Trade Unionism in the North of England, 1833–42', *Northern History*, v (1970).
3. According to Turner the Irish were noted equally as strike leaders and strike breakers; at least one Lancashire union refused to admit them. H. A. Turner, *Trade Union Growth, Structure, and Policy*, pp. 48, 145. See also Handley, *The Irish in Scotland, 1798–1845*, pp. 107–8.
4. On this theme generally see Ch. 9.

In all probability one reason why unionism made little progress among the unskilled was the presence of the Irish, but they were no more than one adverse force among many and it is difficult to envisage significantly more rapid organization in their absence. After 1889 unionism extended among the semi-skilled, and later among the unskilled, but by this time the Irish were no longer a considerable hindrance.[1]

While the evidence marshalled so far suggests that the immigrants reduced regional wage differentials within Britain, attempts to measure their influence are unlikely to reach firm conclusions. One complication is the sporadic existence of an 'Irish differential'. Gilboy noted a case in eighteenth-century London where Irish labourers worked for half the native rate; Caird described farm wages in south Lancashire as 12s. to 15s., '. . . and 9s. a week for Irishmen', and there are reports of a similar differential in parts of Scotland.[2] These cases may not be representative; we know insufficient of immigrant labour to be sure of the extent of the differential, how long it existed, or even to be sure that a general differential did exist. The *Poor Inquiry* (*Ireland*) of 1836 suggested that for identical work the Irish normally received the same pay[3] and it may be that a differential became general when Irishmen were plentiful at the time of the famine but diminished after 1860. Clapham suggested that, although new immigrants often accepted a lower rate, once they were established they received the going wage.[4] And this may have been the general position; Jewish

1. On the expansion of unionism at this time see below, Ch. 9. The Irish community was still distinct in 1890 but they were less resented; there are fewer reports of violence towards Irish workers in the last quarter of the century and their manner of living by then was less deviant. Time, and a substantial decline in the rate of immigration, had effected a measure of integration. The 1889 dock strike was something of a watershed in this respect: the greater part of the London dockers were of Irish extraction and by his sympathy and successful intervention Cardinal Manning won the affection of workers of every persuasion. On these points see Jackson, op. cit., pp. 93–5, 119; Denvir, op. cit., pp. 394–7; Handley, *The Irish in Modern Scotland*, p. 120.
2. Gilboy, op. cit., p. 18; Caird, op. cit., p. 284; Handley, *The Irish in Modern Scotland*, p. 167. See also A. H. John, *The Industrial Development of South Wales, 1750–1850*, p. 68.
3. *Poor Inquiry* (*Ireland*) *Appendix G*, p. ix. Elsewhere in the report, however, there is evidence which suggests they may have received somewhat less. Ibid., p. iii.
4. Clapham, 'Irish Immigration into Great Britain', p. 603.

immigrant wages followed this pattern, and it is consistent with frequent reports of a differential in the 1840s and 1850s.[1] Even if a general differential existed for a substantial period its likely effect is not clear: would its presence substantiate other evidence that the immigrants reduced wages by their willingness to accept low rates or would it perhaps imply that natives and immigrants were to some extent non-competing groups working for different rates in similar, but distinct, sectors of the labour market?

Another possible approach to the problem of assessing the Irish influence on wages consists in examining the differential between rates for skilled work and labouring. The Irish were confined largely to occupations which required no skill and in some towns they accounted for the greater proportion of building labourers. It might be expected, therefore, if immigrants did in fact reduce wages, that in these towns the differential for skill would have been greater than average. There is some evidence that this was the case. The building trade differential in Liverpool and Glasgow was usually wider than elsewhere; in the mid-nineteenth century labourers in London, where the proportion of Irish-born was well below that in Liverpool and Glasgow,[2] earned two-thirds of the artisan rate, in Liverpool they earned 63 per cent of the artisan rate, and in Glasgow 57 per cent.[3] A collection of artisan and labourers' wages in England and Wales compiled by F. W. Lawrence in the 1890s shows that Liverpool labourers received 63 per cent of the artisan rate, a lower proportion than in most cities, and that whereas the average Liverpool artisan wage was exceeded in only 5 out of 92 other centres the Liverpool labourers' average was exceeded in

---

1. See below, p. 316. I found no reference to Irish differentials after 1870.
2. In 1851 the Irish-born comprised 22 per cent of the population of Liverpool, 18 per cent of the population of Glasgow, and 4·6 per cent of the population of London. See text and references above, pp. 291–3.
3. A. L. Bowley, 'Wages in the Building Trades', *J.R.S.S.*, lxiii (1900), 306, 495; lxiv (1901), 104. Not much weight should be placed on these proportions. The Liverpool figure is the proportion that bricklayers' labourers' wages formed of bricklayers' wages—plumbers and carpenters earned less. The paucity of wage statistics in the 1840s and 1850s when the immigrant influence was probably at its maximum is one of the difficulties hindering analysis of this type.

34 centres.[1] Unfortunately labourers' and artisans' wage rates cannot be made to yield more than this. Tests of correlation between the differential for skill in the 1890s and the proportion of Irish-born in various cities produced no meaningful results: if the Irish had any general effect on building differentials outside Liverpool and Glasgow the influence of other variables was too great for it to show in correlation exercises. This position, however, is not incompatible with their having exercised some general and significant influence because the Irish settled in high-wage areas where labour was relatively scarce and where the differential between skilled and unskilled wages might be expected to have been somewhat less than average; in low-wage towns, where few Irish settled, other market forces would tend to produce wide differentials.[2] In this light the absence of a significant correlation between the differential for skill and the proportion of Irish-born is hardly surprising; in fact it might be regarded as a consequence of immigration because had the Irish exercised no influence other market forces may well have produced some correlation between the differential for skill and local wage levels.

# IV

We are left with a substantial body of literary evidence which suggests that immigration reduced wage rates and, because of their spatial distribution, regional wage differentials; but no quantitative assessment of these influences has been possible. The discussion might be left at this point; but not without risk because the analysis, like most contemporary comment, has been restricted to a short-run context. The broader and longer-term consequences of immigration must be considered if short-sighted analysis, of the type evident when trade unions in the United States clamoured for restrictions on immigration to

1. F. W. Lawrence, *Local Variations in Wages*, pp. 12–13.
2. On this point see K. G. J. C. Knowles and D. J. Robertson, 'Differences between the Wages of Skilled and Unskilled Workers, 1880–1950', *Bulletin of the Oxford University Institute of Statistics*, xiii (1951), 113.

protect their wage levels, is to be avoided. Immigration frequently reduced American wages in the short run but few
economic historians would dispute that immigration was one
of the causes of long-term growth and prosperity in the United
States. It would be surprising if the other main recipient of
Ireland's surplus felt no similar advantages.

To the British employer Ireland offered a large pool of
relatively cheap and highly mobile manpower. And there were
times when this proved invaluable: 'The boundless coalfields
beneath us, and the boundless mines of labour, so to speak,
existing for us in Ireland, form together one of the great
secrets of the almost unparalleled prosperity of this part of
Scotland.' [1] This comment, by a Paisley cotton manufacturer,
in one of many similar views from Lancashire and the west
of Scotland in the second quarter of the nineteenth century.
One Lancashire factory master suggested that had the Irish
not moved to Lancashire, manufacturers might have found it
necessary to move to Ireland; a Greenock sugar manufacturer
said that the alternative to using Irish labour was to import
Germans or give up the trade. [2] And there is something in what
they said even after allowance has been made for the exaggeration that flowed naturally from their desire to secure a plentiful
labour supply and forestall attempts to restrict immigration.
Prosperity was frequently interrupted but the long-term
demand for labour in Lancashire, the west of Scotland, and a
few other flourishing centres was extraordinarily buoyant and
they were considerably dependent on distant supplies of labour.

The general case for regarding the Irish in this optimistic
light has often been stated. Some partisan accounts, not
surprisingly, make much of the argument but it also finds a
place in more scholarly accounts[3] although, remarkably, none

1. *Poor Inquiry (Ireland), Appendix G*, p. xxxvii.
2. Ibid., pp. xxxvi–xxxvii.
3. See e.g. Jackson, op. cit., p. 82: 'As casual labourers they found their way
into a wide variety of employment which effectively mirrors the changing
needs and rapid expansion of the country . . . The existence of a large pool
of cheap labour at a time of national expansion proved an *essential* ingred-
ient to the rapid industrial advance'; Handley (*Irish in Modern Scotland*,
p. 319) comments in a similar fashion: 'In their humble way they were
*indispensable* adjuncts of the expansion of industry and agriculture in
nineteenth-century Scotland.' Emphasis mine in each case.

of them goes on to suggest that a likely consequence of situations of this kind was a higher standard of living in immigrant areas. Some accounts, including Redford's, suggest both that the Irish were vital to industrial development and that they lowered wages, a combination which, while not impossible, is so unlikely that is requires discussion.[1]

From a long-term perspective the immigrant effect on economic growth in areas where labour was least abundant, including the growth of working-class incomes,[2] appears considerably more positive than it looked to displaced native workers, and the earlier conclusions that Irish immigration helped to erode regional wage variations after 1850 must be adapted to take account of their long-term influence. Whether it should be reversed or merely modified is difficult to decide; probably it should be no more than modified because the most acute local labour shortages occurred before the second half of the nineteenth century. It is possible to find cases where Irish labour may have raised, rather than reduced, relative wages after 1850—the Irish harvesters who saved farmers the burden of supporting a half-employed labour force for ten months in the year and relieved the men of the low wages this implied were an especial asset—but there were fewer situations of this kind in the second half of the century. Even so, the advantages which immigration conferred after 1850 were probably sufficient to offset at least a part of the erosive influence on regional wage variations suggested by the initial appraisal.

But there is another and more important factor to be taken into account which also modifies the initial impression, and by a margin sufficient to suggest that the over-all influence of Irish immigration was perhaps, after all, to sustain regional wage differentials. The question of what would have been the

1. 'The main social significance of the Irish influx lay in its tendency to lower the wages and standard-of-living of the English wage earning classes' (Redford, op. cit., p. 159). 'It was, indeed, generally assumed that Irish labour was indispensible to the prosperity of both the manufacturers and the agriculture of Great Britain' (ibid., p. 162). See also W. A. Marwick, *Economic Developments in Victorian Scotland* (1936), p. 132.
2. Unskilled as well as skilled although the skilled workers benefited most, see above, pp. 298–9.

pattern of events in the labour market had the Irish not offered their services is worth stating explicitly. And, in a general way and without venturing too far into the never-never world of counter-factual analysis, it can be answered. The consensus answer to the question is implicit in Jackson's comments quoted above: that is, without the Irish and the labour they offered areas like Lancashire and the west of Scotland would have suffered labour shortages and their economic growth would have been less rapid.[1]

The evidence of Chapters Four and Six of this investigation suggest a different answer. Chapter Four showed that large parts of Britain, particularly southern England, rural Wales, and the rural north and south of Scotland, contained a great deal of surplus labour. These areas had much in common with pre-famine Ireland—population rose rapidly, demand for labour slowly—and like Ireland they exported population to more prosperous areas. Chapter Seven suggested that while labour in low-wage rural areas was less mobile than average it was not immobile in any general sense. From this it follows that a part of the answer to the question of what would have happened had the Irish not arrived is that native labour in low-wage areas would have taken advantage of the additional opportunities in London and the north;[2] wages in the latter areas would have been much the same but mobility within Britain and wages in the worst-paid areas would both have been

---

1. Jackson's comment is above p. 300 n. 3. Other comments are in similar terms. Pollard-Urquhart made the point more explicitly than most in his survey of the Irish in east London. 'How many of these latter', he asked, referring to native artisans, 'would be unable to obtain their present superior remuneration if there were not others of Celtic origin to undertake the less desirable and less highly paid, but absolutely essential work, which now falls chiefly to their lot?' As indicated below the correct answer to his question is not the one he implied. W. Pollard-Urquhart, op. cit., p. 745.
2. Competition between immigrants and labour from the low-wage south of England was concentrated in London because few migrants from southern England sought employment in the north (see Ch. 7 section IV). It is possible, however, that the antipathy which many potential migrants felt towards northern industrial towns owed something to the stigma the Irish helped attach to unskilled occupations and the poorer residential districts. In the case of the Highlanders, competition with Irish labour was felt most in central Scotland; migrants from rural Wales competed with the Irish in Lancashire and Cheshire, in south Wales, and in London.

higher. Highly mobile themselves, the Irish retarded mobility among those sections of the British labour force most in need of mobility. Before 1834 the poor law imposed a restraint on this group's mobility: in England and Wales at that time, although not in Scotland, the alternative to the Irish may well have been labour shortages;[1] after 1834, however, the alternative, more and more, was the employment of Britain's own surplus labour. By 1850 the generally favourable view of the value of immigrant labour advanced by Jackson and others is probably wide of the mark, and the analogy between the role of immigrant labour in the British and United States economies no longer valid.[2] The Irish offered cheap unskilled labour to employers in both countries, but whereas in the United States labour was scarce, in Britain it was plentiful: 'Has there ever . . . been a time when employers could not get practically at a moment's notice all the labour they required?'[3] In most years

1. It might, alternatively, have resulted in a new poor law long before 1834. The inquiry into the Irish poor in Britain is one of the few studies, possibly the only one, which considers explicitly the likely state of the labour market in the absence of Irish immigration. The report, based on evidence collected in 1834, stated that without Irish immigration migration from the south of England would undoubtedly have been greater but, owing to the poor law, still insufficient (*Poor Inquiry (Ireland)*, *Appendix G*, p. xxvi). The mobility of labour in Scotland was not impeded in this way (see above pp. 279–80). There, demands for labour expanded with great rapidity —even so the Irish found jobs partly at the expense of the Highlanders. *Poor Inquiry (Ireland)*, *Appendix G*, pp. xxviii–xxx; MacDonald, op. cit., pp. 80–1, and above, p. 290.

  The general points in the 1836 report are undoubtedly correct although in places there are signs of a tendency to ignore or underestimate alternative native supply similar to those found in comments on the post-1834 period. The Highlanders are described as less suitable than the Irish for industrial work because they were a pastoral, fishing, and agricultural people (p. xxix); they were of course, but so were most of the Irish. Commenting on Irish dominance of unskilled work in Liverpool and Manchester the report states that Englishmen were not prepared to undertake such disagreeable labour (p. xxix) whereas most work of this type was undertaken by natives in small towns all over southern England, and for considerably less than they might have obtained in Liverpool.

2. Some similarities, however, remained: the United States had untapped labour supplies of its own in the south which competed with immigrants for jobs in northern cities; restriction of immigration in the 1920s was followed by a substantial quickening of the northward flow of negro labour.

3. W. H. Beveridge, *Unemployment: A Problem of Industry* (1909), p. 69.

substantial numbers left Britain for other parts of the world[1]
and in the low-wage areas Britain had its own reservoir of
unskilled labour which was constantly replenished by a high
birth-rate and the decline in farm and village employment.
Ireland, then, eased its malthusian crisis partly by migration
to Britain but at the expense of delaying the solution of
Britain's milder variation of the same problem. Before 1834
Irish immigration may have conferred a net economic advantage
upon Britain—although this may have been more than offset
by social costs, in particular the influence of immigration on
housing, sanitation, and health—after 1834 Irish immigration
was a net liability.[2]

## V

The Irish, it seems, were another example of non-equalizing
migration. Their arrival failed to reduce regional wage differentials and probably helped to sustain them. Their role in main-
taining differentials was modest compared with that of the

1. One interesting contrast between Britain and America concerns the
destination of the more intelligent and enterprising of the Irish emigrants.
Accounts of Ireland's economic backwardness in the nineteenth century
emphasize the disproportionate loss of Irish talent, overseas and to the
priesthood. Few would dispute that in literature and the arts Ireland's
loss was often Britain's gain; but there are few signs of a similar pattern in
occupations more conducive to economic growth. Those that came to
Britain may have been more enterprising than those left behind, but the
more enterprising of these probably left Britain to exploit the far greater
opportunities of the United States, although even in America the Irish have
been noted far less for economic success and social mobility than for their
role in politics and religion. On the Irish in New York see N. Glazer and
D. P. Moynihan, *Beyond the Melting Pot* (Cambridge, Mass., 1964), Ch. 5.
2. The Irish harvesters were prominent among the more favourable consequences of immigration. They were educated in Ireland, retired there, and
returned there for the winter slack season (see above, p. 290). Scotland
generally was perhaps less a loser by immigration than the rest of Britain;
its textile and heavy industries grew very rapidly before 1860 and found the
immigrants particularly useful. They had a strategic value too because the
natives were slow to enter the early factories. After 1860 Irish immigration
had less to offer Scotland, although it continued to derive the greatest
benefit from Irish harvesters and was perhaps fortunate in that Protestants
featured prominently among the influx. Compared to their Roman Catholic
fellow countrymen the Protestants were sober, industrious, better educated,
less associated with urban social problems, and more easily integrated
(Handley, *The Irish in Scotland, 1798–1845*, pp. 100–7).

patterns of demand for labour and natural increase described in Chapter Four and Chapter Six but it was not insignificant.[1] These conclusions are interesting in two respects; first, because they show that the Irish influence on the regional wage pattern was the opposite of what might have been expected and thus held to explain the extraordinary persistence of regional wage variations; second, because they suggest serious weaknesses in existing assessments of the over-all value of Irish immigration to nineteenth-century Britain.

# VI

## ALIEN IMMIGRATION

The beginning of large-scale alien immigration in the nine-teenth century can be stated with some precision. It was a consequence of the greatly intensified persecution of Russian Jews following the assassination of Tsar Alexander II in 1881.[2] There were other, non-Jewish, aliens who settled in Britain after 1881, but not many, and before this date alien immigra-tion of any kind was of little consequence.[3] The total Jewish community in 1880 was around 60,000 but many of these belonged to families long resident in Britain and half or more were dependent upon commerce, finance, and similar middle-class pursuits and therefore were unlikely to exercise any direct effect on regional wage variations.[4]

1. In the decade 1841–51 the number of Irish immigrants considerably ex-ceeded net out-migration from the south-west of England (Region 2) and the rural south-east (Region 3) (for regions see Map 1).
2. On the general background of Jewish migration see V. D. Lipman, *Social History of the Jews in England 1850–1950* (1954), Ch. 5; L. P. Gartner, *The Jewish Immigrant in England 1870–1914* (Detroit, 1960), Ch. 2.
3. The Jews accounted for between a third and a half of the 285,000 aliens registered in the 1911 census and many of the remainder were seamen and other temporary residents. There were only 118,000 aliens in England and Wales in 1881, fewer than half of 1 per cent of the population and most of these were temporary residents. *Census of England and Wales, General Reports*, P.P. 1883, LXXX, p. 56; P.P. 1904 CVIII, pp. 139–40; Gartner, op. cit., pp. 49, 283; Lipman, op. cit., p. 84. Exact figures of Jewish immigra-tion are not available; the census failed to distinguish immigrants' religion, and many immigrants subsequently left for America.
4. Gartner, op. cit., p. 33; Lipman, op. cit., pp. 9, 65, 78, 84.

Anti-Semitism in Russia was followed by similar persecution in other parts of Eastern Europe. In addition the Jews, like other Europeans, were affected by demographic pressure, factory competition, and the opportunities made available by the combination of cheap transport and America's pressing need of labour. America was always their main destination but sufficient settled in Britain to transform the character of its Jewish community and to exercise a noticeable influence on the labour market. The rate of immigration fluctuated from year to year; the virulence of persecution in Europe, the relative attraction of Britain and America, the cost of crossing the Atlantic, and the ease of entry to either country each affected the rate of flow, but it was always higher after 1880 than before.[1] In all, between 1881 and the First World War some 120,000 European Jews settled in Britain, sufficient, with natural increase, to bring about a fivefold increase in the Jewish community.[2]

In a broader context these figures are less impressive. After 1880 Jewish and Irish immigration occurred at about the same rate, but in the 1840s alone Irish immigration amounted to more than three times the number of Jews who settled in the whole period between 1880 and the war.[3] Shortly before the war, when their relative numbers were greatest, the Jewish community as a whole accounted for a little less than three-quarters of 1 per cent of the population, and foreign-born Jews for under half of 1 per cent, a much smaller proportion than the Irish-born at any time between 1850 and 1914, less too than the proportion of coloured immigrants in mid-twentieth-century Britain.[4] There was no year when the net loss of British population failed comfortably to exceed alien immigration and there were several years in the 1880s and again after 1906 when the annual loss exceeded the whole post-1880 Jewish

1. On these points generally see Lipman, op. cit., pp. 85–7, 141–3; Gartner, op. cit., pp. 36, 45–9. The Aliens Act of 1905 made provision to turn back from Britain the lunatic, the diseased, the criminal, and those with no means of support.
2. Gartner, op. cit., pp. 30, 280; Lipman, op. cit., p. 89.
3. For figures of Irish immigration see Jackson, op. cit., p. 191, and above, pp. 286–7.
4. See above, p. 287 n. 1.

influx. Like the Irish the Jews lived in clearly defined communities; they married young and reared large families so their rate of natural increase was almost certainly above average.[1] For these reasons their influence on the labour market is more accurately reflected by the relative importance of their community than by the number of foreign-born Jews.[2] Further, like most immigrant groups, they were characterized by a high activity rate.[3] But when all these points are conceded it remains unlikely that they ever accounted for as much as 1 per cent of the labour force.

In the light of these figures the amount of public concern aroused by alien immigration appears quite disproportionate; the Jewish question quickly attained the status of a 'national problem'. Concern arose partly from exaggerated notions of the numbers involved; until 1894, when a Board of Trade Report proved the worst fears unfounded, less than due allowance was made for those Jews who moved on to the United States.[4] Matters were not helped by their geographical distribution—most settled in London and there was nowhere that a social problem was less likely to be overlooked. In 1883 there appeared 'The Bitter Cry of Outcast London', the Booth survey was underway by the end of the decade, and a government inquiry on the sweating system appeared in 1887; all these focused attention on the East End where the Jews were congregated.

London, the natural point of access from Europe and the centre of those commercial and financial activities in which the Jews excelled, was always the main centre of settlement. It probably housed at least half the Jewish community in 1850 and in the next twenty-five years increased its share to around

1. There are no accurate statistics on Jewish fertility. On their rate of natural increase see C. Russell and H. S. Lewis, *The Jew in London* (1900), pp. 58, 195–6; Gartner, op. cit., p. 167.
2. This characteristic was partly offset by the relatively high proportion of middle-class Jews among those born or long resident in Britain.
3. Of 7,721 Russians and Poles who arrived in 1893, 54 per cent were men, 26 per cent women, and 20 per cent children. *Reports on the Volume and Effects of Recent Immigration from Eastern Europe*, P.P. 1894, LXVIII, p. 10. See also Gartner, op. cit., p. 171.
4. *Volume and Effects of Recent Immigration*, pp. 1, 134.

80 per cent.[1] Few towns were without a Jewish community of some kind but outside London and a small number of other large centres these were composed mainly of retailers, merchants, and others in similar occupations, so that London's share of working-class Jews by 1875 was probably greater than 80 per cent. Its well-established community life, synagogues, Jewish schools, charities, and employers made it the natural destination for poor immigrants. Even so, at the end of the century London's Jews still accounted for under 2·5 per cent of its population.[2] This was no more than the proportion of Irish[3] but the London Jews were less dispersed, and more apparent—the greater part of the Jewish population lived within a few miles of the junction of the Commercial and Whitechapel Roads.[4] Outside London the largest Jewish communities were in Manchester and Leeds which, like London, were centres of commerce, finance, and the ready-made garment trade.[5] No other town had sufficient Jews to exercise more than a very

1. Lipman, op. cit., pp. 9, 64. Some parts of London had a substantial foreign-born population long before the main influx. In 1861 7·7 per cent of the population of Whitechapel were foreign-born. *Select Committee on Emigration and Immigration (Foreigners)*, P.P. 1889, X, p. vii.
2. London contained over four and a half million and the Jews, native and foreign-born, numbered some 110,000. Lipman, op. cit., pp. 98–100; Mitchell and Deane, op. cit., p. 22.
3. Comparison of these figures with those of the Irish population in Liverpool and Glasgow in the 1840s and 1850s emphasizes the far greater importance of the earlier immigrants (see above, pp. 291–3). 1·3 per cent of London's population in 1901 was Irish-born, the total Irish community was likely to have been at least twice this size. *Census of England and Wales 1911, General Report*, P.P. 1917–18 XXXV, p. 212; and see above, p. 288.
4. There were numerous roads with none but Jewish residents in this area and the foreign-born population of Whitechapel exceeded the proportion of Irish-born in mid-century Liverpool. In 1901 31·8 per cent of Whitechapel's population was foreign-born; in 1861 a quarter of Liverpool's population was Irish-born. In Stepney as a whole the alien proportion of the population was 18·2 per cent, but the Jews, native and foreign-born together, may have accounted for as much as 40 per cent of the population. Lipman, op. cit., pp. 94–5; Lawton, op. cit., p. 48; *Census of England and Wales 1901, General Report*, P.P. 1904 CVIII, pp. 139–40; Gartner, op. cit., p. 172.
5. Manchester had some 25,000 Jews in 1900 and Leeds about 15,000. In Manchester they amounted to less than 5 per cent of the population, about the same as the proportion of Irish-born but considerably less than that of the Irish community. In Leeds their relative importance was slightly less although they far exceeded the number of Irish immigrants. Lipman, op. cit., p. 102. *Census of England and Wales 1901, General Report*, p. 136; Mitchell and Deane, op. cit., p. 25.

marginal influence on the labour market. This uneven distribution implies that the alien immigrants, like the Irish,
probably exercised more influence on the regional wage pattern
than their relative share of Britain's population might suggest.
The Jews were less numerous than the Irish but their geographical concentration was even more pronounced. In so far
as this investigation is concerned mainly with working-class
immigrants, attention can be restricted to London's East End
after 1880 and to similar areas in Manchester and Leeds.

Alien employment also had something in common with the
Irish experience in that both groups were restricted to a narrow
range of occupations. But whereas the Irish occupied the most
menial position in almost every calling, the Jews were found
both at skilled and unskilled work in a limited number of well-
defined trades carried on inside their equally well-defined
residential areas. The most important of these trades was
ready-made tailoring which employed over a quarter of London's
working-class Jews after 1880 and a far higher proportion of
the new arrivals; in Leeds and Manchester its relative importance
was even greater.[1] Immigrants worked in almost every branch
of this trade; they were prominent among the unskilled
'greeners', who worked for a pittance while they learned the
trade, and scarcely less prominent as employers. Much the same
could be said of the other immigrant occupations. A large
number, about a fifth, worked as hawkers and general dealers;
boot and shoe manufacturing came next in importance, and
most of the remainder were occupied in the furniture and
tobacco trades.[2]

Few of the above generalizations applied to middle-class
Jews and this distinction illustrates another contrast with the
Irish. Even the poorest Jews were dedicated self-improvers.
Most thought of themselves not as workers but as potential
capitalists, rentiers, or members of the respectable salaried
élite; and their application was such that a great many realized
their ambitions even if only as small retailers or as employers of
a handful of other Jews in an East End sweatshop. If their

1. Lipman, op. cit., pp. 102–8; Gartner, op. cit., pp. 64, 86.
2. Lipman, op. cit., pp. 106–8; Gartner, op. cit., pp. 76–81.

11

own bourgeois aspirations were unfulfilled their children often provided compensation, for the Jews, again in contrast to the Irish, believed passionately in the elevating properties of education. One consequence of these attitudes was a steady movement of Jews out of the wage-earning sector. This move was often accompanied by a physical movement out of the East End ghetto into the nineteenth-century equivalents of Golders Green and Ilford.[1] Before 1880 this movement was sufficient to cause a continuous and significant increase in the proportion of middle-class Jews but the great majority of the new immigrants were poor and they were more than sufficient to reverse this trend.

# VII

The numbers involved make it obvious that the influence of alien immigration on regional wage variations cannot have been substantial. London, Manchester, and Leeds were all high-wage centres. Like most high-wage centres these towns, particularly London, contained categories of employment where pay compared less favourably with rates elsewhere and the alien immigrants tended to be associated with trades of this type. It seems probable, therefore, that what influence they were able to exercise would tend to reduce regional wage variations. First, by the general influence their arrival might exercise on wage rates in these centres. Second, and more specifically, by their probable influence upon wages in the less-well-paid trades of London's East End and similar employment in Manchester and Leeds; in this respect, by adding to the forces which modified the high-wage characteristics of London, Manchester, and Leeds, they might combine a tendency to reduce regional wage variations with a tendency to reinforce local variations. However, as the Irish case showed, the consequence of adding labour to one area of the country is not necessarily a reduction in its relative wage level.

1. On this theme generally see e.g. B. Potter in C. Booth (ed.), *Life and Labour*, 1st Ser., iii, Pt. 1, Ch. 4; Gartner, op. cit., pp. 230, 237.

There were a great many complaints about the Jews, as there had been about Irish immigration, and native workmen, particularly in the years before 1895, were again among the more vociferous.[1] They saw the Jews as competitors, and accused them of lowering wages, displacing natives, and weakening the unions. The T.U.C., more concerned with what was practical and near at hand than fine-sounding aspirations towards international working-class solidarity, passed motions condemning the influx of 'foreign pauper labour' in 1888, 1892, and again in 1894.[2] More generally the immigrants were associated with the sweating system and, by some, held largely responsible for the long hours, low wages, over-crowding, and insanitary conditions which were considered characteristic of that system and nowhere more obvious than in the East End.[3] By a process of association they were blamed for a great deal of the general distress which afflicted sectors of the London labour market.[4] All these claims are highly consistent with immigration having reduced wages—but not all were warranted.

Religion handicapped trade unionism among the Jews, and so did their language and bourgeois ambitions.[5] But these

1. Joseph Arch, for example, in his autobiography: 'I am very strongly opposed to the immigration of alien paupers; as a man who has the best interests of his country at heart I am bound to be. Owing to bad treatment at home, several thousands of our best men emigrate each year—that is bad enough in itself—but instead of this relieving the congested state of the population, we get in about three times as many worthless pauper aliens . . .' (*Joseph Arch: The Story of His Life*, p. 255).
2. The 1888 motion was seconded by Keir Hardie. S. W. Lerner, 'The Impact of the Jewish Immigration of 1880–1914 on the London Clothing Industry and Trade Unions', *Bulletin of the Society for the Study of Labour History*, xii (Spring 1966), 13–15; H. A. Clegg, A. Fox, and A. F. Thompson, *A History of British Trade Unions since 1889*, i. 181–3. See also Hardie's evidence to the *S.C. on Emigration and Immigration*. The evidence before this committee, in the report on the *Sweating System at the East End of London*, P.P. 1887, LXXXIX, and before the two other parliamentary inquiries (*R.C. on Alien Immigration*, P.P. 1903, IX; *Volume and Effect of Recent Immigration*, P.P. 1894, LXVIII) contains numerous complaints on the effect of immigration upon the wages, employment, and conditions of native workers. For a more detailed examination of trade union attitudes see J. A. Garrard, *The English and Immigration* (Oxford, 1971), Ch. IX.
3. Some of these problems were also evident in the Jewish quarters of Manchester and Leeds. Gartner, op. cit., pp. 88–91.
4. See e.g. E. Aves in Booth (ed.), *Life and Labour*, 1st Ser., iv. 209.
5. On immigrant trade unionism generally see, Lerner, loc. cit.; Clegg, Fox, and Thompson, op. cit., pp. 33, 181–3, 442; Gartner, op. cit., Ch. IV.

personal characteristics were no great handicap because, like the Irish, the Jews worked in an environment which was unconducive to trade unionism among workers of any faith or nationality. Unionism flourished most among skilled and scarce male workers in large organizations characterized by impersonal industrial relations: conditions in the East End were the opposite of these. In this respect the east London trades had much in common with many trades in Birmingham and the Black Country and with conditions on small farms in Wales, the west, and the north where unionism was similarly retarded.[1] In the furniture and tobacco trades and in the Leeds clothing trades, where conditions were less unfavourable to unionism, Jewish attitudes and religion seem to have presented no great handicap; it was the nature of the trade more than the nature of the workmen that retarded unionism.[2]

When we turn to sweating, the Jews are less easily exonerated although they were less to blame than many contemporaries supposed. Their misfortune, as suggested earlier, was to arrive shortly before various social inquiries focused attention upon East End problems. Jews were prominent in the most distressed districts and sectors of the press, the public, and the trade union world too readily diagnosed immigration as the crux of the problem.[3] The first point in defence of the immigrants is that sweating was not new: it may have been expanding but the main change was that it was more noticed. The surveys of the 1880s and 1890s were rediscovering what Mayhew had described thirty years earlier when the number of Jews in the East End was too small to have any significant effect on wages and conditions. The problems, in the 1890s as much as in the 1850s, derived mainly from the nature of the capital's industry. London was Britain's first industrial centre yet a large part of its activity, even at the end of the century, was scarcely affected by the industrial revolution. It depended heavily on the local market whose demand, particularly for

1. See below, pp. 332–3.
2. See Gartner, op. cit., p. 121; Lipman, op. cit., p. 115; Russell and Lewis, op. cit., p. 80.
3. See Booth, *Life and Labour*, 1st Ser., iv. 209, *Volume and Effects of Recent Immigration*, p. 1.

clothes and similar articles, was notoriously subject to seasonal fluctuations and the whims of fashion. This led directly to erratic work patterns and indirectly to the small and lightly capitalized units of production which in one way or another were connected with most of the East End problems.[1] In some trades a man might set himself up as a 'sweater' with no more than a pound in his pocket and the ability to secure a modest amount of short-term credit.[2] When entry to a trade was as easy as this, over-supply was a logical consequence and over-supply put pressure on profits, wages, and working conditions.[3] These problems were the more serious because the multiplicity of workshops and the prevalence of home work made inspection extraordinarily difficult.[4]

Another element in the East End problem was the abundant supply of female labour. Women were both a cause of the distress and, in all probability, its chief victims.[5] They were mainly gentile;[6] some were the wives and daughters of dockers and others in similarly precarious East End occupations, many were widows or otherwise in reduced circumstances,[7] and some

1. Booth considered short-time the most serious problem of the 'sweated' trades. Periods of frantic activity alternated with spells of idleness; the latter were particularly prevalent between December and April. On the nature of London industry generally see Booth, *Life and Labour*, 1st Ser., iv. 53–4, 355–6; P. G. Hall, *The Industries of London since 1861*, Chs. 3, 4, 5, and 7; Gartner, op. cit., Ch. III; G. Stedman Jones, *Outcast London*.
2. Few machines were used and these were not costly; the Singer sewing machine was normally obtained by hire purchase. Booth, *Life and Labour*, 1st ser., iv. 45, 60.
3. The sweaters seldom earned much more than the best-paid of their employees and often worked alongside them. See e.g. Lipman, op. cit., pp. 111–12.
4. The report on the *Sweating System at the East End of London*, P.P. 1887, LXXXIX, found the Public Health Acts and the Factory and Workshop Regulation Acts 'utterly disregarded' and the existing system of inspection 'entirely inadequate' (p. 7). Gartner considers the Factory Act of 1901 the first effective measure against sweated work (op. cit., p. 70) but the 1894 report on *The Volume and Effects of Recent Immigration* (pp. 57–8) recorded a recent marked improvement in workshop conditions.
5. See above, pp. 11–13, 109–10 and below, p. 318; *M.C.* 14 Dec. 1849; Booth, *Life and Labour*, 1st Ser., iv. 45; C.H.d'E Leppington, 'Sidelights of the Sweating Commission', p. 282; *House of Lords S.C. on the Sweating System*, P.P. 1890, XVII, p. xliii.
6. The Jews married early and their wives seldom worked. See Russell and Lewis, op. cit., pp. 58–9, 170, 195–6.
7. See Hall, op. cit., p. 61. He considers this group the most important in the female labour force of the East End.

supported 'the purely parasitic population of East London'.[1] It has been said that this particular problem arose because east London, unlike Nottingham, Leicester, and the towns of Lancashire and the West Riding, lacked a substantial female employment.[2] In a sense this is true, but in another sense tailoring and the other East End trades were east London's staple female industrial employment. The problem arose from the seasonal and highly competitive nature of these trades, from their low productivity, and the prevalence of home work which encouraged women to work for very little.

These various circumstances were at the root of the East End problems throughout the nineteenth century and the Jewish areas in Manchester and Leeds were similarly, although less seriously, affected.[3] Towards the end of the century the older London industries were increasingly challenged by provincial competition and foreign imports. A little before this the greater use of simple machinery, particularly the sewing machine, increased output and competition within London. Both developments aggravated the long-term problems.[4] However, while there can be no doubt that the East End problems were of long standing, they were almost certainly aggravated by immigration. The East End was seldom short of labour,[5] immigrants were attracted there not by jobs and high wages but by the presence of other Jews, and it is difficult to imagine their arrival having beneficial results. The British standard of living was very high by east European standards; because of this, because many could not speak English, and because most lacked any means to defer taking the first available job, new arrivals were easily exploited. Their pay soon improved but not their conditions and there can be little doubt that the Jews helped sustain occupations which otherwise would have

1. Booth, *Life and Labour*, 1st Ser., iv. 62; Hall, op. cit., p. 61.
2. Hall, op. cit., p. 118.
3. Conditions in Leeds, where tailoring production units were relatively large and heavily capitalized, compared favourably with London. See Gartner, op. cit., pp. 88–9. Much the same contrast could be made between East End tailoring and the London tobacco trades. See above, p. 312.
4. Booth, *Life and Labour*, 1st Ser., iv. 339; Gartner, op. cit., pp. 75–85; *S.C. on Emigration and Immigration*, Evidence, paras. 3001–2, 3012.
5. See Hall, op. cit., pp. 59–60.

more speedily succumbed to factory competition to the long-term benefit of everyone concerned.[1] In addition, their bourgeois aspirations caused them to take every advantage of the ease of attaining employer status; thus they intensified the cut-throat competition responsible for so many East End problems. The importance of low wages among these problems deserves a little more attention than was appropriate in Chapter One and Chapter Three.[2] 'Sweating' is usually taken to mean some combination of sub-contracting, poor working conditions, long hours, and low wages. There is no doubt that the first three of these conditions were features of the East End, and there is no doubt that wages in several East End trades compared less well with those in similar trades elsewhere in Britain than was usually the case when comparisons were made between London and provincial rates.[3] But the widespread existence of significantly low wages, although often inferred, has never been established. The wage picture was highly complicated. Earnings varied a great deal in the short run, each trade was extensively sub-divided, each task paid differently and often by the piece. Fortunately others have entered this maze and emerged with some useful conclusions. Wages were not generally low: certainly not as low as other conditions implied, nor as low as native workers suspected. According to Shirley Lerner, 'the Jewish worker was sweated in terms of his working conditions and hours of work, but not in terms of his hourly earnings';[4] this generalization is probably appropriate for most, although not all, East End workers. Contemporaries were misguided on several counts. One source of confusion was the level of piece-rates; the East End trades, compared with similar trades elsewhere in London, made greater use of division of labour, they employed more machinery and less skill. Piece-rates were

1. This was particularly true of the London boot and shoe trade. See *Volume and Effects of Recent Immigration from Europe*, p. 93; Gartner, op. cit., p. 76.
2. See above, pp. 11–14, 109–11.
3. See above, pp. 7, 10–14.
4. Lerner, op. cit., p. 13. Sweating was, in part, an attempt to provide a remedy for the competitive disadvantages imposed upon London manu-facturers by high wages. G. Stedman Jones, op. cit., p. 23; see also Russell and Lewis, op. cit., p. 70.

lower but productivity higher, so crude comparisons of piece-rates inevitably, but wrongly, suggested that earnings in the East End were extremely low.[1] The new arrivals or 'greeners' were another source of confusion; for three months after they landed they were paid only a pittance, subsequently they were paid a little more, and they received the full rate after about a year. It was only at the initial stage in the immigrant's career that he might need to get through the day on the proverbial 'red herring and a cup of coffee' but there was a tendency to generalize his condition to all Jewish workers.[2] In fact, once past the 'greener' stage the Jewish worker was seldom paid less than the gentile for similar work.[3]

A few figures will illustrate these points. Generalizations are least hazardous for the late 1880s when a considerable amount of information on wages and earnings was collected.[4] Male earnings in the tailoring trade for a full six-day week ranged between 30s. and 60s. according to skill; general tailors averaged 43s. 6d.[5] London bricklayers at the time were paid 39s. 4½d. for a full summer week, their labourers received 26s. 3d.,[6] and almost half of the 75,000 adult males covered by the Booth survey earned 30s. or less.[7] From these superficial comparisons the male workers in the tailoring trade emerge quite favourably;

1. On this see *Volume and Effects of Recent Immigration*, p. 132. Earnings were below those of West End craftsmen but this compares skilled workers with unskilled and, often, men with women.
2. *Report on the Sweating System of the East End of London*, pp. 7–8; Lipman, op. cit., p. 110; Booth, *Life and Labour*, 1st Ser., iv. 211.
3. *Volume and Effects of Recent Immigration*, pp. 132–3; Lipman, op. cit., p. 115.
4. The most useful material is in Booth, *Life and Labour*, 1st Ser., iv, Ch. III by Beatrice Potter; and in the Second Report from the *House of Lords S.C. on the Sweating System*, P.P. 1888, XXI, Appendix H. Most of the other government inquiries mentioned in this chapter contain some figures. The *Labour Gazette* for May 1893 contains a useful survey of wages in the Jewish tailoring workshops of Leeds and Manchester. Some of this material is usefully summarized in C.H. d'E. Leppington, 'Sidelights of the Sweating Commission'. The best short summary of the more useful of this material is in Lipman, op. cit., pp. 108–11.
5. See Lipman, op. cit., p. 110; Booth, *Life and Labour*, 1st Ser., iv. 50, 52–3; *House of Lords S.C. on the Sweating System*, Appendix H. P.P. 1888, XXI.
6. See A. L. Bowley 'Wages in the Building Trades', *J.R.S.S.* lxiv. (1901), 104.
7. 45·5 per cent earned 30s. or less, 22·5 per cent earned 25s. or less. Booth, *Life and Labour* 2nd Ser., v. 272.

but they worked far longer for their money[1] and their hourly earnings, at 6¼d., were considerably below the building craftsman and only slightly above the labourer. By London standards 6¼d. was a low rate and of course there were many who were worse paid than the general tailor, but it is hardly so low as to constitute a 'social problem' comparable with East End working conditions.[2] The comparison becomes more unfavourable to the East End when short-time is taken into account. This was one of the worst features of the sweated trades; according to Beatrice Potter most workers could depend on no more than an average of three days' work per week over the year.[3] This gave a general tailor several shillings less than a building labourer in full employment and perhaps similar annual earnings, a position which can still hardly be considered a 'social problem' but which supports the contention that tailoring was badly paid by London standards because it required more skill than labouring and because there were many men in the trade who were paid less than the general tailor. These generalizations may be applied to the Jewish trades as a whole; tailoring was the most important of these, the furniture and footwear trades paid similar rates, the tobacco trades somewhat more.[4]

It is even less easy to generalize usefully about women's wages in the East End: their earnings range was greater and comparisons with other trades are less meaningful. Fortunately this problem too was tackled by one of the contemporary surveys. The *Reports on the Volume and Effects of Recent Immigration from Eastern Europe* compared the Jewish trades with women's work in a variety of provincial trades and several London factories. While London wages in the Jewish trades were below those for mill work in the northern textile towns, and the capital had no clear advantage over the rest of the country, the general comparison was not unfavourable to the

1. 13 to 14 hours a day. Booth, *Life and Labour*, 1st Ser., iv. 51.
2. London wages were the highest in Britain. See above, Chs. 1 and 3.
3. Booth, *Life and Labour*, 1st Ser., iv. 54.
4. Lipman, op. cit., pp. 110, 111, 115. The relative level of wages in the footwear trade subsequently declined. See below, p. 318 n. 3.

East End.[1] However, in most trades, other than those specifically associated with the East End, women's wages in London were the highest in Britain[2] and in this light the indecisive nature of the comparisons with provincial centres suggests that women's wages in the East End, as well as men's, were low by London standards even if not sufficiently low to constitute a 'social problem' on a par with East End working conditions.

It would be quite wrong to use these figures to suggest that low hourly earnings seldom caused distress, but they were not a widespread and general cause of distress. However, there were at least two major exceptions to this generalization apart from the obvious case of the 'greeners'. Earnings might be absolutely low for a time in any trade which fell victim to factory competition or changes of fashion;[3] the Jews had little direct responsibility for distress of this sort although they were responsible in some cases for prolonging the consequences of competition. The other case concerns the female home workers. There were a considerable number in this category; some fared reasonably well but a great many were paid very badly.[4] There were not many immigrants among this class,[5] nor was it a recent phenomenon; poorly paid home workers had featured prominently in Mayhew's survey. On these counts the Jews can be exonerated as a main cause of this distress although they probably bore some responsibility because any increase in labour supply in the East End, or in manufacturing capacity, was bound to affect the home workers adversely.[6]

1. P.P. 1894, LXVIII, pp. 132–3.
2. See above, pp. 109–11.
3. Sectors of the boot and shoe trade were affected in this way by the end of the century. Gartner, op. cit., pp. 75–81, 99, 279.
4. Booth, *Life and Labour*, 1st Ser., iv. 63; Leppington, op. cit., p. 279, and above, pp. 11–14, 109–11.
5. Jewish wives seldom worked; those that did, and their daughters, were found mainly in the workshops of the better-paid branches of the trade. *Volume and Effects of Recent Immigration*, p. 131; G. Drage, 'Alien Immigration', *J.R.S.S.*, lviii (1895), 15.
6. The home workers probably suffered more from immigrant competition than any other branch of the trade. Several contemporary surveys mention the displacement of gentile women by immigrant labour and they were probably also affected by competition from unskilled 'greeners'. Beatrice Potter described how they 'grasp after the leavings of the Jews' (Booth, *Life and Labour*, 1st Ser., iv. 62). 'Greeners' received a normal wage after

In all, the Jewish influence on wages seems to have been similar to their influence on other East End problems; they were not a prime cause of unfavourable conditions but they added a moderate impetus to forces already at work. Their share of responsibility for poor working conditions was probably more serious than their influence on wages because, although wages in the East End were low by London standards, the area was more remarkable for poor working conditions. The immigrants had very little direct influence on wages outside the East End and the Jewish areas of Manchester and Leeds.[1] In each of these cases they tended to reduce wages and as the general level of wages in these towns was above average it seems likely that alien immigration exercised a modest erosive influence on regional wage variations.

# VIII

The conclusion above is tentative because the outcome of the relationship between wages and an increase in supply could be more complex than a simple reduction of wages. Two other ways in which immigrants might have influenced regional wage variations can be dismissed fairly quickly although both required careful consideration in the Irish case. The first of these is what might be called the United States analogy: the possibility that immigration, by relieving labour bottlenecks,

about a year but the supply of immigrants was constantly replenished so that although the membership of this group was transitory it provided constant competition to native workers. See also *Volume and Effects of Recent Immigration*, p. 93.

1. The East End competed with provincial factories but in most cases factory productivity was so much greater that the outcome of the competition was seldom in doubt and provincial wages scarcely affected. Tailors and cobblers in the West End complained bitterly of Jewish competition and there was substance in some of what they said, but most of their complaints were without foundation because the two areas catered for different markets. Much the same might be said of the furniture trade; the East End manufactured almost entirely for a working-class market which had greatly expanded in the last quarter of the century. On these points see Russell and Lewis, op. cit., pp. 67, 80; *Volume and Effects of Recent Immigration*, pp. 73-4, 86; *R.C. on Alien Immigration*, P.P. 1903, IX, p. 20.

stimulated economic growth and wage rates sufficiently to offset the depressing consequences of increased supply.[1] The East End had little in common with nineteenth-century America or with Lancashire and west Scotland in the second quarter of the nineteenth century; there was no shortage of unskilled labour, no bottlenecks to be relieved. Unlike the Irish the Jews did not go where labour was most needed; they were attracted most by their co-religionists and made for the East End almost regardless of conditions in the labour market. Nor did they have any significant indirect influence on wage rates elsewhere in Britain. The Irish took work of a kind which otherwise would have attracted migrants from low-wage areas and thus helped retard wages where they were lowest; the Jews competed with those long-established in the East End but their trades were not the kind that provincial migrants might have entered in significant numbers.

However, the latter point suggests an important question: how many additional jobs would have been available for natives had alien immigration not occurred? The earlier and tentative conclusion that immigration lowered wages obviously assumes some displacement occurred and that immigration adversely affected the relationship between supply and demand. But whereas the Irish brought their labour and little else the Jews also brought enterprise and technical knowledge.[2] The Irish immigrant commenced near the bottom of the occupational hierarchy and his subsequent career, and that of his descendants, was characterized by social and occupational immobility. The alien immigrant began no higher but aspired to greater things and his subsequent career was characterized by rapid vertical mobility.[3] Some entered clerical or professional work but a great many chose a more difficult but potentially more rewarding path to respectability—they set up in business, thus gratifying what Beatrice Webb called 'the

---

1. See above, pp. 299–300.
2. Some also brought capital and useful trade connections (Gartner, op. cit., p. 33). These were especially likely to increase the demand for labour more than its supply but such cases were exceptional after 1880.
3. See above, pp. 309–10.

strongest impelling motive of the Jewish race—the love of profit as distinct from other forms of money-earning'.[1] This path often added to over-capacity with unfavourable consequences for wage earners; the earlier analysis assumed this was the most likely result. There were several cases, however, where Jewish enterprise won new markets and thus stimulated local employment and wage rates. This contribution was recognized in most serious contemporary investigations and one over-enthusiastic commentator likened their contribution to that of the Huguenot weavers who came after the revocation of the Edict of Nantes.[2] In the ready-made clothing trade they pioneered the use of machinery and extensive division of labour and effected a considerable increase in sales.[3] The net effect of Jewish labour, enterprise, and capital upon the Leeds and Bradford textile trades was almost certainly to the advantage of the local community, and immigrant skill was responsible for the development of the Manchester waterproof clothing trade.[4] Ladies' jackets and mantles, previously imported from Germany, were first manufactured in Britain by immigrants and before long exported to Germany; there were similar successes in branches of the tobacco and furniture trades.[5] How much new employment was created in this way is impossible to determine but it may have been sufficient to offset a great deal of immigrant influence on the supply side of the market and thus remove much of the slight moderating influence on regional wage variations noted earlier. Alien immigration it seems, like Irish immigration, should probably be added to those other examples of non-wage-equalizing migration noted in Chapter Seven.

The conclusion that alien immigration may have added to supply and demand in approximately equal proportions in the

1. Booth, *Life and Labour*, 1st Ser., iv. 60.
2. See e.g. *Volume and Effects of Recent Immigration*, pp. 90–1; Drage, op. cit., p. 15.
3. See e.g. Gartner, op. cit., pp. 82–93; Russell and Lewis, op. cit., pp. 63, 72–3.
4. See e.g. the special report on Leeds in *The Times*, 26 Nov. 1969, p. 15; A. R. Rollin, 'The Jewish Contribution to the British Textile Industry', *Trans. Jewish Historical Society of England*, xvii (1951–2); Gartner, op. cit., p. 90.
5. Gartner, op. cit., pp. 74–5; Russell and Lewis, op. cit., pp. 72–4, 80; Lipman, op. cit., p. 114.

same areas and thus had no significant influence on the regional wage pattern, and the contrast with the Irish who brought labour but little enterprise, appears characteristic of the broader economic and social influence of alien immigration. Despite the considerable attention they received one of the most remarkable aspects of Jewish immigration is how little it affected the rest of the community. The immigrants worked in a well-defined range of occupations, usually for Jewish masters, and often for markets created by Jewish enterprise. A cost–benefit analysis of the net economic effects of alien immigration before the First World War would probably discover no marked influence in either direction. The same could hardly be said of the Irish, and given that Britain's was a labour surplus economy[1] it is remarkable that a considerable inflow of mainly unskilled and destitute aliens was not accompanied by considerable disadvantage to native workers. The analogy with their effect on regional wage variations, and the contrast with the Irish, can be extended to their influence on society. Problems of the kind which accompanied Irish immigration and the costs these imposed on the host community were of little consequence in the East End. Contemporary reports suggest that apart from their association with the sweated industries the Jews were not far from being model citizens: ambitious, thrifty, devoted to their wives and children, law-abiding, and temperate.[2] The only problem that seriously inconvenienced existing residents was the overcrowding and high rents which resulted from immigrant determination to settle in existing Jewish settlements, and this was partly mitigated by Jewish enterprise in the form of Rothschild's '4 per cent' housing developments.[3] Many of the new arrivals were destitute and

---

1. See above, pp. 302–4.
2. See e.g. *Volume and Effects of Recent Immigration*; *R.C. on Alien Immigration*, p. 22; Booth, *Life and Labour*, 1st Ser., iii. 191; Garrard, op. cit., pp. 95–102, 188–9. The Jewish authorities established their own health and sanitation inspectorate to ensure new arrivals adopted British standards (Gartner, op. cit., pp. 151–2). H. S. Lewis writing in 1900 noted how several streets which Booth's 1887 survey classified as 'vicious and semi-criminal' by 1900 were 'Jewish and respectable' (Russell and Lewis, op. cit., p. 176).
3. Lipman, op. cit., p. 105; Gartner, op. cit., p. 156.

certainly constituted a problem but for the most part they
were accommodated by the Jewish Board of Guardians and
they seldom fell upon the rates.[1] As in the economic sphere,
the overwhelming impression is of a largely self-contained
community;[2] their lack of influence on the regional wage
pattern derived from this same general independence.

1. In the early 1890s Russians and Poles accounted for 18 per cent of the
   population of Whitechapel but only 1 per cent of its paupers (Drage,
   op. cit., p. 14; Gartner, op. cit., Ch. 2, and pp. 149, 238; Lipman, op. cit.,
   p. 102).
2. '. . . they have introduced new trades as well as new habits, and they live
   and crowd together, and work and meet their fate almost independent of
   the great stream of London life surging round them' (H. L. Smith in Booth,
   *Life and Labour*, 1st Ser., iii. 104).

# 9

## TRADE UNIONS

TRADE union attitudes on differences in pay for similar work are well known: 'The most general precept of trade unions is that differences of pay, though proper between occupations, are wrong within them: there should be one and only one rate of pay for a given job, irrespective of who does it or where it is done.' [1] No aspect of labour history has received more attention than trade unionism yet its effect on regional wage variations before 1914 has been neglected. What we know of their influence since then might suggest that the unions were prominent among the forces which operated to reduce differentials. [2] This was certainly their effect by 1914, but in the second-half of the nineteenth century their influence was quite different. This chapter argues that the erosive influence of unionism on regional differentials was not effective until after 1900 and that for most of the previous half-century their influence was in the opposite direction.

## I

How important was the influence of unions on regional wage variations? Several variables have a part in the answer to this question; the two most important are, first, the extent of their power, their ability to implement union policy, and second, policy itself. Discussion of union power must begin with an assessment of numerical strength.

1. E. H. Phelps Brown, *The Economics of Labour* (New Haven, Conn., and London, 1962), p. 175.
2. There is a considerable literature on trade unions and differentials since 1918, see, in particular, H. A. Turner, 'Trade Unions, Differentials and the Levelling of Wages', *Manchester School of Economic and Social Studies*, xx (1952).

The proportion of nineteenth-century labour history devoted to the unions reflects their subsequent importance, the influence of Marx on history, and historians' preference for writing the history of institutions, but it exaggerates their contemporary significance. Union membership fluctuated violently before 1880 especially in the first half of the century. The short-lived Grand National Consolidated Trades Union, with a total strength of half a million or more but only 20,000 paid-up members,[1] illustrates the early pattern in an exaggerated fashion and suggests too that union effectiveness fluctuated less than membership. The biggest fluctuation in the second half of the century was the great expansion of the early 1870s and its subsequent collapse.[2] In 1880 membership stood at around half a million,[3] about 4 per cent of the working population; for every trade unionist there was one Irish workman,[4] three farm workers, and nearly four domestic servants.[5]

The 'new unionism' expansion which began at the end of the 1880s took membership beyond the level achieved in the early

1. H. A. Clegg, A. Fox, and A. F. Thompson, *A History of British Trade Unions since 1889*, i. 2. Its nominal membership may have reached 800,000. S. G. Checkland, *The Rise of Industrial Society in England 1815–1885*, p. 348.
2. The Webbs, writing in the early 1890s, considered the expansion of the early 1870s one of the three high tides in trade union history. The other two were 1833–4 and 1889–90. S. and B. Webb, *History of Trade Unionism* (1950 ed.), p. 328.
3. In 1880 494,000 were represented at the T.U.C. Not all unionists were represented but this figure probably includes a considerable number who were counted both as trade union and trades council members. B. C. Roberts, *The Trades Union Congress, 1868–1921* (1958), pp. 379–80. In 1884 598,000 were represented at the T.U.C., 379,000 of these were affiliated through trade unions (ibid.; Clegg, Fox, and Thompson, op. cit., p. 3).
4. The Irish well illustrate the disproportionate attention to trade unions in nineteenth-century labour history. Irish workers out-numbered trade unionists in most years before 1889; their influence on economic and social conditions was at least as great, and in the 1840s, 50s, and 60s it was probably greater. Yet, compared with unionism, their study has been neglected.
5. Mitchell and Deane, op. cit., p. 60. Similar comparisons for the 1850s and 1860s would be even less favourable to the unions. In 1874, a peak year, the T.U.C. represented over one million members, but this was nearly three times the total in the previous year (Webbs, *History of Trade Unionism*, p. 326). Hobsbawm talks of the great expansion of the early 1870s raising membership to, 'something like half a million' (E. J. Hobsbawm, *Industry and Empire* (1968), pp. 128–9).

1870s and marks something of a watershed, for membership did not subsequently fall below one and a half million and, although there were still more domestic servants than trade unionists, 10 per cent of the labour force was now organized.[1] In 1900 2 million of Britain's 16 million workers were union members and by 1910 the total reached two and a half million or about 14 per cent of the labour force. The following decade saw rapid expansion which took membership to over 4 million, or some 20–25 per cent of the labour force, in 1914, and to more than 8 million by 1920.[2]

These figures are no more than an approximate guide to union strength. If membership is measured as a proportion of the male labour force the results are more impressive; if as a proportion of adult manual workers more impressive still, something of the order of 10 per cent in 1888, 25 per cent in 1901, 30 per cent in 1910, and approaching 50 per cent in 1914.[3] There is also the question of what constitutes 'a union': some workers acted in unison and enjoyed the advantages of combination although not formally organized,[4] while among the 'formal' trade unions there where always some, and sometimes a great many, who could contemplate neither strike nor depression and be sure they would survive. The trade union

1. Clegg, Fox and Thompson, op. cit., pp. 1–2, 466, 489; Mitchell and Deane, op. cit., pp. 60, 68.
2. Clegg, Fox and Thompson, op. cit., p. 466; Pelling, *A History of British Trade Unionism*, p. 262; Mitchell and Deane, op. cit., pp. 60, 68.
3. These figures, however, include female and 'white collar' unionists. Clegg, Fox and Thompson, op. cit., pp. 466–7.
4. The Scots miners, although not 'organized', exercised some control over wages and employment by restricting output (Pelling, op. cit., p. 44). The miners of the north-east operated similarly and more effectively (H. A. Turner, *Trade Union Growth, Structure and Policy*, p. 188) while the railway navvies and builders' labourers exercised a degree of control over recruiting by their practice of over-loading and harrying new hands (*S.C. on Railway Labourers*, Evidence, para. 1043–5; Handley, *The Irish in Scotland, 1798–1845*, p. 117). The best exposition of this phenomenon is contained in H. A. Turner's examination of the early cotton unions. He argues, convincingly, that the beginnings of continuous 'unionism' in the cotton trades was much earlier than has been suggested by interpretations which equate 'unionism' with 'formally constituted organizations—with documentary constitutions, formally-appointed officers, formally-stated agreements, trades regulations and so on . . .' (Turner, op. cit., (1962), section II, Ch. 1, p. 51).

world of 1874 included many in the latter category[1] and much
of the expansion of unionism among the unskilled in 1889–90
was similarly ephemeral.[2] But the general position is sufficiently
clear: for most of the first half of our period, until the late
1880s, trade unionism, however defined, embraced only a
small minority of British workers; between 1890 and 1910 it
accounted for a substantial minority; and the years immediately
before the war saw the start of the rapid expansion which
carried the movement to a position which enabled the Webbs,
in the 1920 edition of *Industrial Democracy*, to note with
satisfaction that the same critics who in 1897 'ridiculed the idea
of attaching even so much importance to the workmen's
organizations as to write a book about them', were by then
concerned that the unions might 'swallow up all other social
institutions'.[3]

However, unions were still not free of the trade cycle; 1920
had much in common with 1834 and 1874. By 1922 membership
was down to 5½ million and this figure was not substantially
exceeded until shortly before the Second World War.[4] The
close relationship between membership and trade conditions
reminds us that assessment of union influence on wages in-
volves more than counting heads. To a considerable extent
membership was a dependent variable: wages, prices, employment, profits, and union membership rose and fell together.
It is this interrelationship, among other things, that makes it
so difficult to assess union influence on wages—no single
influence within it can be isolated. However, the relationship
by no means denies that unions could influence wages; even if
numerical strength was determined only by the trade cycle—
which it was not—it remains that trade unions were more
likely to secure increases in wages than unorganized labour.

1. The farm labourers for example; some 10 per cent of union members in
   1874 were farm labourers but there were few of these left five years later.
   B. C. Roberts, op. cit., pp. 73, 379; Webbs, *History of Trade Unionism*, p.
   349.
2. See E. J. Hobsbawm, 'General Labour Unions in Britain, 1889–1914',
   *Ec.H.R.*, 2nd Ser., i (1949).
3. S. and B. Webb, *Industrial Democracy*, pp. v–vi.
4. Mitchell and Deane, op. cit., p. 68.

Perhaps the most debated aspect of union influence is whether or not they have the power to affect the share of the national income which goes to labour. For some time the initiative in this debate has been with those who deny the unions any lasting influence. This school of thought concedes an 'impact effect' when unions first appear, some fluctuation in factor shares over the trade cycle, and a long-term decline in the share of rent, but considers that the most remarkable feature of all is the long-term stability between the shares of labour and capital.[1] These conclusions are open to criticism on certain grounds. The usual explanation of the apparent constancy in factor shares depends, in essence, on the fact that at the level of the firm capital controls costs and prices although it may not control pay; hence it is able to defend its 'normal, adequate and reasonable' level of profit.[2] However, at this level factor shares are not constant; bankruptcies and violent fluctuations in profit are commonplace, which suggests that the explanation may rely unduly upon the law of averages.[3] Another problem is that of reconciling capital's resolute defence of its gross share of the national income with its near acquiescence in substantial government redistribution. It is strange too, given the admitted 'impact' effect of the unions, that they failed to increase labour's share substantially between 1850 and 1914. The statistics show least change of all in factor

1. See e.g. E. H. Phelps Brown, *Economics of Labour*, pp. 180–1, 185; Deane and Cole, op. cit., pp. 248, 255. After summarizing the available evidence Deane and Cole conclude that the proportion of the national income going to labour '. . . seems to have changed comparatively little in the nineteenth century and early twentieth century in spite of a structural transformation of the British economy'. The 'impact effect' arises partly from union ability to overcome the influence of custom when customary wages are below what the market will bear. For examples of work which expresses reservations about union inability to influence the share of the national income which goes to labour, see R. M. Solow, 'Relative Shares: A Skeptical Note on the Constancy of Relative Shares', *American Economic Review*, xlviii (1958); A. M. Ross, *Trade Union Wage Policy* (Berkeley, Cal., 1948); R. Ozanne, 'Impact of Unions on Wage Levels and Income Distribution', *Quarterly Journal of Economics*, lxxiii, (1959).
2. For a more detailed explanation see E. H. Phelps Brown, *Economics of Labor*, pp. 184–90.
3. This difficulty is recognized by some of these who advance the 'constancy' thesis; see e.g. E. H. Phelps Brown and P. E. Hart, 'The Share of Wages in National Income', *Economic Journal*, lxii (1952).

shares in these years[1]—yet this was the main period of union growth and custom was a powerful influence in the labour market at the beginning of the period. All this suggests that the apparent stability of factor shares may well owe a great deal to deficiencies in the evidence used to support its existence. However, interesting as it is, this debate has little bearing on the question at hand because union ability to affect regional wage variations depends far less on their ability to change the size of labour's share than to influence its distribution, and of the latter influence there is no doubt at all. Pollard, for example, has shown how the organized skilled workers of Sheffield were able to influence their wage levels;[2] most skilled workers shared this advantage and for several decades after 1850 skilled workers generally used their market influence to increase their differential over the unskilled.[3]

## II

Having outlined some aspects of the nature and limitations of union influence we can begin to examine its likely effect on regional wage differentials. The first question which requires an answer concerns the geography of trade unionism: in what parts of Britain was union influence most likely to be felt?

1. Deane and Cole, op. cit., pp. 246–7.
2. Pollard, *Labour in Sheffield*, pp. 67–71.
3. The unions were especially able to influence the distribution of income between workers when employers acquiesced in their attempts to secure better pay and conditions, either because the total pay of the men concerned accounted for only a small part of total costs or because they were anxious to establish a cartel-like arrangement which eliminated both price and wage competition. In such cases both parties stood to gain at the expense of consumers. The Coventry ribbon trade was for long organized on just such a basis: 'The good masters and the good men were always looking for ways of combining to try to impose their own standards upon the minority who flouted them . . . at no time did they have any difficulty in agreeing about what constituted a just wage.' The country weavers, outside Coventry and excluded from these arrangements, were wretchedly poor. Another, although less enduring, arrangement appeared in the Birmingham metal bedstead trade in 1891. On these various points see Hobsbawm, *Labouring Men*, pp. 291–4; Checkland, op. cit., p. 232; Clegg, Fox, and Thompson, op. cit., pp. 189, 194–5; J. M. Prest, *The Industrial Revolution in Coventry*, pp. 55, 63–4, 70, 75.

The spatial and chronological patterns of union development had much in common; each combined long-term expansion with considerable cyclical fluctuation. Farm labourers everywhere and the least industrialized parts of Britain were both beyond the reach of trade unionism except for short spells in exceptional periods like the early 1870s when geographical and numerical expansion occurred together. In the subsequent retrenchment they contracted together: 'Up and down the country the hundreds of little societies in miscellaneous trades which had flourished during the good years, went down before the tide of adversity. Widespread national organizations shrank up practically into societies of local influence, concentrated upon the strongholds of their industries . . . In some districts . . . Trade Unionism practically ceased to exist.' [1] In broad terms, the 'strongholds' of unionism were in those parts of the country where the labour market most frequently approximated the highly favourable situation of the early 1870s and unions were weakest in those areas where the normal, long-term, relationship between supply and demand was closest to national conditions at the end of the 1870s. Here again it can be seen that union strength was to some extent a dependent variable: in certain areas high wages, strong unionism, and a buoyant demand for labour were found together; high wages and strong unions each owed something to the other and both were consequent upon market conditions. This identity between areas of union strength and areas where market conditions were favourable has a large part in explaining why unionism exercised no erosive influence on regional wage differentials in the nineteenth century.

The low-wage areas in the south of England were comparatively unaffected by union development. In 1900 Luton's town council was trying to attract employers to the town by advertising its low wages and freedom from trade unions; unionism came to Courtaulds' East Anglian plants with the northern workmen they recruited at the end of the century; and the relative weakness of organized labour in the south is

---

1. Webbs, *History of Trade Unionism*, pp. 349–50.

accepted as one reason why the new industries which developed in the inter-war years shunned the traditional industrial areas.[1] The Amalgamated Society of Railway Servants found recruiting was most difficult in rural southern England and easiest in counties like Lancashire, Yorkshire, Northumberland, and Durham.[2] Lancashire was a strong union centre and the only part of Britain where any considerable number of females were organized. Northumberland and Durham was the strongest of the mining centres: this field dominated the short-lived Miners' Association of Great Britain and theirs were the only district associations to survive the crisis at the end of the 1870s.[3] The Webbs have shown the over-all distribution of all trade unionists in 1892: 'Trade Unionists', they noted, 'were aggregated in the thriving industrial districts of the north of England.'[4] Five northern counties contained over half of England's unionists and two-thirds of Scotland's worked in the

1. J. G. Dony, *A History of the Straw Hat Industry*, p. 138; D. C. Coleman, *Courtaulds*, i. 258–60.
2. Membership in rural counties was not only lower in absolute terms, as would be expected, but also when measured as a proportion of those eligible for membership (P. S. Gupta, 'Railway Trade Unionism in Britain, c. 1880–1900', *Ec.H.R.*, 2nd Ser., xix (1966), 136–7.) In 1900, for example, of the 13 areas Gupta shows, the most highly unionized were Durham and Northumberland with 5·9 per cent of eligible workers and 10·8 per cent of members, and Yorkshire and south Wales with 13·7 and 6·4 per cent of eligible workers and 18·1 and 9·3 per cent of members. At the other end of the scale Wiltshire, Hampshire, Dorset, Devon, Somerset, and Cornwall together accounted for 6·2 per cent of eligible workers and 2·2 per cent of members, while Oxfordshire, Buckingham, Bedfordshire, Berkshire, and Hertfordshire together had 3 per cent of eligible workers and 1·1 per cent of members.
3. A. J. Taylor, 'The Miners' Association of Great Britain and Ireland, 1842–8: A Study in the Problem of Integration', *Economica*, xxii (1955), 48, 54–5; Rowe, *Wages in the Coal Industry*, p. 34; Turner, op. cit., p. 190. Of the other major coalfields south Wales was certainly one of the weakest before 1900. It was the last major field to develop a strong union; difficulties of communication, race, religion, and language presented obstacles to organization. After 1900 unionism in south Wales appears to have recovered ground rapidly. Webbs, *History of Trade Unionism*, p. 350; Clegg, Fox, and Thompson, op. cit., pp. 17–19, 105–6, 124–5, 337; B. Thomas, 'Studies in Labour Supply and Labour Costs', pp. 176–7, 189. It seems not unreasonable to suggest that had unionism been less retarded wage levels in south Wales might have been more in keeping with its rate of economic growth (see above, pp. 152–3).
4. Webbs, *History of Trade Unionism*, pp. 425–7, 741–3, and see the appendix to this chapter.

Glasgow area.[1] In Northumberland and Durham a half or more of adult males were organized; at the same time there were ten English counties with fewer than a thousand unionists.[2]

In short, there was an obvious correlation between areas where unions were strong and areas where wages were high. The relationship was not perfect because trade union strength was not entirely a function of the state of the market. Birmingham and London were high-wage centres but hardly union strongholds—no doubt largely because both had a preponderance of small concerns where industrial relations were likely to be more personal, and the distinction between labour and capital less well defined, than in other manufacturing centres.[3] Similar circumstances explain the situation in agriculture: the Swing disturbances, Arch's movement, and the half-hearted revival of agricultural unionism in the early twentieth century all drew their main strength from the south-east and East Anglia. Wages there were low, but it was the area where farms were largest, 'living in' least common, and the distinction between masters and men most pronounced.[4] These cases, however,

---

1. Webbs, *History of Trade Unionism*, pp. 426, 742–3. The five counties were: Lancashire, Cheshire, Northumberland, Durham, and the West Riding.
2. Ibid.
3. G. C. Allen, *Birmingham and the Black Country*, pp. 170–1; Webbs, *History of Trade Unionism*, p. 426. Allen also noted an unusual degree of paternalism in the larger Birmingham firms.

   In London unionism was weakest in the East End where the small master system was most prevalent. There were other handicaps to unionism in the East End; a large proportion of the workers were unskilled, casual employment was commonplace, and a great many of the workers were female. Trade unionism was stronger in other parts of London and in so far as unionism had any headquarters in the second half of the nineteenth century it was London. Some of London's relative weakness was modified after 1890 when it was the centre of the new unionism which began the expansion of organization among the less skilled. C. Booth, *Life and Labour*, 1st Ser., iii. 58; Hobsbawm, *Labouring Men*, p. 275, and in R. Glass (ed.), op. cit., pp. 11–13; Webbs, *History of Trade Unionism*, pp. 299, 323–4, 442; Clegg, Fox, and Thompson, op. cit., p. 86.

   South Wales might to some extent be regarded as another exception to the general pattern (see above, p. 331 n. 3) and so might the West Riding textile area where the great importance of female employment was a handicap to unionism. Clegg, Fox, and Thompson, op. cit., pp. 34, 184–7.
4. On these points generally see E. J. Hobsbawm and G. Rudé, *Captain Swing* (1969), esp. Part I; Hasbach, op. cit., esp. Ch. V. On farm wages see the appendix to Ch. 1.

were the only significant exceptions to the over-all pattern and agriculture was the only occupation where unions were strongest in low-wage areas.

## III

Given the spatial distribution of union strength, the nature and effectiveness of union action on wage variations is of great consequence. Unless they adopted policies to secure equal pay for equal work, and pursued these policies with vigour, their impact was likely to operate in the reverse direction. By securing more pay for themselves they would alter the distribution of labour's share of the national income in favour of the high-wage areas. The influence of unionism in this respect changed during the course of the period and is best considered in two parts. The first part extended at least to 1890 and perhaps to 1911. It covers the years before the emergence of industrial and general unions which catered for the unskilled; there were one or two examples of this type of union before 1889 and a few more after but in 1900 the trade union world was still dominated by skill—by true craftsmen like engineers, printers, and carpenters, and by the cotton workers and coal hewers whose unions and working rules closely approximated those of true craftsmen.[1]

Craft unionism was based upon the scarcity value of skilled workers. Its main concern was to protect this scarcity and it did so by regulating labour supply; therefore it was exclusive and restrictive and neither its structure nor mode of operation was conducive to the erosion of regional differentials.[2] This was not a consequence of union opposition to the removal of regional differentials; most craft unions professed some intention of securing standard wage rates and one of the main objects of

---

1. The Webbs lumped them together: 'The Trade Union World was, .. in 1892, in the main composed of skilled craftsmen. ' (*History of Trade Unionism*, p. 442). H. A. Turner, more recently, has done likewise. Turner, op. cit., p. 200.
2. In Turner's definition these unions were 'closed' in contrast to the later 'open' unions of the unskilled. For more details of the characteristics of the two forms see section III of his book.

the amalgamation which created the Amalgamated Society of Engineers was, avowedly, to secure uniformity in trade policy and to equalize real wages.[1] The difficulty was that in practice this aim conflicted with more cherished priorities, in particular with the desire for a large measure of local autonomy. The margin between principle and practice can be seen in the A.S.E.: some thirty years after it was founded its executive surveyed the great diversity of wages and trade conditions between districts and, far from urging their removal, gave their existence as reason for permitting a substantial degree of branch autonomy[2]. As well as indicating artisan preference for self-government the absence of strong central direction on wage matters reflected a partial acceptance of the conclusions of classical economics. As William Newton put it: 'We are very little concerned in regulating rates and wages. They regulate themselves . . .'[3] The craft unions were not quite as convinced of the omnipotence of the invisible hand as this might suggest; where they could they regulated supply, but their awareness of the strength of market forces, and of the limits within which they could shape these forces to their own end, help to explain the absence of central wage policies and the passive acceptance of regional differentials. There were practical considerations also; craft scarcity depended on careful control and at a time when the labour market was much fragmented this regulation was best carried out by officers familiar with local conditions.

1. Webbs, *History of Trade Unionism*, p. 221.
2. J. B. Jeffreys, *The Story of the Engineers* (1946), pp. 99–100. The extent to which the executive acted on this matter is illustrated by evidence to the *Royal Commission on Labour*, P.P. 1893–4, XXXII, Minutes of Evidence, Group A. Gerald Balfour questioning J. Whittaker, resident official of the A.S.E. at Manchester:
   Q. Your Society consists of a very large number of districts, and great freedom seems to be allowed to each of these districts to determine for itself questions of wages and of hours?—A. Yes.
   Q. I think you said the initiative almost always came from the district?— A. Almost always, except in low rate of wages districts. We have endeavoured, by drawing their attention to it, to get them to move in the matter, and we have in fact, I may say, encouraged them to do so . . .
   For other examples see R. W. Postgate, *The Builder's History* (1923), pp. 294, 353; Turner, op. cit., pp. 203–6; Webbs, *Industrial Democracy*, p. 321.
3. Evidence to *R.C. on Trade Unions* (1867–9), quoted in Jefferys, *The Story of the Engineers*, p. 98.

For these reasons local officials in most of the craft unions, like the masons, 'retained an amount of power which would surprise a modern trade unionist. . .'[1] Their central administrations, which are generally cited as a characteristic of the new model unions, had a very limited influence on wage determination. There is no doubt that in some respects the craft unions were centralized. Many had members throughout the nation and maintained a salaried central executive; one of its functions might be parliamentary lobbying, others might include looking after the union's financial and friendly society affairs, and in each case there were advantages of scale. Strike funds too were usually controlled by head office and in this way it exercised some influence over wage policy. But the activities which affected wage rates most directly—the formulation and presentation of wage demands, negotiation with employers, regulation of hours and apprenticeship—were left to the district,[2] and when head office attempted to circumscribe local power it ran the risk of fomenting considerable opposition, especially in the high-wage branches which had most to lose from centralized policies and their egalitarian tendencies.[3] In the 1870s the modest progress towards centralization and co-operation between unions ended. Branches became increasingly intolerant of national leaders and the slow tendency towards amalgamation was reversed.[4] Unions were shifting their headquarters from London to a variety of centres in the north and as they did so the Junta, with its potential for central leadership, diminished in influence.[5] The Webbs have labelled the years

1. Postgate, op. cit., p. 156.
2. Clegg, Fox, and Thompson, op. cit., p. 8; Jefferys, The Story of the Engineers, p. 99.
3. The tailors provide a very clear illustration; see Clegg, Fox, and Thompson, op. cit., pp. 135–6.
4. Webbs, History of Trade Unionism, pp. 318–25.
5. In time the T.U.C. took over most of its functions but the failure of the T.U.C. to give a strong lead to the union world is well established; convening the first meeting at Manchester was itself a challenge to the authority of the London-based Junta. The T.U.C. came close to being wound up in 1875 and again the following year. On these points, and on the role of the T.U.C. generally at this time, see Webbs, op. cit.; Phelps Brown, Industrial Relations, pp. 244–56; H. M. Lynd, England in the Eighteen Eighties (1945), pp. 253, 257.

1863–85 as a period of sectionalism[1] and the description is apt although it would be wrong to imagine that there was much more in the way of co-operation and central control either before 1863 or for some time after 1885.

In this light the persistence of large regional wage variations, even in occupations where unionism was strong, is less remarkable. In 1900 the engineers and the carpenters, the first of the new model unions, still tolerated rates which gave some members twice as much as others.[2] Not all unions were so indifferent; a few, like the flint-glass makers, regarded the establishment of a national standard rate as a first priority and pursued this end even to the extent of branches in high-wage areas foregoing increases[3]—but cases like this were very exceptional. The main influence of unionism upon spatial differentials occurred at district level;[4] while most unions considered the achievement of a national rate no more than a very distant ambition differentials within the district were regarded with greater concern and many unions succeeded in establishing district standard rates.[5] But before 1900 the levelling process seldom extended further[6]—union influence on local rates contrasts with their indifference to inter-district variations.

District parochialism was at the root of this dichotomy. There are several illustrations of this phenomenon in Hobsbawm's study of the London labour market: 'North of London . . . Watford, St Albans, and Hertford seem to be the

1. The title of Ch. 6 in their *History of Trade Unionism*.
2. See above, p. 1.
3. Webbs, *Industrial Democracy*, pp. 280–1.
4. The 'district' varied in size according to occupation. Some trades recognized several 'districts' within London whereas, at the other extreme, in mining the 'district' usually covered a whole coalfield or all that part of a coalfield within one county.
5. In well-organized trades this latter influence was considerable and in a few trades, like the cotton industry which operated mainly in one small and well-defined area, it went a considerable way towards securing a national standard. The achievement of standard district rates probably came mainly after 1870; this was certainly the case in engineering. On these points, and for further details, see M. L. Yates, *Wages and Labour Conditions in British Engineering* (1937), p. 64; Jefferys, *The Story of the Engineers*, p. 98; Webbs, *Industrial Democracy*, p. 125; J. H. Porter, 'Industrial Peace in the Cotton Trade, 1875–1913', *Yks. Bull.*, xix (1967), 50.
6. Webbs, *Industrial Democracy*, p. 321.

only places within the ken of the London unions.'[1] The London carriage makers feared being governed by Liverpool and took special care to preserve their autonomy, and the Miners' Association of Great Britain, the first attempt to co-ordinate the industry as a whole, is one of several examples from the coal industry in which attempts at unity foundered on the rock of district particularism.[2] The Miners' Association broke up largely because the north-east saw no reason to put its own interests second to the movement as a whole, a waywardness which persisted into the twentieth century. On the Scottish coalfields in the 1860s strikes were operated on a local basis and there was almost no co-ordination between districts.[3] Alexander MacDonald could bring them together at times, but not for long, and although he favoured co-ordination within Scotland he led the pressure group within the National Miners' Association which insisted on a maximum of regional autonomy.[4] The foundation of the National Miners' Association was itself the beginning of a great cleavage which persisted until 1908 based upon conflicting attitudes towards the sliding scale and the eight-hour day.[5] The export fields were reluctant to abandon the sliding scale, and the north-eastern hewers, a well-paid 'aristocracy'[6] who enjoyed a seven-hour day for at least half a century before the 1908 Eight Hours Act,[7] refused to support a movement which might benefit hewers elsewhere and other mine labour on their own field but threatened to upset their

---

1. Hobsbawn in R. Glass (ed.), op. cit., p. 17.
2. E. Aves in C. Booth, *Life and Labour*, 2nd Ser., v. 150; A. J. Taylor, loc. cit. See also Aves's comments on the parochialism of the painters, leather workers, printers, and other trades with a multiplicity of separate societies many of which operated only in London. Booth, *Life and Labour*, 2nd Ser., v. 151.
3. Youngson Brown, 'The Scots Coal Industry', p. 208; *idem*, 'Trade Union Policy in the Scots Coalfields', 1855–85', p. 41.
4. Youngson Brown, 'The Scots Coal Industry', p. 208; G. D. H. Cole, *A Short History of the British Working Class Movement* (1948), pp. 181–3.
5. Webbs, *History of Trade Unionism*, pp. 303, 393; Rowe, *Wages in the Coal Industry*, p. 39.
6. This description is Turner's. He quotes Welbourne who reported that in the 1920s the north-eastern collier was still apt to look upon other miners as navvies rather than miners proper. Turner, op. cit., pp. 186, 189.
7. E. Welbourne, *The Miners' Unions of Northumberland and Durham* (Cambridge, 1923), p. 245.

own working and domestic arrangements as well as their employers' ability to sell abroad.[1]

There were many other trades with two or more societies and the division between them was often geographical. Situations of this kind were seldom tranquil for long and obviously inimical to the emergence of policies likely to secure a national standard rate. For long periods the building trade unions expended more energy on inter-union dispute than in trying to wrest advantages from the masters; the most common feature of these conflicts was a struggle for membership between London and Manchester societies.[2] There were similar problems in the printing trades with London societies, who were anxious to protect their wage differential, refusing to join the Printing and Kindred Trades Federation,[3] and the A.S.E., which had to contend with numerous independent local societies, did not hesitate to encourage its own members to blackleg if by doing so it might weaken those 'absurd and irritating institutions'.[4] These divisions, between trades and within trades,[5] and the lack of central guidance and control are nowhere more apparent than in the despairing comments of sympathetic middle-class observers who were usually more convinced than the men themselves of the propriety and potential advantages of working-class solidarity: 'Too many unions and too little unity', wrote

---

1. Rowe, *Wages in the Coal Industry*, p. 169; Phelps Brown, *British Industrial Relations*, p. 316.
2. Postgate, op. cit., pp. 85, 294, 308, 355, 359, 362–3, and Ch. 3, *passim*.
3. Clegg, Fox, and Thompson, op. cit., p. 133.
4. Liverpool district delegate of the A.S.E. quoted in Webbs, *Industrial Democracy*, pp. 117–18.
5. Sectionalism was even more apparent between trades and occupations than among men who worked at the same trade in different parts of the country. It was especially evident in craftsmen's attitudes towards the unskilled— best summed up in a remark by the boiler-makers' secretary, Robert Knight, to the *Royal Commission on Labour*. When asked whether there were divergences of interest between his own and the Tyneside Labour Union Knight replied: 'There ought not to be if we could only get the labourers to keep their places' (quoted in Lynd, op. cit., p. 263). In the shipyards unskilled unions were formed to fight the artisans as much as the masters; the unskilled were recruited and paid by the artisans. On this theme generally see Hobsbawm, 'The Labour Aristocracy in Nineteenth-Century Britain', in *Labouring Men;* H. A. Turner, op. cit., section 4, Ch. 1.

Aves; '. . . trade unionism is to be regarded rather as representing an expanded form of individualism than any thorough collectivism.'[1] The Webbs attributed 'nine-tenths of the ineffectiveness of the Trade Union world' to 'competition between overlapping unions'.[2] As well as underlining the reasons advanced to support the thesis that unions had little erosive influence on regional wage differentials these comments are a reminder of the folly of imposing upon the multitude of parochial and self-interested groups labels which imply collective interests and ambitions: there was no single working class before the end of the nineteenth century and precious little solidarity.

# IV

Given the large measure of district autonomy in the nineteenth century, together with the positive correlation between union strength and spatial wage variations, it follows that whatever influence the unions were able to exercise upon regional wage variations helped to sustain them, just as the unions helped the well-paid to maintain and increase their differentials over the unskilled.[3]

How strong this influence was is impossible to determine precisely. The proportion of the labour force likely to be affected directly as union members was described earlier; it was not substantial, never more than one worker in eight before 1900. However, the uneven geographical distribution of membership allowed unionism to exercise a greater influence on regional differentials than this proportion might suggest and the effect of the union was not confined to its own members. Although not formally organized, non-union workers in districts where unionism was strong were likely to be able to secure at least some of the advantages of organization because they operated in the same favourable market conditions which were a necessary

---

1. E. Aves in C. Booth, *Life and Labour*, 2nd Ser., v. 147, 150.
2. Webbs, *Industrial Democracy*, p. 121.
3. E. J. Hobsbawm, *Labouring Men*, p. 293.

condition for strong unionism.[1] To some extent favourable market conditions were also created by the unions; they protected their position by restricting supply and excluding the unskilled and similar groups. The latter measures brought no direct benefit to the unorganized but another part of union policy was the encouragement of emigration and by the interest they aroused and the provision of information the unions encouraged the emigration of all classes of workmen.[2] In this, and in other ways, they helped to restrict labour supply in areas where the relationship between supply and demand was already favourable to the labour force[3] and, as was noted earlier, this influence is probably a part of the explanation of some of the differences in mobility inimical to the erosion of regional wage differentials which were discussed in Chapter Seven.

The 'demonstration effect' of unionism extended beyond encouraging emigration. Where unionism was strong the unorganized not only operated in a more favourable market environment, they were also more likely to exploit these favourable market opportunities because they had before them the example of the formal union. They might secure some control over entry to the trade and were more likely to defend traditional practices, including the maintenance of a customary proportion between effort and reward.[4] Other working-class

1. See above, pp. 325–7, 330–2.
2. On this point see above, pp. 277–8. The carpenters referred to emigration as the natural outlet for 'surplus labourers and mechanics' produced by the 'prolific character of the Anglo-Saxon Race'. Pelling, op. cit., p. 57; see also Clements, op. cit., p. 171.
3. The unions not only encouraged a relatively high rate of out-migration in high-wage areas, they also at times did what they could to stem the inflow of labour from low-wage areas; the Scots miners' response to the arrival of an advance guard of unemployed Cornishmen in 1866 was to dispatch 5,000 notices to Devon and Cornwall imploring others not to come and suggesting that employers were trying to create surplus population in Scotland (Youngson Brown, 'The Scots Coal Industry', p. 198). The unions were especially likely to take action of this sort when in dispute with their employers. Their generally gloomy pronouncements on local wages, unemployment, and the cost of living, as well as the fact that they encouraged emigration, may have convinced many potential migrants in low-wage areas that they were as well off where they were. Union emigration policy, in fact, was partly a response to the challenge of migration from low-wage areas. See Clements, op. cit., pp. 169, 177.
4. See above, p. 326 n. 4.

organizations, which were usually strongest where the unions were strong, might aid these endeavours; friendly societies made available the means to secure a measure of independence and co-operative societies provided both another example of self-help and, in some cases, facilities for organization and credit to men on strike.[1] The working man's vote was most likely to be of consequence in the same areas; this was particularly true in local elections and the local authorities, whose pay and employment policies might thereby be affected, were substantial employers of unskilled labour.[2]

Another way in which some of the benefits of organization were distributed to other working classes was through the force of customary differentials.[3] Let us suppose that in any one area labourers' wages traditionally maintained a level around two-thirds of the craftsmen's rate. Suppose further that the craftsmen then joined a union and the union was strong enough to raise pay and thus increase their margin of advantage over similar, but unorganized, craftsmen in other areas. Their differential over local labourers might widen too, and in many cases it did,[4] but the force of custom was such that the craftsmen would tend to pull their labourers up behind them thus moderating the influence of unionism on the differential for skill even if not eradicating it entirely: in either case the consequence was a widening of the differential between the labourers' wage and labourers' wages in areas unaffected by unionism.

In these various ways some of the benefits of unionism were shared with other workers in the same areas and made union influence on regional wage differentials greater than the number

1. Turner, op. cit., p. 120; B. Drake, *Women in Trade Unions* (1921), p. 27. For co-operative and friendly society membership distribution see Gosden, op. cit., pp. 29–30, and above, pp. 98–9.
2. On this point see below, pp. 348, 352.
3. This was a powerful influence, even more so in the nineteenth century than today. E. H. Phelps Brown and S. V. Hopkins have shown how the ratio between building labourers' and craftsmen's wages persisted with little change over five centuries ('Seven Centuries of Building Wages', *Economica*, N.S. xxii (1955), 202). With very few exceptions workers and unions were far more concerned to preserve traditional differentials between occupations than to break down traditional differentials between regions.
4. See above, p. 329.

organized might suggest.[1] It might be argued, with justification, that the same customary differentials which helped spread union gains among the unorganized also placed limits on the amount of gain and thus on union ability to increase spatial differentials. Employers were aware of the force and sanctity of occupational differentials and doubtless resisted union claims the more strongly when they felt that concessions would be followed by concessions to the remainder of their labour force. But the sanctity of traditional occupation differentials was also a powerful obstacle to those unions which made some attempt to erode spatial differentials. It was impossible to secure London rates in areas where most men received half or three-quarters of those rates without doing violence to occupational differentials. The union might nibble away at the regional differential over a long period, but any attempt to reduce the gap substantially was likely to increase the number of men prepared to work for less than the union rate; the alternatives were either to accept local market rates or set a higher rate and exclude the vast majority of potential members. Most unions, accordingly, tempered principle with expediency: the printers, for example, in 1867 tried, unsuccessfully, to enforce a national minimum—twenty-five years later they considered the minimum, 'not an imperative rule, but a standard to be aimed at'.[2] Other unions came to a similar conclusion:

Q. But does your Society not recognize that district rates differ from one another?

A. Yes.

1. It is interesting to consider how the influences described affect Turner's thesis that the early organization of the skilled and the exclusive character of their unions retarded union development among the majority of the working classes (Turner, op. cit., section 4, Ch. 1). Even if it is agreed that the 'labour aristocracy' retarded union growth among other classes it seems likely that it shared with them the benefits of organization. There were exceptions of course both to Turner's thesis and to the generalizations put forward above. Some craft unions, like the cotton spinners who organized the female operatives, deliberately fostered unionism among weaker workers to protect their own position. Some unions, and some influential individuals, did the same thing for more altruistic reasons, but there were few such examples before the advent of new unionism at the end of the 1880s.

2. A. E. Musson, *The Typographical Association*, pp. 191–2. The minimum was well below the rate paid in large towns but the union found expansion impossible in low-wage areas like the south of England unless the rule was waived.

Q. Why do you recognize them?

A. Because we cannot do anything else . . . our union is not strong enough to enforce the higher rates in those districts.[1]

In short, customary differentials imposed limits on the amount by which unions could either increase or diminish regional differentials, but whereas few unions made more than half-hearted attempts to erode regional differentials all tried to improve the pay and conditions of their members. Thus, whatever influence unions possessed was directed mainly against the obstacles that custom imposed to a widening of spatial differentials; at the same time the force of custom spread some of the benefits of unionism to unorganized workers in the same areas.

There were other restraints on union ability to influence differentials which should be included in an assessment of their importance relative to other forces in the labour market. A union might be too successful at raising wages where they were strong and thereby force capital to move, thus helping to erode regional differentials by pursuing a course which seemed likely to have exactly the opposite effect. The edge-tool trades which expanded in the west midlands at Sheffield's expense, mainly due to the 'tyranny' of the Sheffield unions, illustrate both the ability of unions to affect local wages and one limit to their power.[2] However there were not many such cases because the general correlation between high wages and high productivity, and the continuous increase in productivity, gave unions considerable scope to raise wages without fear of

1. Evidence of the general secretary of the United Pattern Makers Association to the *Royal Commission on Labour*, P.P. 1893–4, XXXII, para. 22459–60. See also *Report of the Fair Wages Committee*. P.P. 1908, XXXIV, pp. 13–14 and paras, 824–6 and 4369–74 of evidence. An alternative to forcing up pay in low-wage areas was to forgo increases or actually reduce rates in well-paid districts. But this course was unlikely to commend itself to most unions because not only did it openly allow capital to take what could easily go to labour, it also upset traditional occupational differentials and invited splinter movements. Even the threat of such action was likely to provoke opposition from the better-paid districts. See e.g. Musson, op. cit., pp. 376–7, and the cases mentioned above, p. 335 and below, p. 349.

2. Allen, *Birmingham and the Black Country*, p. 67. The same sort of pattern occurred in the Nottingham textile trades. Church, *Victorian Nottingham*, pp. 277, 299, 305.

precipitating industrial mobility.[1] At the same time low productivity imposed formidable obstacles to wage increases in
areas where wages were low and unions weak.[2]

These various points help to explain the general nature and
limitations of union ability to erode or consolidate regional
wage variations in the first of the two periods but they provide
no way of estimating its magnitude. We must be satisfied with
stating that the union influence on wages operated within
limits set by more powerful market forces; that it was nevertheless greater than might be suggested by the proportion of the
labour force in trade unions; and that it helped to strengthen
existing spatial differentials. The only significant exception to
these generalizations was agriculture which was noted earlier
as the one important occupation where unionism was strongest
in low-wage areas. Whatever influence the unions exercised
upon farm wages helped to erode regional differentials but
it could not have been substantial because unionism was insignificant except for a few years in the early 1870s. In these
years wages rose where the union was strong but, as is well
known, they rose by at least as much in the north of England
where the union had fewest members.[3]

1. The Sheffield unions wanted too much of both worlds: they forced up wages
   and resisted attempts to raise productivity. Allen, *Birmingham and the
   Black Country*, p. 67.
2. See e.g. union policy in relation to wages on the low-productivity Somerset
   and Forest of Dean coalfields above, pp. 16, 198.
3. See e.g. Hasbach, op. cit., pp. 277–84. The situation suggests that the
   influence of Arch's union was slight although not that it was non-existent
   because the strong hold of tradition upon farm wages provided scope for
   more union influence than in most other occupations. Doubtless some
   increases would not have been obtained without the union and there were
   probably also fewer irrational local variations by the time the union

Net out-migration as a proportion of the population at the beginning of
the decade in areas most affected by agricultural trade unionism between
1872 and 1874.

|         | Region 3 (rural south-east) | Norfolk | Suffolk |
|---------|-----------------------------|---------|---------|
| 1851–61 | 8·2 per cent | 12·0 per cent | 12·4 per cent |
| 1861–71 | 5·6 per cent | 10·3 per cent | 9·4 per cent |
| 1871–81 | 7·3 per cent | 9·5 per cent | 11·7 per cent |
| 1881–91 | 5·4 per cent | 10·1 per cent | 10·5 per cent |

*Sources:* As for Table 7–1.

# V

By the First World War the circumstances which placed the unions among the forces bolstering regional wage differentials were weaker; the unions were becoming, or were already, one of the influences responsible for the erosion of differentials. The changes which brought about this transformation affected not just the unions but the whole framework of industrial relations; there were few signs of them before 1890 and the transition was most rapid after 1910. The most obvious index of change was a fivefold increase in membership accompanied by a significant increase in the size of the average union; in 1888 unionists were outnumbered 3 to 1 by domestic servants, in 1914 nearly half of all adult male workers were organized.[1] In this expansion unionism tightened its grip on the traditional high-wage strongholds but at the same time spread geographically so that its influence was felt over far more of Britain.[2] Just as important as the magnitude of expansion was the form it took. In 1888 organization was the prerogative of the skilled: the expansion between then and the war, and particularly after 1910, embraced large numbers of unskilled and semi-skilled workers. Their qualities and aspirations dictated unionism of a novel kind. Where the craft unions were closed, exclusive, and conducive to the strengthening of wage differentials, both for

subsided. Perhaps the greatest and most enduring influence in this occupation arose from union encouragement of migration; it told farm labourers of opportunities in the north and overseas, arranged transport, and subsidized the cost of moving. However, although many were helped to move in this way they were not sufficient to leave any clear sign of the union's activity either upon the pattern of regional wage variations (see Ch. 1 above), upon the rate the farm labour force declined, (See Mitchell and Deane, op. cit., p. 60), or upon figures of net migration (see table, p. 344).

1. There were approximately 750,000 unionists in 1888 and 4,145,000 in 1914. This expansion was achieved without increase in the number of unions. Clegg, Fox, and Thompson, op. cit., p. 466; Mitchell and Deane, op. cit., pp. 60, 68.
2. See e.g. Phelps Brown, *Industrial Relations*, p. 331; E. J. Hobsbawm, 'General Labour Unions in Britain, 1889–1914', p. 140. Hobsbawm talks of general unions helping to organize areas like Devon and parts of the Midlands which had previously been neglected by unionism.

skill and between regions, the general and industrial unions were open, inclusive, and likely to exercise an erosive influence on differentials.[1]

The organization of the unskilled began in 1888 and continued in some measure until the end of the period. However, the expansion begun by the match-girls and dock workers was less of a watershed than once believed. The year 1889 was the most prosperous since 1873 and 'new unionism' had much in common with the short-lived expansion of the early 1870s. When the boom subsided in 1892 employers began to recover ground and in this retrenchment the least skilled unionists fared worse; the London dockers were among the first to succumb.[2] At the turn of the century coal, cotton, and the craftsmen still dominated the union world; substantial and enduring expansion among the unskilled came after 1900 and mainly after 1910.[3] The more egalitarian and centralized character of the new unions began with their members' lack of scarcity value. The craft unions represented a privileged minority; their mainstay was their members' skill and effective unionism depended upon keeping this skill in short supply, upon the exclusion of outsiders. The new unionists had few skills to defend and were threatened by blacklegs at every turn; in these circumstances orthodox unionism offered no solution. The remedy lay in the opposite direction—to include within the union as many as possible: if all were members then none could blackleg. Lacking scarcity the new unions aimed for solidarity, and the logic of the situation suggested that unions, like men, were

1. Their influence on the differential for skill was not marked before 1914 although after 1890 the differential was probably stable whereas in the previous fifty years it widened. Their failure to narrow this differential was, no doubt, due largely to the fact that the traditional unions shared in the rise of membership and dominated the expansion until 1910. In the long run union influence on the differential for skill was substantial. Hobsbawm, *Labouring Men*, p. 293; Turner, loc. cit.
2. Clegg, Fox, and Thompson, op. cit., Ch. 2.
3. Hosbawm distinguishes three stages in these developments: 'the old fashioned general unionism of 1889–92; the cautious, limited and conservative "sectional" unionism of 1892–1910; and the revolutionary urge for amalgamation, the industrial union or the articulated "general" organization of the modern Transport Workers, which arose out of the expansion of 1911–20' ('General Labour Unions in Britain, 1889–1914', p. 135).

stronger united than or their own—hence the enthusiasm for amalgamations and alliances which reached its furthest point in the Triple Alliance of 1914. The craftsmen's ability to regulate wages by exercising subtle pressure on labour supply had helped to preserve local autonomy and in some respects it acted as a substitute for executive control; but these remedies were not open to the unskilled. Accordingly, they looked more to their head offices and to Westminster, and from head office regional wage variations appeared both more obvious and more anomalous.

It was not only the structure of the new unions that made them more likely to put pressure upon regional wage variations—their priorities inclined them in the same direction. They were distinguished by egalitarian sentiment of a kind seldom in evidence before 1890 and which derived partly from their own status—under-privileged themselves, they felt a compassion for others similarly placed—and partly from the fact that they developed at a time when society as a whole was becoming more receptive to such attitudes and more sensitive to social inequality. These new attitudes were a consequence of many influences and events; they owed a great deal to the investigation into poverty and changes in education.[1] Educated men were more aware of privilege in any form, and they were more likely to challenge it, and to formulate remedies for its removal; they also had higher expectations. These trends were given further impetus by the revival of socialism. Few unionists rushed to embrace ideas that involved the wholesale transformation of society but the activists who did, and others outside the unions, were able to foster feelings of injustice and channel resentment in directions which led to demands for egalitarian solutions, most obviously in the widespread agitation for 'a living wage'. Socialism was also among the influences which encouraged mutual sympathy between men whose loyalty once extended little beyond their own trade and locality.

1. Booth's survey began to appear in 1889 and was widely imitated. On the influence of education see Phelps Brown, *Industrial Relations*, pp. 43–51, 334.

Against this background inequalities no greater than many which had existed for decades now give rise to demands that something be done, and in many cases it was the government that was expected to act. Often this was because remedy required legislation; it was also because the new unions were both highly centralized and relatively weak and so looked naturally to the government to give them what they could not win directly from their employers. Their demands were not unheeded; from about 1890 the flow of social welfare legislation quickened and after 1906 it increased again. There were two measures which influenced wage differentials directly by putting a floor under the lowest wage rates in areas where labour was most plentiful. The first of these was the 1891 Fair Wages Resolution, designed to prevent the award of government contracts to employers who paid 'unfair' rates. No national minima were set ('fair' rates were those paid by 'good' employers in the district), but like most steps towards central determination of wages the resolution was probably accompanied by some narrowing of regional differentials.[1] The Trade Boards Acts went a step further. The first of these, which set minimum rates in tailoring, chain making, box making, and the lace finishing trades, became operative only in 1913 and affected women's wages more than men's but their influence on wages is of some interest and has been better investigated than the effects of the Fair Wage Resolution. Tawney showed that the act regulating the tailoring trade had little effect in the north of England but raised wages in the low-wage south; and according to Bulkley the box-making industry was similarly affected.[2]

While the attitudes which have been described were most discernible among semi-skilled and unskilled workers they were also found among the old unions. In 1914 the old unions still

---

1. The 1908 report of the Fair Wage Committee considered the measure was working reasonably well and noted that local authorities had adopted similar measures. *Report of the Fair Wage Committee*, P.P. 1908, XXXIV, Report and Appendices VI and VII.
2. R. H. Tawney, *Minimum Rates in the Tailoring Industry*, pp. 69–71, 80–1; M. E. Bulkley, *Minimum Rates in the Boxmaking Industry*, see especially p. 89.

showed many signs of traditional attitudes[1] but there were also
signs of the changes which had come in with 'new unionism',
not least a blurring of the class divisions between the 'aristocracy' and the unskilled. There were already indications that
this gap would eventually diminish during the expansion at
the end of the 1880s; the help rendered the London dockers by
Tom Mann and John Burns is well known, and others followed
their example.[2] The change was especially marked among the
miners who were among the most receptive to socialist propa-
ganda; in 1888 unionism in the mines was weak and fragmented
but in that year the Miners' Federation of Great Britain was
formed and in 1893 it was engaged in a strike which involved
nearly four-fifths of all underground workers;[3] the 1908
Eight Hours Act opened the way for reconciliation between
the north-east and the rest of the industry and by 1912, thanks
to government assistance, the right to a national minimum wage
had been established. The miners were forced to accept greater
regional variations in the minimum than they would have liked
but there were several signs that spatial differentials were increasingly under challenge.[4]

The process whereby the old unions abandoned some of their
exclusive attitudes and extended the hand of friendship to the
'labour element' was not entirely of their own devising—to a
considerable extent the two were thrust together. New machines
and methods of workshop management obscured the old
distinctions by expanding the number of 'semi-skilled' workers
who fitted easily into neither of the traditional categories[5].
At the same time a new militancy was apparent among the

1. See e.g. Clegg, Fox, and Thompson, op. cit., p. 488. The National Union of
   Railwaymen had great difficulty in persuading craftsmen to abandon
   traditional regional differentials. P. S. Bagwell, *The Railwaymen* (1963),
   p. 425.
2. See e.g. Clegg, Fox, and Thompson, op. cit., pp. 57-8, 65, and Buckley's
   account of unionism in Aberdeen. K. D. Buckley, *Trade Unionism in Aberdeen, 1878-1900* (Edinburgh, 1955), pp. 33-9.
3. Rowe, *Wages in the Coal Industry*, pp. 35-6.
4. See e.g. Phelps Brown, *Industrial Relations*, pp. 324-8; Clegg, Fox, and
   Thompson, op. cit., p. 461; R. H. Campbell, *Scotland since 1707*, pp. 314-15;
   G. A. Phillips, 'The Triple Industrial Alliance in 1914', *Ec.H.R.*, 2nd Ser.,
   xxiv (1971), 61.
5. Phelps Brown, *Industrial Relations*, pp. 89-98.

employers; it began as a reaction to 'new unionism' but later extended to unionism in general.[1] The 'counter-attack' highlighted the mutual interests of those under attack and could hardly fail to promote a growth of working-class consciousness. The protracted lock-out of 1897 in the engineering industry and the employers' victory were milestones in these developments but the most significant event was the Taff Vale judgement in 1901—no measure could have been more effective in closing union ranks, reducing the gap which separated old unionism from new, and underlining the necessity for independent political representation.[2]

By 1914 the novel features which characterized 'new unionism' had spread throughout much of the union world. It is easy to exaggerate the changes that had occurred; they were still more evident among unions where the skilled were in a minority and were accepted far more readily by young skilled workers than by those whose attitudes were moulded before 1890.[3] But a great deal had happened in twenty-five years. Before 1890 unionism consisted of a privileged minority which furthered its own ends regardless of the interests of the majority of workers and sometimes at their expense; class consciousness existed but it was a divisive element. In 1914 these exclusive attitudes were much less in evidence. By then unionism embraced almost half of all male workers and, by means of the Labour Party, extended its concern and protection to those outside the unions who were generally most in need of assistance. The British working class and the working-class movement, long heralded, finally appeared sometime between 1890 and the First World War: one consequence of their creation was that towards the end of the period covered by this investigation the unions ceased to hinder, and began to hasten, the erosion of regional wage differentials.

1. For details and a general account of the 'counter-attack' see Clegg, Fox, and Thompson, op. cit., Chs. 2 and 4.
2. 'The Taff Vale Case created the Labour Party', G. D. H. Cole, *A Short History of the British Working Class Movement*, p. 291. For general accounts of the Taff Vale case and its affect on union attitudes see Clegg, Fox, and Thompson, op. cit., Ch. 8, and Phelps Brown, *Industrial Relations*. On the engineering lock-out see Clegg, Fox, and Thompson, op. cit., pp. 161–8.
3. See e.g. Phelps Brown, *Industrial Relations*, pp. 313, 319.

# VI

Trade unions were the most dynamic element in industrial relations but not the only element nor the only one that changed after 1890. Alongside the expansion of unionism there were similar developments on the employers' side with similar consequences on regional wage differentials. The size of the average firm had probably been increasing throughout the century but it grew faster after 1890[1] and large firms were both more likely to be aware of conditions throughout the labour market and more likely to raise the question of wage levels elsewhere during industrial bargaining. If they operated where wages were high they might resist unions' demands on this ground: if they knew that local rates were less than average they might more easily yield concessions. And when large companies acted in this fashion market forces would carry their influence throughout the areas where they operated.

In those cases where the increase in company size involved the acquisition of additional branches pressure on regional differentials was especially strong because different rates for the same job appeared more anomalous when the men worked for a single employer. The railway companies were among the first to be affected in this way: they were substantial employers long before 1890 and railway pay varied less between different regions than pay in most other occupations.[2] Doubtless this was partly because railwaymen were highly mobile and had ample opportunity to compare rates, but it probably also owed something to the fact that the companies occasionally met to discuss wage policy.[3] Some banks were in a similar position;

---

1. This was a consequence of new manufacturing methods, cheap money, company promoters, and the growing strength of trade unions. This feature is well established; see e.g. P. L. Payne, 'The Emergence of Large-scale Companies in Great Britain, 1870–1914', *Ec.H.R.*, 2nd Ser., xx (1967).
2. See above, p. 57.
3. P. W. Kingsford, 'Labour Relations on the Railways, 1835–75', *Journal of Transport History*, i (1953–4), 76.

several which had a large number of branches scattered throughout the country found it necessary to devise a policy on regional
differentials and means of coping with the problems that arose
when staff were transferred from one area to another.[1] The
government, the greatest individual employer of all, was perhaps
more aware than most employers of differences in pay and
possibly more amenable to their removal.[2] Its commitment to
'fair wages' in 1891, its general support for 'sweated' workers,
and measured sympathy for the doctrine of 'the living wage'
inclined it in the direction of uniform wage rates; local government was similarly affected.[3] In addition government employees
were perhaps more sensitive to regional differentials than most
other workers; postmen were demanding national standard
rates early in the 1890s,[4] the Association of Municipal Employees submitted a similar claim in 1905,[5] and shortly before
the war the National Union of Teachers began a vigorous
campaign for the establishment of a national scale.[6]

There was another development which helped to spread
some of the influence of these events to small companies and
industries that were little affected by industrial concentration.
This was the substantial expansion of employers' associations
that occurred mainly after 1890. The timing of this development
is partly explained by the growth of union strength and the
emergence of 'new' unions with their tendency to widen
disputes,[7] and partly by the conspicuous success of the relatively small number of joint boards of conciliation set up in the

1. H. Higgs, 'Workmen's Budgets', p. 265; see also Webbs, *Industrial Democracy*, p. 776.
2. The government imposed upper and lower limits on police pay which varied
less than pay in several other occupations. See above, pp. 57, 75–6.
3. Webbs, *Industrial Democracy*, p. 775, and see above, p. 460.
4. However, they were still agitating in 1914 and rates still varied substantially
over short distances: three scales were paid in different parts of Bristol
and seven in the London area. See Nat. Joint Committee of Postal and
Telegraph Assocs. correspondence. Webb Trade Union Collection, Coll. E.
Sect. B. CXIII. British Library of Political and Economic Science.
5. Clegg, Fox, and Thompson, op. cit., p. 361.
6. S. E. Barnes, 'Individual, Local and National Bargaining for Teachers'
Salaries in England and Wales, 1858–1944', Ph.D. thesis, University of
London (1959), pp. 81–131.
7. See above, pp. 346–7, and, for further details, Phelps Brown, *Industrial
Relations*, pp. 264–7, 341.

previous thirty years. Two influences made these examples
seem especially worthy of imitation in the 1890s: one was a
number of long and costly disputes in major industries;[1] the
other was the encouraging conclusion of the *Royal Commission
on Labour* which reported industrial relations at their best when
both sides were well organized and able to reach agreement by
an established procedure set up by themselves.[2] While the
development of employers' associations initially was largely a
response to union growth, once they were established employers
found that the widening of collective bargaining offered certain
advantages. In particular there was the fact that collective
settlements imposed equal labour costs on all competitors
within the bargaining area. This knowledge made employers
less reluctant to grant increases and provided a constant encouragement to widen the area of bargaining—a process almost
certain to diminish regional wage differentials. In some cases,
particularly where craftsmen were involved, it was the employers who set the pace, imposing increasingly centralized
bargaining upon unions whose long-established structure was
still geared to local bargaining. Before the lock-out of 1897–8
the engineering employers had no national association. In the
course of this dispute and its immediate aftermath an industry-
wide employers' organization was created which took the
initiative and forced the A.S.E. to participate in bargaining on
a wider scale.[3]

The pace of these developments varied from one industry to
another; in building for example, where the craft unions were
strong and employers had little to fear from competitors outside their locality, centralization occurred slowly.[4] The pace

1. Clegg, Fox, and Thompson, op. cit., p. 362.
2. Phelps Brown, *Industrial Relations*, p. 184. This finding also encouraged
   the Board of Trade to extend the practice whereby whenever it was invited
   to act as conciliator in a dispute it tried to persuade the two parties to set
   up a joint board (ibid., pp. 184–8, 338).
3. This development influenced wage negotiation less than negotiation on
   working conditions; wage negotiation was affected mainly at district level.
   On these points and the role of employers' organizations in the widening
   of the bargaining area see, Clegg, Fox, and Thompson, op. cit., pp. 161–8,
   341, 471 ff; Phelps Brown, *Industrial Relations*, pp. 123, 142, 161–3,
   359–60; Rowe, *Wages in Practice and Theory*, p. 135.
4. Clegg, Fox, and Thompson, op. cit., pp. 153, 354; Rowe, *Wages in Theory
   and Practice*, pp. 69, 145–6.

also varied according to the subject at issue. There were few obstacles to national bargaining over apprenticeship, manning arrangements, and similar matters but the very magnitude of regional wage variations at the end of the nineteenth century imposed limits on the rate of transition to central wage bargaining.[1] There was a general transition from local wage negotiations to district or regional bargaining but the extension to industry-wide collective bargaining began in earnest only just before the war at about the same time as the great expansion of unionism among the unskilled.[2] We might conclude therefore, although to do so means generalizing about a pattern which varied a great deal from trade to trade, that until about 1890 trade unions and the whole environment of industrial relations in Britain helped to sustain regional wage differentials, over the next two decades they exercised no clear influence in either direction, but by 1911 they were a force helping to reduce differentials.

1. Phelps Brown, *Industrial Relations*, p. 281.
2. I. G. Sharp has distinguished three phases in the development of conciliation and arbitration in Britain: in the first, between 1870 and 1900, negotiation was mainly on a local basis; in the second, which began at the end of the nineteenth century, negotiation was mainly at district level; the third phase, the development of negotiation on a national scale, began shortly before the war. I. G. Sharp, *Industrial Conciliation and Arbitration in Great Britain* (1950), p. 6. For other accounts and details of the process in particular industries see: Phelps Brown, *Industrial Relations*, pp. 145, 162, 358–9, 361–2; Turner, op. cit. (1952); Yates, op. cit., pp. 64–6; Rowe, *Wages in Practice and Theory*, Chs. 4, 7, and 8; Jefferys, *The Story of the Engineers*, pp. 153–4; Musson, op. cit., pp. 193, 376–9; Orwin and Felton, op. cit., pp. 250–1; Bagwell, op. cit., pp. 349, 380.

# APPENDIX TO CHAPTER NINE

### TABLE 9–1
### Distribution of Trade Unionists in England and Wales
### in 1892: Counties

| | Trade unionists per cent of population | | Trade unionists per cent of population |
|---|---|---|---|
| Northumberland | 11·23 | Kent | 1·69 |
| Durham | 11·21 | Cambridgeshire | 1·45 |
| Lancashire | 8·63 | Wiltshire | 1·44 |
| East Riding | 7·42 | Somerset | 1·29 |
| Leicestershire | 7·34 | Shropshire | 1·26 |
| Derbyshire | 6·82 | Norfolk | 1·06 |
| S. Wales and Monmouth | 6·70 | Hampshire | 0·96 |
| Nottinghamshire | 6·14 | Oxfordshire | 0·96 |
| West Riding | 5·73 | Devon | 0·95 |
| Gloucestershire | 4·74 | Essex | 0·85 |
| *England and Wales | 4·55 | Westmorland | 0·80 |
| Cheshire | 4·52 | Hertfordshire | 0·52 |
| Staffordshire | 4·49 | Sussex | 0·51 |
| Suffolk | 4·21 | Buckingham | 0·44 |
| Warwickshire | 4·19 | Berkshire | 0·36 |
| Northamptonshire | 3·96 | Herefordshire | 0·34 |
| Cumberland | 3·86 | Bedfordshire | 0·33 |
| London | 3·52 | Surrey | 0·26 |
| North Riding | 3·49 | Cornwall | 0·20 |
| Lincolnshire | 2·03 | Dorset | 0·16 |
| North Wales | 1·96 | Huntingdonshire | 0·04 |
| Worcestershire | 1·86 | Rutland | 0·00 |

*Source:* S. and B. Webb, *The History of Trade Unionism* pp. 741–3.

# SUMMARY AND CONCLUSIONS

The outstanding features of the pattern of spatial wage variations in Britain between 1850 and 1914 were the magnitude of the variations and their extraordinary persistence amid so much that made for change. Wage differentials reflected other spatial differentials which are easily overlooked in studies of the national economy, and in the course of examining the causes of wage differentials this investigation has thrown light upon several other aspects of the economic history of Britain after 1850; it has been shown, for example, that regional analysis of the labour market is a powerful antidote to overdoses of pessimism concerning the effect of industrialization on living standards and casts doubt both upon the view that nineteenth-century labour was relatively immobile and that Irish immigration was beneficial to the British economy. Another feature of the labour market which emerges prominently is the plight of the rural labourer of southern England and parts of Wales and northern Scotland—in this period there is no major occupational group more worthy of compassion.

The differences in male wage rates were not offset by compensating differentials in either the cost of living or family earnings; with regard to prices generalizations which assume a high degree of homogeneity in the economy are not far wide of the mark, except when they refer to rent, and differences in men's earnings were more often augmented than compensated by the earnings of their wives and children. The pattern of male wage differentials was largely a consequence of events in the eighteenth century and the first decades of the nineteenth. Perhaps the most powerful of the forces which sustained the pattern after 1850 was the nature of demand for labour which, for the most part, worked to maintain the advantages of already prosperous areas—capital was not drawn to low-wage areas in the fashion postulated by neo-classical general equilibrium theory. The diversity of regional experience in this respect raises questions about the appropriateness of terms like 'the Great Depression' and similar historical generalizations; the label may be entirely appropriate for the Black Country, but it is not easily attached to an area like south Wales, and while the Black Country had clearly experienced an 'industrial revolution' by 1880, there were many parts of the country still hardly more industrialized than they were two centuries earlier. The reason why employers continued to invest heavily in areas where the demand for labour was already substantial and wages high was that high wages were compensated by variations in productivity; changes in technology after 1750, and associated changes in the nature and importance of capital, management, and labour in the production process, broke down the positive relationship between wages and labour costs, so that, despite improving communications, the likelihood that large spatial wage variations would continue failed to diminish and probably increased.

Population growth was another influence which helped to account for the remarkable persistence of regional wage variations. Regional variations in labour supply were, directly or indirectly, almost entirely a consequence of migration—high birth-rates were commonplace both where labour was needed and where it was abundant, and their ubiquity helped to maintain wide disparities in regional prosperity. Internal migration, however, had quite different effects. There were variations in mobility between different groups of workers and between different areas, some of which helped sustain wage differentials, and it seems likely that railways made little contribution to the erosion of differentials before the last quarter of the century; but there is little evidence to support the view that nineteenth-century labour was relatively immobile. The extraordinarily slow reduction of differentials before 1914 was not due to low labour mobility, nor was their rapid erosion after 1914 a consequence of greater mobility.

13

Differentials remained because the market forces making for regional inequality were such that considerable mobility was required to prevent a widening of differentials. An examination of the effect of immigration and trades unionism adds a little more to the explanation of the persistence of differentials. Neither Irish nor alien immigration did much to reduce differentials, and Irish immigration probably helped sustain them; and while the trade unions played an important part in the erosion of differentials after 1900, for most of the previous half-century their influence was in the opposite direction.

Differentials were considerably greater in 1850 than they were sixty years later, but until the First World War what was remarkable was how slowly change occurred. Rapid change commenced with the war and continued after 1918;[1] the accelerated decline of differentials was due to the introduction of one new force in the labour market and changes in the nature of several others. The new force was inflation. By 1910 prices had begun to rise steadily; during the war money wages more than doubled, and the practice of awarding across-the-board cost of living increases left regional differentials intact in money terms but proportionately much reduced.[2] But inflation could not have had the effect it did without changes in the economic forces responsible for the persistence of wide differentials in the previous half-century. Some of these changes began before the war and have already been indicated. There was, for instance, the change in trade

1. For some indication of the extent of this change see L. G. Reynolds and C. H. Taft, *The Evolution of Wage Structure* (New Haven, Conn., 1956), pp. 278–80. The best general accounts of changes in differentials after 1914 are probably those of J. W. F. Rowe, *Wages in Practice and Theory*, and H. A. Turner, 'Trade Unions, Differentials and the Levelling of Wages'. See also A. L. Bowley, *Prices and Wages in the United Kingdom, 1914–1920*, and, for details of change in the engineering and printing trades, M. L. Yates, *Wages and Labour Conditions in British Engineering*, and A. E. Musson, *The Typographical Association*.

2. The differentials for skill and sex were similarly affected; for example, shortly after the war it was agreed that building labourers, who were traditionally paid about two-thirds as much as craftsmen, should henceforth receive at least three-quarters of the craftsmen's rate. Rowe, *Wages in Practice and Theory*, p. 161.

union influence—whereas in the second half of the nineteenth century collective bargaining bolstered the existing pattern of wide differentials, after 1911 its influence was more as we would expect it. By 1900 there were also indications of change in the spatial pattern of demand for labour; the relative decline of employment prospects in the rural south was coming to an end and the attractions of the great urban manufacturing centres appeared less compelling. After 1918 more drastic change occurred, bringing heavy unemployment to several of the regions where demand for labour had been most buoyant in the second half of the nineteenth century. Finally there was the fall in the birth-rate; this began to affect the labour market after 1914, and although mobility itself was no higher after the war the fall in birth-rate increased its effectiveness.

# SELECT BIBLIOGRAPHY

Abbreviations used are those shown above. Those books with no indicated place of publication were published in London.

## A. Books, Articles, and all other sources except British Government Publications

ACLAND, T. D., 'On the Farming of Somersetshire', *J.R.Ag.S.*, xi (1850).

ADAMS, D. R., 'Some Evidence on British and American Wage Rates, 1790–1830', *J.E.H.*, xxx (1970).

ALEXANDER, D. G., *Retailing in England during the Industrial Revolution* (1970).

ALLEN, G. C., *The Industrial Development of Birmingham and the Black Country, 1860–1927* (1929).

ARCH, J., *Joseph Arch: The Story of his Life* (1898).

ASHBY, J. and KING, B., 'Statistics of some Midland Villages', *Economic Journal*, iii (1893).

ASHBY, M. K., *Joseph Ashby of Tysoe, 1859–1919* (Cambridge, 1961).

ASHWORTH, C., 'Hosiery Manufacture', in *V.C.H. Leicestershire*, IV (1958).

ASHWORTH, W., 'Changes in the Industrial Structure 1870–1914', *Yks. Bull.*, xvii (1965).

BAGWELL, P. S., *The Railwaymen* (1963).

BARKER, T. C., and HARRIS, J. R., *A Merseyside Town in the Industrial Revolution, St. Helens 1750–1900* (1959).

——, McKENZIE, J. C., and YUDKIN, J. (eds.), *Our Changing Fare* (1966).

BARNES, S. E., 'Individual, Local and National Bargaining for Teachers' Salaries in England and Wales, 1858–1944', Ph.D. thesis, Univ. of London (1959).

BARTON, D. M., 'The Course of Women's Wages', *J.R.S.S.*, lxxxii (1919).

BAXTER, R. D., 'Railway Extension and its Results', *J.R.S.S.*, xxix (1866).

BECK, G. A. (ed.), *The English Catholics, 1850–1950* (1950).

BELLAMY, J., 'Occupations in Kingston upon Hull, 1841–1948', *Yks. Bull.*, iv (1952).

——, 'A Note on Occupational Statistics in British Censuses', *Pop. Stud.*, vi (1952–3).

BELLERBY, J. R., 'Distribution of Farm Income in the U.K., 1867–1938', *Procs. of the Agricultural Economics Society*, x (1953).

BLACK, C. (ed.), *Married Women's Work* (1915).

BLACKMAN, J., 'The Development of the Retail Grocery Trade in the Nineteenth Century', *Business History*, ix (1967).

BLAUG, M., 'The Myth of the Old Poor Law and the Making of the New', *J.E.H.*, xxiii (1963).

——, 'The Poor Law Report Reexamined', *J.E.H.*, xxiv (1964).

BOOTH, C., 'Occupations of the People of the United Kingdon, 1801–81', *J.R.S.S.*, xlix (1886).

—— (ed.), *Life and Labour of the People in London* (1902–3 edn.).

BORTS, G. H., 'The Equalization of Returns and Regional Economic Growth', *American Economic Review*, 1 (1960).

—— and STEIN, J. L., *Economic Growth in a Free Market* (New York, 1964).

BOSANQUET, H. (ed.), *Social Conditions in Provincial Towns* (1912).

BOWLEY, A. L., 'The Statistics of Wages in the United Kingdom during the Last Hundred Years: Parts I and II, Agricultural Wages; Parts VI, VII, VIII, Wages in the Building Trades; Part IX, Wages in the Worsted and Woollen Manufactures of the West Riding of Yorkshire', *J.R.S.S.*, lxi (1898), lxii (1899), lxiii (1900), lxiv (1901), lxv (1902).

——, *Wages in the United Kingdom in the Nineteenth Century* (Cambridge, 1900).

——, 'Rural Population in England and Wales', *J.R.S.S.*, lxxvii (1914).

——, *Prices and Wages in the United Kingdom, 1914–1920* (Oxford, 1921).

BRASSEY, T., *Lectures on the Labour Question* (1878).

——, *Work and Wages* (1916).

BREMNER, D., *The Industries of Scotland* (Edinburgh, 1869).

Bricklayers: Operative Bricklayers Society, Annual Reports from 1862. Library of the Amalgamated Union of Building Trade Workers, Clapham.

BRIGGS, A., 'Social History since 1815', in *V.C.H. Warwickshire*, vii (1964).

—— and SAVILLE, J. (eds.), *Essays in Labour History* (1960).

BROUDE, H. W., 'The Significance of Regional Studies for the Elaboration of National Economic History', *J.E.H.*, xx (1960).

BROWN, E. H. PHELPS, *The Growth of British Industrial Relations: A Study from the Standpoint of 1906–14* (1959).

—— and HART, P. E., 'The Share of Wages in the National Income', *Economic Journal*, lxii (1952).

—— and HOPKINS S. V., 'Seven Centuries of Building Wages', *Economica*, N.S. xxii (1955).

——and HOPKINS, S. V., 'Seven Centuries of the Prices of Consumables, compared with Builders' Wage-Rates', *Economica*, N.S. xxiii (1956).

BROWN, A. J. Y., see A. J. Youngson Brown.

BROWN, L. M., 'Modern Hull', in *V.C.H. Yorkshire: East Riding*, i (1969).

BUCKATZSCH, E. J., 'The Constancy of Local Populations and Migration in England before 1800', *Pop. Stud.*, v (1951–2).

BUCKLEY, K. D., *Trade Unionism in Aberdeen, 1878–1900* (Edinburgh, 1955).

BULKLEY, M. E., *Minimum Rates in the Boxmaking Industry* (1915).

BULLEY, A. A. and WHITLEY, M., *Women's Work* (1894).

BURNETT, J., *Plenty and Want: A Social History of Diet in England from 1815 to the Present Day* (1966).

BUTLER, C. V. in BOSANQUET, H. (ed.), *Social Conditions in Provincial Towns* (1912).

BYTHELL, D., *The Handloom Weavers* (Cambridge, 1969).

CADBURY, E., MATHESON, M. C., and SHANN, G., *Women's Work and Wages* (1906).

CAIRD, J., *English Agriculture in 1850–51* (1852).

CAIRNCROSS, A. K., *Home and Foreign Investment 1870–1913* (Cambridge, 1953).

—— (ed.), *The Scottish Economy* (Cambridge, 1954).

——, in R. Miller, and J. Tivy, (eds.), *The Glasgow Region* (Glasgow, 1958).

CAMPBELL, R. H., *Scotland since 1707: The Rise of an Industrial Society* (Oxford, 1965).

CARRIER, N. H., and JEFFERY, J. R., *External Migration: A Study of the Available Statistics 1815–1950* (1953).

CARROTHERS, W. A., *Emigration from the British Isles* (1929).

CHADWICK, D., 'On the Rate of Wages in Manchester and Salford and the Manufacturing Districts of Lancashire, 1839–59', *J.R.S.S.*, xxiii (1860).

CHALONER, W. H., *The Social and Economic Development of Crewe, 1780–1923* (Manchester, 1950).

CHARLES, E., and MOSHINSKY, P., in L. Hogben, (ed.), *Political Arithmetic* (1938).

CHECKLAND, S. G., *The Rise of Industrial Society in England, 1815–1885* (1964).

CHURCH, R. A., 'Technological Change and the Hosiery Board of Conciliation and Arbitration 1860–84', *Yks. Bull.*, xv (1963).

——, *Economic and Social Change in a Midland Town: Victorian Nottingham, 1815–1900* (1966).

CLAPHAM, J. H., 'The Transference of the Worsted Industry from Norfolk to the West Riding', *Economic Journal*, xx (1910).

——, 'Irish Immigration into Great Britain in the Nineteenth Century', *Bull. of the International Committee of Historical Sciences*, v (1933).

CLEGG, H. A., FOX, A., and THOMPSON, A. F., *A History of British Trade Unions since 1889*, i (Oxford, 1964).

CLEMENTS, R. V., 'Trade Unions and Emigration, 1840–80', *Pop. Stud.*, ix (1955–6).

CLIFFORD, F., *The Agricultural Lock-out of 1874* (Edinburgh and London, 1875).

——, 'The Labour Bill in Farming', *J.R.Ag.S.*, 2nd Ser., xi (1875).

COLE, G. D. H., *A Short History of the British Working Class Movement* (1948).

COLEMAN, D. C., 'Growth and Decay during the Industrial Revolution: The Case of East Anglia', *Scandinavian Economic History Review*, x (1962).

——, *Courtaulds: An Economic and Social History*, 2 vols. (Oxford, 1969).

COLEMAN, T., *The Railway Navvies* (1968 edn.).

COLLET, C., 'Women's Work in Leeds', *Economic Journal*, i (1891).

COLLINS, E. J. T., 'Harvest Technology and Labour Supply in Britain, 1790–1870', Ph.D. thesis, Univ. of Nottingham (1970).

CONSTANT, A., 'The Geographical Background of Inter-Village Population Movements in Northamptonshire and Huntingdonshire, 1754–1943', *Geography*, xxxiii (1948).

CORNWALL, J., 'Evidence of Population Mobility in the Seventeenth Century', *Bulletin of the Institute of Historical Research*, xl (1967).

DALZIEL, A., *The Colliers' Strike in South Wales* (Cardiff, 1872).

DARBY, H. C., 'The Movement of Population to and from Cambridgeshire between 1851 and 1861', *Geographical Journal*, ci (1943).

DAVIDOFF, L., 'The Employment of Married Women in England 1850–1950', M.A. thesis, Univ. of London (1956).

DAVIES, D. J. 'The Condition of the Rural Population in England and Wales, 1870–1928', Ph.D. thesis, Univ. of Wales (1931).

DAVIES, M. F., *Life in an English Village* (1909).

DAVIES, V. C., 'Some Geographical Aspects of the Decline in the Rural Population of Wales', *J. Merioneth Historical and Record Society*, ii (1953–6).

——, 'Some Geographical Aspects of the Depopulation of Rural Wales since 1841', Ph.D. thesis, Univ. of London (1955).

DAY, C., 'The Distribution of Industrial Occupations in England, 1841–61', *Trans. Connecticut Academy of Arts and Sciences*, xxviii (1927).

DEANE, P., and COLE, W. A., *British Economic Growth 1688–1959* (Cambridge, 1962).

DENVIR, J., *The Irish in Britain* (1892).

DODD, A. H., *The Industrial Revolution in North Wales* (Cardiff, 1933).

DODD, G., *The Food of London* (1856).

DONY, J. G., *A History of the Straw Hat Trade* (Luton, 1942).

DRAGE, G., 'Alien Immigration', *J.R.S.S.*, lviii (1895).

DRAKE, B., *Women in Trade Unions* (1921).

DRUCE, S. B. L., 'The Alteration in the Distribution of the Agricultural Population of England and Wales', *J.R.Ag.S.*, 2nd Ser., xxi (1885).

DUNCAN, R., 'Case Studies in Emigration: Cornwall, Gloucestershire and New South Wales, 1877–1886', *Ec.H.R.*, 2nd Ser., xvi (1963–4).

DUNLOP, J. C., 'The Fertility of Marriage in Scotland', *J.R.S.S.*, lxxvii (1914).

DYOS, H. J., 'The Suburban Development of Greater London south of the Thames', Ph.D. thesis, Univ. of London (1952).

EASTERLIN, R. A., 'Regional Income Trends, 1840–1950' in S. E. Harris (ed.), *American Economic History* (New York, 1961).

EDWARDS, J. K., 'Communications and the Economic Development of Norwich, 1750–1850', *Journal of Transport History*, vii (1965).

EDWARDS, K. C. (ed.), *Nottingham and its Region* (Nottingham, 1966).

ERICKSON, C. J., 'The Encouragement of Emigration by British Trade Unions 1850–1900', *Pop. Stud.*, iii (1949–50).

——, 'Who were the English and Scots Emigrants to the United States in the late-Nineteenth Century?' in D. V. Glass and R. Revelle (eds.), *Population and Social Change* (1972).

EVANS, G. E., *Ask the Fellows who Cut the Hay* (1965 edn.).

EVERSLEY, D. E. C., 'Industry and Trade, 1500–1880', in *V.C.H. Warwickshire* VII (1964).

Lord EVERSLEY, 'The Decline in Number of Agricultural Labourers in Great Britain', *J.R.S.S.*, lxx (1907).

FOX, A. WILSON, 'Agricultural Wages in England and Wales during the last Fifty Years', *J.R.S.S.*, lxvi (1903).

FREEMAN, C., *Luton and the Hat Industry* (Luton, 1953).

FRIEDLANDER, D. and ROSHIER, R. J., 'Internal Migration in England and Wales, Part I', *Pop. Stud.*, xix (1965–6).

FUSSELL, G. E., and K. R., *The English Countrywoman* (1953).

GARRARD, J. A., *The English and Immigration* (Oxford, 1971).

GARTNER, L. P., *The Jewish Immigrant in England 1870–1914* (Detroit, 1960).

GILBOY, E. W., *Wages in Eighteenth Century England* (Cambridge, Mass., 1934).

GILFILLAN, J. G. S. and MOISLEY, H. A. in R. Miller and J. Tivy (eds.), *The Glasgow Region* (Glasgow, 1958).

GLASS, D. V. in L. Hogben (ed.), *Political Arithmetic* (1938).

——, *Population Policies and Movements in Europe* (Oxford, 1940).

——, 'A Note on the Under-Registration of Births in Britain in the Nineteenth Century', *Pop. Stud.*, v (1951–2).

—— (ed.), *Introduction to Malthus* (1953).

GLASS, R. (ed.), *London: Aspects of Change* (1964).

GOLLANCZ, V. (ed.), *The Making of Women* (1918).

GOSDEN, P. H. J. H., *The Friendly Societies in England, 1815–75* (Manchester, 1961).

GRAHAM, P. A., *The Rural Exodus* (1892).

GRAY, M., *The Highland Economy, 1750–1850* (Edinburgh, 1957).

GULVIN, C., 'Wages and Conditions in the Border Woollen Industry about 1890', *Trans. Hawick Archaeological Society* (1967).

GUPTA, P. S., 'Railway Trade Unionism in Britain, c. 1880–1900', *Ec.H.R.*, 2nd Ser., xix (1966).

GWYNN, D., 'The Irish Immigration' in G. A. Beck (ed.), *The English Catholics 1850–1950* (1950).

HALL, P. G., *The Industries of London since 1861* (1962).

HAMMOND, J. L., and B., *The Village Labourer* (1966 edn.).

HANDLEY, J. E., *The Irish in Scotland, 1798–1845* (Cork, 1943).

——, *The Irish in Modern Scotland* (Cork, 1947).

HARE, A. E. C., 'Labour Migration. A Study of the Mobility of Labour', Ph.D. thesis, Univ. of London (1933).

HASBACH, W., *A History of the English Agricultural Labourer* (1908 edn.).

HAWKE, G. R., *Railways and Economic Growth in England and Wales, 1840–70* (Oxford, 1970).

HEADS, J., 'The Internal Migration of Population in England and Wales 1851–1911', M.Sc. thesis, Univ. of Cambridge (1955).

HEATH, F. G., *The English Peasantry* (1874).

HENDERSON, W. O., *The Lancashire Cotton Famine, 1861–1865* (Manchester, 1934).

HEWITT, M., *Wives and Mothers in Victorian Industry* (1958).

HIGGS, H., 'Workmen's Budgets', *J.R.S.S.*, lvi (1893).

HILL, A. B., Internal Migration and its Effects upon the Death Rate., *Medical Research Council Reports* No. 95 (1925).

HIRSCHMAN, A. O., *The Strategy of Economic Development* (New Haven, 1958).

HOBSBAWM, E. J., 'General Labour Unions in Britain, 1889–1914', *Ec.H.R.*, 2nd Ser., i (1949).

——, 'Custom, Wages and Workload' in A. Briggs and J. Saville (eds.), *Essays in Labour History* (1960).

——, *Labouring Men* (1964).

——, 'The Nineteenth Century London Labour Market', in R. Glass (ed.), *London: Aspects of Change* (1964).

—— and RUDÉ, G., *Captain Swing* (1969).

HOGBEN, L. (ed.), *Political Arithmetic* (1938).

HOOKER, R. H., 'On the Relation between Wages and the Numbers Employed in the Coal Mining Industry', *J.R.S.S.*, lvii (1894).

HOUSE, J. W., *Rural North East England 1951–61*, Papers on Migration and Mobility in North East England No. 1 (Newcastle, 1965).

HOUSTON, G., 'Farm Wages in Central Scotland from 1814 to 1870', *J.R.S.S.*, Ser. A, cxviii (1955).

——, 'Labour Relations in Scottish Agriculture before 1870', *Agricultural History Review*, vi (1958).

HUNT, E. H., 'Labour Productivity in England Agriculture, 1850–1914', *Ec.H.R.*, 2nd Ser., xx (1967).

HUNTER, L. C., and REID, G. L., *Urban Worker Mobility* (Paris, 1968, O.E.C.D.).

HUTCHINS, B. L., 'Statistics of Women's Life and Employment', *J.R.S.S.*, lxxii (1909).

——, and HARRISON, A., *A History of Factory Legislation* (1903).

INNES, M. R. H., 'Chelmsford: The Evolution of a County Town', M.A. thesis, Univ. of London (1951).

JACKSON, J. A., *The Irish in Britain* (1963).

JEFFERYS, J. B., *The Story of the Engineers* (1946).

——, *Retail Trading in Britain, 1850–1950* (Cambridge, 1954).

JEVONS, H. S., *The British Coal Trade* (1915).

JEWKES, J., and CAMPION, H., 'The Mobility of Labour in the Cotton Industry', *Economic Journal*, xxxviii (1928).

JOHN, A. H., *The Industrial Development of South Wales, 1750–1850* (Cardiff, 1950).

JONES, G. STEDMAN, *Outcast London* (Oxford, 1971).

KEBBEL, T. E., *The Agricultural Labourer. A Short Summary of his Position* (1893 edn.).

KERR, B., 'Irish Seasonal Migration to Great Britain, 1800–1838', *Irish Historical Studies*, iii (1942–3).
——, 'The Dorset Agricultural Labourer, 1750–1850', *Procs. Dorset Natural History and Archaeological Society*, lxxxiv (1962).
KINDLEBERGER, C. P., *Europe's Postwar Growth: The Role of Labour Supply* (Cambridge, Mass., 1967).
KINGSFORD, P. W., 'Labour Relations on the Railways, 1835–75', *Journal of Transport History*, i (1953–4).
KNOWLES, K. G. J. C., and ROBERTSON, D. J., 'Differences between the Wages of Skilled and Unskilled Workers, 1880–1950', *Bulletin of the Oxford University Institute of Statistics*, xiii (1951).
LANDES, D. S. in H. J. Habakkuk and M. M. Postan (eds.), *Cambridge Economic History of Europe* (Cambridge 1965), vi, Part I, Ch. 5.
LAWRENCE, F. W., *Local Variations in Wages* (1899).
LAWTON, R., 'Population Migration into and from Warwickshire and Staffordshire, 1841–1901', M.A. thesis, Univ. of Liverpool (1950).
——, 'Irish Immigration to England and Wales in the Mid-Nineteenth Century', *Irish Geography*, iv (1959).
LEE, C. H., *Regional Economic Growth in the United Kingdom since the Eighteen Eighties* (1971).
LEIBENSTEIN, H., 'The Theory of Under-employment in Backward Economies', *Journal of Political Economy*, lxv (1957).
LENNARD, R. V., *Economic Notes on English Agricultural Wages* (1914).
LEPPINGTON, C. H. d'E., 'Sidelights of the Sweating Commission', *Westminister Review*, cxxxvi (1891).
LERNER, S. W., 'The Impact of the Jewish Immigration of 1880–1914 on the London Clothing Industry and Trade Unions', *Bulletin of the Society for the Study of Labour History*, xii (1966).
LIPMAN, V. D., *Social History of the Jews in England 1850–1950* (1954).
*Liverpool Economic and Statistical Society* 'How the Casual Labourer Lives' (Liverpool, 1909).
LONGSTAFF, G. B., 'Rural Depopulation', *J.R.S.S.*, lvi (1893).
LYTHE, S. G. E., 'Shipbuilding at Dundee down to 1914', *Scottish Journal of Political Economy*, ix (1962).
MCCONNELL, P., 'Experiences of a Scotsman on the Essex Clays', *J.R.Ag.S.*, 3rd Ser., ii (1891).
MACDONALD, D. F., *Scotland's Shifting Population 1770–1850* (Glasgow, 1937).
MCKINLEY, R. A., and SMITH, C. T., 'Social and Administrative History since 1835', in *V.C.H. Leicestershire*, iv (1958).
MADDEN, M., 'The National Union of Agricultural Workers', B.Litt. thesis, Univ. of Oxford (1957).
MAKOWER, H., MARSHAK, J., and ROBINSON, H. W., 'Studies in Mobility of Labour: A Tentative Statistical Measure', *Oxford Economic Papers*, i (1938).
——, 'Studies in Mobility of Labour: Analysis for Great Britain Part I', *Oxford Economic Papers*, ii (1939).
——, 'Studies in Mobility of Labour: Analysis for Great Britain Part II', *Oxford Economic Papers*, iv (1940).
MANN, H. H., 'Life in an Agricultural Village in England', *Sociological Papers*, i (1904).
MARSHALL, J. D., 'The Lancashire Rural Labourer in the Early Nineteenth Century', *Trans. Lancashire and Cheshire Antiquarian Society*, lxxi (1961).
MARTIN, J. P., and WILSON, G., *The Police: A Study in Manpower* (1969).
MARWICK, W. H., *Economic Developments in Victorian Scotland* (1936).
——, *Scotland in Modern Times* (1964).
MATHIAS, P., *Retailing Revolution* (1967).

MAYHEW, H., *London Labour and the London Poor* (1861–2).

MILLER, R., and TIVY, J. (eds.), *The Glasgow Region* (Glasgow, 1958).

MITCHELL, B. R., 'The Economic Development of the Inland Coalfields 1870–1914', Ph.D. thesis, Univ. of Cambridge (1955).

——, 'The Coming of the Railway and United Kingdom Economic Growth', *J.E.H.*, xxiv (1964).

—— and DEANE, P., *Abstract of British Historical Statistics* (Cambridge, 1962).

MOLLAND, R., and EVANS, G., 'Scottish Farm Wages from 1870 to 1900', *J.R.S.S.*, Ser. A, cxiii (1950).

MOLLAND, R., 'Agriculture 1793–1870', in *V.C.H. Wiltshire*, iv (1959).

*Morning Chronicle* Survey of 'Labour and the Poor', published by the *Morning Chronicle*, commenced Oct. 1949.

MORRIS, J. H., and WILLIAMS, L. J., 'The Discharge Note in the South Wales Coal Industry, 1841–98', *Ec.H.R.*, 2nd Ser., x (1957).

——, *The South Wales Coal Industry, 1841–75* (Cardiff, 1958).

MOUNFIELD, P. R., 'The Location of Footwear Manufacture in England and Wales', Ph.D. thesis, Univ. of Nottingham (1962).

MUSSON, A. E., *The Typographical Association* (1954).

MYRDAL, G., *Economic Theory and Under-Developed Regions* (1957).

NEWTON, M. P., and JEFFERY, J. R., *Internal Migration* (1951).

NOWELL-SMITH, S. (ed.), *Edwardian England, 1901–4* (1964).

ODDY, D. J., 'The Working Class Diet, 1886–1914', Ph.D. thesis, Univ. of London (1971).

O.E.C.D. *Wages and Labour Mobility* (Supplement No. 1) (Paris, 1966).

O.E.C.D. *Urban Worker Mobility* by L. C. Hunter and G. L. Reid (Paris, 1968).

OGLE, W., 'The Alleged Depopulation of the Rural Districts of England', *J.R.S.S.*, lii (1889).

OKUN, B., and RICHARDSON, R. W., 'Regional Income Inequality and Internal Population Migration', *Economic Development and Cultural Change*, ix (1961).

Operative Bricklayers Society. Annual Reports from 1862. Library of the Amalgamated Union of Building Trade Workers, Clapham.

ORWIN, C. S., and FELTON, B. I., 'A Century of Wages and Earnings in Agriculture', *J.R.Ag.S.*, xcii (1931).

OSBORNE, R. H., 'Internal Migration in England and Wales, 1951', *Advancement of Science*, xii (1955–6).

——, 'The Movements of People in Scotland, 1851–1951', *Scottish Studies*, ii (1958).

——, 'Population and Settlement', in K. C. Edwards (ed.), *Nottingham and its Region* (Nottingham, 1966).

PELLING, H. M., *A History of British Trade Unionism* (1963).

PERLOFF, H. S., DUNN, E. S., LAMPARD, E. E., and MUTH, R. F., *Regions, Resources and Economic Growth* (Baltimore, Md., 1960).

PIGOU, A. C., 'A Minimum Wage for Agriculture', *The Nineteenth Century and After*, lxxiv (1913).

PINCHBECK, I., *Women Workers and the Industrial Revolution, 1750–1850* (1930).

POLLARD, S., 'The Decline of Shipbuilding on the Thames', *Ec.H.R.*, 2nd Ser., iii (1950–1).

——, 'Wages and Earnings in the Sheffield Trades, 1851–1914', *Yks. Bull.*, vi (1954).

——, *A History of Labour in Sheffield* (Liverpool, 1959).

——, *The Genesis of Modern Management* (1968 edn.).

POLLARD-URQUHART, W., 'Condition of the Irish Labourers in the East of London', *Trans. National Association for the Promotion of the Social Sciences* (1862).

POSTGATE, R. W., *The Builder's History* (1923).

PREST, J. M., *The Industrial Revolution in Coventry* (Oxford, 1960).

PURDY, F., 'On the Earnings of Agricultural Labourers in England and Wales, 1860', *J.R.S.S.*, xxiv (1861).

——, 'On the Earnings of Agricultural Labourers in Scotland and Ireland', *J.R.S.S.*, xxv (1862).

RATHBONE, E. F., 'The Remuneration of Women's Services' in V. Gollancz (ed.), *The Making of Women* (1918).

RAVENSTEIN, E. G., 'The Laws of Migration', *J.R.S.S.*, xlviii (1885); lii (1889).

READ, C. S., 'On the Farming of South Wales', *J.R.Ag.S.*, x (1849).

REDFORD, A., *Labour Migration in England, 1800–50* (Manchester, 1964 edn.).

REYNOLDS, L. G., and TAFT, C. H., *The Evolution of Wage Structure* (New Haven, Conn., 1956).

RICHARDSON, C., 'Irish Settlement in mid-Nineteenth Century Bradford', *Yks. Bull.*, xx (1968).

RICHARDSON, H. W., *Regional Economics: Location Theory, Urban Structure and Regional Change* (1969).

RIMMER, W. G., 'Leeds and its Industrial Growth: 4 The Working Force', *Leeds Journal*, xxv (1954).

ROBERTS, B. C., *The Trades Union Congress, 1868–1921* (1958).

—— and SMITH, J. H. (eds.), *Manpower Policy and Employment Trends* (1966).

ROBERTSON, D. J. in A. K. Cairncross (ed.), *The Scottish Economy* (Cambridge, 1954).

ROGERS, E., 'The History of Trade Unionism in the Coal Mining Industry of North Wales', *Trans. Denbighshire Historical Soc.*, xii–xvii (1963–8).

ROLLIN, A. R., 'The Jewish Contribution to the British Textile Industry', *Trans. Jewish Historical Society of England*, xvii (1951–2).

DE ROUSIERS, P., *The Labour Question in Britain* (1896).

ROWE, J. W. F., *Wages in the Coal Industry* (1923).

——, *Wages in Practice and Theory* (1928).

ROWNTREE, B. S., *Poverty. A Study of Town Life* (1908 edn.).

—— and KENDALL, M., *How the Labourer Lives* (1913).

RUSSELL, C., and LEWIS, H. S., *The Jew in London* (1900).

RUSSELL, R. C., *The Revolt of the Field in Lincolnshire* (Boston, Lincs., 1956).

SAVILLE, J., *Rural Depopulation in England and Wales 1851–1951* (1957).

SHANNON, H. A., 'Migration and the Growth of London, 1841–91', *Ec.H.R.*, v (1934–5).

SHARP, I. G., *Industrial Conciliation and Arbitration in Great Britain* (1950).

SHEPPARD, J. A., 'East Yorkshire's Agricultural Labour Force in the mid-Nineteenth Century', *Agricultural History Review*, ix (1961).

SHEPPERSON, W. S., *British Emigration to North America* (Oxford, 1957).

SHORTER, A. H., 'The Historical Geography of Manufacturing Industry in the South-west of England in the Nineteenth Century', M.A. thesis, Univ. of Manchester (1948).

SHRIMPTON, W., *Notes on a Decayed Needleland* (Redditch, 1897).

SMART, W., *Women's Wages* (Glasgow, 1892).

SMITH, A., *The Wealth of Nations*, ed. E. Cannan (1950 edn.).

SMITH, B. M. D., 'Industry and Trade, 1880–1960', in *V.C.H. Warwichshire*, vii (1964).

SMITH, C. T., 'The Movement of Population in England and Wales in 1851 and 1861', *Geographical Journal*, cxvii (1951).

SPRINGALL, L. M., *Labouring Life in Norfolk Villages, 1834–1914* (1936).

STRANGE, J., 'On the Money Rate of Wages of Labour in Glasgow and the West of Scotland', *J.R.S.S.*, xx (1857).

TAWNEY, R. H., *Minimum Rates in the Tailoring Industry* (1915).

TAYLOR, A. J., 'The Miners Association of Great Britain and Ireland, 1842–8: A Study in the Problem of Integration', *Economica*, xxii (1955).

THOMAS, B., 'The Migration of Labour into the Glamorganshire Coalfield', *Economica*, x, (1930).

——, 'Studies in Labour Supply and Labour Costs', Ph.D. thesis, Univ. of London (1931).

——, 'The Movement of Labour into South East England', *Economica*, N.S. i (1934).

——, 'The influx of Labour into London and the South East, 1920–36', *Economica*, N.S. iv (1937).

——, 'The Influx of Labour into the Midlands, 1920–37', *Economica*, N.S. v (1938).

——, *Migration and Economic Growth* (Cambridge, 1954).

—— (ed.), *The Welsh Economy* (Cardiff, 1962).

THOMAS, D. S., *Migration Differentials*, Social Science Research Council Bulletin No. 43 (New York, 1938).

THOMPSON, F. M. L., 'Agriculture since 1870', in *V.C.H. Wiltshire*, iv (1959).

TIVY, J. in R. Miller and J. Tivy (eds.), *The Glasgow Region* (Glasgow, 1958).

TRANTER, N. L., 'Population and Social Structure in a Bedfordshire Parish', *Pop. Stud.*, xxi (1967).

TURNER, H. A., 'Trade Unions, Differentials and the Levelling of Wages', *Manchester School of Economic and Social Studies*, xx (1952).

——, *Trade Union Growth, Structure and Policy* (1962).

*Victoria County History* Lancaster, ii (1908); Leicestershire, iv (1958); Warwickshire, vii (1964); Wiltshire, iv (1959); Yorkshire, East Riding, i (1969).

WALTON, K., 'Population Changes in North East Scotland, 1696–1951', *Scottish Studies*, v (1961).

WEBB, J. W., 'The Natural and Migrational Components of Population Change in England and Wales, 1921–31', *Economic Geography*, xxxix (1963).

WEBB, S., and B., *Industrial Democracy* (1920 edn.).

——, *History of Trade Unionism* (1950 edn.).

*Webb Trade Union Collection*, British Library of Political and Economic Science.

WELBOURNE, E., *The Miners' Unions of Northumberland and Durham* (Cambridge, 1923).

WELTON, T. A., 'By-Products of the Census: A Study of the Recent Migration of English People', *Trans. Manchester Statistical Society* (1904–5).

——, *England's Recent Progress* (1911).

WHETHAM, E. H., 'The London Milk Trade, 1860–1900', *Ec.H.R.*, 2nd Ser., xvii (1964).

WILKINS, W. H., *The Alien Invasion* (1892).

WILLIAMS, D., *The Rebecca Riots: A Study in Agrarian Discontent* (Cardiff, 1955).

WILLIAMSON, J. G., 'Regional Inequality and the Process of National Development', *Economic Development and Cultural Change*, xiii (1964–5).

Women's Industrial Council, *Married Women's Work*, ed. C. Black (1915).

WOOD, G. H., *A Glance at Wages and Prices since the Industrial Revolution* (Manchester 1900).

——, appendix to B. L. Hutchins and A. Harrison, *A History of Factory Legislation* (1903).

——, *The History of Wages in the Cotton Trade during the Past Hundred Years* (1910).

WOOD, G. H., Collection of Wage Rates at the Library of the Royal Statistical Society and Library of the Department of Employment and Productivity.

Wood, J. D., 'Scottish Migration Overseas', *Scottish Geographical Magazine*, lxxx (1964).

Wood, T., *Autobiography* (1956).

Wrigley, E. A., *Industrial Growth and Population Change* (Cambridge, 1961).

Yates, M. L., *Wages and Labour Conditions in British Engineering* (1937).

Youngson Brown, A. J., 'The Scots Coal Industry 1854–1886', D.Litt. thesis, Univ. of Aberdeen (1952).

——, 'Trade Union Policy in the Scots Coalfields, 1855–85', *Ec.H.R.*, 2nd Ser., vi (1953–4).


## B. British Government Publications — Arranged in Chronological Order

*Annual Reports of the Registrar General.*

*Census of England and Wales, Scotland, and Great Britain 1831–1961.*

*Poor Inquiry (Ireland) Appendix G to Report*, 1836, XXXIV.

*Employment of Women and Children in Agriculture*, 1843, XII.

*S.C. on Railway Labourers*, 1846, XIII.

*Sixth Report of the Medical Officer of the Privy Council*, 1864, XXVIII.

*Commission on the Employment of Children, Young Persons, and Women in Agriculture*, 1867–8, XVII; 1868–9, XIII; 1870, XIII.

*Report on the Diminution in the Number of Migratory Labourers from Ireland*, 1884, LXII.

*R.C. on the Housing of the Working Classes*, 1884–5, XXX, XXXI.

*Reports of Inspectors of Constabulary*, 1886, XXXIV.

*Sums Received and Expended for the Purposes of the Metropolitan Police*, 1886, LIII.

*Amount Expended for In-maintenance and Out-door Relief in England and Wales*, 1887, LXX.

*Report on the Sweating System at the East End of London*, 1887, LXXXIX.

*Returns of Wages published between 1830 and 1886*, 1887, LXXXIX.

*S.C. on Emigration and Immigration (Foreigners)*, 1888, XI.

*House of Lords S.C. on the Sweating System*, 1888, XX, XXI; 1889, XIII, XIV; 1890, XVII.

*Return of Rates of Wages in the Principle Textile Trades*, 1889, LXX.

*Return of Rates of Wages in the Minor Textile Trades*, 1890, LXVIII.

*Return of Rates of Wages paid by Local Authorities and Private Companies*, 1892, LXVIII.

*Labour Gazette*, i (May 1893), 'Wages in Jewish Tailoring Workshops in Leeds and Manchester'.

*Wages of the Manual Labour Classes*, 1893–4, LXXXIIIii.

*Royal Commission on Labour*, Various parts, in particular: *The Agricultural Labourer*, 1893–4, XXXV–VI; 1893–4, XXXVII ii; *Appendix on The Employment of Women*, 1893–4, XXXVIIi; 1894, XXXV; *Final Report and Secretary's Report on the Work of the Office*, 1894, XXXV.

*Reports on the Volume and Effects of Recent Immigration from East Europe*, 1894, LXVIII.

*Statistics of Employment of Women and Girls*, 1894, LXXXIii.

*R.C. on Agricultural Depression*, 1894, XVIi, XVIii; 1896, XVI; 1896, XVII.

*Report on the Money Wages of In-door Domestic Servants*, 1899, XCII.

*Report by A. Wilson Fox on the Wages and Earnings of Agricultural Labourers*, 1900, LXXXII.

*Reports and Tables relating to Migratory Agricultural Labourers*, 1900, CI.

*R.C. on Alien Immigration*, 1903, IX.

*Memoranda, Statistical Tables and Charts on British and Foreign Trade and Industrial Conditions*, 1903, LXVII.

*Second Report by A. Wilson Fox on the Wages, Earnings and Conditions of Employment of Agricultural Labourers*, 1905, XCVII.

*Report on the Decline in the Agricultural Population of Great Britain, 1881–1906*, 1906, XCVI.

*Report of the Fair Wages Committee*, 1908, XXXIV.

B. of T. *Inquiry into Working Class Rents, Housing and Retail Prices*, 1908, CVII.

*Earnings and Hours Inquiry I. Textile Trades*, 1909, LXXX; *III. Building and Woodworking Trades*, 1910, LXXXIV; *V. Agriculture*, 1910, LXXXIV.

*Standard Time Rates of Wages in the United Kingdom*, 1910, LXXXIV; 1914, LXXX.

*Fifteenth Abstract of Labour Statistics*, 1912–13, CVII.

B. of T. *Inquiry into Working-Class Rents and Retail Prices*, 1913, LXVI.

*Seventeenth Abstract of Labour Statistics*, 1914–16, LXI.

*Financial Results of the Occupation of Agricultural Land and the Cost of Living of Rural Workers*, 1919, VIII.

*Wages and Conditions of Employment in Agriculture*, 1919, IX.

*Coal Industry Commission*, 1919, XI, XII, XIII.

*Report of the War Cabinet Committee on Women in Industry*, 1919, XXXI.

*Time Rates of Wages and Hours* (H.M.S.O., 1950).

*Census Reports of Great Britain 1801–1931*, Guide to the Official Sources No. 2, (H.M.S.O., 1951).

Studies on Medical and Population Subjects 5. *Internal Migration*, by M. P. Newton and J. R. Jeffery (H.M.S.O., 1951).

Studies on Medical and Population Subjects 6. *External Migration: A Study of the Available Statistics, 1815–1950*, by N. H. Carrier and J. R. Jeffery (1953).

*Manual of Nutrition* (1961).

'Notes on Regional Labour Statistics 5. Inter-Regional Migration of Employees in Great Britain', *Ministry of Labour Gazette* (July, 1965).

# INDEX

Aberdeen, earnings, 55–6, 67, 69–70; trade unionism, 349n.

Aberdeenshire, earnings, 11, 20, 53–6, 63, 69–70; employment, 178–80; *other references*, 54

Abergavenny, earnings, 24n., 68

Accommodation, 45, 49, 51n., 65, 76–8, 87–92, 102, 103n., 204n., 322; *see also*, living-in, rent, tied cottages

Acle (Norfolk), 19n.

Activity rate, *see* women, children

Africa, 204, 210

Agricultural depression, 18, 122, 206, 208

Agricultural labour, diet, 10, 14–15, 45, 78, 86, 96–7, 121, 205, 208–13, 215, 274n.; earnings, 1–2, 4–5, 9–66 *passim*, 67, 71, 73, 78, 82, 85, 87–93, 96, 113, 116, 121–3, 124n., 126, 135n., 137, 145–6, 161n., 170, 173n., 175, 177n., 178–9, 205–15, 222–3, 233n., 234, 237n., 251, 272–5, 284, 297, 301–2, 344, 356; employment, 4, 65, 67, 129–84 *passim*, 195–6, 213–4, 237, 257, 265–7, 271, 275, 280–1, 289, 293n., 304, 325, 332, 344n., 345n.; productivity, 205–15; trade Unionism, 277n., 312, 327n., 330, 332–3, 344; women's earnings and employment, 112–5, 118–23, 126; *other references*, 47n., 97, 100, 105, 126; *see also*, accommodation, hand threshing, hinds, living in, mobility of labour, orraman, ploughman, poverty

Agriculture, *see* agricultural labourer, grain production, harvest, livestock production, management

Aire and Calder navigation, 268n.

Alcohol, 109, 212, 322; *see also*, brewing

Aldershot, 207

Alexander II, 305

Alien immigration, *see* Jewish immigration

Allen, G. C., 198, 217

Allotments, *see* gardens

Amalgamated Association of Mineworkers, 151n.

Amalgamated Society of Carpenters, 1; *see also*, carpenters, trade unionism

Amalgamated Society of Engineers, 334, 338, 353; *see also*, engineers, trade unionism

Amalgamated Society of Railway Servants, 331; *see also*, railway workers

America, *see* United States

Anglesey, earnings, 24–7, 62; employment, 153–5; population, 219n.

Anguilla, 283n.

Angus, earnings, 53–6, 63, 69; employment, 178–80, 207–8

Annan, earnings, 49

Apprenticeship, 151n., 335, 354

Arch, J., 277n., 311n., 332, 344

Argyll, cost of living, 82; earnings, 53–6, 63, 69; employment, 178–80; population, 219n.

Armour, P., 96

Ashby, J., 29, 65n., 105

Ashby-de-la-Zouch, earnings, 30n.

Ashton-under-Lyne, 37, 90n.

Asia, 204, 210

Association of Municipal Employees, 352

Atcham (Salop.), 30

Atwater, Prof., 212

Australia, 253, 281

Aves, E., 339

Ayrshire, earnings, 50–3, 63; employment, 174–7; women's earnings and employment, 117n.

Backwash effects, 3n., 181, 199, 218, 356–7; *see also*, dualism, growth poles, investment, productivity